Also by James MacGregor Burns

ROOSEVELT
The Lion and the Fox

JOHN KENNEDY
A Political Profile

THE DEADLOCK OF DEMOCRACY
Four-Party Politics in America

ROOSEVELT
The Soldier of Freedom

LEADERSHIP

THE AMERICAN EXPERIMENT
Vol. 1: The Vineyard of Liberty
Vol. 2: The Workshop of Democracy
Vol. 3: The Crosswinds of Freedom

DEAD CENTER

*Clinton Core Leadership
and the Perils of Moderation*

James MacGregor Burns
and Georgia J. Sorenson

with Robin Gerber
and Scott W. Webster

A LISA DREW BOOK

SCRIBNER

A LISA DREW BOOK/SCRIBNER
1230 Avenue of the Americas
New York, NY 10020

SCRIBNER and design are trademarks of Macmillan Library Reference USA, Inc., used under license by Simon & Schuster, the publisher of this work.

A LISA DREW BOOK is a trademark of Simon & Schuster, Inc.

DESIGNED BY ERICH HOBBING

Set in Electra

Manufactured in the United States of America

1   3   5   7   9   10   8   6   4   2

Library of Congress Cataloging-in-Publication Data
Burns, James MacGregor.
Dead center : Clinton-Gore leadership and the perils of moderation /
James MacGregor Burns and Georgia J. Sorenson ;
with Robin Gerber and Scott W. Webster.
p.   cm.
"A Lisa Drew Book."
Includes bibliographical references and index.
1. United States—Politics and government—1993– 2. Political
leadership—United States. 3. Moderation—Political aspects—United States.
4. Clinton, Bill, 1946– .5. Gore, Albert, 1948– . I. Sorenson, Georgia Jones.
II. Gerber, Robin. III. Webster, Scott W. IV. Title.
E885.B88   1999
320.973'09'049—dc21   99-34871
CIP

ISBN 0-684-83778-1

To our friends and colleagues
at the University of Maryland

CONTENTS

Contents

Contents

Turning and turning in the widening gyre
The falcon cannot hear the falconer;
Things fall apart; the centre cannot hold;
Mere anarchy is loosed upon the world,
The blood-dimmed tide is loosed, and everywhere
The ceremony of innocence is drowned;
The best lack all conviction, while the worst
Are full of passionate intensity.

Surely some revelation is at hand;
Surely the Second Coming is at hand.
The Second Coming! Hardly are those words out
When a vast image out of Spiritus Mundi
Troubles my sight: somewhere in sands of the desert
A shape with lion body and the head of a man,
A gaze blank and pitiless as the sun,
Is moving its slow thighs, while all about it
Reel shadows of the indignant desert birds.
The darkness drops again; but now I know
That twenty centuries of stony sleep
Were vexed to nightmare by a rocking cradle,
And what rough beast, its hour come round at last,
Slouches towards Bethlehem to be born?
— "The Second Coming,"
WILLIAM BUTLER YEATS

Fast Trip to Falls Church

September 12, 1992

We—Bill Clinton and the two authors—are squeezed into the backseat of a small sedan, on the Washington Mall. The noise from the crowd outside is deafening. Clinton reaches through the window and pumps the hands of some children. In an instant we are off to the next campaign stop, the Virginia suburb of Falls Church.

For weeks Clinton has been ranging across the country castigating, Harry Truman–style, the Republicans for see-nothing, do-nothing government. Could *he* do any better? we asked. He ticked off the presidents who could: Jefferson, Lincoln, the two Roosevelts, Kennedy. These would be his leadership models.

Sixty years earlier, in 1932, FDR had run a shrewd, calculating, foxlike campaign to oust the Hoover Republicans. "Do you feel you are running that kind of campaign," we asked, "and if you are, do you think you'll be a lion as a president?"

"Oh, absolutely." Clinton spoke clearly through the wailing sirens. "Our system has benefited from electing people who at moments of change were able to be—to use your term—transforming leaders, who could get people to move beyond party and beyond the little boxes in which we normally think and vote and live . . ."

"Transforming leaders." This word *transforming* had come into vogue as meaning the most radical kind of change, both of outward form and inner character, as with "a frog transformed into a prince," according to our *Webster's*. It meant rising above everyday accommodation, expediency, "pragmatism," and seeking instead real, intended, and lasting change, measured by fundamental values of security, liberty, equality, justice, as unforgettably dramatized in FDR's Four Freedoms—freedom of speech and religion, freedom from want and fear.

"At the end of the cold war," Clinton went on, "the fundamental reality is that most competition between nations will be economic, that military power is a mixed blessing but a clear responsibility of the United States, that history will judge us based on whether at this moment we make the changes we need to make." Clinton was waving vigorously through the closed window at everyone he spotted on the sidewalks—at everything that moved, it seemed. "We must improve the productivity and efficiency of our work, increase our levels of investment to improve and advance our capacity to educate all of our people. To solve some of our thorny social problems, which other nations have been more willing to deal with, chief among them health care and quality of life in our vast urban areas."

But could he do all this without changing the system? we asked. Franklin D. Roosevelt—if he really was one of Clinton's models—had enjoyed the usual hundred-day honeymoon and had then became fouled up in the checks and balances, the very system of deadlock he tried to reform. If Clinton as president began to run into trouble in his second or third year and felt that he too had been stymied by the system, "what could you do?"

Two or three things, he said. First, "keep a coherent and powerful vision of change before the American people." Second—laughing—"wear them down!"

"A lot of it is who lasts longest," Clinton went on, warming up to the subject. "I'm good at that. I do a good job at that. And the third is to generate popular support."

That was how it was in Arkansas, he said. When he was politicking at the State Fair for a fifth term as governor, "this old fellow in overalls" asked if Clinton was going to run again. He remembered that Clinton would "nag, nag, nag" to put his programs through. "I wouldn't put up with that at home for ten years"—still, yes, he'd vote for Clinton again.

But if Clinton did meet gridlock in Washington, we persisted, would he call for constitutional change? No, he said, he had tried that in Arkansas and it hadn't worked. But he would favor *institutional* change, such as regulation of lobbying or setting up a National Security Council and Economic Council. He would like to see changes in the process by which we elect members of Congress. What about a relatively minor constitutional change? we asked—four-year terms for representatives? He had never thought about it, he said.

By now we had left the drab city blocks and were speeding through the Virginia suburbs, the sirens still howling. There were no pedestrians to wave at. Clinton seemed completely relaxed, yet focused on the dialogue.

Years before, Oliver Wendell Holmes had famously summed up Franklin Roosevelt: "a second-rate intellect but a first-rate temperament." This interview had inadvertently become a test of that temperament. Because of a mix-up at the Mall, Clinton had had to intervene with the Secret Service to get us into the car, amid a clamorous crowd pressing around us. Two of the three tape players did not work. We were sitting partly on top of one another in the car. We gathered that the meeting with African-American leaders at the Mall had been difficult.

But here he was, during the few moments before the next venue, when he might have wanted some quiet, talking with two academics raising long-run, theoretical questions, while he was intent on winning an election seven weeks away. Still, he answered our questions thoughtfully, articulately, without a flicker of impatience. Grace under pressure.

In retrospect what struck us most about Bill Clinton was his calm, almost blasé confidence that he could take leadership, among the continuing disasters and turmoils of the twentieth century, to bring about transforming change. He had no experience of foreign-policy-making, he had presided over the economy of one of the smaller states, and he had little background for the throbbing, uncontrolled, and inequitable economy of the financial capital of the world. But he claimed to be a potential transforming leader who would bring about the comprehensive change that had eluded most of his Democratic and Republican predecessors.

Granted, he would enter the White House when the cold war was assuredly over, when the United States had brilliantly deployed its military might in the Gulf War, when the economy appeared stable, when most of the New Deal–Great Society reforms had survived the Reagan and Bush eras reasonably intact. As presidential historians, though, we wondered if we were witnessing in the Clintons, the Gores, and their youthful, exuberant campaigners the makings of that "ceremony of innocence" that William Butler Yeats had noted at the end of an earlier world war, when idealistic Americans embraced the League of Nations and savored the heady prospect of world government.

Could poets be more prophetic than politicians? The innocent Warren G. Harding had become president around the time Yeats was envisioning a world far different from the rosy hopes that followed World War I. With piercing insight Yeats saw past the "peace" of Versailles to the anarchy that would rule the world. He sensed the rising tumult that would reach across Europe, from the religious extremists in Ireland to the revolutionaries in Russia. But he saw much farther—to the desert lands in northern Africa and the Middle East and Asia that would let loose the blood-dimmed tides following the next world war.

Bill Clinton possessed none of this pessimism. He constantly invoked the image of a peaceful and prosperous twenty-first century that he and Gore would shape during their administration. Still, some historians remembered a similar optimism at the start of the twentieth century, when Theodore Roosevelt entered the White House. Aside from America's lethal civil war and Europe's colonial oppressions around the globe, the nineteenth century had laid the foundations, it was hoped, for expanded peace and prosperity in the twentieth. On the contrary, that century has been the most ghastly in history—decimation of whole populations, deliberate murder of weak and unarmed ethnic groups, worldwide pestilences, the tyranny of "rough beasts" named Hitler, Mussolini, Stalin, Mao, Pol Pot, and scores of others.

During the 1990s some analysts were predicting an upcoming century of menacing overpopulation—especially of jobless youth, tidal flows of refugees across national borders, endless struggles over diminishing resources—with global crime and violence.

The leadership coming to power in America were well aware of some of these possibilities. Assuredly they would cope with tumult as it arose. They would rapidly adapt to global change. But history might ask for more—not only to react and adapt to change, but to plan and manage change—to take leadership of democratic transformation away from the worst, full of passionate intensity.

How to explain Clinton's self-confidence, even cockiness, as he entered the White House, the global command center that would confront tumult abroad and sharp conflicts at home? A politician's self-esteem hardly suffers, of course, when he pulls off the supreme triumph in American politics—beating an incumbent president. But Clinton had another reason to feel confident. He was bringing to the White House a strategy of leadership, a "game plan" that had been crafted in a string of Arkansas victories and carefully fashioned with his friends in Washington.

This strategy would come to be called centrism, embracing bipartisanship, consensus, incrementalism, moderation in policy, "pragmatism." Other men had come to the presidency with tactical skills and experience. Clinton had a formula for leadership and change, a kind of do-it-yourself kit for an office that had defied efforts by journalists and scholars to generalize as to how to make it effective. He was fortified in this strategy by Al Gore, who had helped to shape it. Clinton would be challenged in the strategy by a person even closer to him in the White House, Hillary Rodham Clinton.

Still, transforming leadership in the White House would require more than grace and aplomb. It had to be a catalyst for change, taking leadership in risky initiatives: controversial reforms such as in campaign finance and even in the transformation of institutions such as the presidency or Congress or political parties. Transforming leadership would demand more than day-to-day incrementalism and fine promises; it would call for intellectual and moral creativity leading to real, purposeful, and lasting change.

Was Clinton capable of that kind of leadership?

PART I

TURNING AND TURNING

CHAPTER ONE

Presidential Heroes and
Moral Failures

Why, we asked Bill Clinton, did he not use his full name? William Jefferson Clinton—what a perfect name for a Democrat. In other times, at least, an aspiring politico would have been tempted to steal it off a gravestone. But now it was just plain Bill. He seemed curiously uninterested in the question. He hadn't thought much about it, he said. "Probably I should use it." We hoped he would use his full name, if elected, at least in taking the inaugural oath. He wasn't sure.

All this struck us as a rather casual attitude toward the "founder of the Democratic Party"—the party that had honored Clinton with its presidential nomination, the party whose *D* or *Democratic* would sit across from his name on millions of ballots across the nation. Admittedly, we were biased, as students of presidential history, but duly impressed that he had not claimed any descent from or kinship with the great Virginian. Still, his casualness did seem a bit self-effacing, historically, in a year when Democrats were invoking the party saints.

It was not just a question of sentiment. A Democratic president in the 1990s would face some of the same problems that had confronted the great party-builders two centuries before. In the 1790s, Thomas Jefferson and James Madison took the first steps in building a national party out of discordant and quarreling factions. At first they had no national political strategy—they were fashioning their platforms as their anti-Federalist party expanded. But people wanted something more than simple denunciation of Hamilton and the other "elitists"—a purpose, a vision of the century ahead.

As party leader, Clinton would encounter a dilemma that had faced the Jeffersonians—the widespread view that political parties, or at least their vigorous combats, were threats to national unity and hence were unpatriotic. So in his 1801 inaugural Jefferson had proclaimed, "We are all republicans, we are all Federalists," but he didn't really mean it. Rather he took strong ideological and policy leadership of his party, in dealing with Congress and with the press, and he selected a party cabinet. Like the party

19

leaders that followed over the decades, the Jeffersonians would promise to "rise above party" and "speak for all Americans," while assiduously pursuing party advantage and party spoils.

Jefferson demonstrated his political sagacity when, in the 1790s, he recognized the need—indeed the inevitability—of robust party conflict in a democracy. Would Bill Clinton recognize this need in the 1990s? Or would his centrist strategy compel him to make deals with the Republican opposition in a calculated bipartisan strategy? Or—a third alternative—would he switch back and forth between principled partisanship and pragmatic deals with the GOP as the shifting political situation seemed to dictate?

We did not have the heart to ask Clinton about the political symbolism of his *last* name—about the "northern" Clintons. He claimed no family kinship with them either, of course, but he might have jovially hinted of a "Clinton connection" while campaigning, say, in upstate New York. For George Clinton, and his nephew De Witt Clinton, were fierce New York anti-Federalists over a span of almost half a century. In choosing George Clinton as his running mate in 1804, Jefferson recognized the vital need for a Virginia–New York alliance, which would broaden out over the years to a North-South coalition in the Democratic party. Oddly, it was precisely that historic coalition that would be integral to Clinton's winning electoral strategy in 1992.

HEROIC LEADERS IN THE WHITE HOUSE

Bill Clinton, Hillary Rodham, and Al Gore grew up in an era of transcending leadership. It was the era of three great presidents in a row: FDR, Harry Truman, Dwight Eisenhower. Of senators like Robert Taft, Hubert Humphrey, and Arkansas's own William Fulbright. Of generals like George Marshall and Omar Bradley, who actually won wars. Of justices like Earl Warren and William J. Brennan Jr., who not only interpreted law but made law. Of first ladies Eleanor Roosevelt, Jacqueline Kennedy, Lady Bird Johnson.

In Washington, schoolchildren flocked to monuments celebrating earlier heroes. These were mainly presidents—Washington, Jefferson, Lincoln, in particular. After decades of presidential glorification, it was hard to find monuments even to the legendary senators like Henry Clay and Daniel Webster. The implication for youngsters like Bill Clinton was clear. To be really famous it was not enough to be a senator or a governor—you had to be president. And it was not enough to be president—you had to be a moral leader and a courageous innovator.

We can assume that whatever texts and storybooks about great presidents were available in Hot Springs, young Clinton would greedily seize them. We can also assume that many in Arkansas remembered Woodrow Wilson's grassroots campaign for the League. Some might have recalled Teddy

Roosevelt, perhaps having even served with him in the Rough Riders. Certainly the heroic memory of TR still vibrated fifty years later. It was not only the physical image—bristling mustache, gleaming eyeglasses, crenellated teeth—but the posture of constant combat couched in moral outbursts that was so vividly recalled.

Any schoolchild would be impressed by the story of the sickly boy, fatherless at twenty, who had tracked down bad guys in the Dakotas, fought his way into the rough-and-tumble of Manhattan politics, charged up San Juan Hill, succeeded to the presidency when hardly out of his thirties, and as commander in chief sent the American fleet around the world. All this was well remembered, because TR made it memorable through assiduous "public relations." He first exploited the press as New York police commissioner; later he reported on himself in countless magazine articles and political speeches. He invented the bully pulpit.

Still, if Roosevelt was the first media president, as historian John Milton Cooper Jr. has noted, he was in many other respects the first modern president. Political power that previous "strong" presidents such as Lincoln had evoked only in wartime, TR mobilized without the help of a timely war, as had Jackson.

During the high tide of American financial and industrial capitalism, Roosevelt took on the "trusts," and if his posturing sometimes outran his performance, he established for good the responsibility of the federal government to monitor the marketplace. Both through his peacemaking and his saber rattling he established his nation's place among the great powers. Resoundingly elected to his own term in 1904, he turned even more "left" in fighting for railroad regulation and pure food and drug legislation. And if in the end he was carved in stone on Mount Rushmore, few felt that he was an interloper among the Big Three.

After Roosevelt emerged as the very model of the warrior-king, Woodrow Wilson headed toward his own destiny as the tragic hero in the White House. His ultimate failure was all the more poignant because he had entered the White House in 1913 with more definite views about political leadership than any other president before or after. Public opinion, he believed, must be molded by a moral leader who could convert the inchoate wants and needs of the community into grand principles that would embody spiritual and even poetic insights. "The ear of the leader must ring with the voices of the people," he believed. "The forces of the public thought may be blind; he must lend them sight; they may blunder; he must set them right." But leadership was not a one-way process; national renewal would spring from the followers, the people. Nor was it a one-person process—only by "leading minds was the will of a community stirred to a guiding control of affairs." After the bloodletting of the "Great War," diplomats and civilians alike hailed the peacekeeping role, however feeble, of the new League.

The test of this noble concept of leadership came swift and hard in Wilson's campaign for American membership in the League of Nations. Senate Republicans, led by Henry Cabot Lodge, vowed to accept membership only with "reservations" that, in Wilson's view, would cripple even the limited peacekeeping power of the League. There followed a contest between Lodge's masterly transactional leadership, as he brokered support among his partisans in the Senate, and the President's effort at transformational leadership as he carried the battle to the people. Greeted by cheering crowds, the scholarly Princetonian was transformed into a model of courage and conviction. But Wilson's epic campaign for the League across the country ended in his own physical breakdown. The fight for the League finally collapsed when the Democratic ticket of James Cox and Franklin Roosevelt carried the issue into the 1920 election and lost.

Twelve years later, when Wilson was mainly remembered as a leader who had gone down fighting for his ideals, Franklin Roosevelt invoked the concept of the presidency as "preeminently a place of moral leadership." All our great presidents, he said on the eve of entering the White House, were "leaders of thought at times when certain historic ideas in the life of the nation had to be clarified." The presidential office was a "superb opportunity for reapplying, applying in new conditions, the simple rules of human conduct to which we always go back. Without leadership alert and sensitive to change, we are all bogged up or lose our way."

Roosevelt moved through a series of leadership roles during his long presidency: the crisis president pushing through emergency legislation in 1933–34; "Dr. New Deal" turning left in 1935 as he shaped the enduring New Deal of social security and regulatory measures; the partisan president winning his huge reelection victory in 1936; the reform president of 1937 seeking to liberalize both the judiciary and the Democratic party; the interventionist president of the late thirties cautiously reorienting the nation toward the menace of Hitlerism; the nonpartisan "Dr. Win the War" during the struggle against the Axis; the leader in the establishment of the United Nations, achieving the American participation that Wilson had sought in vain.

For young Clinton, Wilson and the two Roosevelts were role models in courageous leadership. But—especially in FDR's case—they were also models of caution and compromise. Was there one leader behind these many roles? "A chameleon on plaid," Herbert Hoover had labeled FDR during the 1932 election campaign, and until FDR's final days leaders in both parties were trying to pin him down ideologically. But he was a moving target, shifting adroitly to meet new exigencies. Viewed in retrospect, however, he always appeared to return to "true north"—to TR progressivism, Wilsonian internationalism, Democratic party liberalism. Thus during World War II, when he might have sacrificed social reforms to military needs, he established housing, health, education, jobs, and "equality of opportunity" programs far surpassing the achievements of the earlier New Deal.

If Bill Clinton's schoolbook histories were behind the times, he probably did not read much about the New Deal. But he did not need to, to learn about the recent heroes in the White House. For the hero worshipers were all around him in Hot Springs—men and women who had survived on the WPA (Works Progress Administration), who had clung to their homes through mortgage relief, served in the CCC (Civilian Conservation Corps), benefited from soil-conservation and farm-electrification programs, gone to college under the GI Bill of Rights. The lesson for Bill Clinton was clear: leadership could make a difference in people's lives.

During the decade after Roosevelt's death American politics fell into a pattern of coalition and conflict that would shape the political landscape for most of the next half century. The crucial political division lay not in the age-old seesaw of two-party politics but in the bitter conflicts within the major parties. The liberal presidential wing of the Democratic party warred with conservative southern Democrats still entrenched in Congress despite FDR's earlier efforts. And the victory of the military hero Dwight Eisenhower, an internationalist and moderate conservative, over the right-wing Robert Taft for the GOP presidential nomination in 1952 presaged the long battle between presidential and congressional Republicans. Americans had in effect a four-party system: liberal (Truman-Stevenson) Democrats, moderate (Rockefeller) Republicans, and two conservative parties entrenched in Congress and in most rural areas of the country.

Bill Clinton was only six when Harry Truman left the White House after Eisenhower's victory over Adlai Stevenson in 1952, but a dramatic confrontation in Arkansas brought presidential politics almost to the youth's door. Late in 1957, Governor Orval Faubus mobilized the state national guard in Little Rock to block court-ordered desegregation of Central High School. Despite his own reservations about integration, Eisenhower called out airborne troops and dispatched them to the state capital to enforce the court decree. The nation was mesmerized by news photos of brawny soldiers escorting apprehensive black girls into the building. Eleven-year-old Bill Clinton was frustrated by Faubus's defiance, his mother recalled, but he had seen up close a demonstration of naked presidential power.

Burdened by repeated cold war crises, frustrated by a heavily Democratic Congress, Eisenhower appeared relieved to turn over the presidency to John F. Kennedy in January 1961. The exuberant young president presented a vivid contrast to the aging military hero. Kennedy's inaugural address was a bracing celebration of freedom. Yet even more than most inaugural talks, it reflected the nation's—and his own—uncertainty and confusion over the meaning of freedom. Americans still had their old revolutionary beliefs, but the torch had passed to a new generation. Americans would "pay any price" and "bear any burden" to protect liberty, but Kennedy decried the cost of arms. "Let us never fear to negotiate," but "let us never negotiate out of fear."

The Kennedy presidency reflected these ambivalences as it offered a new alliance for progress to Latin America but mounted an invasion of Cuba, renewed New Deal and Fair Deal programs but within severe budget restrictions, forced the Soviets to turn back their missiles headed for Cuba but on the basis of a secret deal to dismantle U.S. missile bases in Turkey. Despite Democratic party criticism of Eisenhower's covert intervention in Vietnam through military "advisers," Kennedy considerably enlarged the U.S. "advisory mission" in Vietnam and assigned American forces to combat-support missions.

Transcending Kennedy's moderate policies and limited initiatives was the charismatic personality of the young president. Whether appearing as a hawk or a dove, as a moderate Democrat or dedicated New Dealer, he radiated excitement, intensity, commitment—even while he practiced caution and compromise. To some there seemed to be four Kennedys: the rhetorical radical delivering ringing speeches; the policy liberal constantly balancing human wants against limited resources; the fiscal conservative always intent, like FDR, on balancing the budget, though not succeeding; and the institutional conservative who hoped that, instead of reshaping the traditional constraints on the presidency, he could revitalize the torpid governmental system by applying jolts of New Frontier electricity.

All this was a long way from the day-to-day routine of Hot Springs, Arkansas. A high school hero-worshiper like Bill Clinton could only gape at this hero from afar. But then a wonderful opportunity opened up. Through intensive politicking he got himself chosen by Boys' Nation in Arkansas as a "senator" who would travel to College Park, Maryland, and then to Washington for a presidential reception at the White House. Clinton carefully maneuvered to be in front of the group in the Rose Garden and to have his picture taken with John F. Kennedy. He was elated to shake hands with the President of the United States. He was even more elated, it appeared, to have a *photograph* showing him shaking hands with the President.

For young Clinton it was the Kennedy legacy of leadership that he most wanted to inherit. If historians saw JFK as a profile in caution as well as courage, this was a legacy for Clinton too. But when it came time for Clinton to take office thirty years later, it was JFK's youthful élan and glittering style that Bill Clinton most wanted to emulate.

THE "CENTER OF MORAL LEADERSHIP"

Bill Clinton launched his presidency amid more than the usual inaugural effusions. He saluted his predecessor, George Bush, for his half century of service to America and thanked the "millions of men and women whose steadfastness and sacrifice triumphed over depression, fascism, and communism." Then he quickly reechoed his campaign theme of change. Over a dozen times he spoke the language of transformation.

"Today we celebrate the mystery of American renewal. . . . America, to endure, would have to change. . . . The urgent question of our time is whether we can make change our friend and not our enemy. . . . To renew America, we must be bold . . . must revitalize our democracy. . . . Together with our friends and allies, we will work to shape change, lest it engulf us."

Yet even this trumpet call had muffled notes. Clinton appeared to equate the terms *change* and *renewal,* but these words had highly diverse implications. He used *change* itself ambiguously—was it something out there, an enemy to head off, or a constructive force to be embraced and employed? Perhaps these questions demanded too much of a short speech, but presidents-elect and their staffs fuss over the inaugural language because it stands historically as the authentic statement of intention.

Whatever his purpose, an inviting array of powers lay spread out before the new president—law-writing, budget-making, treaty proposing, electronic pulpit-exploiting, appointing friends, and disappointing enemies. This was the fabled "power of the president." The presidency was superbly equipped as a vehicle for conducting transactional leadership among a host of competing actors and agencies. But could such quid pro quo tactics produce real change, or at least renewal, or merely continuation? The fundamental question was, leadership by whom, for what, when, how, and at what cost?

A huge paradox dominated this question. The presidency was weak where it should be strong as a tool of majority rule. It was strong where it should be weak in a democracy. And, by the time Clinton took office, the presidency had become morally compromised as an institution; how would he cope with this?

Weak where it should be strong—this was the cardinal issue: the constitutional constraints on the presidency are familiar to all students of American government—the power of Congress to pass or bottle up laws, its power to override presidential vetoes, its fiscal authority carefully protected by the Framers. These powers are buttressed by extraconstitutional arrangements, such as the Senate filibuster and the fragmented committee systems. And the Constitution established a federal system that put state politics and policy far beyond the influence of most presidents.

A single legislator can thwart even persuasive or overpowering presidents. In December 1963, when Johnson was receiving plaudits for taking over so firmly after JFK's death, he complained to legislative leaders about Congressman Otto Passman of Louisiana, who was blocking a foreign aid appropriation. "I'm really humiliated that I'm President and I've got a friendly Speaker and I've got a friendly Majority Leader . . . and Otto Passman is king. I think that's disgraceful. . . . I think it's awful that a goddamn Cajun from the hills of Louisiana has got more power than all of us. . . . If I ever woke up in the cold of the night and a rattlesnake's out there about ready to get him, I ain't gonna pull him off. I'll tell you that."

Commonly called the separation of powers, this system is really the intertwining of powers among separated institutions. In effect this intertwining distributes veto power throughout the whole presidential-congressional system. Activist presidents—and indeed activist congresses—confront permanent barriers of conflict and deadlock.

It would take a president of rare courage to challenge this structure. When we asked Bill Clinton in our campaign interview whether he would support some kind of institutional change—party or even constitutional change—to overcome gridlock, he replied "not constitutional." He mentioned FDR's court-packing plan. In fact that plan was not to change the Constitution, but for Congress to authorize FDR to appoint up to six more justices to modernize—really liberalize—the high court. His plan failed— and remains as a warning to Clinton and other presidents not to essay basic reforms that even *look like* constitutional change.

Deadlock and delay on domestic policy help explain one of the most consistent presidential patterns—decline in presidential legislative support from Congress. Eisenhower's support dropped from 89 percent at the start of his presidency to 65 percent at its end, Johnson's from 88 percent to 75, Reagan's from 82 percent to 47, Bush's from 63 percent to 43. This pattern in turn helps explain another phenomenon, the drop in popular approval ratings during presidencies. All the last presidents prior to Clinton lost popularity—Truman from 81 percent to 29 percent from start to finish, Eisenhower from 68 to 61, Johnson from 74 to 42, Carter from 63 to 41, Bush from 64 to 40. Liberal Democrats and centrist Democrats, moderate Republicans and conservative Republicans—they all lost support of people and politicians suffering from blighted hopes and crushed expectations. For Clinton this was a dire aspect of the presidential legacy.

What can presidents do when faced with dwindling support? One thing they have done, with some consistency, is to focus on areas where they can act more on their own—foreign policy, war making, crisis control. And this is the area where the presidency has most been strengthened—but also twisted and perverted. While the Constitution granted Congress the authority to declare war, to raise and support armies and a navy, and to regulate the armed services, from almost the start early presidents—even the strict constitutionalist Thomas Jefferson—bent the war-initiating power by launching secret operations against Barbary pirates and other miscreants, sending secret agents abroad, and denying relevant information to Congress.

The larger and more critical the war, the broader the president's war-making role. Abraham Lincoln simply conducted the early Civil War without Congress, which was not in session. On his own authority he expanded the army and navy, spent unauthorized funds, and even suspended habeas corpus—the last a most dramatic action for a Whig who had opposed federal power. Fully aware he was violating the Constitution, "honest Abe" was candid about it: "Was it possible to lose the nation and yet preserve the Constitution?" Often a limb must be amputated to save a life, but a life was never wisely given to save a limb.

At least Lincoln's actions were public. In 1941, Franklin Roosevelt launched secret naval operations in the North Atlantic against German U-boats to protect American lifelines to Britain. He also sent troops to Iceland without congressional authorization. "Roosevelt, like Lincoln, relied on his sense of popular demand and public necessity," Arthur Schlesinger Jr. wrote. Since Congress had authorized arms to Britain as national policy, "then, inferentially, national policy was to make sure the arms got to Britain." But Congress was sidetracked.

Nor did Congress have a formal role in the foreign-policy decisions and crises of the 1960s—in John Kennedy's disastrous Bay of Pigs gamble, in his skillful handling of the missile crisis, in Johnson's escalations in Vietnam. The grimmest irony of all was that, despite all the constitutional limitations on presidential foreign-policy-making, the president of the United States had separate and exclusive control of nuclear weapons—and hence the power to precipitate global holocaust. Presidents have intervened in explosive situations around the world—Theodore Roosevelt and others endlessly in Latin America, FDR in the North Atlantic, Harry Truman in Korea—without formal congressional sanction and often without true consultation with Capitol Hill. Congress might still possess the war-declaring power, but the president controlled the war-making power.

Much of this intervention has been defended as an inevitable and necessary response to a turbulent and threatening world, but assumptions of power and abuse of power have marred the domestic presidency as well. Watergate is too fresh in memory, with its myriad cover-ups, violations of constitutional rights of citizens, and other illegalities, to need detailing here. But Watergate so dwarfed other presidential transgressions as to make these earlier ones seem trivial. They were not.

When Congress dragged its heels on a crucial price-control bill during World War II, Roosevelt told the legislators that if they did not enact the bill within three weeks, "I shall accept the responsibility, and I will act." Congress passed the bill in three weeks and the people cheered FDR, but a dangerous precedent had been established. During World War II, FDR, in another far-reaching act of executive authority, allowed the army to incarcerate tens of thousands of Japanese-Americans in concentration camps. Harry Truman established by executive order a "loyalty" program requiring loyalty checks and "oaths" of all federal employees and applicants—a program that even his admiring biographers have called a shameful mistake.

Clinton inherited other malign legacies of the presidency: When Joseph R. McCarthy called General George Marshall a traitor, Dwight Eisenhower dropped from his campaign speech a defense of his former boss's patriotism.

Eisenhower and John F. Kennedy—or the administrations they presided over—connived in assassination attempts against foreign heads of state.

Lyndon Johnson carried FDR's manipulative tactics to an ugly extreme, pressuring and bullying people to his will.

President Gerald Ford pardoned ex-president Richard Nixon.

At a critical moment of loss of popular confidence in his leadership, Jimmy Carter sacked three cabinet members.

After preaching "fiscal responsibility" for years, Ronald Reagan lowered taxes and triggered an almost catastrophic budget imbalance.

George Bush conducted a campaign for president against Michael Dukakis that was scurrilous even by late-twentieth-century standards.

Such was the presidency that Bill Clinton inherited, with its real heroes, constitutional authority, political powers, lofty visions, occasional creative leadership, and also with its fake histrionics, unconstitutional and illegal actions, unconscionable overpromising, shabby compromise, endless dealing and brokering. The "center of moral leadership" was also a center for moral failure. This mixed legacy would offer Clinton ample leeway but little guidance.

All this assumes that Bill Clinton knew American history—at least presidential history. Evidently he did. He had good history teachers in school and university, and he read omnivorously. But even more, he—and Rodham and Gore, along with many of his future colleagues in politics and government—grew up among people who had watched Wilson and the Roosevelts and the other activist presidents firsthand, who knew of their achievements and their failures, who understood the power and the impotence and the occasional perversions of the presidency. Did Clinton see a presidential legacy embodied in them?

WHERE ARE MY FOLLOWERS TO LEAD ME?

Bill Clinton's assumption of office early in 1993 would mark the two hundredth anniversary of George Washington's inauguration to a second term. It would mark an even more significant anniversary, though generally unnoticed—Secretary of State Thomas Jefferson's effort to plant the seeds of an opposition party. Incensed by Treasury Secretary Alexander Hamilton's fiscal policies and political ambitions, Jefferson during 1790–93 joined James Madison in setting up the *National Gazette* to propagandize the Democratic-

Republican cause, and the two men made a long excursion to New York and New England to sound out anti-Federalist feeling. Jefferson's resignation from the cabinet in 1793 marked his decisive break with the Federalists.

Since the two Virginia leaders looked on their trip as a "botanical" as well as political expedition, they could hardly have known that they were setting two great precedents. One was for disaffected leaders to mobilize opposition elements in the hinterland, thus laying the basis for two-party combat. The other was to turn from the transactional maneuvering within the capital to potentially transformational politics in a much wider arena of conflict, with profound implications for the conduct of presidential leadership.

Jefferson, with Madison and thousands of republican activists, led the way to the first voting realignment in American history with their victory over John Adams in 1800. Jefferson became the first—and some historians say the strongest—party leader of the nineteenth century. He worked closely with Democratic-Republican leaders in Congress, mapped party strategy for upcoming legislation—but above all he starred as a symbol of democratic leadership for the whole country. Later, Andrew Jackson exercised Democratic party leadership even before he entered the White House. Shut out of the presidency in 1824 as a result of what he considered to be a corrupt bargain between John Quincy Adams and Washington insiders, he appealed to the country—especially the South and West—so forcefully that he beat Adams, 178 to 83, in the 1828 electoral college.

The Jeffersonian and Jacksonian "revolutions," while not really revolutionary, laid the ground for major changes in fiscal policy, foreign relations, territorial expansion, tariffs, internal improvements. In between these transformational eras, leaders returned to the familiar brokerage, trading favors, fixing things up, giving a little here and getting a little there. Most Americans appeared content with this transactional style of leadership. Most of the issues were economic and quantifiable—additive, divisible, multiplicative.

But what would happen in the face of moral, qualitative, incalculable problems? As conflict heated up over the transcending issue of slavery and as both zealous abolitionists and fanatical secessionists stoked the flames, all political arithmetic was altered. The "grand compromises" of Henry Clay and Daniel Webster and others took on an almost mythic importance, but they merely postponed civil war. The masterly mediators and compromisers utterly failed to deal with the supreme moral issue of the century.

In a four-way party split of the electorate—Lincoln Republicans, Stephen Douglas Democrats, old-time Whig Unionists, and Southern secessionists—Abraham Lincoln was elected president in 1860. He prepared to take office as southern states were seceding, charging northern aggression against their "domestic institutions." Civil war would now be the ultimate test of the American people, their democracy, their values; it was also a test of the presidency. It would incidentally prove that a man could be elected with less than a majority, as would later be the case with many candidates including Bill Clinton, and still govern.

Lincoln soon faced not only a big war with the South but a small war with leaders of the abolitionist movement. Some of them assailed him as vehemently as did Confederates. "The conviction that SLAVERY IS A SIN is the Gibraltar of our cause," Wendell Phillips proclaimed. William Lloyd Garrison publicly incinerated a copy of the Constitution because it protected slavery. Lincoln, Phillips proclaimed, lacked "the boldness to declare an emancipation policy, until by a pressure," which Phillips and others created, the administration would be forced to do it.

The abolitionists made their priorities clear—emancipation first, union second. Lincoln made his clear, in reply to Horace Greeley: "If I could save the Union without freeing any slave I would do it, and if I could save it by freeing all the slaves I would do it, and if I could save it by freeing some and leaving others alone, I would also do that."

Never in American history has the clash of values been sharper or more consequential. For Lincoln the supreme need was *order*—the security of the North, the survival of the Union. But the issue was not that simple. Only by subduing the South, Lincoln believed, could the slaves finally be freed. Only by emancipation, Phillips and others believed, could the President invoke the moral fervor and popular support necessary to win the war. The issue was resolved, temporarily, not by rational debate, but by soldiers and guns. Perhaps Frederick Douglass, impassioned though he had been over the issue, rendered a more lasting judgment. Had Lincoln "put the abolition of slavery before the salvation of the Union, he would have inevitably driven from him a powerful class of the American people and rendered the resistance to rebellion impossible," the former slave wrote. "Viewed from the genuine abolition ground, Mr. Lincoln seemed tardy, cold, dull, and indifferent; but measuring him by the sentiment of his country . . . he was swift, zealous, radical, and determined."

Second only to slavery as the supreme moral issue facing Americans was the rights of women. In Woodrow Wilson's administration votes for women sharply posed both the moral and political dilemma of his presidency. Early in the century, after decades of frustrations, blocked by the "veto traps" in the constitutional system and often divided among themselves, many women suffrage leaders had concluded that a constitutional amendment was necessary and that the president, even though he had no formal role in the amending process, was key politically to a successful drive to mobilize popular backing. In 1912 they were heartened by Wilson's support for votes for women, at least in principle but seemingly not in political practice. Women were not lacking in boldness. While Wilson was speaking against monopolies at the Brooklyn Academy of Music, Maude Malone suddenly rose in the audience.

"Mr. Wilson, you just said you were trying to destroy a monopoly, and I ask you, what about woman suffrage? The men have a monopoly on that."

"Woman suffrage, madam, is not a question that is dealt with by the national government at all, and I am here only as a representative of the national party."

"I appeal to you as an American, Mr. Wilson."

"I hope you will not consider it a discourtesy if I decline to answer this question on this occasion. . . ."

Amid rising hubbub a burly detective swooped down on Maude Malone and carried her out.

Slowly over the next few years, letter by letter, conference by conference, setback by setback, suffrage leaders thrashed out tactical questions of intellectually baffling complexity. To what extent should the women's movement try to work through either or both major parties, or leverage between them, or form its own party as of old? How strongly should it link with labor and consumers and even farmers? What political tactics should be used—electioneering (with most women voteless), propaganda, personal influence, militancy, even violence?

New leaders were rising, notably Carrie Chapman Catt and other militants. Early in 1917, on the eve of America's declaring war, suffragists began picketing the White House itself. Standing motionless outside the gates, they held banners demanding "How Long Must Women Wait for Liberty?" Violence escalated as passersby tore the banners from their hands, and police began to arrest pickets rather than the malefactors. Thrown into a notorious workhouse, women protested their brutal treatment, underwent hunger strikes, suffered forced feeding—and became martyrs.

Catt's ablest lieutenant was Helen Gardener, a wealthy Washingtonian who had personal access to Wilson. As a crucial House vote neared in late 1917, Gardener played on the commander in chief's newest and strongest motivation by urging him to support suffrage as a war measure. Wilson finally agreed. With the president's help the suffragists and their allies pushed the voting amendment through the House of Representatives by exactly the required two-thirds majority. Then the Senate, a tougher obstacle. Redoubling her White House operation, Gardener persuaded Wilson again and again to intervene with vacillating senators. In September 1918, on her urging and that of party leaders, the President staked his prestige on a sudden personal appearance before the Senate.

"This is a people's war," he said. "Democracy means that women shall play their part in affairs alongside men and upon an equal footing with them." But the magic two-thirds still could not be won in the Senate, which would wait another year to vote it through. It would take the women's movement still another year to push the amendment through three-quarters of the states. It was a splendid but flawed victory for the suffragists, with implications for presidential leadership too. Why did Wilson, the fervent apostle of freedom, take such a moderate, cautious, centrist position on women's suffrage, at a time when rivals such as Theodore Roosevelt and even Charles Evans Hughes, Wilson's Republican foe in 1916, were taking bolder stands? In a country dedicated to liberty, equality, and the pursuit of happiness, and rededicated to equality by Lincoln, how could he accept the grossest inequality in women's right to participate in democratic politics? Wilson took refuge, of course, in supporting state-by-state suffrage, but all knew that this was a hopeless alternative.

Finally Wilson came around, but on what basis? Not liberty or equality but mainly because of the suffragists' militance. Some women, perhaps forgetting that their own efforts had often been disconnected from those of millions of other Americans lacking freedom, complained that Woodrow Wilson lacked moral leadership. He could in turn complain that he lacked effective followership.

Twenty years later this could have been the lament of Wilson's protégé Franklin D. Roosevelt, as well. Midway in his second term FDR was heard to remark glumly, "It takes a long, long time to bring the past up to the present." How could *he* say this—the President who had exuberantly presided over the "one hundred days" of emergency measures in 1933, the reformer who had put through the "permanent" New Deal in the progressive legislation of the "second one hundred days" of 1935, the grand reformer who had won all but two states in his reelection campaign? He could say it because the great mandate he had appeared to receive in 1936 had been followed by some painful defeats—the ignominious failure of his effort to "pack the court," the dismal results of his attempt to "purge" the Senate of reactionary southern Democrats, the shocking "recession" that sent joblessness spiraling again.

Critics came up with various explanations for these setbacks—FDR's lionlike boldness and radicalism; FDR's foxlike cautiousness and centrism; the ferocity and resources of the conservative opposition; the constitutional checks and balances that inhibited comprehensive planning and action, as dramatized by the Supreme Court's vetoes of major New Deal measures; the control of congressional committees by conservative southern Democrats.

The fundamental cause lay much deeper, in Roosevelt's failure to mobilize a strong and dependable followership and his followers' failure to gain a definable and dependable White House leadership.

"Mobilization of the masses" would have been difficult even for a masterful politician such as FDR. The "masses" were not massed, but rather fragmented or inert. Millions of Americans whom FDR had excited and politicized later followed strange populist gods—the anti-Semitic hate monger Charles Coughlin and his National Union for Social Justice, the populist Senator Huey Long and his Share the Wealth plan, the radical oldster Dr. Francis Townsend and his movement for federal pensions of $200 a month for everyone over sixty. These protest organizations were united only in their opposition to Roosevelt.

Unionists and populists and oldsters rallied to FDR's banner in 1936, but many would be fair-weather friends as the New Deal faltered. What about the Democratic party? In most democracies party support would be the leader's most dependable backing, but the Democrats too were divided between New Dealers and southern conservatives, with old Al Smith Democrats still on the outs with FDR. Like most presidents, Roosevelt had treated his party essentially as a campaign adjunct, rather than developing long-range organization at the grass roots. It was not there when he needed it during his second term.

Roosevelt's basic problem—and that of Wilson too—was not leadership. It was the failure of followership—of followers' failure to mobilize for him for still stronger leadership—and thus a lesson for all future presidents, including Bill Clinton.

Roosevelt's political fate might have been as dismal as Wilson's but for the advent of World War II. Despite his public role shift from domestic to war leadership, he not only continued but expanded his New Deal programs in the form of war projects. Jobs, housing, nutrition, health, incomes—all expanded amid war prosperity. In the grimmest of paradoxes, Americans had never had it so good—aside from those who died and their loved ones. Roosevelt's rhetoric matched reality. It was during the war, not the New Deal period, that he enunciated not only his famous Four Freedoms but also his Economic Bill of Rights, which set forth the agenda of liberal Democrats over the next half century.

For the man to be inaugurated in January 1993, were there lessons in all this—in Lincoln's handling of emancipation, Wilson's cautiousness on suffrage, FDR's search for a winning political strategy?

One stark fact was the role of war as the forcing house of reform. It could be any kind of war—world war, civil war, even regional war—but it must be a winning war and the reform had to be linked to winning the war. Lyndon Johnson learned that lesson as Vietnam divided his followers and brought an end to his Great Society hopes.

But Clinton was coming into the White House at a time of relaxed tensions, especially with Moscow. Was there a substitute for war—an example of a twentieth-century presidency that acted out of domestic needs and pressures? Only one: Theodore Roosevelt's. TR did not have a war. But he had powerful convictions about "malefactors of great wealth," poisonous food and drugs, ravaged timberlands, rebate evils, and much else. And he had a crucial ally—a militant press. He had the muckrakers to whip up reform frenzy—Ida M. Tarbell, who investigated Standard Oil; Upton Sinclair, who exposed conditions in Chicago meat-packing plants; Lincoln Steffens, who wrote about the "shame of the cities"; David Graham Phillips, who dramatized the "treason of the Senate"; and scores of others.

So, for a new president dedicated to "change," much would depend, in the absence of galvanizing war, on sheer conviction—his own, his followers', and that of the liberal media.

What other lessons could the new president, reportedly a voracious late-night reader of history, learn from Presidential Leadership 101?

That absent the transcending moral conviction of a Lincoln or a Theodore Roosevelt or the global activism of a Woodrow Wilson or an FDR, a president must depend on the ancient arts of transactional leadership; that a chief executive has huge resources for such brokerage but rarely enough to put through his most ambitious programs and sustain them; that presidents must employ both the cunning of the fox and the power of the lion, as Machiavelli advised, but that knowing when to use which tactic is extraordinarily difficult; that traditional party and ideological foundations of presidential influence are increasingly yielding to a politics of money, media, and personalism; that vaunted "presidential authority" is in fact elusive, volatile, complex, and even illusory; and indeed that the famed "power and the glory" of the White House cannot substitute for mobilizing followers and then following *them*— and this strategy of leadership is extraordinarily difficult.

LEADERSHIP: CONVICTION AND CHARACTER

In 1747, at the age of fifteen, George Washington copied out 110 "rules of civility." Most of them involved "Decent Behaviour in Company and Conversation"—how to sit, stand, dress, eat, drink, walk. "If you Cough, Sneeze, Sigh, or Yawn," read the fifth rule, "do it not loud but privately; and Speak not in your Yawning, but Your handkerchief or Hand before your face and turn aside." Or no. 71: "Gaze not on the marks or blemishes of Others and ask not how they came. . . ."

Toward the end of his list young Washington moved beyond day-to-day behavior to matters of conviction and conscience:

"108: When you Speak of God or his Attributes, let it be Seriously & with Reverence . . .

"109: Let your Recreations be Manfull [sic] not Sinfull [sic].

"110: Labour to keep alive in your Breast that Little Spark of Celestial fire Called Conscience."

Forty-two years later, when the secretary of the Confederation Congress rode to Mount Vernon to inform Washington of his election as president of the United States, the address paid tribute to the moral leader that Washington had become: ". . . the proofs you have given of your patriotism and your readiness to sacrifice domestic separation and private enjoyments to preserve the liberty and promote the happiness of your country . . ." The secretary did not exaggerate. Throughout his life Washington embodied the qualities he began to write about as a boy: self-discipline, probity, resoluteness, constancy, courage. If his cutting down the cherry tree was a fiction, it became a national fable because his whole life exemplified honesty and integrity.

The "father of his country" shared these qualities with many of his class and breeding; what distinguished Washington throughout his adult life as a revolutionary, a constitution maker, and a president was his fixed belief that what Americans most needed was security at home and abroad. Whether fulminating against Shays's Rebellion in western Massachusetts in 1787 or firmly putting down the Whiskey Rebellion in Pennsylvania as commander in chief, whether resisting British rule in the 1770s or threats from French revolutionaries in the 1790s, Washington consistently stuck to this principle.

In both character and conviction Washington set a standard for all future presidents. When William Butler Yeats lamented in 1920 that "the best lack all conviction," he was reflecting the disillusion with the rulers who had poured millions of their subjects into the "blood-dimmed tide" of World War I. Decades later did Bill Clinton's presidential heroes contradict Yeats's rejection of modern leaders' lack of conviction? Did they, rather, exemplify courage and commitment, moral principle and political vision? With a few exceptions, it was hard to find that kind of commitment—and even less so in the Vietnam-era and post-Vietnam presidents that Clinton had so closely observed.

Not that these latter-day presidents lacked ideas. They—or their speechwriters and brain trusters—came up with a host of ideas. But these ideas suffered from a tendency Tocqueville noted over a century and a half ago. In the United States, he said, "ideas are extremely minute and clear or extremely general and vague; what lies between is a void." This gap between grandiose oratory about "liberty" or "justice" or "equality" and day-to-day "practical" specifics—with no firm analytical linkage among values, priorities, and day-to-day actions—has continued through most of the presidencies to this day.

Consider the leadership of John F. Kennedy, Clinton's topmost presidential hero. Kennedy's inaugural address and the policies that followed for a year or two after were perfect examples of the "Tocquevillian void." "Let every nation know," he proclaimed to an enthusiastic crowd, "that we shall pay any price, bear any burden, meet any hardship, support any friend, oppose any foe, to assure the survival and the success of liberty"—but within three months he refused to back up the Cubans he had encouraged to launch the Bay of Pigs invasion. Only "when arms are sufficient beyond doubt," he orated, "can we be certain beyond doubt that they will never be employed." But the armed forces he now commanded were vast beyond doubt, yet they were employed in Vietnam. He expressed high hopes about "New Frontier" domestic policies, but these had hard going in Congress.

Still, the Kennedy White House was proud of its day-to-day achievements, its hardheaded practicality, its piecemeal improvements, its "pragmatism." The only problem was that its achievements lagged far behind the promises of the presidential campaign and inauguration. Forced to negotiate with the Republican/southern-Democratic coalition in Congress, Kennedy was unable to pick up support on the Hill in the midterm congressional elections. "Every president," he said, "must endure a gap between what he would like and what is possible."

By 1963 it was evident that Kennedy's centrist, transactional leadership was not working in the face of continued cold war stalemate, sharpening black protest, a deepening quagmire in Vietnam, and the impending election campaign. During that year he moved toward far more purposeful leadership with two remarkable speeches. At American University in an address that historian Herbert Parmet called a landmark in postwar Soviet-American relations, he said that the United States wanted not a "Pax Americana" but "general and complete disarmament, including a treaty to outlaw nuclear tests." In the same month, June 1963, after asserting that Americans faced a "moral crisis as a country and people," JFK announced that he was sending an omnibus civil rights bill to Congress. Also in 1963 he began planning an attack on chronic poverty, which was the prelude to Lyndon Johnson's "war against poverty." In all three areas he left an irreversible legacy for his successor. Thus John Kennedy began to fill in his Tocquevillian void.

Kennedy's shift to a principled liberal position, followed by LBJ's egalitarian domestic policies, placed them in history as men of conviction. Whatever their expediencies and evasions, their "pragmatism" had ultimately served their values, rather than the reverse. Their successor provided an instructive contrast.

Richard Nixon prided himself on his political realism, his flair for electoral cut-and-thrust, even his cynicism. Consider his comment on a matter that had nothing to do with Watergate or other crises, but with the independent voter. "The media go on about the 'undecided voter,'" Nixon said to a reporter. "Ha! Undecided voter. That's bullshit. Believe me, people decide about politics early on. You take the average guy. You know? Sipping beer and eating his pretzels." This kind of realpolitik had nothing in common with Wilsonian idealism.

Still, during his first term Nixon's presidential skills so impressed voters, including independents, that in 1972 they gave him the electoral vote of every state save Massachusetts. Those transactional skills included formidable innovations in policy, flexibility in bargaining position, adroit exploitation of media, and opportunistic choice of congressional friends and enemies. But even before Watergate voters were finding it difficult to place Nixon politically. The man who had inveighed against big government proposed a host of new federal interventions in environmental policy, social security expansion, urban mass transit, occupational safety and health. The lifelong Quaker waged ferocious war in Indochina. The man who had virtually constructed his career out of anticommunism undertook brilliant diplomacy in opening up détente with China and Russia.

No wonder Nixon came to be called Tricky Dick. But other presidents—not least FDR and LBJ—have been manipulative and disingenuous. Nixon won the deception prize because he shifted so readily between liberal and conservative postures. He evidently felt that it left him preempting the strategic center. On the contrary, it left him appearing to lurch from left to right, right to left, with no connection between the two—thus revealing his own Tocquevillian void.

After this procession of presidential "pragmatists" and centrists, what would a principled leader look like in the White House? The answer came from a most unlikely personage—a onetime liberal Democrat, Hollywood actor, and General Electric spokesman. As governor of California and president, Ronald Reagan was an ideologue—a term that cries out for definition. In its main dictionary meaning, an ideologue supports a body of doctrine that guides an office, social movement, or institution, as well as himself, resulting in a political or social program. Ideology has a second meaning: speculative theorizing of a visionary or impractical nature. Reagan was the first kind of ideologue, but widely seen as the second type.

Reagan had won his doctrinal laurels first of all by sticking to his conservatism despite defeat. In 1976 he had challenged President Gerald Ford in the Republican primaries, judging him as another namby-pamby Republican and pro-Rockefeller centrist—and Reagan had lost. Urged to turn more "pragmatic" and modify his conservatism, he steadfastly proclaimed that he would stick to his right-wing stance and thereby win the next time. That is what he did in 1980, capturing the nomination handily and trouncing President Carter in the fall.

Reagan was not, nor did he pretend to be, an original or creative conservative thinker. But he had the guidance of leading intellectuals during a sunburst of conservative thought in the seventies and eighties. The conservative renewal, stimulated by a host of foundations, publications, and think tanks, produced a considered and collective effort by rightists of various schools to build their intellectual case. Many of them were political activists too. Their strategy assumed that potent ideas themselves were the most steady and powerful propellants of political action. *Ideas Are Weapons*, the liberal Max Lerner titled his book. *Ideas Have Consequences*, conservative Richard Weaver titled his.

As president, Reagan was derided for vagueness on details, excessive delegation of authority—indeed, as a marionette controlled by puppeteers in his administration and outside. The critics did not understand. Like a Hollywood director, he had only to preside over an agreed-upon script enacted by actors themselves united by ideology. This ideological conservatism was far more coherent than long-fragmented liberal doctrine. While White House liberals had feverishly pursued step-by-step, day-by-day policy-making, the Reagan White House pursued their values of social order, individual liberty in the marketplace, and property rights.

The prime minister of Britain warmly supported her friend in the White House. "From the strong fortress of his convictions," she said, "he set out to enlarge freedom the world over at a time when freedom was in retreat—and he succeeded." But Ronald Reagan was no Margaret Thatcher. He was laid-back, folksy, charming, a good though not always attentive listener. In between his homilies in the Oval Office, though, he was out on the hustings, as the quintessential rhetorical president, drumming conservative ideas throughout the American heartland. This onetime New Dealer had now, as a conservative, filled in his own Tocquevillian void.

Conviction—strong beliefs anchored in a set of explicit values and held over time—had long been the supreme test of great presidential leadership. Conviction had to be applied with skill, of course, and it had its dangers. Thus Reagan delegated power excessively in the Iran-contra affair. Other strong presidents made comparable errors. Conviction was not always adequate; it was only necessary. The strong presidents were strong because they stood for something. Hence they—from Washington to the committed New Dealers—were leaders.

If a politician assumed the presidency without an ideology rooted in a set of values, would the White House provide this foundation for leadership? The presidency had long been glorified as an office that steadied and even ennobled its occupants, converting politicos into statesmen. Perhaps in the earlier days of the presidency, when chief executives were firmer partisans, the White House had broadened and deepened their programmatic leadership. But the presidential heritage of great party debates—between a Lincoln and a Douglas, a Bryan and a McKinley, an FDR and a Landon or Dewey—had been lost in an era of "pragmatic" brokerage and accommodation. There was no presidential legacy, only legacies, amorphous and ambivalent.

If the White House came with no instruction booklet for presidential leadership, neither did it provide a home creed for moral leadership and ethical conduct. Virtually all the presidents had been churchgoers and hence well indoctrinated with Ten Commandment virtues, but did that impact on presidential behavior? You shall not use the name of your God in vain—but presidential tapes were full of profanity. You must not lie—but presidents had often uttered untruths or withheld the full truth, especially in war making. You must not commit adultery, but probably more than half of the presidents in the past half century had violated this commandment before or during their presidencies.

Nor did the White House legacy offer much guidance in everyday "ethics-virtues"—gratitude, kindness, generosity, or honesty, rectitude, integrity, and self-discipline. These virtues were observed or ignored depending on day-to-day "practical politics." The Golden Rule was not a White House rule.

If the state of personal virtues in the presidency was not impressive, what of the role of overarching *values*, in the dictionary definition of what is right, principled, and moral in the public domain? This is the domain of "abstract" but crucial qualities of justice, fairness, compassion, of security and survival, of liberty, equality, fraternity (or community), of "life, liberty, and the pursuit of happiness." However hazy in definition, incompatible with one another, changeable in application over time, these were the ultimate tests of presidential character, presidential leadership, presidential *conviction*.

So for a young politician entering the White House in January 1993, ambitious to be a great president, the historical legacy he would encounter there was not a roster of moral guidelines but a thicket of dilemmas. Did the American people want a decent and caring "common man" there, or an "uncommon" hero or visionary leader? Did they prefer an innovative, creative president, or a "pragmatist" operating close to the policy and ideological center? Were they calling for another partisan president, Andrew Jackson or Harry Truman style, or a nonpartisan leader who could govern "above politics"? Did they, in sum, want a transactional or transformational leader, or some complex combination of these strategies? Of course they might be lucky and get both—but what if they had to choose?

The White House beckoned to the forty-second president, with three dozen real-life models to choose from. Much would depend on the moral and intellectual luggage the new occupants would bring with them, from home and school, church and precinct. Could Clinton combine moral conviction and personal character? Or would he have to make a choice between the two?

CHAPTER TWO

The Education of Three Politicos

Bill Clinton told us in 1992 that he was not only ready for change, he would master change. Would this turn out to be an idle boast, a piece of Clintonian grandiloquence? It would be hard enough to force changes at home through a conservative Congress and tradition-bound courts. But even more formidable would be to cope with massive alterations by CEOs consolidating and downsizing companies, scientists producing breathtaking ventures in space and biochemistry, revolutionaries and terrorists readying their plans in dozens of countries, European experiments in new international organizations. Some environmental perils were accelerating much faster than humans' puny efforts to cope with them.

These changes raised even tougher moral than managerial choices. These decisions were especially acute for the young men and women who would emerge out of the struggles over civil rights and Vietnam. In the 1850s, agitators such as Frederick Douglass and politicos like the young Abraham Lincoln had confronted the burning issue of slavery. A century later Al Gore and Bill Clinton would face—and one would evade—the issue of Vietnam, and as young southerners they would run into explosive questions of civil rights and equality of opportunity in their states. But other moral issues were equally acute.

The misnamed cold war, which had erupted in flames in Korea in 1949, was smoldering in Cuba and Berlin and in a dozen other places in Asia, Africa, and Latin America ten years later. Were Americans yet ready for a grand compromise with Russian and Chinese communists?

At home the New Deal–Fair Deal reforms of the 1930s, however beneficial, were not resolving rooted problems of poverty and inequality a generation later. A resurgent conservatism had challenged Lyndon Johnson's Great Society in the 1964 election and failed; it would reassert itself. Should young liberals forge a new progressivism, as "muckrakers" had done at the turn of the century?

Transcending these dilemmas was the rising anarchy and bloodletting in Africa, the Middle East, and southern Asia. Should the United States, now a dominant world power, intervene in civil wars and tribal butcheries, with all the dangers and costs involved?

For many in the new generation these were remote, even theoretical questions. Then in rapid succession two issues erupted at home, one involving thousands of human lives and hopes, the other the integrity of the nation's election process—Vietnam and Watergate. These issues would call for the standard skills of young politicians and MBAs schooled in transactional management and mediation. But even more, they would test the moral character and political conviction of those who would aspire to lead their country in the 1980s and 1990s.

SCHOOLS THAT MADE A DIFFERENCE

Of all the forces giving birth to great leaders, the most mysterious are the sources of leadership potential in the early lives of men and women who will make history rather than merely live it. Historians, said Erik Erikson, blithely forget a crucial fact: that everyone was once a child. Social historians poke fun at political psychologists who emphasize psychological factors at the expense of economic and social influences that play on leaders all through their lives. "Chance" and "chaos" theorists say that it's all a matter of contingency—the rise of leaders is a great pinball machine in which a few lucky ones bump mindlessly into the bells and flashing lights.

In the wake of Sigmund Freud, analysts explored infancy for sources of later behavior; in the wake of Erikson and others, they looked also at the years of adolescence. All searched for early deprivations leading to compensatory reactions that in turn led to the drive for power and leadership. The worst deprivation was damaged self-esteem.

Because of his abandonments as a child, Bill Clinton has been irresistible game for this kind of psychologizing from a distance. But Clinton did not lose his balance; he survived with his ego intact and a high level of functioning in the world outside his home. School gave him a psychological safety zone. After being teased for his awkwardness and unskillfulness in play and sports, he naturally bonded with his schoolmates, and he won affection and recognition from his teachers.

Hence the key element in Clinton's early development was his growing self-esteem, based in turn on others' regard for him. The pathbreaking psychologist Abraham Maslow saw the need for self-esteem as comprising "the desire for strength, for achievement, for adequacy, for mastery and competence, for confidence in the face of the world, and for independence and freedom," "the desire for reputation or prestige . . . status, dominance, recognition, attention, importance, or appreciation."

The early need for self-esteem and recognition was true also of Al Gore and

Hillary Rodham. Whatever their small childhood and family traumas, they experienced little of the deprivation that affected Clinton. Yet they almost equaled him in their high school and college ambitions as they won friends and competed for student offices. This was crucial, for it is often in childhood years that the path toward future leadership roles assumes rough form and direction. Following that path may call for a sense of political efficacy—children's confidence that they have the competence to take part in group and political affairs. This feeling, like general political awareness, develops early in the United States, starting around third grade, and tends to increase with the child's rising self-esteem and participation in school activities.

What, then, was the major influence on all three future leaders as they moved through the early stages of their lives? Their schooling. This was part of a broader heritage. For many centuries societies have sought the key to identifying and educating possible political talent. In Greece, young men were tested to see who possessed the essential qualites of leadership—common sense, intellectual capacity, devotion to the public welfare. In the fifteenth century Niccolò Machiavelli and other sages wrote tracts on how princes should be educated and how rulers should govern. The "public" schools of England, such as Eton and Harrow, and private academies in America such as Groton and Exeter, purposefully educated their youths in citizenship and leadership.

Somehow an eclectic mix of American schools—Hot Springs and Park Ridge high schools, Wellesley College and Georgetown and Yale Universities, and, in Gore's case, St. Albans and Harvard—provided this threesome with the formal education and the self-esteem that would sustain them in the trials ahead.

Most American presidents grew up in small towns. Archetypical was Calvin Coolidge, born in the Vermont hamlet of Plymouth Notch in 1872 and sworn in as president fifty-one years later by his father, a farmer and storekeeper, under the light of an oil lamp in the farmhouse living room. It might be argued that an urbanizing America would need presidents who had grown up in large cities, like Theodore Roosevelt, but Americans felt reassured when their leaders emerged with small-town values from small-town America.

And so it was that people appeared pleased, when Bill Clinton began his presidential quest, to learn that he had been born in the little Arkansas town of Hope, its bucolic image refurbished by campaign publicists. There were portraits of a young Tom Sawyer type growing up on the banks of the Mississippi, which inconveniently lay 150 miles or so to the east. Here was a young man who would incorporate the small-town values of simplicity, neighborliness, trustworthiness, and kindness.

Soon skeptical biographers were demolishing this bucolic picture. The "man from Hope" lived there only six years. Later Clinton's campaign propaganda boasted that he won the "prettiest baby" contest when he was two. Not noted was the fact that his birth name was William Jefferson Blythe III, that his father had died in an auto wreck just before he was born, that he was raised by his mother and grandmother, that he was fatherless until four, when his mother remarried, to a man named Roger Clinton.

Least noted of all was the community the Clintons moved into, and the family life of mother, grandmother, stepfather, and child. Hot Springs offered not a country spa for the genteel but a collection of casinos for two issues pleasure-seekers, gamblers, and hustlers. Clinton's mother, Virginia, who had left for two years during his infancy to train as a nurse anesthetist in New Orleans, was a Hot Springs good-time gal who spent most evenings and weekends in the life of the casinos. Roger Clinton proved to be an alcoholic, philanderer, and abusive husband. Much of the time Billy was left in the care of Virginia's mother, whom the daughter was said to despise as jealous, possessive, and perpetually sharp-tongued. The home was less a hotbed of violence than a place of tension and near anarchy, with its unpredictable comings and goings, emotional scenes, and silent anger. It was less dysfunctional than nonfunctional. Billy was adored, doted on, by both Ma and Grandma, but much of the time they were not there, even when physically present.

In effect Billy suffered four abandonments—from the father who left him before he was born, the mother who was absent so much, the stepfather who was first loving and then abusive, and the grandmother who was caring but could be overwhelmed by dark emotion. His home life was seen later as the clue to varied aspects of Clinton's adult character—his desperate need for friendships, his search for self-esteem, his overwhelming ambition, his compassion for the have-nots, his bursts of rage.

Yet the unanswered question was why the chaotic life at home did not disable Clinton as a boy. Why did he not fail abjectly in school—the fate of so many abandoned youths? The answer lay in the schools themselves.

Clinton did not merely attend the Hot Springs schools—he devoured them. Well tutored by his grandmother, he first enrolled in a Catholic grade school where, according to biographer David Maraniss, he stuck his hand up so much in class that the nun gave him a C for being a busybody. Then on to fourth grade at the public school, where he was soon at home, making friends and winning top grades. But it was in high school where young Clinton soared. Paul Root, who taught world history to sophomores, remembered that Clinton "loved to read. He loved to understand. He just enjoyed world history, and that was a little unusual. Most tenth-graders are not in love with world history. But he wanted to know about the world, about relations between nations and people." And, Root added, "he was glad to tell you what he knew."

Clinton ran for almost every elective position he spotted. In his senior year the principal, Johnnie Mae Mackey, told him he could not run for student body president, for his strenuous participation in the school's big-band program was enough in itself. Clinton refused to accept her decision. He had been president of the junior class, he reminded her. He and a friend pushed the principal so hard on the issue that she broke into tears—partly because she liked him too much to stand in his way.

Was there some kind of narcissistic wound working here, a desperation to take leadership? He ran against one of his closest friends, Carolyn Yeldell, for class secretary, a post usually reserved for a girl. He accosted her. "So help me, if you beat me for this, I'm never going to forget it." She did beat him, and they managed to make up. Later she felt that it was not an ill-spirited demand on his part. "It was just kind of fun." Or was it just healthy young ambition?

Yet Clinton had somehow reversed the psychological situation. In the gap between home and school, he brought his schoolmates into his home rather than letting the family turmoil dominate his life in school. He entertained his friends in his bedroom, the largest in the house, with its own bath; he had full access to the ample freezer; and he had use of the family's big Buick to run his friends around town. At the same time he was widening his own activities beyond school. He spoke to the Elks, Kiwanis, and other organizations. His saxophone paved the way into clubs and dances. It was only natural that he would try out for Boys' Nation delegate and succeed and thus meet President Kennedy.

Clinton's school life in Hot Springs indicated, in short, that his psyche was influenced much more by his day-to-day exchanges with his teachers and schoolmates than by his childhood abandonments. Whatever "oedipal" forces were at work were to a major extent dissolved in the oceanic tide of mutualities and reciprocities at school. This made it all the more crucial that he gain teachers' and schoolmates' esteem—that he earn high grades, win school elections, achieve community recognition. In this way narcissistic wounds suffered at home were bandaged and cured—at least temporarily.

This pattern was repeated at Georgetown University, which Clinton entered in the fall of 1964. Why Georgetown? With his standing as fourth in his class at Hot Springs and as a community activist, Clinton could probably have gained admission to a Harvard or a Stanford. But Georgetown had a fine teaching faculty and an admired school of foreign service, which Clinton joined. Even more, the university was in Washington, where he could make job and political contacts. And the capital was full of Kennedy glamour, still, and Lyndon Johnson electricity amid mounting conflict over LBJ's call for civil rights and for the Tonkin Gulf Resolution.

But first Clinton had to validate himself. He was well aware of his status as a hillbilly among eastern urbanites, a Southern Baptist in a Roman Catholic institution. He had hardly set foot on the campus when he began to run for freshman class president, enlisting help, printing leaflets, pumping hands, beguiling women students, and campaigning against a vague "Long Island power slate." He won. He ran for sophomore president the next year and won again. Hardly the crusading leader, he focused on parking problems, food prices, and other campus issues. He was not one to defy the administration. When, in his junior year, he lost to a foe who called him the "establishment candidate," Clinton fell into a depression.

He did not slight his courses, mainly because they excited him. Catholic universities such as Georgetown were at this time taking advantage of the liberal atmosphere ushered in by Pope John XXIII. From a multilingual Hungarian-born China expert who taught a course nicknamed "Buddhism for Baptists," he learned about Asian religions, including Hinduism and Taoism. With a young Jesuit philosopher he explored absolutist as against relativistic thinking in a world of confusion and chaos. In a hotbed of theological debate he learned about the middle ground.

Professor Carroll Quigley, a quirky product both of Harvard and Boston's Irish ghetto, influenced him the most. In a required freshman course Quigley lectured passionately about the rise and fall of civilizations. Spurning "absolutists," he struck at Plato as a precursor of fascism, dramatizing his onslaught by ripping out pages from *The Republic* as he spoke and scattering them from the window. Tragedy could be avoided, he contended, only by toiling through pain and setbacks. He gleefully pricked the dogmas on both the right and the left. Clinton was paying attention.

Clinton spent much of his time reaching out beyond the campus to the movers and shakers in Washington. He wrote home excitedly that he had seen President Johnson, Vice President Humphrey, Robert and Edward Kennedy, Senator Thurmond. But the senator he was most attracted to was J. William Fulbright of Arkansas. A former university president and Rhodes Scholar, Bill Fulbright became a role model for Clinton, who won a bottom-level staff job on Fulbright's committee. This allowed him to roam the Capitol and make connections.

What Clinton did not do during these years is more important historically. While the South was seething over desegregation, Fulbright voted against LBJ's civil rights bills as a matter of political expediency, and Clinton would doubtless have done the same. He faced a small civil rights issue at Georgetown over the funding of students headed south to support the civil rights crusade. Clinton at first sought a compromise on the amount, then backed it. He first supported Johnson on Vietnam, then turned moderate dove as Fulbright battled against LBJ's policies.

When Martin Luther King Jr. was shot down early in April 1968, however, Clinton responded with his heart as well as his head. His old friend Carolyn Yeldell happened to be visiting him the next day. She and Bill had talked a lot in high school about their segregated community. They agreed that the Little Rock integration crisis in 1957 had been a "catalytic time for the whole nation to come to grips with attitudes about race." Now on the morrow of King's death this seemed another such time.

Loading the Buick with relief supplies, she and Bill made their way into Washington neighborhoods that had been burned and looted. The riots made him believe more strongly in King's message of nonviolence. "He wanted to take the torch from Martin," Carolyn Yeldell recalled. But he did not repudiate Fulbright's stand against civil rights legislation. In the summer of 1968 the just-graduated Clinton worked in Arkansas for Fulbright's reelection.

And it was Fulbright who helped boost the recent graduate up on his next academic and career step. This was the prestigious scholarship, the Rhodes. Clinton had sound credentials for the honor, but he had something else—a letter of recommendation from the senator. So he was among the thirty-two Rhodes Scholars, along with future notables Robert Reich and "Strobe" Talbott, who embarked on the S.S. *United States* early in October 1968.

For decades, the ancient university at Oxford had challenged the ability of American students to cope. They arrived with dreams of lofty spires and formal gardens, of cobblestone streets and grand philosophical discourses at high table. The reality was more often cold rooms, endless rain, boring lectures, and wretched food at low table. A flap at the porter's lodge suggested the tenor of things when Clinton and three comrades arrived at University College on High Street. The porter—an extreme example of the lodge martinet who guarded his turf by cowing masters and students alike—took one look at the quartet and insulted them collectively and individually. To the diminutive Robert Reich, he growled, "You're the goddamn bloody shortest freaking American I've ever seen in my life." Here, clearly, was a man to avoid. But not in Bill Clinton's mind. Within weeks, he was swapping stories with the porter, helping him run the lodge, and winning special dispensations.

Clinton was not a consistently brilliant student at Oxford. Despite his inflated claim later that he had read for a degree in the famed PPE (Politics, Philosophy, and Economics), he started as a literature student and later shifted to political science. His program called for weekly tutorials, a dissertation at the end of two years, and an examination in political science subjects. He did not finish it. But he could shine when a subject captivated him. His tutor was a Polish-born, anticommunist ex-Nazi prisoner who had been liberated by the British. He gave Clinton an advanced course in American, British, and totalitarian politics.

For his don, Clinton wrote an essay on political pluralism in the Soviet Union. His writing penetrated the monolithic facade of the Kremlin, describing factions struggling for power in a nation confronting the West. He avoided the usual simplicities about Soviet tyranny. Rather, he speculated on alternative futures for the USSR—continued bureaucratic oppression, more pluralism within the one-party system or outside it, parliamentary democracy, or, more likely, degeneration and collapse. His tutor found the paper a model of clarity and synthesis.

At Oxford, Clinton made no effort to hide his provincial background— rather he exploited it. He fascinated and perplexed staid dons with his stories about southern "ole boys" and Hope watermelons. But most of the talk was about politics. He took part in a "floating seminar" that moved from student rooms to low table to local restaurants. The topics, according to Maraniss, ranged "from the Soviet invasion of Czechoslovakia to the sorry state of American politics to the ideology of Mao Zedong to the British influence in nineteenth-century crimes," and of course to the war in Vietnam.

In two respects the schoolboy from Hot Springs never changed. He had brought with him, historian Roger Morris noted, "the ubiquitous lists and three-by-five cards he had faithfully tended, as one might an impassioned diary, since high school." He filed these away for the future. His ambition did not grate on everyone, though. Clinton, said one acquaintance, "was ambitious in the same way Ella Fitzgerald is a great singer—so good you barely notice it." And his English friends were amazed at the ease with which he charmed women, juggling love affairs in Oxford and London even while posting romantic letters to old friends back home, including a Miss Arkansas.

Clinton loved the Oxford freedom that enabled him to push the boundaries of his world farther and farther from Arkansas. He drove through the country, seeing most of the British Isles. During one long vacation he made his own version of a grand tour, beginning not on the Riviera but in Scandinavia, thence to Moscow, and finally to Czechoslovakia, hardly a year after Warsaw Pact tanks had crushed the Prague Spring. Clinton did not come back disenchanted with communism—he had never been enchanted by it.

On one enveloping issue, though, the moral philosophy taught at Georgetown and Oxford could not help Clinton—and it was one he could not escape. The war at home over Vietnam had escalated along with the war in Vietnam, from university teach-ins in 1965 to massive demonstrations across the nation, to a march from the Lincoln Memorial to the Pentagon in 1967, where over fifty thousand protesters were met by massed troops with fixed bayonets. Early in 1969, Hanoi launched a new general offensive that cost U.S. troops heavy casualties. Despite the talk by newly inaugurated President Richard Nixon of withdrawing American troops and the "Vietnamization" of the war, planning for even more massive antiwar demonstrations continued. Clinton ardently wished not to fight in a conflict condemned by so many of his peers as irrational, immoral, or both.

This was the supreme personal dilemma of his early life. He faced it with a mixture of moral concern, shrewd self-protectiveness, and agonizing uncertainty because of the interminable peace negotiations and his own vulnerability to the draft. The only constant in the process was his continuously recalculated self-interest.

By the end of his first year at Oxford, Clinton began to take part in organized opposition to the war. In the summer of 1969, he returned from Oxford to work in Washington for the Vietnam Moratorium Committee. He went to Martha's Vineyard one weekend that summer to meet with other activists for a discussion of ways to continue the work begun by Eugene McCarthy and the late Robert Kennedy. The next summer, he worked for Operation Pursestrings, an antiwar lobbying organization.

Some at Oxford condemned the war as an example of American imperialism. Clinton's opposition was more pragmatic and less ideological. The war, it seemed to him, was a gross miscalculation, a big mistake, rather than the manifestation of evil intent. His opposition was tempered as well by other concerns. There was the matter of equity. Young Americans his age were dying in Vietnam. Should he not fight too? And there was the matter of his own political ambition. He knew that most of the great American presidents had fought in wars and that most Americans held "draft dodgers" in contempt. As his draft status changed, these conflicting concerns caused him to twist and squirm, trying to avoid both Vietnam service and any step that would compromise his career plans. The more he evaded the issue, the more he agonized over it.

Like any other undergraduate, Clinton had obtained a II-S student deferment when he enrolled at Georgetown. It had been extended three times. But this deferment did not cover graduate school. Between his graduation from Georgetown and his enrollment at Oxford, his status changed to 1-A, denoting his eligibility for the draft. In April 1969, he received his second and final notice from the Hot Springs, Arkansas, Draft Board No. 26. He was to return home for military service. In desperation, in the summer of 1969 Clinton visited Colonel Eugene Holmes, director of the University of Arkansas Army ROTC program. He told Holmes he planned to enroll at the University of Arkansas law school in the fall of 1970 and would like to join the Army ROTC program, become an officer, and possibly serve in Vietnam. He signed an agreement with Holmes to that effect. That done, he was able to return to Oxford for his second year in the fall of 1969.

Meanwhile, opposition to the draft was growing, and in the fall of 1969, President Nixon instituted a lottery system. Bill Clinton received a high draft number on the first day of December 1969. Given Nixon's reductions in U.S. troop levels, this meant that it was highly unlikely Clinton would be called. Two days later, on December 3, 1969, Clinton wrote Colonel Holmes a long letter notifying him that he no longer planned to enroll in ROTC and would, instead, expose himself to the draft.

It was probably the most self-revealing letter he ever wrote. After he had signed his ROTC letter of intent, he told Holmes, "I began to wonder whether the compromise I had made with myself was not more objectionable than the draft would have been, because I had no interest in the ROTC program in itself and all I seemed to have done was to protect myself from physical harm." He said that he had decided to accept the draft because he felt "compelled" to try to lead "a political life characterized by both practical and political ability and concern for rapid social progress. It is a life I still feel compelled to try to lead." But, Clinton added disingenuously, he wanted to maintain his "political viability within the system."

Clinton had schemed and calculated, on every mile of a tortuous road, to evade both ROTC and the draft, making use of connections both in Arkansas and in Washington. Clinton did not want to go, but he wanted to be a patriot and to be seen as a patriot. He knew that when rich and middle-class men did not go to war, the poor, who were disproportionately black, did. He flunked his first test of moral leadership. A harbinger of things to come?

The war was a problem for Bill Clinton because it presented him, perhaps for the first time, with a situation he could not manage or manipulate. Only the luck of the lottery and some personal connections saved him. A young man who had made ambition and adaptability work in harness now found them at odds. A would-be leader of his generation failed to meet the supreme test facing that generation. Taking a principled stand neither to fight nor to resist, he brought to the issue all his qualities except principled conviction.

Vietnam haunted Al Gore, too, but he arrived at a decision different from Clinton's, perhaps partly as a result of his upbringing. Gore's early life is a study in strong community and powerful concentration on values. The Gores gave careful thought to their son's rearing. While Pauline Gore had little idea they were attending to the education of a future president, Al Gore Sr. at least considered the possibility. "I didn't rule it out," he would say, laughing, years later.

The elder Gore's position in the U.S. Senate permitted Al Gore Jr. to see how power worked, how it looked, and how it sounded. Young Al worked for a month as a Senate page, sometimes standing behind his father in committee hearings. At fifteen, he accompanied the senator on a trip to Central America and served as his interpreter. One evening he even answered the home telephone to hear a White House operator announcing that President Kennedy wanted to speak to Senator Gore. Al junior could not resist the urge to listen in on an extension as Kennedy complained, in vivid and vulgar terms, about something that had happened that day on the Senate floor. "I didn't know presidents talked like that," young Al later told his father.

Much as Kennedy fought with congressional colleagues, so did the elder and younger Gore occasionally spar with one another. "A powerful father and a strong-willed son is not always an easy relationship," Al junior's friend Martin Peretz later observed. But in his father, Gore still had two things Bill Clinton did not: a mentor and a powerful model.

Grooming his son for public office, in the elder Gore's opinion, meant two things, in addition to academics: leadership and work. In effect he designed a childhood to provide training in both. "I think we were both very conscious that if Al grew up in Washington, he would have been totally in an upper stratum of life and would never get to know the lessons that he would learn growing up on a farm," Pauline Gore recalled.

The senator believed firmly in the formative value of the labor of his own early years. So Al junior spent summers and one entire year living on the Gore farm, in the home of a tenant couple whom he came to regard as his second mother and father. There was no running water, and there were always chores to do—hoeing, feeding cows, and plowing. The farm experience was intended, the elder Gore admitted, to make Al "self-reliant, to teach him to work and know the value of work." He learned the discipline and moderation that would serve him well in future years.

Later at Harvard, at a time when many undergraduate careers veered off in radical, uncontrolled directions, Gore was a study in moderation and self-control. He smoked some pot, but not very much. He went out for sports, without overdoing it. Even his positions on the great overriding issue of the day, Vietnam, were calibrated, though still decisive. One of his instructors, Graham Allison, occasionally provided students with hypothetical case studies in which students assumed various roles. Gore enjoyed them and was quite good at them. One thing in particular stood out. "He was never unable to make a decision," Allison said. Gore later wrote a senior thesis examining the impact of television on the American presidency, impressing Professor Richard Neustadt, an expert in the nuances of presidential power.

Gore graduated cum laude in 1969, in time to face fully the question of service in Vietnam. After much consideration he came to a decision that would contrast sharply with that of his future running mate. "I'll go, obey the law," he told his parents after several emotional exchanges with them, in which they pledged to support any decision he made. "I'll volunteer tomorrow."

Gore served in Vietnam for several months as an army reporter near Saigon with the Twentieth Engineering Brigade. He witnessed combat by his second day there. But his decision to enlist did not help things at home. His father, an opponent of both the war and southern segregation, was engaged in a difficult reelection battle in 1970. And even though the senator sought to soften his controversial anti-Vietnam stance by appearing with his son in a television ad in which the elder advised the younger always to love his country, Gore senior still suffered a bitter election defeat.

After Vietnam, Al Gore had time to enjoy his marriage to high school sweetheart Mary Elizabeth "Tipper" Acheson, whom he had wed before departing for Southeast Asia. Gore also had time to ponder some "troublesome questions" raised by Vietnam, and he enrolled in the Divinity School at Vanderbilt University. But he did not, he confided to his father, intend to become a minister. He considered the school an intellectual challenge and haven rather than a place to train for a vocation. Soon, Gore signed on as a reporter in his home state for the Nashville *Tennessean.* "He wrote exceptionally well. He was fearless. He had a moral compass. He understood the First Amendment values and was committed to fairness and accuracy," recalled John Seigenthaler, then the *Tennessean*'s editor in chief. Gore made a mark for himself uncovering a story of massive corruption in city government and testifying at the resulting trials. Soon after, he enrolled in Vanderbilt Law School.

As he had at his prep school, St. Alban's, and at Harvard, Gore impressed the law school faculty. Don Hall, who taught Gore in two courses, remembered him as "well-prepared, bright," and very willing to debate issues. A classmate, Andrew Shookhoff, remembered Gore as thoughtful and analytical. He was also cautious and deliberate about what he said. Gore "would not make a comment that seemed out of left field," said Hall.

Thus by the mid-1970s, while still in their twenties, Clinton and Gore were each well educated and well on the way to careers in public life. "Youth's innocence" may have faded, but a strong residue of optimism remained. Both had been influenced by the upheavals of the preceding decade, a decade of war and assassinations, but also a decade of liberation for women and minorities. And even more than Clinton or Gore, Hillary Rodham's political coming-of-age reflected these transformations.

THE THREE HILLARY RODHAMS

A friend who knew Bill Clinton and Hillary Rodham in their law school days remembered them vividly even before they became famous. What initially struck Susan Thomases about Hillary Rodham was that she spoke in paragraphs—"full-formed, intelligent paragraphs—it's all there," though "sometimes too long." She had already heard of Rodham because of her Wellesley graduation speech, which had become celebrated in college circles. Thomases had distinct memories of Bill Clinton too, looking "like this giant red lion because he had bushy hair and he had a beard that went all the way around." But what she most remembered was that Clinton was so much in love with Rodham. "He talked about her in all sorts of ways that he had never spoken about other women."

In the decades ahead, through horrendous vicissitudes, that love would endure even as it was altered and tempered. When Rodham "stood by" her faithless husband, many women could not comprehend it. It seemed harder than ever, wrote Margaret Talbot in *The New Republic* in February 1998, "to scrunch our eyes shut and construe Hillary Clinton as a feminist icon, a role model for young women of talent and imagination." With a womanizing husband, some said, she had made a demeaning bargain that allowed her to gain power at the cost of her dignity.

That feminists could be surprised by Rodham Clinton's "bargain" proved that she was still a perplexing symbol after years of leadership in Arkansas and the nation. But this confusion was understandable because the First Lady herself was confusing. She incorporated three personal histories, each with implications for leadership and its dilemmas. Even as she shifted from one phase of her life to another, residues of each would affect her public roles. Yet there remained three distinct personalities.

The first of these emerged out of the cocoon of a caring, demanding family, in a big-brick, Georgian house, on a tree-lined street with gaslight-style streetlamps. Many of the neighbors belonged to the big Methodist church that helped bring the community together on Sunday. *Community* was the word for Park Ridge, Illinois, with its upper-middle-class families, its clubs and societies, its conservative businessmen-fathers and stay-at-home mothers, all in a suburban enclave well protected against intrusion from the huddled masses in Chicago, a commuting-trip away.

The Rodhams were hardly a nonfunctional family, as compared to Bill Clinton's. But neither was everything serene for Rodham and her two young brothers, once past the infant stage. Her father, Hugh Rodham, had not grown up in such agreeable surroundings. After working as a coal miner during the Great Depression, he won a football scholarship to Penn State University. Eventually he owned a Chicago business that sold custom-made draperies to hotels and airlines. He was a "tough guy—gruff, big, and overweight," a friend of Rodham's recalled. And why not—"life is hard out there," he would tell his children. He had definite ideas about how to raise his offspring. They must not be spoiled. They should earn their own spending money. They must not even be paid for chores around the house. Dorothy Rodham was different. Lacking a college education, she had learned on her own at local junior colleges. She was a secret Democrat, some suspected, perhaps a closet intellectual and even a feminist who wanted no doors closed to her daughter. But she did not stand up to her husband when it came to discipline or politics.

On one matter the parents fully agreed—their children would have the best education. "Learning for learning's sake," Dorothy would say. "Learning for earning's sake," Hugh would add.

Above all Hugh Rodham was a rock-ribbed Republican who believed in rugged competition. Hillary Diane Rodham combined her father's competitiveness with her mother's strong boosting to the daughter's self-confidence in school. She could outplay the boys in softball and throw herself into swimming, tennis, skating, and skiing. In her large consolidated high school she won not only high grades but close friendships with her teachers. And she carried a series of student elections even though some of her schoolmates viewed her as a bit cold and distant, dubbing her Sister Frigidaire.

Her choice of college might have triggered a confrontation with her father, for Hugh Rodham had little tolerance for eastern schools with their liberal faculties and rambunctious students. But here again the overriding issue was the best education. Rodham was allowed to apply to Radcliffe, Vassar, Smith, and Wellesley; she chose Wellesley partly because a high school teacher had liked it, but partly because it struck her as familiar and reassuring, in a leafy suburb outside Boston, removed from the racial and ethnic tensions of the city to the east but close to its cultural attractions. Driving from Park Ridge in their Cadillac, her parents deposited her at the college in the fall of 1965. Soon she was repeating her high school successes, winning student offices and top grades, along with the admiration of faculty members.

Rodham's most notable feat at Wellesley came in the act of leaving it. Pressured by her class, the college had agreed for the first time to adorn commencement with a student speaker, and of course Rodham was that speaker. She set the audience to buzzing when she first rebuked the guest speaker, Republican senator Edward Brooke of Massachusetts, for a speech without substance, then attacked "our prevailing, acquisitive, and competitive corporate life, including, tragically, the universities." It was a small but courageous act of student leadership.

Had Wellesley radicalized Hillary Rodham? Sitting in the audience, her father could have had no fear. His daughter had inherited the family and community Republicanism. In high school she had headed the membership committee of Students for Goldwater; in college she had led the campus Young Republicans; in the Wellesley Internship program she had worked for Republican congressmen. But she appeared to be moving toward moderate Republicanism in 1968 when she volunteered for Nelson Rockefeller's abortive campaign for president.

At twenty-one Rodham was, in heart and mind, essentially the product of Park Ridge—of its upper-middle-class culture, Ten Commandments Methodism, pervasive Republicanism, of its suburban isolation from the tumult over Vietnam and civil rights and urban poverty. But a second Hillary Rodham had been germinating in Park Ridge and Wellesley, to flower in other places. Even Park Ridge could not fend off the penetration of ideas—especially when the ideas emanated from the youth minister of the venerable Methodist church, Don Jones. Touting his own self-image as a "pragmatic centrist with a strong dose of political realism," Jones proudly called himself "no raving radical." Rather he believed in thinking that emphasized "decision-making, commitment, and responsibility," according to Rodham biographer Donnie Radcliffe.

Rather heady stuff for a teenager, but Jones also took his charges into the world outside Park Ridge. He took them to Chicago to see art by Picasso, urged them to read the poetry of e. e. cummings, invited them to listen to Bob Dylan as well as Pat Boone. He escorted them to encounters with inner-city youths and to an electrifying meeting with Martin Luther King Jr. following King's speech to a huge city audience. Here Rodham witnessed a transformational leader in action. Long after she left for college and Jones had been sacked by the church as too liberal, she corresponded with her mentor. They discussed theologian Reinhold Niebuhr and his brilliant application of philosophy to political action. "I wonder," she wrote Jones, "if it's possible to be a mental conservative and a heart liberal?" Was it possible, Jones replied, to take Niebuhr's utterly realistic, unsentimental approach to life and yet still be an idealist about the human potential?

Jones also introduced her to Saul Alinsky, the noted grassroots radical, and later she talked with Alinsky about her undergraduate thesis, on community action programs. Rodham had the temerity to challenge Alinsky's basic notion that the poor were poor because they lacked power and must hence be empowered through local organizing. She saw such grassroots activism as necessary but hopelessly inadequate. Her own solution? Evidently better leadership—from above?—but she was vague about this.

Events too were turning her left. The civil rights struggle had swept through the South and spread to Chicago and other northern cities. As Vietnam convulsed college campuses, she put aside her Republicanism to join Wellesley students working for Eugene McCarthy in the New Hampshire primary of 1968. Then—a few months later—King was assassinated. Her roommate remembered the door to their room flying open.

Rodham flung her book bag into the wall. "She was yelling. She kept asking questions. She said, 'I can't stand it anymore. I can't take it!' She was crying."

By the time Rodham arrived at Yale Law School in the fall of 1969, she had become the second Hillary, a confirmed liberal. But she was less a Gene McCarthy or Robert Kennedy type of progressive than an "old-fashioned" FDR–LBJ–New Deal–Great Society liberal. She was above all a policy liberal, concerned with governmental action to address specific problems. On this she would be most consistent, year after year, studying and politicking for the rights of children, migrant workers, penniless defendants before the law, inmates, and—always—children needing better education. She was proud of being a "practical" liberal always seeking specific and timely *results*. Thus she would be an expedient, "pragmatic" leader.

Later there would be conflicting reports as to who approached whom in the Yale Law School library, but it didn't much matter. Rodham and Clinton were bound to meet—both political activists, moderately liberal Democrats, and burning with ambition. It was clear that he would return to Arkansas for his political career, and that she, enamored of him, would at some point follow. What could not be known was the impact of Arkansas on her life and ambitions—and the shaping of a third Hillary Rodham Clinton.

Meantime they had to get their law degrees. It was not serendipitous that they had both chosen Yale, for the law school had a politically involved faculty, a permissive curriculum, and a pass-fail grading for the first semester of the first year. While Rodham concentrated more on her studies, Clinton took advantage of the ample time available to take part in election contests—notably Joseph D. Duffey's for U.S. senator from Connecticut and George McGovern's presidential campaign. Both candidates failed, but Clinton left with a card file of new contacts. Rodham, finishing Yale a year before Clinton, worked in Washington first for the Children's Defense Fund and then for the House Judiciary Committee's inquiry staff on the impeachment of Richard Nixon. She was learning more about the frustrations and failures of leadership than the successes.

While Rodham brought her pro-McGovern, anti-Nixon bias to her work for the committee, she found the job more a sobering experience than a moral crusade. Listening to the Nixon tapes hour after hour gave her insights into the complex machinery of the White House. She learned first-hand that a president can be brilliantly innovative in making both domestic and foreign policy and yet be utterly self-destructive in his personal conduct. It was a lesson she and the rest of America would soon enough revisit.

One of three women on the forty-three-member staff, and one of the most highly regarded by her bosses, she was happy enough to leave the fetid political atmosphere of Washington to join Clinton in Arkansas.

Nothing delighted Bill Clinton more than taking out-of-state friends—and now Rodham—on a tour of Arkansas. He liked to start in Hope, even noting places where his school bus had stopped. Driving through the state, down the Arkansas River Valley toward the Mississippi, he would point out the heavily forested mountain areas, the gleaming lakes, the "hollers" where the invisible poor lived, and of course villages where he had campaigned—all embellished with stories about "ole boys." But concealed behind the rustic charms lay a state in political and social disarray.

And no one had made a more penetrating analysis of Arkansas politics than southern political scientist V. O. Key Jr. In his classic *Southern Politics,* Key summarized Arkansas politics as one of factional fluidity—"pure one-party politics of personal organization and maneuver." Because all serious contenders for office were Democrats, save for a few "mountain Republicans," conflict in Arkansas tended to be more over populist politicians and less about issues and ideology—more about personal followership than policy leadership. It was king-of-the-hill politics, old-boy politics, and not very hospitable to women. Above all, it was hard on the poor. In Arkansas, Key wrote, "more than in almost any other southern state, social and economic issues of significance to the people have lain ignored in the confusion and paralysis of disorganized factional politics." With its wide-open Democratic party headed by garrulous "bubbas," and its party primaries dominated by friends and neighbors, Arkansas politics was made to order for a young politico with a seductive personality, boundless ambition and energy, and a thick pile of index cards. In Arkansas, Rodham learned more about personal politics than policy or program leadership.

In American state politics the ladder of success is often long and creaky. First you run for school board or town council, then take a shot at county commissioner, then move up to the state legislature, all the while with an eye on the glory of the governorship. Clinton had a different ladder in mind, a national one. Like his mentor Bill Fulbright he would run for Congress, then for statewide office. He was twenty-eight years old.

He immediately showed facility in a special feature of Arkansas primaries—the lively dance of coattail seizing and shunning. The problem was his long association with Fulbright, whose political fortunes were now sinking. The governor, Dale Bumpers, was contesting Fulbright's Senate seat. Clinton spent much time with Bumpers at campaign meetings, incidentally picking up tips from the governor's skill at captivating rural audiences. Clinton's allegiances seemed ephemeral, his brand of personal politics flavored by who could most advance his ambitions when. Bumpers beat Fulbright by the humiliating margin of three to one. It was another lesson for Clinton: his mentor, a national leader, had fallen victim to the parochial politics of Arkansas.

Clinton beat his primary opponent for Congress, a state senator. This should have been the end of the story in a southern state in the 1970s, where a Democratic nomination was tantamount to election. But the Arkansas highlands had long been friendlier to the GOP than the rest of the state, and now Clinton faced a tough Republican incumbent, John Hammerschmidt. Taking him on was a bold move for the young challenger, but Clinton thought he had a secret weapon. Late in July 1974 the House Judiciary Committee had voted articles of impeachment of Richard Nixon. Clinton would make Hammerschmidt's friendship with the beleaguered president his key issue. Then, on August 9, Nixon suddenly resigned.

But this setback brought a boon—as would so often happen in Hillary Rodham Clinton's career. Her job with the Watergate inquiry having ended, Rodham arrived at campaign headquarters to help out. She quickly took over a disorganized campaign. In the final weeks, with Nixon unavailable as a target, Clinton tried a populist, Trumanesque strategy against his foe. He denounced the GOP as the party that wanted to keep corporate profits high and wages low, that caused recessions and then told the working classes to tighten their belts. Off the stump, though, he honored another Arkansas Democratic party tradition by raising money from big business—especially the huge Tyson Food, Inc. But Hammerschmidt too knew how to raise money. He edged Clinton with 51.5 percent of the vote.

Clinton worried for a time over his loss, but—in a pattern that would characterize his whole career—he soon recognized the seeds of future success in his defeat. He had taken on the strongest Republican in the state and almost beaten him. The lesson was to choose his target more carefully. He set his sights on the race for attorney general as a likely stepping-stone to the governorship. With only weak opposition in the primary, his major problem was organized labor, which had backed him for Congress but now wanted him to boost their campaign to repeal the state's right-to-work law. Clinton, now seeking to moderate his liberal image from the congressional campaign, balked at repeal. The state AFL-CIO was furious, even when Clinton came to their state convention, the press reported, "with tears in his eyes."

Clinton won a majority of the primary votes, thus avoiding a runoff. And then he was spared the general election contest, for no Republican had run for the nomination. At the age of thirty Bill Clinton was attorney general of Arkansas. But even now he had his mind on a wider scene. Between the primary and the election he helped run the Jimmy Carter campaign in Arkansas, while Rodham took over a more trying assignment—field coordinator in Indiana for the Georgia governor. She emerged from the campaign season with a political reputation markedly different from Clinton's. Reversing the usual gender stereotypes, Rodham was applauded for her decisive, no-nonsense, sometimes abrasive style, while Clinton retained his image of the ever-schmoozing, self-promoting political salesman.

The endless campaigning had a happy interlude. Rodham and Clinton married in the fall of 1975. But it was more a political marriage, some friends felt, than a deeply committed one—a "kind of bargain," one said. But Clinton carried it off with his usual aplomb, and Rodham looked radiant. She made it clear, though, that she would keep her own name, much to the distress of Clinton's mother, Virginia—and, as the couple would discover, to the distress of Arkansas voters too.

While Bill Clinton and Hillary Rodham moved smartly along the path they had set for themselves, Al Gore was slowly changing his mind about politics. The events of the late 1960s and early 1970s, especially his father's reelection defeat, had soured him on political life. But his tenure as a newspaper reporter and a law student produced an outer transformation that reflected an inner awakening, one that his friends and mentors had always expected would come with time. His father's tough congressional defeat had toughened the son.

In 1974, John Seigenthaler had been after Gore to consider public service, but Gore wanted more time. Two years later, on the morning that the wire service Teletypes brought word that a seat in Congress would be open, Seigenthaler again called Gore.

"We talked about it. And I was encouraging him—no pressure, but I was encouraging him. I always thought that he was made for journalism, but I also think he's made for politics. I think primarily he's made for public service. That's what he wants his life to be about. By that time, the disillusionment with politics had passed and he saw this as an opportunity to serve."

Gore decided to run. The first call he made was to his parents, who were in California. "This call came about four in the morning—it was real, real late," remembers Al Gore Sr. "I grabbed the phone and Pauline was on the extension and I said, 'Hello.'

"He said, 'Dad?'

"I said, 'Son, are you hurt?'

" 'Nothing's the matter. The seat is open. I'm running.'

"Well, it took my breath away, and I said, 'Look, Son, I'll vote for you.' "

In what proved his most difficult election fight ever, Gore defeated eight primary opponents and prepared to go to Washington. There he stayed—in the House and the Senate—for nearly the next twenty years before making his way to the White House, which his father aspired to but was never quite able to reach.

Bill Clinton did not use his Arkansas attorney generalship merely as a stepping-stone to his next objective, the governorship. His limited goals as attorney general—lowering utility rates and boosting energy conservation—were good policy as well as good politics. His strategy was to wait for outside pressure to "force" him to act boldly. Only after a judge had called Arkansas prisons "dark and bloody" under Orval Faubus did Clinton try seriously to reform the system. But by now all political calculations were turning on the next race. When the incumbent governor announced for the Senate, Clinton declared for governor. In 1978, he trounced a little-known and poorly financed Republican two to one.

Clinton's governorship could serve as a textbook example of the young, activist, ambitious leader coming up against a state's heavily fragmented and personalized transactional politics. Executive power was amply checked—especially by a legislature that could override vetoes by a simple majority. The governor's two-year term made for short-run, expedient leadership rather than sacrifice or planning for long-term gain.

Clinton assembled a staff much like himself—educated, opportunistic, brimming with ideas. He proposed a big roads program requiring higher licensing fees, only to see it blocked by the trucking industry's legislative lobby. He then proposed shifting the major tax burden to cars and pickup trucks, only to kindle the wrath of drivers across the state. Tighter regulation of the timber industry triggered counterattacks. Even setting up a task force to consider restrictions on timber companies' ravaging of virgin forests set off what Clinton called a "buzz saw" of criticism from timber owners, sawmill workers, log wrestlers, and state lawmakers from the forestry counties. The governor backed off.

He also had a piece of sheer bad luck. The Carter administration decided to send to Fort Chaffee in Arkansas thousands of Cuban refugees who had been boatlifted from Mariel. Confined in what they called a concentration camp, several hundred Cuban militants broke out of Chaffee and fought a brief pitched battle with state police. Helicoptering up from Little Rock, Clinton met with the military and activated the National Guard, but there were some casualties and then quarrels as to whom to blame for the fracas—Washington, the local military, or the governor.

It was a poor reward, Clinton grumbled, for his work for Carter in 1976. "You've fucked me!" he fumed at the Carter White House.

Encouraged by Clinton's rising vulnerabilities, several candidates decided to contest his 1980 reelection. Frank White, whom Clinton had vanquished in an earlier Democratic primary, now turned Republican and jumped into the race. A Little Rock savings and loan executive, White commanded plenty of money and television time. Clinton could not counter with a striking list of achievements. The man who had wanted to transform the state could list only good but limited advances—a school for gifted children, a hazardous-waste code, an intensive care unit for newborn children, promoting overseas markets for state products. White won decisively.

In American politics, if nothing succeeds like success, nothing fails like failure. Defeat not only stunned Bill Clinton, it mortified and humiliated him. It was one thing to miss capturing that Republican congressional seat; it was far, far worse to be thrown out of the governorship he had held. And Little Rock was not kind. The "wunderkind of Razorback politics" was suddenly not so wonderful. And to be beaten by a Republican in a Democratic state! The defeat now put enormous pressure on the Clintons. They could not flunk again; a second defeat would mark them as failures—*losers.*

The financial pressure intensified too. Defeat made money all the more important and at the same time harder to raise. Clinton lost his $35,000 annual salary as governor, but the most profound impact was on the working life and psychological outlook of Hillary Rodham. She had joined the Rose Law Firm, one of the most financially high-powered partnerships in the state. That provided a quick introduction to the world of big money and political influences of the big corporations headquartered in Little Rock.

This was a world of land speculation, investment gambles, kaleidoscopic market changes, roller-coaster incomes, reputed "rip-offs," and worse. It was not a wholly alien environment for Rodham; her father had tutored her about stocks and bonds. Since she could be as competitive in finance as she and Clinton were in politics, doubtless she gained some satisfaction from pitting her wits against the "pros." But this was a world where financial success could produce more envy and suspicion than admiration; when, with the help of colleagues, she made $100,000 profit in cattle futures on a tiny original stake, she was more censored for this than commended.

The exact nature of her dealings and wheelings would be determined years later, perhaps in the courts. But there was little question about the impact on her. If Arkansas politics brought out the worst of Bill Clinton as a compromiser and manipulator, Arkansas economics brought out the "other side" of Hillary Rodham as a transactional dealer. Yes, it was "hard out there," more so in Arkansas than Washington. But the third Hillary Rodham was neither the straight arrow of Park Ridge nor the compassionate liberal of the 1960s.

The third Rodham Clinton took out her financial and political frustrations on the governor's people. Typically businesslike and professional in her legal ventures, she could not abide the occasional slovenliness and incompetence of some on the governor's staff. She would burst into tirades in the governor's office, swearing like a trooper in a way that made the real troopers wince. Much of this was exacerbated by her concern as to where Clinton was, what he was doing, what women he might be with. She provoked mutual suspicion and animosity in an entourage under constant pressure.

Both Clinton and Rodham tried to make some sense of the defeat, but she still found it almost incomprehensible. "I've been thinking a lot about the irrationality of politics," she wrote her old mentor Don Jones. One irrationality was the critical buzz about her continuing use of her maiden name. Letters had arrived at the gubernatorial mansion: "Doesn't your wife love you?" Keeping her name had been important to her; it made her "feel like a real person," she had insisted. But now, for electoral reasons, she would use her married name.

Bill Clinton too was learning, about Arkansas politics and leadership. He worked out some political maxims:

Most people are for change in general but not in particular.

You're most vulnerable in politics when you think you're least vulnerable.

Whenever someone tells you "It's nothing personal," he's about to stick it to you.

Under enough pressure, most people—but not everybody—will stretch the truth on you.

Never look past the next election. It might be your last.

There's no such thing as enough money.

Don't drink in public. You might act like yourself.

After her immersion in Arkansas politics, Hillary Rodham could hardly disagree. George Washington would hardly comprehend.

COMEBACK—AT ANY PRICE

They must not fail this time. The campaign to dislodge Governor Frank White began eighteen months before the election, in the spring of 1981. Trying to wipe the slate clean, Clinton apologized on television for mistakes in office. He and Rodham revamped his staff, calling in Betsey Wright, who had impressed the Clintons in the McGovern campaign, and bringing back political consultant Dick Morris, forced out by Clinton in a dispute during the 1980 campaign. They tried to bypass the hostile press through huge mailings and paid commercials. They began relentless grassroots tours. Above all, they raised money, hundreds of thousands of dollars from the usual corporate and special interest sources. They needed every dollar, barely surviving a lethal primary fight. Then they vanquished White, with almost 55 percent of the vote.

It was Clinton's critical victory; he would never lose another state or national election. He would hold on to the governorship in campaign after campaign, but these were now prepresidential contests, covered by the national press. The Clintons also realized, though, that they had to demonstrate policy leadership as well as election skills. So Clinton resolved to become the "education governor." He would dramatize the problem and then dramatically combat it. During his first term he had sponsored an official assessment of primary school education, with appalling—and predictable— revelations. Back in office after his 1982 win, he set up an education standards committee under Rodham Clinton, who was renewing her leadership role in the administration and had by now assumed her husband's surname. For four months Rodham Clinton and the investigators toured the state, holding hearings and dialoguing with parents, teachers, students, and administrators. The findings were again, predictably, appalling. The committee proposed a longer school year, smaller classes, more counseling and monitoring, and other solid, traditional liberal-reformist changes. It was only a first step toward a Bill-Hillary coleadership strategy.

The "education governor" received good press, especially after he called a special education session of the legislature. But then he ran into a political thicket—educators opposed to "teacher testing," businessmen hostile to an education tax hike, labor and consumers long pledged against a higher sales tax. Some limited steps were taken, enough to bolster Clinton's image in the national press but not enough to prove Clinton's commitment or skill in transformational leadership of educational reform. And the coleadership was viewed with suspicion by some Arkansas voters, including women.

Clinton's governorship presaged his leadership style as president. Close observers noted his moderate, centrist strategy. He had "powerful core principles," observed an admirer, political scientist Diane Blair, but he was "very much a pragmatist when it comes to getting things done." Said another friend, "He sought out the middle of the road. . . . He would push for an agenda that would be regarded as fairly liberal, and then he would back away from it" as "political reality came to him. He would compromise for something pretty much middle of the road."

How "practical" was it all? Despite intense politicking by the governor and valiant help from Rodham Clinton, Arkansas remained at or near the bottom in education. Other southern states did a bit better. Arkansans could no longer bank on their old consolation: "Thank God for Mississippi."

For scholars studying presidential elections, no question has remained more mystifying than why did Bill Clinton, "this young man from nowhere," win the presidential election of 1992? The how of his win has long been clear: campaign skills, ample money, running scared, underestimation of him by President Bush's campaign people until too late. But the why of Clinton's win suggested other explanations.

Clinton, to be sure, had won some national attention. He had politicked to become chairman of the National Governors' Association, both for the honor of it and the speeches he could make around the country. He was active in the Democratic Leadership Council (DLC), the controversial lobby and think tank for moderate and conservative Democrats. But the main national memory of the southern governor in the Democratic party was his nominating speech for Michael Dukakis in the 1988 Democratic convention—so long and boring that delegates were shouting "give him the hook" before the television cameras.

The answer to the why of his win lies more in the realm of conjecture: the absence of potentially strong opponents and the presence of Hillary Rodham Clinton. The 1992 election would be remembered as the year that inherently strong candidates, including Senators Bill Bradley of New Jersey, Jay Rockefeller of West Virginia, and Al Gore of Tennessee, decided not to enter the race. Clinton's people were most concerned that Governor Mario Cuomo of New York would run. A December 1991 poll showed the governor leading all possible rivals by a considerable margin. Cuomo changed his mind about taking the plunge, more often, someone once said, than a novice parachutist. Finally, as a chartered plane warmed up on the runway to fly him to New Hampshire, he made up his mind. He was out. "Cuomo would have been hell in a primary," Clinton campaign adviser James Carville admitted.

Three senators—Paul Tsongas of Massachusetts, Bob Kerrey of Nebraska, and Tom Harkin of Iowa—were in the New Hampshire race, along with Virginia governor Douglas Wilder and former California governor Jerry Brown. All had better-known policy positions than Clinton. But the primary schedule, which displayed all the electoral logic of a used-car lot, began of course with New Hampshire. The primaries would as usual combine the politics of personality, a fierce vote-getting entrepreneurship, and elaborate ploys to attract media attention. Serious issues and choices would take a backseat. All this was markedly to Clinton's advantage, except for one huge potential pitfall. In a race turning on personalities and publicity, he had left himself highly vulnerable through his womanizing.

When the news broke in early 1992 at the New Hampshire headquarters that back in Arkansas a woman named Gennifer Flowers was talking to a tabloid newspaper about a twelve-year affair with Clinton and had a tape recording as evidence, it was Rodham Clinton who remained cool and collected in the crisis. With her husband she worked out a carefully calculated joint interview on CBS's *60 Minutes.* Clinton admitted he had known Flowers but the relationship was "very limited." Rodham Clinton said, "I don't think being more specific about what's happening in the privacy of our life is relevant to anyone besides us. We're proud of our marriage, we've kept it going, and we hope that's what we can convey to the American people." It was clear she still loved her husband, whether or not she trusted him.

Much has been made of how Rodham Clinton "stuck by her man," then and later. Less has been made of the drive and direction she brought to the whole campaign—to the degree that David Brock called her the "cocandidate." "The Clintons were an awesome political team, complementing one another's talents perfectly," Brock wrote. "With her education plan, Hillary had given Bill the political identity as the 'education governor' that he used to get reelected three times and that served him as a springboard to the presidency. She had cut some corners in her legal practice to boost the political partnership. She had changed her name, her hairstyle, and even her public persona for political gain. She went on television to defend Bill against charges of infidelity and then assembled one of the most effective political damage-control operations in the history of American politics." What was even less known was the grim determination that gripped Rodham Clinton as she fought to preserve Clinton's nerve and morale—and the extent to which it toughened further the "third Hillary."

The Arkansas governor came in second in the New Hampshire primary to Tsongas—curiously considered a great victory, while third place would have been viewed as the automatic death knell for his candidacy. Then came Super Tuesday—five southern primaries—which Clinton had to win as the only southern candidate. He carried them all, ranging from a two-to-one win over Tsongas in Florida to eight-to-one in Mississippi. Evidently the South was ignoring the prodigal son's indiscretions—another harbinger of things to come? Thereafter Clinton's momentum carried him through the critical primaries of Illinois and Michigan and to impressive wins in New York and even in California, where he beat native son Jerry Brown.

Again the question arose, how did Clinton win these primaries so decisively? One answer bordered on the cynical. Name recognition was essential in elections where voters, confused by the barrage of ten-second images and the whole crazy-quilt nomination process, groped for some cue. Suddenly two names emerged from the cacophony, a name projected in big headlines and on late-night shows: Bill Clinton and the wife who stood by him. Once again, Bill Clinton had it both ways.

Aside from one decision, the 1992 Democratic National Convention would be but another quadrennial orgy of celebration and pontification. The party platform, carefully designed to foster Clinton's chosen image as a "New Democrat," played up the theme of "opportunity with responsibility." This phrase, with all its ambiguities, was the key concept that Clinton offered in his acceptance speech. But one notable and potentially historic act took place at the convention—the nomination of Al Gore Jr. for vice president.

Most of the delegates had some knowledge of Gore: that he was the son of a much admired senator from Tennessee who had lost his seat in part because of his opposition to Vietnam; that Al junior had grown up mainly in Washington, with summers back on the family's Tennessee farm; that he had attended both law school and divinity school, followed by a few years as a journalist; that he had plunged into the 1988 presidential primaries with a big head of steam that had evaporated by the time of the Illinois and Michigan primaries; and even that he was a self-styled "raging moderate" who favored a strong defense and opposed gun control. And now, in 1992, they knew the most crucial immediate fact about Gore—he was Clinton's selection for running mate.

The choice of Gore was both conventional politics and calculated risk. It was conventional in the sense that Clinton obviously felt comfortable with Gore, a fellow member of the DLC, a southerner, and a baby boomer with a reputation as a straight arrow, a square shooter, and a team player. It was risky in that it rejected age-old nostrums about balancing a ticket by religion, geography, and age. Both men were Baptists. They came from adjoining states. They were only a year apart in age. Some derided this ticket of two "baby bubbas." With the South turning increasingly Republican, Clinton was determined to win Dixie back to the Democrats with his all-southern ticket.

But did Clinton know how much Gore had changed since they had come to know one another at DLC events? The Tennessee senator had undergone virtually a personal metamorphosis. Generating this change were potent forces: Gore's misgivings about his role in the poll-driven, media-dominated presidential campaign of 1988; the near death of an adored son struck by an automobile, producing personal and family introspection; a

65

spiritual reawakening; and a heightened interest in the global implications of environmental crises he had long been concerned about. He published his views in January 1992 in *Earth in the Balance,* a work that impressed many critics with its philosophical inquiry, psychological insight, and grasp of both ecology and technology.

"This life change," Gore wrote, "has caused me to be increasingly impatient with the status quo, with conventional wisdom, with the lazy assumption that we can always muddle through. Such complacency has allowed many kinds of difficult problems to breed and grow, but now, facing a rapidly deteriorating global environment, it threatens absolute disaster. Now no one can afford to assume that the world will somehow solve its problems. We must all become partners in a bold effort to change the very foundations of our civilization." Like Clinton he was preaching change, but was he taking a bolder approach to it? And how might this play out over the course of their White House partnership?

Gore criticized himself. "I have become very impatient with my own tendency to put a finger to the political winds and proceed cautiously. The voice of caution whispers persuasively in the ear of every politician, often with good reason. But when caution breeds timidity, a good politician listens to other voices. For me, the environmental crisis is the critical case in point; now, every time I pause to consider whether I have gone too far out on a limb, I look at the new facts that continue to pour in from around the world and conclude that I have not gone nearly far enough. . . . And the time has long since come to take more political risks—and ensure much more political criticism—by proposing tougher, more effective solutions and fighting hard for their enactment."

He called for a higher level of leadership. "Especially in times of rapid change, the ability of leaders to provide vision and to catalyze appropriate responses to danger is critical." But Gore's book proposed no strategy for such leadership. He evaded the gritty obstacles facing committed leaders—the weakness of parties, the deadlock and disarray in government, the domination of politics by media and money. The "political system is simply not working," he said, but he offered no plan for fundamental or structural changes.

A critic of the election process, a denouncer of muddling through, a preacher of visionary leadership, an advocate of boldness, a practitioner of self-transformation—this was the man Clinton was calling to his side as a partner in a grand effort to recapture the presidency for the Democrats. And this was the man who had agreed to plunge into the very kind of campaigning and politicking that he had excoriated in his high-minded testament.

The Clintons and the Gores began their quest with a grassroots campaign innovation—a bus tour. If the 1992 campaign was a symbolic quest, a traveling down the pathways to political power, they would make the idea real.

The bus was personal, fun, and tremendous political theater. The vehicle itself was not a poor man's "trailer," but a streamlined, forty-five-foot custom cruiser with table space for Clinton to play his favorite card game, hearts, and a sound system for them all to listen to the bluesy rock singer of their generation, Bonnie Raitt. For almost a week, the bus traveled a thousand miles from media market to media market in New Jersey and Pennsylvania, and then through the Appalachians into the Midwest heartland, ending up in St. Louis.

Taking the bus allowed Clinton to play the role he most loved, the man who touched people. For Gore, rolling up his shirtsleeves to toss footballs with real voters peeled some of the bark off the wooden image the press carved for him early on. The bus also gave the campaign a chance to show off the two smart and engaging wives. When Tipper Gore and Hillary Rodham Clinton emerged from the bus, the crowds came alive with shouts and screams and whistles, pushing the male candidates to the background.

Derided by the opposition as just another political stunt, the bus was in fact part of a carefully revamped election strategy. Clinton had emerged from the primaries as "Slick Willie," skillful in evading questions about his womanizing and vague about most issues. Distrust toward Clinton was part of a national mood of cynicism toward almost all candidates, disillusionment with government, and blighted expectations about past and current leaders. Despite his sweep of the primaries Clinton feared that he was not truly engaging with the voters, at least not as he had once done on the back roads of Arkansas. He needed to create the same personal linkage on a national scale. The brainchild of national campaign director David Wilhelm, the bus trip—on the most populist kind of transportation, at out-of-the-way stops, with an eye to local television, with family on board—helped accomplish that.

But the bus tour, with its quick, noisy stops, did little to achieve Clinton's goal of forcing the media to pay more attention to major issues, to the programs he advocated. He had elaborately spelled out his views in a policy-rich document, aimed directly at the voter, entitled *Putting People First.* Its main section, "Putting America to Work," laid out in detail his jobs, investment, tax, "welfare-to-work," transportation, environmental, and child-support proposals. A key theme was "quality, affordable health care." For campaign literature, this document was unusually forthright. On the issue of "tax fairness" it promised, "We will lower the tax burden on middle class Americans by forcing the rich to pay their fair share. Middle class taxpayers will have a choice between a children's tax credit or a significant reduction in their income tax rate." To be sure, there was no equivalent concession to the working class or the poor. But this was the kind of substantive document Clinton accused the media of ignoring or minimizing.

This was not entirely the fault of the media. The press was still having a hard time defining Clinton. Was he running as a liberal or a centrist? An old-fashioned Democrat or a New Democrat? A pragmatic politician or a moral leader? Clinton had no wish to help the journalists by pinning himself to a particular point on the political spectrum. But the voters needed political labels—handles.

The two-party situation didn't help, either. Positions can best be firmed up and clarified in the heat of interparty competition. But as July turned into August, the Republicans were still busy hashing out their own differences. The best news of the summer for Clinton was not anything he generated. It was the disarray in the GOP. In 1991, when so many prospective Democratic candidates had decided not to run, George Bush had enjoyed a seemingly invincible approval rating of nearly 90 percent. But the slightly sour aftermath of the Gulf War—Saddam Hussein was still in power—combined with an economic downturn, sent Bush's approval ratings tumbling.

Worse for Bush, he had not firmly captured the loyalty of his party's base, the conservative movement. Bush had not emerged from the conservative wing. His long years of Washington service—as a congressman, chairman of the Republican National Committee, director of Central Intelligence, and vice president under Reagan—had irrevocably stamped him as a member of the government establishment so reviled by conservative activists. He had failed certain right-wing litmus tests, especially on abortion, and he had broken his pledge not to agree to new taxes. So when he tried to shore up his support on the right by such measures as reaffirming Dan Quayle's place on the 1992 ticket, it smacked of pandering to the conservatives. And it did not deter Patrick Buchanan from mounting a nettlesome challenge in the primaries. By the time of the Republican convention, Bush had higher negative poll ratings than any previous president seeking reelection.

It was late summer 1992 before Bush, by then trailing in the polls, could train his sights on Clinton. The Democrats expected a series of harsh attacks. They were not disappointed.

Bush assailed his opponent's draft record, patriotism, and trustworthiness—and even his trip to Russia during his Oxford years. "I say level with the American people on the draft, whether he went to Moscow, how many demonstrations he led against his country from a foreign soil," cried the embattled President. Most tellingly, he charged that Clinton had raised taxes in Arkansas 128 times. This number, according to strategist James Carville, was an exaggeration of Clinton's actual record, but that hardly deterred the Republicans from trying to make it as familiar to voters in 1992 as Willie Horton had been in 1988.

For Clinton, Bush was a moving target, shifting from an above-the-battle presidential stance to hard-line Reagan conservatism to navy-hero patriotism to street fighter, labeling Gore the "Ozone" man and claiming that Clinton had about as much foreign policy experience as the White House dog, Millie. Later on, Dan Quayle would complain about the Bush presidency that there was no "sense of purpose, direction, no theme, no focus, no guiding message or vision." There was little for Clinton to grab hold of. But Clinton, who was now alternating between centrism and old-fashioned liberalism, presented an equally moving target to Bush. It was like blindman's bluff, with neither candidate clearly seeing the other.

Before either Bush or Clinton could even draw a bead on the other, a third gunslinger reentered the fray and changed its dynamics. Ross Perot had already launched, directed, and terminated an independent presidential campaign in 1992. Now, proclaiming his dissatisfaction with both aspirants, Perot was back in full campaign form. Unlike Bush and Clinton, the billionaire populist was the leader of a movement. Perot's office in Dallas was instantly flooded with calls. Soon he was heading up a third-party campaign empowered by millions of Americans who were embittered by government in general and corruption in particular, worried about the economy and disappointed with the limited choice that the Republicans and Democrats offered them at the polls.

One month before election day, Clinton still maintained a lead over Bush, but there were signs that the gap was narrowing. Candidates now were making trips to their targeted key states. Gone were the days when presidential campaigners moved majestically across the country in trains with rear platforms, stressing environmental issues in the West, farm needs in the Midwest, economic problems in the industrial heartland, foreign policy or urban issues in the Northeast. Now candidates darted here and there, picking out targets of opportunity, making brief television appearances on talk shows or in malls or at sports events. It was almost as kaleidoscopic as the primaries had been.

Perot's electoral strategy was to rack up the highest possible percentage of the popular vote with an eye to running again in 1996. Bush and Clinton followed an electoral college strategy of targeting key districts in key states as the crucial battlegrounds. It was expected that Bush would carry the South and Clinton would win California, New York, and Pennsylvania. The key battlefronts were heartland states such as Illinois, Missouri, and Ohio.

When the returns came in on election night with Clinton winning those three states and most other states in the Midwest and East, as well as on the West Coast, the Bush people knew they were beaten. Clinton took 44.9 million votes to Bush's 39.1 million and 370 electoral votes to Bush's 168. Perot, whose support doubled in the final weeks of the campaign, got 19 percent of the popular vote, but no electoral votes, because he could not carry a single state.

After the bitter exchanges in the final campaign weeks, the election ended on a higher note when President Bush sent his congratulations to Clinton, who then, speaking to a jubilant crowd in Little Rock, asked them to join with him in expressing gratitude to Bush for "a lifetime of service."

*　　　*　　　*

The permanent campaigner had won the top prize through some good luck, much persistence, a skillful staff, and his mastery of electioneering techniques peculiar to the American way of choosing leaders. No one could gainsay the sweep of his victory—decisive wins all the way from the six New England states across the wide midriff of America to the West Coast, where he carried all three states. The most striking aspect of Clinton's vote was his strength in the industrial "rust belt" states contrasted with his defeats across the South, where he carried only Georgia, Louisiana, Gore's Tennessee, and his own Arkansas. After his opportunistic efforts to achieve some kind of moderate or centrist posture in the Deep South, he did little better there than had McGovern or Mondale, in terms of electoral votes. Clinton's losses were Bush's gain: the twenty-year drift of the South toward the Republican party had now peaked with a near sweep by a man from Maine and Texas over a man from Arkansas.

How well informed was the public about the election? In the last three months of the campaign all three major networks spent more than a third of their evening news broadcasts on election coverage. By the end of the campaign C-SPAN had transmitted over 1,200 hours of campaign coverage, and CNN had spent $10 million on its reports. While 77 percent of a national sample questioned within a week of the election said they had learned enough to make an informed choice, the media had dwelt far more on personal aspects of the candidates than on issues.

So most voters were interested in the election, felt informed and entertained by it. But did they feel truly connected with it? Clinton's idea of connection was simple and practical—face-to-face meetings in small groups, with the usual round of handshaking and hugging. In contrast, Perot's straight talk triggered intense political activism that inspired thousands of local committees, which in turn took on a direction and dynamism of their own. If personal contact was a way to connect with people through their hearts, explicit and principled leadership on issues, however controversial, was the way to reach people through their heads. Principled leadership meant a coherent set of goals with clear priorities, firmly built into a roughly structured set of ideas. This is what the Bush-Clinton campaign lacked.

"In the microcosm of Bill Clinton's election," political scientist W. Lance Bennett found signs "of an institutional breakdown in the psychological ties that once bound citizens to parties, candidates, and, in turn, to each other in the American polity." The "psychology of the public political experience has become devoid of the stable cues and identifications that once allowed individual citizens to feel part of solid political groups" and to have confidence in leaders, Bennett wrote.

The prime device in America for linking politicians and people, leaders and followers, into a political vehicle of power and principle was the political party. Clinton campaigned as a Democrat and often appeared with Democratic contenders for state and local office, but his campaign in essence was a huge entrepreneurial effort using marketing techniques adjusted to the personal needs of himself, Rodham Clinton, and Gore. Instead of campaigning on a foundation of party members, local activists, committees, and platform—in short, political organization—Clinton operated in a milieu of volatile media opinion, changing policy angles, shifting interest-group allegiances, and lack of real connection.

He emerged from the election without a strong and stable party base. In olden days, newly elected presidents had carried with them into the White House the heft and reach of a nationwide party built into the wards and precincts, the cities and the states, supplying partisans who would stick with their leaders in the White House. But the culture of the modern campaign did not provide for that. The main gatherings organized by the national Democratic party in recent times have been fund-raising fêtes. When planners of the party's bicentennial decided to invite grassroots party activists from the state and local committees, no lists of such rank-and-file members could be found. But the party's computer could easily produce the names of $25 donors. "The result," according to Bennett, "is an electoral system in considerable disarray, with politicians, the press, and the public all coming in for their share of the blame."

Unlike such contests as FDR's in 1936, Harry Truman's in 1948, LBJ's in 1964, the campaign hardly provided Clinton and Gore with a foundation for strong leadership. This would make the president-elect all the more dependent on his own step-by-step strategy of incrementalism. Could this strategy produce the transformational change that Clinton had promised?

PART II

INNOCENCE IS DROWNED

CHAPTER THREE

Leadership—for a Change?

"What do we do now?" Exuberant Clintonites were still celebrating on the lawn of the Old State House in Little Rock when a campaigner threw this question at reporters who were trailing him. They knew what he was quoting—Robert Redford's last line in the film *The Candidate,* about a feckless campaigner who knew everything about running for office except the ultimate purpose. Did Clinton?

Early in the campaign Clinton had told aides that what he needed most from them was "focus" and "clarity." Campaign adviser James Carville famously posted near his desk:

> Change vs. more of the same.
> The economy, stupid.
> Don't forget health care.

In spite of his challenge to the status quo, Clinton had not in fact called for comprehensive change in his campaign. He had called for a huge menu of specific changes, economic, social, and political. But these could be superficial, mere showpieces, or they could be big enough to rival the transformations that Abraham Lincoln, the two Roosevelts, and Lyndon Johnson had achieved during their early years in the White House.

The problem was that Clinton lacked a war crisis, an economic emergency, or the civil rights struggle that had inspired and hardened the leadership of those four predecessors. The cold war, which had produced so many presidential victories in Congress, from Truman to Reagan, was over.

In the new Congress, the press reported as final returns came in, the President would have slim Democratic majorities in both houses. But Clinton, with his 43 percent of the popular vote, would be dealing with Democratic legislators who had, in many cases, won much clearer majorities. He could not claim a single congressman or senator who had ridden in on his coattails. They had all done better than he in their districts—and they all knew it. The continuing Democratic majorities in both houses contained their usual diverse elements, with conservative southerners still able to hold the balance of power on issues like civil rights. With the largest class of freshmen congressmen since 1949, House support for the new administration was unpredictable at best.

In voting against Bush, an electoral majority had shown the courage to vote for change. The national debt had quadrupled in the Reagan-Bush years to over $4 trillion. Ten percent of the population was on food stamps, and one in eight were living in poverty. These were not small problems.

Other shifts in the political environment awaited Clinton, and they were unique to the last decade of the twentieth century. Americans' faith in government was at an all-time low. When Clinton took office, only 12 percent of the public reported having a great deal of confidence in the executive branch. Seven in ten Americans believed the level of ethics and honesty had fallen over the last decade; the same numbers felt the country was controlled by special interests. From the 1960s onward, even the most rudimentary of democratic responsibilities—voting—had declined by a quarter.

In Roosevelt's time the vast majority of Americans looked to the federal government for assistance and leadership. Before 1960, nearly three-quarters of the public felt they could trust the government to do the right thing all or most of the time; less than one-quarter felt that way in 1993.

Historical cross-cultural comparisons have concluded that four conditions are present in deteriorating democracies: dependent and apathetic followers; low-quality policies coupled with a lack of constituent support; the mystification of the decision-making process; and in some cases, social strife and aggression. Bill Clinton's election and his dream of a changed America coincided head-on with precisely these conditions.

Would Clinton have the courage to lead a change? He had promised some kind of transformational leadership, but he also had limited political clout to offer such vigorous and sustained leadership. He knew that "virtually all major initiatives involving governmental action at the federal level," in the words of presidential scholar Bert Rockman, "gravitate or emanate from the President." As a governor he could buck up tough issues to the White House. As president he knew where the buck stopped.

Clinton faced hard questions at the outset of his presidency—whether he would serve as a transformational or transactional leader, whether he would go straight to the people if negotiating with Congress failed, whether he would pursue a "liberal" or "moderate" strategy.

Remarkably, for a politician long prone to expediency and opportunism, Clinton did have a strategy of presidential leadership—centrism. This strategy had been hammered out in the Democratic Leadership Council (DLC), the Washington think tank of moderate Democrats in which Clinton and Gore had leading roles. The "populism of the center" was one of four secret campaign themes closely adhered to by his inner circle of political consultants. The strategy in essence was sincere on its face—Clinton would position himself, his administration, and his party at the center of the ideological and policy spectrum. From that center he could move left or right as day-to-day needs arose, but he would always return to the middle, somewhere between moderate Republicans and moderate Democrats, and hence he could patch together bipartisan coalitions in Congress. As an electoral strategy, centrism was tactical—it aimed for the huge numbers of voters presumed to be massed or "triangulated" between liberal and conservative "extremists." But how would centrism play out as a governing strategy or as a leadership strategy?

Not for eighty years—not since Woodrow Wilson had come to office—had a new president offered such a considered strategy of leadership. Wilson, like most of his predecessors, was a strong partisan who could operate from his party base. Franklin Roosevelt, amid dire economic crises, pursued tactics of expediency and experimentation, picking up support across the two-party spectrum. John Kennedy entered the White House with a proclivity for wielding influence through personal skills and brokerage rather than party strategies. Jimmy Carter resorted to moral exhortation that transcended party. Clinton's would be a strategy not of party but of a fluid though inconstant coalition of factions and interests.

Thus Clinton's presidency would be a test of political and philosophical centrism as a strategy of leadership. The day after his election, centrism was a general plan of action rather than an explicit ordering of means to established ends. Many details and problems remained to be worked out from day to day. But the somewhat unpredictable foundations and hazy contours of the approach did not dim the certainties of the DLC theorists.

Ultimately centrism would be a test not only of a particular brand of leadership in the White House but also of the longer-term question of whether new presidents pledged to great changes could find the right political strategy to effect those changes—could find the formula for linking practical means to transformational ends.

THE TIME OF THE TROIKA

After a campaign promising change, and despite the alleged leadership powers of the presidency, Clinton could only immediately transform one part of Washington—the personnel in the executive branch. But he had to move fast: like Bush, he had decided against establishing a preelection transition office. But unlike Bush, who could rely on Reagan appointees already in place, Clinton had to begin anew—it had been twelve years since the Democrats had held the White House. He had about ten weeks for the transition.

Actually that was more time than most democracies allowed: in such countries as England and France shifts in power occurred almost overnight, with an established party leadership ready to move into office at any moment.

Clinton had no such leadership during the interregnum, but he already had a mini-cabinet—Gore, Rodham Clinton, and himself. Barring catastrophe, Clinton and Gore could not be removed unless impeached, nor Rodham Clinton removed from the first ladyship unless divorced. While all three stood somewhere a bit left of center, they had their disagreements over priorities. Gore would guard against any cabinet aspirant who might be soft on environmentalism, but otherwise he opted for deficit reduction and other conventional economic policies. He wanted Clinton to be courageous in the FDR style, but courageous for deficit reduction.

Hillary Rodham Clinton stood aloof from some of these postelection discussions. "She wanted mostly to listen, but she also wanted to be sure that everyone at the table was thinking about the real lives behind their decisions," wrote Bob Woodward. Her decisions were not abstract. She had running through her mind a movie of the thousands of people she and her husband had seen on the bus trips and the rallies over the last year. These people had come and clutched his hands, her hands. They had supported Clinton, she felt, because they believed that as president he would pay attention to their concerns.

However tender-minded about people, she was tough-minded in protection of her future turf. Early on it was agreed that the First Lady would have an office in the White House "power center," the West Wing. Her top staff assistants would be intertwined with Clinton's and Gore's, with additional offices in the Old Executive Office Building next door. And she would have her own chief of staff, just like Clinton and Gore, who for the first time would have a dual title that included "Assistant to the President." They would act as a team of three—a kind of "troika."

The transition planning formally began the morning after the election. Bone-tired from grueling months of day-and-night politicking, the campaigners gathered in the first-floor study of the governor's mansion in Little Rock. It had already been decided for the time being to keep most of the transition team in Arkansas rather than Washington. Some suspicion of the distant capital was already evident. Having played the "southerner running against Washington" during the campaign, they could hardly pick up camp and move there overnight.

A clash of ambitions, too, marred the first transition meetings. Campaign chairman Mickey Kantor, working closely with the centrist Democratic Leadership Council and a small, informal group of transition advisers, presented a detailed transition plan essentially proposing that he, Kantor, be in charge. Clinton had had no time to think ahead during the campaign. "It's a real problem, the way we elect presidents," James Carville acknowledged, "the presidential candidate never has any time to think about anything." Clinton looked at the prepared document. Doubtless feeling that he was being prematurely pressured—even "rolled"—the President-elect took the plan and then cut the meeting short, dismissing the group and walking out with the document in hand.

The next day, longtime friend Vernon Jordan was put in charge of handling the Washington transition, and Warren Christopher was to oversee the cabinet selection in Arkansas. Now the process would operate not by Kantor's plan, but more "by guess and by golly," as the Little Rock transition team struggled with the perplexities of linking tentative appointments with tentative policies. John Kennedy had asked Clark Clifford and Richard Neustadt to prepare separate memorandums on the transition process and on the organization of the White House, which had helped immeasurably. But Clinton had been superstitious about such planning and now he had to play catch-up.

The President-elect took a largely mediating role as cabinet selection began. He faced ideological and institutional constraints. He did not want anyone too far to the left of his personal political spectrum. And he hesitated to draft experienced members from the Senate and House because his narrow majorities there might be threatened.

He knew historically that cabinets were increasingly underutilized. In his first year, Jimmy Carter held thirty-six sessions of the full cabinet; by his last year he was down to six. Bush's Vice President, Dan Quayle, had pronounced cabinet meetings "anachronisms." Still, Clinton aspired to a cabinet of thinkers and advisers. As presidential scholar Harold Laski suggested, cabinets were supposed to be groups "where the large outlines of policy can be hammered out in common, where the essential strategy is decided upon, where the president knows that he will hear, both in affirmation and in doubt, even in negation, most of what can be said about the direction he proposes to follow." The quality of the cabinet members, as individual heads of agencies, and as a group, would be crucial. Transformational change hung in the balance.

An effort was made for a structured and organized cabinet-selection process. Christopher would gather a group of five or six people at the Arkansas governor's mansion every day—Clinton, Gore, Bruce Lindsey, and Roy Neel, Gore's longtime aide. Rodham Clinton was often there too, even on the business of lesser appointments. Clinton had invited Neel to accompany Gore, but the President-elect dragged his feet about including his own senior staff. Already Gore's organized, proactive style contrasted with Clinton's open-ended leadership style, which over time would privately frustrate the new vice president.

"Each session began with a kind of high-minded discussion about what the mission of this agency or department or office should be," Neel remembered. "And they were really quite extraordinary.... Rarely were there jokes, personal things, and anecdotes. The process was kept very serious." The group talked at great length about Clinton's preferences, and how so-and-so might fit into his administration. Rodham Clinton would often have some strong views—particularly about Health and Human Services and Justice.

Philosophically, they decided they wanted a team approach, like their own troika structure—with White House and cabinet members sharing in decision-making powers. They would not have the "Cabinet Government" of recent administrations, in which control was delegated to the departmental level. Thus collegiality among the cabinet members became one of three selection criteria, along with diversity and mending political fences within the Democratic party.

From the long, halting deliberations a cabinet was slowly shaped. Embracing Neustadt's wisdom, they named the economic leadership early: Texan Lloyd Bentsen, influential moderate Democrat and chairman of the Senate Finance Committee—famous for his put-down of Dan Quayle, "You're no Jack Kennedy"—was named treasury secretary; and Robert E. Rubin, a multimillionaire investment banker and Clinton fund-raiser, was made head of the National Economic Council. Leon Panetta, announced with the cabinet members of the economic team, would head up the budget office. The foreign affairs team: Warren Christopher, an old State Department hand and strong internationalist, as secretary of state; Anthony Lake, a former Carter administration official and foreign policy scholar, as national security adviser; and Madeleine Albright, another academic, as ambassador to the United Nations. Les Aspin, chairman of the House Armed Services Committee, was named secretary of defense.

Spurred by Rodham Clinton, the troika strove for a diverse cabinet. They chose three women—more than in any other administration since the cabinet was established in 1789. But there were some hidden politics. The paucity of senior black campaign staffers and some difficulties with Jesse Jackson throughout the campaign made the selection of prominent African-American cabinet members difficult. The largest minority group not represented were Asian-Americans, who complained and were promised subcabinet positions.

Whether the cabinet represented a new, deeper diversity was open to question. Like all previous administrations, the appointees were drawn overwhelmingly from the most-privileged, upper-class and upper-middle-class segments of America. Eight of the fourteen members had received their education at Harvard, Yale, or Stanford, and almost all had advanced degrees. Here again Clinton responded by promising more variety in sub-cabinet appointments.

The zeal for racial and gender diversity exacted its price. Particularly for attorney general, the troika wanted a woman. The post might well have gone to Rodham Clinton herself but for legislation, passed after the

Kennedy years, that prohibited the selection of a president's family member. Pushed by their own Christmas Eve deadline, Clinton chose Zoe Baird, a high-salaried counsel for a major insurance company. Shortly after, the *New York Times* ran a front-page story that Baird and her husband had hired illegal immigrants and not paid social security taxes for them. After a flurry of opposition in the Senate and agonizing discussions, Baird was dropped. Clinton announced a seemingly supersafe replacement, Janet Reno, Dade County state attorney in Florida. Still, her vetting required more than two hundred phone calls and a relentless investigation to ferret out anything that might, broadly defined, embarrass the president. She would be the last to take her seat at the cabinet table, on March 12, more than four months after the search for the first woman attorney general began.

Political diversity, crafted to mend Democratic party fences after a difficult primary season, as well as to provide "the mix of new and old hands" that Clinton thrived on, continued as a top aim. Clinton chose leading members of the more conservative wing in Lloyd Bentsen and Les Aspin, of the moderate wing in Warren Christopher, and of the more liberal wing in Donna Shalala, Robert Reich, and Bruce Babbitt.

Perhaps the most striking aspect of the new cabinet was its lack of notability, or at least of notables. There was no Henry Wallace or George Marshall, no Henry Kissinger or Robert Kennedy. The emphasis on diversity had narrowed the choices, putting fair representation over noted accomplishment. Agriculture was wide-open when Mike Espy passed a note to Clinton in early December at a black-tie DLC dinner, indicating his interest in the job. And too, searches for women and minorities slowed the process considerably, as the team had to look beyond its immediate circle. But diversity offered the great hope that lesser-known appointees would make their own mark as leaders, a strategy of political empowerment that had served Clinton well in Arkansas.

During the tough cabinet-selection process the framework of a troika fully emerged, the first such approach to the presidency in history. The President-elect, First Lady, and Vice President–elect would complement one another's strengths and weaknesses, as well as function in a collaborative leadership structure. U.S. senator Harris Wofford acknowledged that, at least in the early going, these three constituted "three centers of power in the administration, and they worked together most of the time. . . . They each have a circle [of influence], and each have a range of issues, and each have a lot of power."

It was easier to stake out Rodham Clinton's space than it was to specify her responsibilities. During the campaign, the Republicans had exploited her image as a policy-maker who rejected the traditional role of wife. She even had a parallel staff during the campaign, with her own chief of staff, communications director, and strategy. "Elect one and get two," Clinton often remarked to audiences of women activists.

But Rodham Clinton even early on was an issue. Most women, proclaimed Marilyn Quayle, wife of the 1992 Republican vice presidential nominee, "do not wish to be liberated from their essential natures as women." The GOP chairman accused Rodham Clinton of likening "marriage and family to slavery." Now the Republicans were warning that the First Lady would be co-President. To the Clintons and their Little Rock advisers, the easy countermove was to make Rodham Clinton a key domestic policy adviser, but with no title.

Very soon, though, it was evident that Hillary Rodham Clinton would become the de facto director of White House domestic policy, save for fiscal policy, which she had no desire or experience to control. This raised two immediate problems. Fiscal and budget decisions, in many respects, drove domestic policy. How could she do general policy-making without understanding the fiscal implications? How could the White House have an effective long-range political strategy if fiscal matters and domestic policy were not integrated?

Then there was the question of publicizing her role. The White House could have announced that the professional woman who had campaigned with her husband, stood by him in defeat and obloquy, and played a leading role in his victories would now be domestic policy director. But that made some advisers skittish. They wanted her to be seen as focusing on "women's issues" such as health and children, and they got their way. But there was a cost. Inevitably, not being totally open about the scope of Rodham Clinton's role meant that a vague hint of duplicity would attend everything she did.

As for Gore, few questioned the legitimacy of his role on matters large and small—or the President's implicit trust of him. Gore quickly became one of Clinton's most able and esteemed advisers. This was no estranged vice president, as some had been. He too took up offices in the West Wing. When the Tennessee senator entered into discussions in the summer of 1992 with then-candidate Clinton about the number-two slot, Gore's father had urged his son to ensure that he obtained "a clear understanding" as to his role in the administration.

The agreement that emerged was clear—and flexible. The President- and Vice President–elect may have been from the South, but they were no bubbas. They knew that White House governing might demand of them things beyond their imagination as mere candidates. Clinton had long been comfortable sharing the Arkansas spotlight; it appeared that he would treat the more intense lights of Washington no differently.

A troika leadership system, harkening back to the Marcus Aurelius Roman triumvirate, would offer both creativity and complexities. "Human triangles"—three interrelating people—in general tend to complicate things.

All the more so when the triangle is composed of no less than a President, Vice President, and First Lady. Triangles are never truly triangles, but two plus one. Although the membership of the pair can change from moment to moment, there is always "two on the inside" and "one on the outside." The odd person in a triangle can break up the relationship between the other two, withdraw from it, or support it by being an interested observer. Thus, the odd person's stance is crucial to the functioning of the troika leadership system, and this trio of self-confident young leaders—Clinton, Rodham Clinton, and Gore—would prove masterful at supporting one another. But it also meant time lost, at least in the appointment process, as staff "needed to coordinate several intersecting power centers." Given the troika's lack of precedence and inherent instability, how long could it last?

ARROGANCE, IGNORANCE, AND ADRENALINE

The joyous moment on election night when the deciding returns had come in to campaign headquarters was also a wrenching moment of change in the relationship of top members of the campaign staff. For months they had been united in one simple overriding aim—defeating Bush. Conflicts and tensions had mainly revolved around the best ways and means of doing that. Suddenly everything was changed. The campaign coordinators were now competitors for the top jobs. They were filled, in political scientist Richard Neustadt's words, with "arrogance, ignorance, and adrenaline." It was not a pretty sight.

And there was no time to lose. Presidents-elect traditionally chose their cabinet members and then their key staff people. But cabinet choosing went so slowly that Clinton's "official" and "unofficial" cabinet appointments were intertwined with potential White House staff appointments. So the men and women who would staff the Executive Office of the President in one of the world's largest leadership bureaucracies fell into disarray at times bordering on chaos.

Did the President-elect in fact want this clutter and scramble? Did he know that Franklin Roosevelt and other presidents had been much admired for deliberately creating conflict among their advisers in order to keep more control—and for the sheer fun of it? As a reader of presidential best-sellers, Clinton knew of FDR's way of bringing together very different points of view, hopefully leading to a productive tension. But the disorganized selection process was probably more a matter of circumstance than plan. The campaign had utterly drained everyone's sleep, time, and energy, and it was easier to operate from day to day, trying at the same time to be accessible to all, at the expense of reflective thinking.

"Not only had the process of governance been generally ignored during the campaign," observed political scientist Shirley Anne Warshaw, "the transition process itself had been ignored during the campaign." Infighting and frenzy reigned for weeks after the election.

With Jordan and Christopher chairing the transition team, DLC founder Al From served as transition director of domestic policy, and Bruce Reed, former DLC press secretary, was installed as deputy. Although DLCers were notably absent from all other policy areas, clearly the moderate Democrats would be in charge of the domestic agenda. Counterbalancing the moderates, Clinton selected liberal Robert Reich, a Michael Dukakis and Ted Kennedy adviser, to be transition director for economic policy.

Delays in the top cabinet selections held up those below at the staff level. By December, onetime campaigners were wild with hope, disappointment, rumors, rivalries. Christmas was another interruption, and then January 20, 1993, inauguration day, loomed large. Few of the White House staff had been chosen. The nonchosen were pleading, pressuring, blackballing.

Part of the problem was the President-elect's difficulty in delegating decisions. One Democratic insider who helped with vetting during the transition observed, "Clinton was very deeply involved in all of these decisions, whereas other presidents have delegated more." Clinton reviewed every position in the White House and met with those selected one-on-one. Even junior-level staff members had time with the President-elect to discuss their future roles.

But Clinton would argue he was careful out of necessity. The first two-thirds of the century were marked by a relatively easy transition and appointment process; in recent decades the process had become turbulent in light of special interest campaigns, partisanship, ethics and personal-background checks, the media, FBI investigations, and financial reviews. Also, the number of presidential appointments that require Senate confirmation has more than doubled.

Looking back, it was a chaotic transition, worsened by leadership and management flaws. "All of these things conspired to slow down the process," remembered Roy Neel. Decisions "didn't get pounded out [and] presented to the President" for him to sign off on "in time to get these people working together for some number of weeks before we had to take office. So we named the senior White House staff" only days before the inauguration. "It was extraordinary. And many of them didn't know each other, very few of them had worked together.

"Meanwhile," continued Neel, "all these people who had worked in the campaign in senior positions—and some not so senior—had no idea what they'd be doing. They were working through the transition; most of them— or the senior people—were still getting nominal paychecks. But they had no idea what was next. No one was giving them a clue." Chief of Staff Thomas F. "Mack" McLarty "did not feel like he was in a position to offer anybody a job. You had just a bunch of people who really didn't know what they were going to be doing."

By the New Year, the transition from campaigning to governing had not been accomplished. Indeed, the question of governance hardly interested the staff at that stage. What preoccupied them were their own survival, status, the title on the door, and where in the pecking order they would end up. They were people with enormous egos, suddenly inflated further by their winning campaign. During that campaign, when there had been little hierarchy, they had disciplined themselves not to discuss jobs with one another. Confiding ambition was bad form, even a jinx. Clinton himself was superstitious about it, believing that too much talk or preparation before election night did not demonstrate the proper humility. It could be dangerous too. In the looming king-of-the-hill competition to be on top in the Clinton White House, who would be a friend, who foe? So they had nursed their hopes in secret; now they had to seize their opportunity.

"The White House is not simply a spoil of victory," observed Harrison Wellford, a former White House official. "It's the nerve center of the greatest government in the world, and we ought to at least give it the same respect that you do when you take over a second-rate corporation." Some of these rivalries would carry over into the administration. And some of the old campaigners would prove far less effective at governing than they had been at electing.

What about the hundreds of office seekers who had no hope of White House jobs but who aspired to political appointments in the departments and agencies? Résumés by the thousands—fifteen thousand a week during the early transition period—inundated the transition offices. Résumés arrived in the mail, by fax, by electronic mail, by hand, over the transom. One staffer told of parking his car in his Washington apartment garage late at night. As he walked toward the elevator, a figure in a trench coat approached him from out of the shadows. The figure grabbed his lapel, stuck a folded résumé in his coat pocket, pivoted, and walked away without saying a word.

The résumés bore the imprimatur of governors and senators, aged politicos, relatives, and numerous FOBs—Friends of Bill. And Bill had many friends. Some had the endorsement of their local or state party committee—not very persuasive with Clintonites, many of whom were almost as suspicious of Democratic party organizations as of Republican.

"In political times, windows of opportunity quickly close," according to a Twentieth Century Fund report on the Clinton transition. "When presidents are unable to fully exercise leadership simply because they have no administrative team to back them up, the quality of governmental performance is diminished and the public trust erodes further. Yet this is now the norm. The new president takes office promptly on January 20, but the president's team trickles in slowly over the following year. The momentum of the election dissipates before there are leaders in place to translate it into policy initiatives." By contrast, in 1960 the average Kennedy appointee had been confirmed within eight weeks. Thirty years later the average confirmation time had lengthened to eight and a half months.

In general the Clintonites from Arkansas were unduly optimistic about their capacity to govern. They had not forgotten, of course, the kind of legislative obstruction and administrative sabotage they had encountered in Arkansas. But the governor's skillful mediating and compromising had often cleared the track for his programs. And, after all, was state government not written up in political science texts as the training ground for national leadership?

It would not take long for even the optimists to discover that Washington, D.C., was not merely Little Rock writ large. The checks and balances at the national level were far more powerful, interlocked, and resistant to executive leadership than in the states. The great prestige and independence of the Senate, the power of factions in the House of Representatives, the huge corporate lobbies, the national press that variously encouraged and thwarted bold leadership, and above all the legacies of the great presidents of the past constantly invoked by politicians and press—all these dwarfed anything that the governor's men and women had experienced in a state that still lived up to political scientist V. O. Key's portrait as rife with "one-party politics of personal organization and maneuver."

Presidential transitions—especially from one party to the opposition party—are an early and harsh test of incoming presidencies. Close observers of the process have given low grades to the presidential leadership qualities revealed in recent party transitions, even though incoming presidents have recognized the critical importance of planning before and during the transition. Jimmy Carter's team consulted with the outgoing Ford administration but paid little attention to the advice received. The eager but inexperienced young men and women from Georgia appeared not to comprehend the complex leadership of the Congress. When the Reagan transition team arrived in Washington four years later, they appeared uninterested in learning from the Carter mistakes. Matters got off to an awkward start when the outgoing and incoming presidents met. Carter felt that Reagan was polite but remote, hardly bothering to take notes.

What were the basic problems with these earlier transitions? "Newness, haste, hubris, and naïveté," concluded two experts on the topic. The worse failing was doubtless hubris—the conviction of the new crowd that they could do much better than the dunderheads who were leaving office.

How did the Clintonites make out, after all this experience with transition difficulties? While Clinton saw the critical importance of this eleven-week period, and while Vice President Gore was given a major role, the transition team was slow in forming, while finally ballooning into a huge, complex structure. Their consultations with the Bush people were agreeable but hardly more than a formality.

Vernon Jordan's ten agency-cluster teams in Washington had been charged with conducting agency reviews, which would be used by cabinet officers as a blueprint for running their departments. In reality, it became a mass of reports without structure and with little coordination. Jordan did not provide much direction to the various teams, which operated relatively autonomously. The lack of leadership from Clinton as well as Jordan during this time meant the new administration had little focus. It was a lost opportunity.

INAUGURATION: HISTORY AND HYPE

The installation of William Jefferson Clinton as president began in Thomas Jefferson country, in January 1993, at the graceful Monticello home of the slave owner. The first black governor of Virginia, L. Douglas Wilder, greeted the inaugural party. Then, in a nice mix of hyperbole and nostalgia, the Clintons and the Gores bused, in their old campaign style, through the small towns and long valleys of Virginia, across the old Civil War battle areas, to the nation's capital. There followed several days of preinaugural celebration, Hollywood style, with a national bell-ringing, astronauts live from a space shuttle, film and television stars, live HBO, traffic jams, and gleaming stretch limousines. It would cost one hundred American corporations more than $25 million.

The bus had followed Jefferson's route to Washington, but otherwise inauguration day, 1993, could hardly have contrasted more sharply with inauguration day, 1801. The tall, loosely framed Virginian had moved quietly out of his boardinghouse near the Capitol and, disdaining a coach-and-eight and even a horse, strolled with a motley throng of congressional and other politicos to the north wing of the unfinished Capitol. Jefferson gave his inaugural address in a low, flat tone that few in the audience could make out unless they had a copy of the *National Intelligencer*, which had somehow managed to publish the speech in advance.

The Jefferson-Clinton contrast was even more striking in substance than appearance. Clinton's inauguration came on the two hundreth anniversary of Secretary of State Jefferson's decision to break with the ruling Federalists by resigning from Washington's cabinet. Ultimately this move led to the creation of a "loyal opposition" to the Federalists and the creation by Jefferson and James Madison of the Democratic-Republican party, which defeated the John Adams Federalists in 1800. Jefferson in his inaugural speech uttered the famous words of conciliation, "We are all republicans; we are all Federalists." Yet he made a more significant though less quoted statement that "the sacred principle of the will of the Majority is in all cases to prevail, though that will to be rightful must be reasonable." Jefferson proceeded to carry out the majority rule of the Democratic-Republicans, while in general accepting the Federalists' right to oppose.

Essential to this doctrine was not only the peaceful transfer of power but, in Jefferson's words, the restoration to "social intercourse" of "that harmony and affection, without which liberty, and even Life itself, are but dreary things." This was also the spirit of 1993. At the end of a century that had seen crushed oppositions and subverted elections around the globe, Bill Clinton's inauguration was saturated in good feeling, starting with the cordial welcome extended by President and Mrs. Bush at the White House on inaugural morning. But all the sweetness and light could not conceal the hard fact: after twelve years of Republican rule, power in the White House had shifted to the opposition leadership.

The chief justice administered the oath of office. Rodham Clinton held the Bible that Virginia Kelley had given her son. It lay open to the selected passage "For he that soweth to his flesh shall of the flesh reap corruption; but he that soweth to the Spirit shall of the Spirit reap life everlasting." It was a rather odd selection, given Clinton's temptations of the flesh in years past, and little noted at the time. Had Hillary selected it? Had he?

Then the new President turned to face the crowd. Stretching directly ahead to the Washington Monument, over on the right past the Robert A. Taft bell tower, over on the left toward the invisible Jefferson Memorial, the crowd was massive, stupendous—the most genuine and significant reality in all the inaugural festivities.

The address itself, written by a squad of speechwriters and carefully edited by the new First Lady, offered the usual pieties: "Though we march to the music of our time, our mission is timeless. . . ." "There is nothing wrong with America that cannot be cured by what is right with America. . . ." "Let us give this capital back to the people to whom it belongs. . . ." "Today we do more than celebrate America. We rededicate ourselves to the very idea of America. . . ." And so on.

But struggling to make its way through all the banalities was an ambivalent message. Clinton teetered between a summons to be bold and a restatement of conservative texts and Republican war cries. He repeatedly asked Americans to meet challenges, but he also proclaimed that "we" should "cut our massive debt," adding, "it is time to break the bad habit of expecting something for nothing from our government or from each other."

But the nation must also have vision. "We know we have to face hard truths and take strong steps," exhorted the new President, "but we have not done so; instead, we have drifted. And that drifting has eroded our resources, fractured our economy, and shaken our confidence. Though our challenges are fearsome, so are our strengths. Americans have ever been a restless, questing, hopeful people. And we must bring to our task today the vision and will of those who came before us. From our Revolution to the Civil War, to the Great Depression, to the civil rights movement, our people have always mustered the determination to construct from these crises the pillars of our history."

Bold change. Dramatic change. Renew, reform, reinvent, revitalize America. The heroic words resonated throughout the address. They were nothing new; he had called for change during his long campaign. But what kind of change? Change for what? The problems were clear, at least to the President, the First Lady, the Vice President, and many of their fellow Democrats: the stagnant economy, massive debt, inadequate health care, political corruption. How to overcome these intractable ills?

Clinton's answer was presidential leadership. But what kind, given the varied leadership styles of American presidents? Some hoped that the new President, in the spirit of the two Roosevelts and other great presidents, would use transformational strategies of setting lofty economic goals and fighting to achieve them whatever the frustrations and setbacks along the way. Clinton believed in a centrist strategy of transactional brokerage and compromise, producing incremental change. Was there an inherent conflict between his ends and means?

At the heart the question was whether Clinton would merely cope with change, responding to economic and technological and environmental changes created by others, or whether he would force the economic and social changes that he and his fellow Democrats had been trumpeting for ages. A centrist strategy would imply the former. But one passage in Clinton's inaugural suggested a stronger leadership for change: "Thomas Jefferson believed that to preserve the very foundations of our nation, we would need dramatic change from time to time. Well, my fellow citizens, this is our time. Let us embrace it." Were these platitudes, or did the new President mean it?

Clinton concluded in a burst of eloquence: "From this joyful mountaintop of celebration, we hear a call to service in the valley. We have heard the trumpets. We have changed the guard. And now, each in our way, and with God's help, we must answer the call."

Though his inaugural address contained flashes of poetry, Americans waited to see whether this new President would end up governing in prose.

CHAPTER FOUR

The Gauntlet of Leadership

The new President was offering some kind of change—but what did the people want?

"Change," wrote Niccolò Machiavelli, "has no constituency." He was right. Calls for change expose would-be reformers to a raucous cacophony of resisters, foes, rivals, adversaries, doubters, and just plain naysayers. Change agents, complain their opponents, are doomsdayers who distort reality. They call for too much too soon. Or demand too little with too much patience. Though conceived in the sixteenth century, Machiavelli's maxim holds no less true on the cusp of the twenty-first. The observation is particularly valid in democratic societies, where the line between leader and follower is blurred, and where many voices are inherently part of governing. To lead is to foment change. And change is messy.

Yet change is precisely what Americans expected from William Jefferson Clinton in January 1993. Had not the self-styled New Democrat promised as much during his campaign? The new President stayed on message during his first day in office too. Clinton's inaugural address pledged to make government "a place for what Franklin Roosevelt called bold, persistent experimentation." Shortly into his first year, the President similarly trumpeted to the National Governors' Association, "I am convinced that what this nation really needs is a vital center, one committed to fundamental and profound and relentless and continuing change." Clinton's linking of "change" and "centrism" seemed counterintuitive, though. Could genuine change occur through moderation? Clinton was masterful at glossing over contradictions.

Clinton had so successfully marketed himself as Mr. Change-Is-Good that 53 percent of Americans on the eve of his inauguration were either "excited" or "optimistic" about his administration. "I don't know any president in my lifetime that has come into office with such a range of things that he wanted to get done," calculated former John Kennedy aide and U.S. senator Harris Wofford. In several areas Clinton faced higher anticipations than did George Bush when he assumed office in 1989. Fifty-one percent of Americans expected Clinton to make "substantial" progress in reducing poverty; only 37 percent expected as much of Bush. Likewise, 68 percent expected Clinton to make "substantial" progress on environmental matters, whereas 57 percent foresaw as much from Bush. On other issues, Clinton similarly aroused hopes: 63 percent of Americans anticipated that he would make significant progress healing the nation's economic ills; and 62 percent expected him to reduce unemployment.

These numbers made some in the Clinton White House nervous. High expectations could quickly translate into widespread disappointment among voters if the anticipated progress faltered. And that could spell disaster for a new president hoping to exercise leadership. White House Political Affairs Director Joan Baggett feared what this might mean for Clinton's first year in office: "Nobody could have filled those expectations. . . . [They] were unbelievable. . . . People thought we'd get health care in the first hundred days." What's more, worried Baggett and her colleagues, if Clinton could not curry favor with his followers during the first few months of his tenure, he'd spend the rest of his term fighting to win them back. That was no way to lead. The new President needed to have the voters follow him, not the other way around.

Opinion poll results were not the only numbers causing Clinton administration officials to fret. Democrats gained no seats in either the House or the Senate in the 1992 elections. They now held 258 seats in the House, to 176 for the Republicans, plus 1 independent. Thus if more than thirty conservative Democrats voted with GOPers, not an unlikely prospect, any presidential initiative could be defeated. In the Senate, the margin was 57 to 43—revealing that Democrats did not have the requisite 60 votes needed to break a filibuster. No other Democratic president this century had begun his first term with so small a congressional majority as did Clinton in 1993. Still, some administration officials nursed a faint hope for the honeymoon that Congress was supposed to accord a new president.

These hopes were soon blighted. Within three months the Senate killed the first major economic proposal from the White House, an "economic stimulus" package. During the next few months the White House made frantic, cliff-hanging efforts to put through its main economic program, but at the cost of jettisoning major components of that package.

What happened was, in part, a collision between the new President's expectations and the realities of the system. Hopes had been pumped up high by Clinton's campaign promises, his plan to hit the ground running, and the mythology of the "first hundred days." Ever since FDR's brilliant legislative leadership in the desperate days of 1933, the media had applied this test to new administrations. But such a quick and fulfilling honeymoon between president and Congress had never happened again, largely because the 1933 situation—an activist, dominating president, an acquiescent Congress, a savage economic depression, and a public demanding "action, and action now"—has never been replicated. In the early months of 1993, Bill

Clinton discovered that the halls of Congress nurtured few supplicants and that few voters were themselves prepared to be silent sycophants.

WITH HONEYMOONS LIKE THIS . . .

In promising so much change, Clinton had at least one historical precedent to ponder. Theodore Roosevelt, FDR's distant cousin, had also approached the presidency with an impatient fervor. Though expectations of TR were not initially as high as those of Clinton—TR's sudden accession following William McKinley's assassination did not allow for bold campaign promises—Roosevelt still managed to exhort, cajole, bully, and persuade Congress into enacting some of the most significant social and economic reform legislation in American history. The lesson for Clinton was that TR did all of this in the absence of a compelling national or international crisis. No war. No depression. No famine. Could Clinton perform likewise in an era similarly devoid of mammoth crises? Could Clinton muster the leadership skills to convince Americans to follow his vision of change?

If he could, the legislators at the other end of Pennsylvania Avenue would surely figure into the equation. The normal relationship between Congress and president was what the Framers of the Constitution had planned two hundred years before— friction. Clinton knew it too, commenting in December 1993 that what bothered him was "when I think somehow the system is keeping us from doing what we need to do for the American people." The legislative and executive branches of government represented different though overlapping constituencies. Deadlock was not an epithet; it was an expectation. At times, the conflict had been somewhat softened by party leadership and unity. In the House and Senate, presidents could deal with majority and minority leaders who could often deliver votes. But as parties declined in power and interest groups gained critical influence, picking up congressional support was often like picking up water.

In their plight, presidents for decades had resorted to "blarney, boodle, and bludgeon" in winning support from Congress. But presidential favors and discipline were now less effective. Members of Congress were becoming more autonomous, more dependent on their own resources. The photograph with the president in the Oval Office, the pen handed out at a bill-signing in the Rose Garden, the warm presidential endorsement, were no longer major sources of presidential influence. Indeed, as Clinton's popularity appeared to sink midway into his first term, some members of Congress decided to shun him at election time 1994 rather than be pictured embracing him.

Enough conservative Democrats were in Congress to tip the balance toward the GOP on close votes. This too was an old problem for Democratic presidents. Stymied by southern Democratic senators during his second term, FDR audaciously invaded their states to ask voters in primaries to dump them. The voters wouldn't. Democratic presidents even from the South—such as Jimmy Carter from Georgia—had little to offer them. Presidents came and went, while the Senate barons went on and on, exploiting their seniority on committees and their vaunted independence.

The President's paltry reservoir of steady congressional support was also, in part, a reflection of political liabilities peculiarly Clintonesque. His mandate was questionable, given the greater percentage of the popular vote won by Congress than by himself. Too, Clinton's legislative experience was confined to a small state with unique customs and procedures. This background proved limiting in the big leagues of national politics. "One of the best preparations for being president is to be governor of a large state," argued a Clinton aide. "One of the worst preparations is to have been governor of a small state. Because if you're governor of a small state, you develop a very personalized relationship not only with the executive branch [but] with the legislature, and you're accustomed to being able to do everything on a very free-floating, noninstitutionalized basis. And the U.S. presidency simply can't work that way."

The White House further compounded the problems with its own strategic errors. Life inside the Clinton White House was something like an old-fashioned round dance, with couples meeting, stepping off, and uniting again in shifting combinations. If not chaotic, the atmosphere was at least frantic, admitted William Galston, who served as deputy assistant to the president for domestic policy. Much was made of conflict within the President's staff, as reports leaked out of angry exchanges and toe-to-toe confrontations. While agreements were constantly being worked out, some decisions might last only a day or so, while other groups worked up other agreements. Groups were composed variously of regular staff members, external consultants, inside and outside pollsters, cabinet or subcabinet members, ad hoc visiting advisers. It was easy for the media to caricature the group as a collection of adolescents, with their jeans, T-shirts, sneakers, and much juvenile use of the F-word.

To cope with this disarray in the early months, "working groups" were organized out of the White House and the departments. These were usually formed around shifting policy issues and hence had a tentative character. Some stability and continuity were provided by the National Security Council, the Domestic Policy Council, and the National Economic Policy Council, but their staffs added complexity and fragmentation as well as a measure of coordination. Another solution was meetings—endless meetings stretching through the night and carried over into weekends.

"Clinton," noticed Labor Secretary Robert Reich, "has a preference for people who are going to collaborate, express their ideas, help him with his continuous process of thinking about policy, and help him reach conclusions about what's to be done." Certainly Clinton encouraged disagreement by seizing on new ideas, calling discussion meetings, including in them virtually any aide who might be involved or interested. Yet the President also, curiously, confessed to a friend, "I love the power and the order that the military provides a man. . . . I know what it's like to live without structure and an authority figure in my life. It's important for individuals and it's important for the country." Perhaps it was the commander in chief in him that was speaking. For hardly the first time, Clinton was a study in contrast.

In his first year, the President was personally accessible, as FDR had been, to almost anyone with a plausible reason to see him on a policy matter. Of all the "meetingest" people in the White House, Treasury Secretary Lloyd Bentsen called him the "meetingest fellow" he had ever seen. But the conferences took a heavy toll on the President's relaxation time, sleep, energy, and opportunity to transcend day-to-day issues and do some reflective thinking. "There was nobody there imposing an order on the White House," admitted Robert Reich. "There was no process policeman, and that got us into a lot of problems."

In the early months, much of the President's momentum, as well as political capital, was sapped by bungled cabinet nominations. The most inglorious of these was the proposed appointment of Lani Guinier as assistant attorney general for civil rights. She seemed the ideal candidate: an old friend of the Clintons' from Yale Law School, an African-American who had specialized in voting rights cases for the National Association for the Advancement of Colored People (NAACP), with experience earlier in the Civil Rights Division under President Carter. Additionally, she had the strong support of Hillary Rodham Clinton, who had taken a special interest in Justice Department appointments. But Guinier, alas, had also written some academic lucubrations—challenging conventional views about majority rule, for instance, as well as the cherished idea that electing African-Americans to legislatures was the way to guarantee civil rights—and these views affronted enough Washingtonians, including blacks, to take on the appearance of Very Dangerous Ideas.

As a drumbeat of opposition sounded in the Senate, White House advisers, including Rodham Clinton, had second thoughts about the appointment. Gore, who had had doubts from the start, took a strong stance against Guinier. For her part, Guinier complained of being victimized by sound-bite allegations that misrepresented her views; she demanded a hearing to defend herself and was alarmed by the President's silence. "He was good at playing hide-and-seek. But is that how he wanted history to know him?" she asked. Guinier saw her nomination as "a test of presidential leadership, a window on the presidential soul. The manner in which the president of the United States would treat a friend was an insight into his character as a

human being, but it was even more than that. It would become an unexpected peek into his character as a leader." If so, the picture was bleak.

It was clear that the appointment was dead in the Senate long before Clinton agreed to withdraw it. Meantime the issue simmered in the media for
many days and then blazed up in a firestorm as the White House dawdled.
With his usual compassion toward friends and political victims, in June
1993 the President had Guinier in for a talk about her writings. He did not
tell her in person of his decision to drop her; instead, Clinton presented the
news in a phone call, shortly after Guinier had left the Oval Office. A few
hours later he tearfully told the press that Guinier's writings did not represent the views he "held very dearly," even though there was much in them he
agreed with. Clinton dubbed his friend's writings "antidemocratic." Guinier
was humiliated and incensed.

Fumbled though the nomination was, the White House could nonetheless contend that it involved tough decisions in a sensitive political context.
The botching of the White House travel office firings had no such defense;
it was a case of pure mismanagement. In May 1993 the seven employees in
this low-level office were summarily sacked without a hearing, on allegations of mishandling finances. They were holdovers from previous administrations, part of the small, low-visibility "permanent civil service" in the
White House. Soon the press was reporting that the office would be taken
over by a Little Rock travel agency and headed by a former campaign
worker and distant cousin of the President's. The incident soon became a
media bungle-of-the-week, as the White House dithered, explained, complained, rehired the ousted seven—and then put them on leave without pay.

Most damaging of all, the travel office incident strongly suggested that
the First Lady was wielding enormous influence within the White House—
and among staff members who supposedly worked for the President. Chief
of Staff Mack McLarty's handwritten notes, for instance, told of "HRC pressure." White House administration director David Watkins composed a
memo charging that Rodham Clinton was the motivating force behind the
firings. White House aide Lorraine Voles's notes reported that the First
Lady's friend Susan Thomases admonished McLarty, "Hillary wants these
people fired." The public increasingly came to view Rodham Clinton as
uncompromising and unfair—and unelected. For a time, her popularity ratings were lower than her husband's.

Other mishaps and setbacks plagued the President too, from Clinton's
treating himself to a $200 haircut at Los Angeles International Airport while
planes were allegedly delayed, to the near-appointment and then disappointment of a candidate for the Supreme Court, to the shocking and inex-
plicable suicide of the Clintons' close friend Vincent Foster. These issues
were not of historic importance, but they crucially shaped the popular image
of the White House as incompetent and drifting. All were inflated by the

media into political tempests that obscured the progress that the administration was making—notably passage of the Family Leave Act hardly two weeks after inauguration day and of Clinton's budget during March.

Were Clinton's difficulties, then, those that every new administration experienced in learning the ropes? The problem lay deeper. "They really weren't ready to govern," charged New York's senior senator, Daniel Patrick Moynihan. The Clintons assumed that the campaigners who had brought off a near-miraculous election victory over the GOP had the finesse, the imagination, and the toughness to win victories over bureaucrats, congressmen, and media people. They underestimated the need for seasoned presidential administrators who had been "through it all" before. Previous presidents had understood this need; thus FDR had kept on the veteran "executive clerk," Rudolph Forster, whom coworker Grace Tully described as unobtrusive, nonpartisan, "correct" in his relationships with eight presidents, and with a "passion for anonymity." Such aides had a special nose for political booby traps and administrative snares. The new White House tenants had not even made a real effort to recruit available personnel from the Carter administration. And as time wore on, it became clear that some of Clinton's aides relished the media spotlight and lucrative book deals as much as they took to policy-making.

If Clinton was the chief source of the mishaps, he was also the prime victim. Even in the early months he had a desperate feeling of time running out, opportunities missed, work undone. Why the rush? In part, it was political: "He knows that one way or another all of this is fleeting," reckoned a White House aide. "One of the things he learned in his devotion to the Kennedy presidency," and having been turned out of office himself in 1980, "is that he has no idea how long he's going to govern." In part, it was personal too: "I have been living with the idea of my father's death and therefore my own mortality since I was a kid," Clinton told an interviewer in 1991, "and that's maybe why I competed so hard and wanted so much." Even on his honeymoon, Clinton toted along Ernest Becker's *Denial of Death,* a searching philosophical work seeking to explain man's "urge to heroism" in his fear of death. For all of the new President's vaunted optimism, he also nursed a ubiquitous and eerie—and fairly private—sense of mortality.

Clinton initially hoped to build momentum via a quick, popular, and symbolic victory on the Hill with the revived Family Leave Act. Twice during the Bush administration, the Congress had passed this bill, which required businesses to give up to twelve weeks of unpaid leave annually to workers with family needs, such as births, adoptions, or the serious illness of a child or parent. Twice, President Bush had vetoed it.

Not that the bill was likely to affect the lives of many people. Its provisions were modest in comparison to the benefits afforded workers in Western Europe. The working poor could hardly afford to take much unpaid leave. Even the bill's backers conceded that it was only a foot in the door, not the kind of support that working people with families needed. But on a symbolic level, the bill struck the right chords. It targeted the problems of people Clinton had charged were neglected during the 1980s, people with jobs and families who struggled to stay in the middle class. It was a bill that the Republicans had rejected as an unfair burden on employers. It was a bill that demonstrated the changed attitude Clinton intended to bring to all governmental decisions. And it was a bill that resonated with what the First Lady saw as one of her husband's driving principles—"social justice with respect to income inequality."

But by the time of the signing ceremony in the Rose Garden early in February 1993, it was a bill being largely ignored. Instead, public attention was riveted on a controversy that could do Clinton little good, the controversy over gays in the military.

During the campaign, Clinton had promised, as one of the first acts of his administration, to issue an executive order reversing the armed services' ban on gay personnel. This pledge was a key element in his successful courtship of the nation's big, largely Democratic, and politically active homosexual community. But neither the pledge nor its timing had been carefully thought out. Many gay activists, including David Mixner, the most prominent gay leader among the semiofficial Friends of Bill, thought Clinton should first have introduced a gay civil rights bill in Congress. That way, it could have been debated and a popular consensus might have emerged in support of progressive change. By contrast, an executive order could be— and was—depicted as an effort by a president who had ducked military service to impose his views on the military by fiat.

"Where would we be today," complained Mixner to Democratic National Committee chairman David Wilhelm, "if people had remained silent in the civil rights movement? This is not an issue to be addressed only when it's politically convenient. . . . We desperately need courageous moral leadership." Clinton and his aides balked at such ingratitude, maintaining that the President deserved credit for giving the issue prominence in the first place and that the outcry over the President's proposal represented anything but political convenience. In a telephone call with Mixner, White House aide Rahm Emanuel huffed, "You've already had too much. . . . You have got to learn to be a team player and stop being so damn self-righteous."

Clinton soon found himself up against some of the most powerful people in Washington. Colin Powell, the chairman of the Joint Chiefs, was openly skeptical of the measure's likely effect on morale and combat readiness. Senator Sam Nunn, the Georgia Democrat who chaired the Armed Services Committee, threatened to introduce legislation to codify the existing military policy banning gays. And, he added, he might well attach it to Clinton's cherished Family Leave bill, effectively killing both measures. Gore urged the President to issue the order, stand by it as a matter of principle, and let Powell and Nunn do what they would to change it.

But Clinton slowly and painfully backed off, seeking a compromise in the form of the ambiguous and tenuous "Don't ask, don't tell" policy: military service branches would refrain from asking personnel their sexual orientation; in turn, officers and enlistees could not discuss it. After the compromise policy was announced, Representative Barney Frank, an openly gay congressman from Massachusetts, confessed, "My disappointment is at the political reality, not the President. Bill Clinton was quite courageous to take it on." But was the President courageous, or was he suffering from a dangerous elixir of naïveté, arrogance, and political miscalculation? He certainly seemed to stumble into this fix without any sense of the intensity of the military's resistance.

If Clinton was truly courageous and intent on bringing about change through presidential leadership, why did he not capitalize on the fact that he, after all, was the commander in chief of the nation's armed forces? Or, if wary of appearing so heavy-handed, why did Clinton not at least venture to gauge privately the temperature of and then debate—the military brass behind closed doors, rather than quibbling so publicly? Was what Frank dubbed courageous actually a colossal misstep? One of the basic tenets of successful leadership is knowing the context in which one is operating— knowing what is likely to be acceptable and what is likely to encounter opposition. Clinton woefully misjudged reactions in this instance.

Clinton supporters and Democrats generally had looked to the new administration to fulfill Clinton's pledge to take the government back from "the privileged few" and "put people first." The move to jettison the military's ban on homosexuals looked like a skewed priority, like pandering to a special constituency. It also looked like Clinton-the-liberal-Democrat, rather than Clinton-the-centrist-Democrat. Worse, it began the process of replacing the image of a bold new leader with the image of a young man in over his head and vulnerable to being pushed around.

In time, Clinton did regain his footing and repair his relations with many in the gay rights community. He spoke out against antihomosexual ballot initiatives in 1994 in Idaho and Oregon; established a Presidential Advisory Council on HIV and AIDS; increased funding for the Ryan White Act by 108 percent; and became the first sitting president in history to endorse a piece of gay and lesbian civil rights legislation when he lent his support to the Employment Non-Discrimination Act in 1996.

But in early 1993, Clinton was like a canoeist trying to paddle through a long and dangerous rapid. A precise, well-timed entrance into the rapid is essential to set the canoeist on the proper route and make the turns and drops downstream possible to negotiate. Clinton had made a sloppy entrance and failed to find the right route. Now the current, in the form of the budget process, was pushing him toward the rocks.

THE TESTING OF THE TROIKA

Nothing so concentrates the mind as an impending execution, Samuel Johnson noted—but he forgot impending budgets. The inexorable schedule of the appropriations process had faced Clinton since the day after winning office. Now it put an end to the postelection luxury of talking endlessly about plans and initiatives. Budgets don't debate alternatives. They set priorities. They are priorities.

To move broadly and coherently along the fiscal front would demand a unity among the White House economic decision-makers that had not yet been achieved. Budgeting and the whole economic plan in particular would test Clinton's leadership abilities as never before.

The troika—the unique collaborative leadership arrangement among Clinton, Rodham Clinton, and Gore—would be tested too. Each member came to the table with shared visions but somewhat different priorities and policy expertise. They came with different styles too—the President reflective, loquacious, but also a good listener; the First Lady cogent, direct, forceful, and insisting always on getting to the point; the Vice President blunt, tenacious, self-confident, and yet conscious of his number-two status. All three had staffs that tended to reflect the attitudes of each principal. The three power centers could stand together or pull each other apart.

Clinton had entered office with a heavy load of visionary goals and political promises. He reminded some of a kid in a candy store, intent on filling up his pockets with one of everything. He had a million ideas: boosting investment in education and training and technology; cutting taxes for the middle class; stimulating the economy with a fast-track spending program on public works and other projects; maintaining entitlements; passing major health-care reform; and reducing the deficit by half in four years. Those easy campaign pledges now faced the brutal reality of the economic situation of the spring of 1993. A year earlier, when Clinton was making his promises, the Bush administration had projected a deficit of around $250 billion. Now the economists were saying it would be closer to $350 billion in fiscal year 1997.

The Clinton White House professed to be shocked by this inheritance from the Bush administration, in the time-honored manner of all new administrations finding the economic situation even worse than they had been warned about during the campaign. In fact, the higher projection had been no state secret.

No matter, Clinton was in a budget bind. What to do? His advisers were divided among centrists and populists, budget balancers and investment boosters, entitlement protectors and welfare trimmers, deficit hawks and deficit doves, tax cutters and tax hikers.

Into this unstable equilibrium there now entered a formidable outside force—Alan Greenspan, the Republican head of the Federal Reserve Bank, in effect the fourth branch of the federal government. Clinton had invited him to Little Rock weeks before the inauguration after Treasury Secretary–designate Lloyd Bentsen had urged Clinton to develop a trusting relationship with the head of the Fed. Greenspan had treated the President-elect to a long lecture that had one clear bottom line—deficit reduction. Nothing would help the economy more than keeping long-term interest rates low. Deficit spending led to inflation, which led to higher interest rates. As unpretentious and agreeable in manner as he was powerful in fact, Greenspan found Clinton knowledgeable and an avid listener.

A week after the inauguration the President invited Greenspan to the White House. The Fed chairman warned Clinton that after 1996, the deficit would mount precipitously, as would the interest on the debt. This could produce a financial catastrophe. Clinton must act now, he added, with a big deficit-reduction program. Over the next few weeks, the word from the Fed and from Clinton's centrist advisers became a mantra—deficit reduction, deficit reduction, deficit reduction.

White House efforts were now focused on a major address the President would make to Congress just four weeks after taking office. The usual fights erupted among his aides and outside advisers over the size and timing of investment, health care, spending, taxes, entitlements, and, yes, deficit reduction. Clinton, not missing a detail, was at the hub of most conferences, mediating, encouraging, placating, admonishing, flattering, postponing. Small pressure groups formed around every major issue, as one side or another, rebuffed in a summit meeting in the Oval Office or cabinet room, would rally its supporting forces throughout the executive branch and take the issue back to the boss. Rather than resolving the differences, Clinton more often shared them.

"The dynamic is inside himself," aide George Stephanopoulos observed to journalist Elizabeth Drew. "There is always a tension between wanting to get this big program and knowing you have to reduce the deficit and get future growth and also make investments. It's a conflict among several sides of him: the part of him that's committed to children's programs and investing in jobs and highways; the part of him that knew the middle class has gotten screwed in the 1980s, that the middle-class tax cut was an important symbol; the part of him that's cut spending time and time again in Arkansas, but also the part of him that knows the intense pain caused by each cut; the part of him that understands the role of Wall Street, and the part of him that knows that ordinary people have been screwed by those sources."

In part, presidents' responses to this eternal leadership predicament follows the fault line that divides great chief executives from the rest of the field. Contrary to popular myth, particularly in the absence of identifiable and imminent crises, leadership from the Oval Office demands more than an impassioned speech here or a timely presidential visit there. Presidents do not twitch their nose, snap their fingers, or click their heels to get things done. As with achieving any goal, prioritizing and persistence are essential. Bill Clinton's desire—though laudable—to do as much as he could in a relatively short time risked securing only Pyrrhic victories. To sacrifice the heart of policy proposals merely to claim victory for the evening news cycle was myopia of the worst sort. The President might boast of a list of accomplishments a mile wide, but, substantively speaking, if each was only an inch deep, what change had he really effected? What leadership had he brought to bear?

The campaign consultants, who had the run of the White House whether employed there or not, watched for every hint that Clinton was turning away from campaign promises on which they felt they had won. They were especially critical of the conservative "elitists" who were obsessed with deficit reduction. "Why," implored Paul Begala of Clinton, "are you listening to these people? They did not support you. It's not what you're about." He needed them, the President shot back. "We can't do anything for people unless we reduce the deficit."

By mid-February the White House populists had lost their top-priority cause. They realized this when they saw the State of the Union speech draft, and even more when they spotted Greenspan sitting next to the First Lady as the senators and representatives took their seats—Greenspan as guest of honor! Clinton's hour-long address was an oratorical triumph for deficit reduction. He pledged that the deficit would dwindle to $140 billion a year by 1997—the figure Greenspan had privately recommended to the White House. Later, the head of the Fed approved this sum publicly.

Clinton's transactional leadership of budget tactics contrasted significantly with the Vice President's and the First Lady's stances. During the early weeks Gore was not a central policy-maker (though no one was, except perhaps for Greenspan). He was feeling his way along the muddy terrain that separated vice-presidential authority from presidential. He could influence Clinton, in day-to-day exchanges between them, without fear of overstepping the boundary because of the trust each had developed in the other. Some aides even pointed to a near-brotherly relationship that had evolved between the President and Vice President. Gore's mother, herself married to a former U.S. senator who had flirted with the vice presidency, approved of the bonding. "It really doesn't make sense that we have gone this long without this kind of relationship," said Pauline Gore. The Clinton-Gore intimacy was becoming a milestone in the annals of presidential/

vice-presidential history, surpassing even the largely frictionless Carter-Mondale interaction.

Clinton's concession of power to Gore was no novel act for him either, according to Clinton friend Diane Blair, a political scientist. "One of the most consistent themes evident in Clinton's career is the joy he has taken in elevating others," she insisted. "He is constantly praising others, calling attention to them, giving people responsibilities that they may feel they are not quite ready for. But he encourages them." The Vice President, of course, hardly needed Clinton's encouragement to assume responsibility; Gore's own bid for the White House in 1988 had proved he coveted the office. Yet he still needed Clinton's permission to hold the wagon reins from time to time. Even more, Clinton trusted Gore implicitly. And, at least in the first term, Clinton knew that Gore knew that any hope for a Gore presidency would be considerably affected by the Clinton legacy. Gore would be a good soldier, at least for the time being.

Still, Gore had to be careful not to cross top advisers who had their own cherished access to Clinton. For a time the Vice President pursued his own strong interests in environmental and energy matters, yet he also took a strong line on general investment policy. He endeared himself to some staff members by urging Clinton, in long, meandering discussions, to come to closure—but with mixed success.

If Gore's work habits complemented Clinton's, Rodham Clinton's stood in sharp contrast with her husband's. Where Clinton circled around problems, invited and played with competing ideas, listened to one and all, she often went straight to the point as she saw it, conferring with persons who could help her do so and bypassing the others. Whereas Clinton, knowing the impact of the power of the presidency, took care not to hurt feelings, she left some staff members shaken and diminished. "She is a litigator par excellence," recalled an aide, "and she is hard-edged. . . . People were afraid of her." She was almost invariably tough-minded, knowledgeable, and unforgiving of incompetence. She sometimes asked questions—about health or social security—that aides could not answer. When it came to interacting with the President, the First Lady admitted, sometimes he solicited her "recommendation or advice on something," and sometimes "I have volunteered it." But Rodham Clinton paid a price for her assertiveness. Aides were occasionally reluctant to spar with her over the merits of particular policy parameters, for fear of inciting her.

"It was hard for her to know when she was getting the straight truth," noted presidential adviser David Gergen. "It's like being terribly wealthy." This compromised the Clinton White House's ability to polish internally some of its legislative proposals before sending them down Pennsylvania Avenue.

The First Lady stuck closely to her principles. She had the talent, when advisers were bogged down in humdrum details of budgets and bonds, to transcend the immediate event in a way that brought her close to the views of her husband. She liked to remind people of the battles she and Clinton had fought in Arkansas on education and other issues. She liked to talk about the "real people" out there who had put their hopes in the new administration. She would mention Clinton's acceptance speech in 1992 when he quoted Proverbs, "Where there is no vision, the people perish." She desperately wanted a White House that would carry out that vision.

For those who knew the Clintons' history and who came to see their close working relationship in the 1992 campaign, there had been little doubt that Rodham Clinton would have a central policy-making role in the White House. She did not request such a role—she assumed it. In May 1993, Bill Moyers asked the First Lady what it was like to govern. She began to answer, "It's been exhilarating, frustrating, eye-opening"—then rushed to add, "Just to set the record straight, I'm not really governing either." Many Americans sided with Texas governor Ann Richards, who quipped, "If you believe that, I've got a bridge I'd like to show you."

Privately, Rodham Clinton was serving as a de facto chief of staff, which added to White House disarray because there was already a public one, Mack McLarty. One journalist even proclaimed, "She's like a second vice president." The President's aides—with Clinton's approval—took pains to play down Rodham Clinton's actual role.

The First Lady was willing to challenge anyone on the administration's direction. At a late-January 1993 Camp David retreat for the cabinet members and top staffers, Warren Christopher suggested that the White House should narrow priorities and do first things first. Rodham Clinton objected. Why not push for the whole program? "Why are we here if we don't go for it?" she implored.

The answer was self-evident to Christopher. His experience in the Carter presidency had sensitized him to the limitations of presidential power. But the exuberance and arrogance of many in the Clinton camp blinded them to such concerns. Reflecting on his years in the Oval Office, even an experienced lawmaker like Lyndon Johnson warned his successor, "Before you get to the presidency, you think you can do anything. You think you're the most powerful leader since God. But when you get in that tall chair, as you're gonna find out, Mr. President, you can't count on people. You'll find your hands tied and people cussin' you. The office is kinda like the little country boy found the hoochie-koochie show at the carnival, once he'd paid his dime and got inside the tent: 'It ain't exactly as it was advertised.'" The Clinton administration overlooked such advice.

Clinton had swallowed the conventional wisdom that the new administration must move quickly, score dramatic points during the first hundred days, build up political clout and reputation that would carry it through tougher days ahead. "I know I can pass a sweeping package of legislation during the first hundred days of my administration," boasted candidate Clinton in the summer of 1992. "It will be the most productive period in modern history." Months later, knowing he was failing on this score, the President at times became morose, indecisive, and angry. He flared up at his staff, phoned old friends to complain, walked out of a press conference. He was giving the job his all, he felt, without much luck, and he was bone tired. The man who had spent his entire adult life climbing the greasy pole of politics was finding it slickest at the top.

The fate of the stimulus bill in early spring 1993 was an ominous forewarning of trouble ahead on the Hill. A rather modest proposal compared to the major economic plan still in the works, the stimulus bill was designed as a $16 billion spending shot in the arm. Pulled together hastily from agency and congressional proposals, it was a grab bag of items, ranging from boosted Head Start funding and free immunization for children to community-development grants to the kind of boondoggles that Republicans still associate with the New Deal. The White House expected an easy victory. The bill appealed to many interests; and Senator Robert Byrd, the chairman of the Appropriations Committee, had given assurances that it would breeze through. But the GOP was not dealing. The bill passed in the House by a party-line vote and headed toward the Senate.

Despite charges later that an arrogant White House was unwilling to negotiate, Clinton and his aides spent hours seeking to placate conservative Democratic senators, moderate Senate Republicans, and others. But they had one enemy that they had not prepared for—a Senate filibuster and the man behind it, minority leader Bob Dole. It was understandable that the White House could hardly anticipate a stoppage, especially in the early weeks of a "honeymoon." A relic of nineteenth-century parliamentary rough-and-tumble, the filibuster was a Senate contrivance that carried out the constitutional spirit of protecting minorities. This obstructive device had lost much of its appeal when it was used by southern conservative politicians in the 1950s and 1960s to thwart passage of civil rights laws. A reform-minded Senate had reduced to sixty the number of votes required to close off debate. But in 1993, this would not help—in a party-line split, the Senate Democrats would have only fifty-seven votes.

So there was Bob Dole, standing in the aisle in front of his determined band, blocking Clinton's first economic initiative. The President might have taken the issue to the country, as his fellow Democrat Woodrow Wilson had done in 1917 when he denounced the "little group of willful men" who had filibustered against a measure to arm American merchant ships seeking protection from aggressive German U-boats. Clinton preferred to keep dealing, saving his anger for aides who had failed to work out an antifilibuster strategy. He proposed compromises and even journeyed to Pennsylvania to win over Senator Arlen Specter, who would not give in to presidential pressure. Clinton tried a last-minute negotiation with Dole, who stood fast as "a matter of principle" even as he harbored hopes to try again for the presidency.

Utterly frustrated, the President struck his colors. His handling of the issue left the Democrats in disarray, at least inside the Beltway. House Democrats resented his retreat after they had voted for the bill expecting he would go all the way. An ally in the Senate, Robert Byrd of West Virginia, had wanted to fight the filibuster by "bringing in the cots" and outstaying them; when Clinton aides told him that their boss was quitting, Byrd would not believe them and insisted on getting the surrender word from the President.

He had tried so hard to work things out, Clinton complained to the press. He then placed the blame on his own shoulders. He had misgauged the situation, he told reporters. He hoped he could learn something. "I've just been here ninety days."

Hillary Rodham Clinton blamed the White House staff for inadequate planning. If a bill this "minor" could be waylaid, what might happen to the big bills ahead?

What lay ahead was the budget, the centerpiece of Clinton's economic plan. Like all presidents he faced a double hurdle, the House and the Senate, carefully contrived by the Constitution to represent different and competing arrays of interests and areas. No other large democracy confronted executive leadership with this potential double bind, but Americans took it for granted; it was part of the normal order of things.

Clinton faced the burden of history too. "Caps" on discretionary spending had been set in 1990 in a budget agreement between Bush and the Democratic Congress of that time. Any tax change or entitlement program had to be paid for on a year-by-year basis under the pay-as-you-go rules. Even worse for the President, the Congressional Budget Office stepped up its deficit projections so sharply as to require steep tax hikes if the deficit was to be kept below $300 billion.

The agitation for deficit reduction directly threatened Clinton's great personal interests—investment in education at all levels, children's programs, strengthening infrastructure, worker training, and health care. These were all programs he believed would pay off in the long run. Then there were high-technology programs of acute interest to Gore. But the relentless pressure for deficit reduction was reinforced by the recognition that the deficit threatened all the other goals. The only other option was a sharp general tax increase, which was the last thing Clinton wanted to do. If he tried to give something to everybody, he could end up giving nothing centrally important to anybody.

The conflicting choices were reflected in fragmented Democratic politics inside and outside the White House. Clinton's staff, political pollsters and consultants, economic and budget advisers, and Treasury people continued to be deeply divided. So were their constituencies. The Democratic majorities in Congress were split among old-line liberal Democrats, the Black Caucus, and New Democrats, among other divisions, while the Republicans were strongly united in opposition to almost all of Clinton's proposals. And hardly a day passed when the President was not reminded that he had won only 43 percent of the vote. Ross Perot, who had made some friendly remarks about the new President after the election, was back on the offensive again, charging that if Clinton sought a position in private industry, "you wouldn't consider giving him a job anywhere above middle management."

The result might have been almost comical if it had not involved such serious issues. A large, amorphous, diverse, and conflict-ridden guerrilla army in the White House came into combat with a similarly large, amorphous, diverse, and conflict-ridden Congress.

Still, Clinton was the politician-in-chief who somehow had to pull together his disheveled supporters to put through a budget bill that was increasingly becoming a test of his leadership, especially after the defeat of the stimulus bill. Since he could not rely on party discipline or strong popular support, his only recourse, he felt, was to exploit every scrap of presidential influence to form ad hoc coalitions in the House and Senate. Clinton threw himself into this battle. He was willing to deal, which meant adjusting to the power structure rather than seeking to bypass, transcend, or transform it.

The first test would come in the House. With the media ready to pounce on every mishap or concession, the administration managed to salvage the bill in the Ways and Means Committee by making concessions to the oil and other industries on the proposed energy tax. On high-tech issues, the White House agreed to abandon the investment tax credit. A proposed boost in corporate taxes was reduced. Under pressure from conservative Democrats, Clinton even accepted a cap on entitlement spending. The troika was throwing victims to the wolves and screams of pain arose, mainly from liberal Democrats and the congressional Black Caucus.

As the House vote neared, the White House resorted to one-on-one telephone calls. Clinton, Gore, and the cabinet dipped into their store of favors, offering hometown projects, military-base improvements, appearances at fund-raisers, promotion of exports. Clinton and Gore worked side by side as they combed the congressional wish list. At the last moment they made further concessions on tax spending and entitlement cuts. Even so, the bill barely passed the House, 219–213. Despite the President's calls for bipartisan harmony and for rising above politics, the Republicans were solid in their opposition.

Would the Senate battle be any easier? Members of the upper chamber had broader, more diverse constituencies. They had more security with their six-year terms, and some were old friends of Clinton's from the campaign trail. Such friendships might have appeared likely to improve prospects for Clinton's budget bill, but they did not. Senators might like Bill Clinton personally, but they could not help wondering, as the new President stumbled and bumbled during the first months, why Bill Clinton? Why not me?

Senator David Boren, Oklahoma Democrat, typified this breed, though at fifty-one he had less seniority than many of his colleagues. He too had been a Rhodes Scholar. He too had been governor. And he too was a "New Democrat"—though some suspected that he used this to disguise his basic conservatism. Then there were Pat Moynihan, the New York philosopher-politician; Bob Kerrey, the Vietnam war hero who could still not fully comprehend why he had lost in the presidential primaries to Clinton, or why he had been passed over as a running mate; Jay Rockefeller of West Virginia, also a former governor and an impassioned liberal; and John Breaux of Louisiana, another DLC conservative, who wanted to play on the national stage even as he guarded his state's oil and gas interests. None of them was the kind of man to fall in quickly and amiably behind someone else's lead.

Clinton did have strong party support from George Mitchell, the majority leader in the Senate, as he did from the House leadership. But, lacking much power to reward and discipline, they could not guarantee the votes of their members—and certainly not those of the Senate barons.

Once again the White House returned to battle. Tired of horse-trading—or at least of appearing too much the horse trader—the President launched a new tactic. Now he would appear more presidential, more principled, transcending the political stock exchange. He wanted to refocus public attention on his economic plan as part of his overall program and vision. With the First Lady sitting nearby, he spoke to the League of Women Voters' leaders in the Rose Garden on long-run investment, tax fairness, welfare reform, spending reductions. But the more Clinton tried to stay above the battle, the more the struggle was played out by the transactors in the arena. Negotiating all the while with Boren, Mitchell worked out a Finance Committee deal for a cut in the House bill's $80 billion of taxes, more spending cuts, some Medicare reductions, and a small rise in the gasoline tax. The straight party vote in the Senate Finance Committee—eleven Democrats versus nine Republicans—heralded a close split in the full Senate.

The President tried to rally support by speechifying out in the country, but it was too late—the great battle over the economic plan had become an inside-the-Beltway fracas. Lobbyists—on behalf of truckers, the retired, oil drillers, deficit reducers, tax cutters, entitlement backers—worked closely with their favorite senators. And always there loomed the Republican opposition, led by the increasingly militant Dole. He kept his forces united against the economic plan, while challenging conservative Democrats to cross party lines.

As the Senate vote approached, it became clear that it would be close.

Clinton could not take a loss on this, his big bill. After a string of setbacks, this would be a political death blow. Hour after hour, working closely with Mitchell, the White House maneuvered and traded with great transactional fervor. Vice President Gore was in the thick of the struggle; when the Senate split 49–49, he triumphantly broke the tie at three o'clock in the morning on June 25, 1993.

The White House had little taste for celebrating. The President, who had been urging his staff for some weeks to "give me a strategy," now deplored the lack of one for securing a principled economic plan. Hillary Rodham Clinton was even more distressed at the absence of a winning plan for a strong bill. She and the President were leaving for Japan, and by the time they returned, she wanted, she told the staff, not only a plan but a "war room," as in the campaign days. Gore was distressed that key political advisers favored dropping the energy tax, which had already been buffeted by Boren and his allies.

The White House lacked even time to celebrate. The House and Senate had passed different bills, which had to be reconciled. To a degree, the battle had to be fought all over again in each chamber and within the White House. Both the political consultants and the policy advisers urged the President to take more leadership. But what kind of leadership? The consultants wanted him to be bold, principled, presidential. Economic advisers urged a cautious, step-by-step strategy, steering clear of highly controversial measures such as a major tax increase, except on the rich. All agreed on setting up the war room, which was soon spewing out statements, monitoring the media, recruiting speakers, and instantly rebutting hostile charges, just as in the old campaign days. No other White House in history had been so adept at media "quick response" and "spin." In fighting off subsequent scandals du jour—Whitewater, Paula Jones, Monica Lewinsky—this aptitude would help salvage some of Clinton's political capital.

By summer 1993, the pressure on the White House to perform was more acute than ever. White House polls showed that voters were following the bill knowledgeably, they understood the taxing and spending implications, and how it might affect their lives. As usual, they wanted decision and action. But Clinton was more conscious than ever of the system's propensity for gridlock. "For a very long time," he told Senate and House negotiators on the bill, "there has been a kind of political paralysis in this country, where we always knew what we had to do, but we could never quite bring ourselves to do it. Our children and our grandchildren will remember whether we were bashful or bold. They will remember whether we showed courage, or whether we turned away from the challenge. They will remember whether we gave in to gridlock and the kind of rhetoric that has come to dominate our politics of the last few years, or whether we govern."

Step by step, member by member, the administration and House leaders tried to construct a majority for the new version of the budget deal in the lower chamber. White House aides appealed to party loyalty, but the Democratic rank and file was too divided into a left, right, and center, and too distant from the Democratic party organization, to follow the administration line. The aides appealed to loyalty to the President—they must not let him fail—but the representatives' greater concern was to avoid their own failure in the next election.

On the day of the final House roll call, August 5, the White House was still scrambling for votes. The President, Gore, and Rodham Clinton were still phoning wavering members. The roll-call vote was a scary roller coaster until the White House went over the top 218–216. Every compromise, including a last-minute bow to conservatives for more deficit reduction, had counted.

And then the Senate again. And again it went step by step, target by target. But the fighting arena was much smaller in the upper chamber. The GOP still presented a solid phalanx of opposition. The White House, with Mitchell and other friends on Capitol Hill, had to hunt down every Democratic vote. When Boren and other conservative Democrats made clear that they opposed the bill, the White House saw that once again it would be a Hairbreadth Harry script in the Senate, with a tie vote as the best possibility. All attention focused on Bob Kerrey. Rarely has a key politico played as "hard to get" on a major bill as the young senator from Nebraska.

From the first, as a longtime deficit reducer and budget cutter, Kerrey had leaned against the bill. But the main problem seemed less economic than psychological. When the President telephoned Kerrey with a plea for loyalty—otherwise, said Clinton, "my presidency's going to go down"—the senator flared up. He said he resented Clinton's argument that "I'm responsible for your presidency surviving." The call erupted into a furious argument that ended with expletives and the banging down of telephones. Indeed, as Al Gore had learned firsthand as a child from that innocent eavesdropping on the phone conversation between his father and John F. Kennedy, presidents did get a little hot from time to time.

Presidential aides met with Kerrey. Was there any way they could win his vote? No way, the senator said at first. But, it seemed, he had a proposition. After a long monologue about sacrifice, personal responsibility, excess entitlement, and the like, he indicated that his own experience and economic understanding should be made available to Clinton. After more meetings with the aides and talks with Clinton, during which Kerrey denounced the budget bill, it developed that what Kerrey really wanted was a bipartisan commission to propose ways and means of reducing the deficit—to be set up after the Senate vote and with Kerrey as the chairman. Though concerned that such a commission might infringe on both Gore's and the Treasury's role, Clinton acceded, provided the announcement was made long after the Senate vote so that people would not suspect a deal.

Kerrey voted aye. So did forty-nine others, leading to the anticipated 50–50 split. Once again, Gore exercised his constitutional prerogative. Battered and bruised, the troika had stood firm.

ORDEALS OF CHANGE

"What we heard tonight at the other end of Pennsylvania Avenue was the sound of gridlock breaking," Clinton proclaimed elatedly after the Senate vote. This was not easy, he added, "but change is never easy." Technically called the reconciliation bill, the budget measure did indeed reconcile a multitude of interests. For conservatives and moderates: deficit reduction by almost $500 billion over the next five years, over $50 billion in Medicare cuts; a 4.3-cent hike in the gasoline tax. For liberals: a boost of approximately 40 percent on the tax on incomes over $250,000; $1 billion for a new project to finance family preservation efforts. There was something for almost everyone except Al Gore, who lost his prized energy program in favor of the gasoline tax step-up.

The loss of the energy tax, which Gore had championed week after week, strengthened his awareness that vice-presidential status gave him no commanding position in the White House—but he could also note that being president didn't fortify Clinton's power all that much either. Both he and Clinton were disappointed by the thinning out of support for the investment priorities they had touted.

Gore made no secret of his disappointment. In dealing with staff and with people on the Hill, the Vice President tended to be more direct, more blunt, than the President. He often couched his advice in terms of values— what was right, or what was the brave thing to do.

Still, there was no erosion in the relationship between the President and Vice President. The relentless pressure on the White House seemed only to tighten both their friendship and their working partnership. "In the thirty years that I have been in and out of Washington," said Clinton's second chief of staff, Leon Panetta, "I have never seen a vice president play as large a role in terms of policy development and maintain as close relationship to the president on issues and on the conduct of government [as] Vice President Gore." Clinton informed his cabinet at the first meeting, "If Al asks you for something, you should consider it as me asking." Recalled economic adviser Gene Sperling, "If [staffers] think the President has really gotten off on a wrong track on something, [the Vice President] is the person you would go talk to, who you think would have the most influence" on changing the President's mind.

At times, the presidential and vice-presidential staffs were difficult to distinguish. Gore's chief of staff, like Rodham Clinton's, was also an assistant to the President—historic firsts—and could attend any meeting he wished. As well, members of the Vice President's staff, from communications to domestic policy to national security, regularly attended meetings with their counterparts on the President's staff.

Often, Gore followed the President's lead on policy; when Clinton shifted, Gore shifted with him. Gore was more likely to differ on ways and means, especially on questions of schedule and timing. He sometimes cut into Clinton's ruminations to urge coming to a conclusion, making a plan, setting a series of specific dates for decision and action. "The Vice President rarely second-guesses himself or his senior staff," recalled aide Roy Neel. "He has always been extremely disciplined about decision-making, even when that means disappointing or aggravating some people." In an unspoken good-cop/bad-cop relationship, Gore was willing to be bad cop—Clinton never.

Hillary Rodham Clinton had little compunction about differing with Bill Clinton when she felt strongly about a question, whether of ends or means. Of her husband's strengths and weaknesses she had a wifely knowledge greater than even the closest of advisers. She taxed the staff relentlessly on better planning, organizing, communicating, scheduling. But she looked on the White House efforts also as an intensive learning experience, so she was critiquing her own performance even as she admonished advisers to improve theirs. That experience seemed mainly to strengthen her, and as her husband continued to negotiate and compromise, she appeared even more determined and focused.

Did she share her husband's values and goals? Values, yes, stemming from years of talking and campaigning together and from a mutually intense, if often private, religiosity. Goals, not always. Working closely with the campaigners and pollsters, who felt they had special knowledge of the people's mandate, she usually took an advanced position on issues, and not only health. Most of all, Rodham Clinton argued for a strategy that would link values and goals to policies and execution.

Like a three-legged stool, there were balances and imbalances within the troika that made for an unstable equilibrium, with all the dynamics and dangers pertaining thereto. As with the Russian troika, they were a trio of strong horses running abreast but with the middle horse as the acknowledged leader. Individually, Gore's and Rodham Clinton's and even Clinton's powers were limited. By running so strongly together they magnified their total influence.

And that middle lead horse? The most easily accessible chief executive ever, Clinton continued to charm those who had a few minutes with him face-to-face. On this score, aide William Galston did not mince words: "Bill

Clinton is the most intelligent, most charming, and most persuasive man I have ever met in my life, hands down." To Lani Guinier, Clinton possessed "living-room charisma." Ann Lewis, eventual White House communications director, was prepared to "follow Bill Clinton to the south pole without a sweater." Clinton flattered people by soliciting their views, letting them talk, listening intently, responding quickly, and promising to get back to them—which he often did, sometimes after midnight by phone.

"When the phone rings at midnight," recalled a friend, "your first reaction is 'What's wrong?' The second reaction is that you sort of think this sounds like Bill Clinton. Do you think it really is? The third reaction is when you realize it is [Clinton] and you're five minutes into the conversation and he's just as alert as he can be and you're trying to figure out where you are, trying to get your mind organized. . . . And your wife is saying, 'Who is that on the phone? Is something wrong? What do they want?'"

Clinton impressed friends and foes alike with his knowledge of policy alternatives. "I think he is one of the most intellectual people I have ever known in politics," said an aide. "Sometimes he is not as effective politically because he overplays the rational aspects of policies." "It just blows me away whenever I meet with him to see how thorough his understanding is of a whole range of issues," a former congressman admitted. Somehow, though, the presidential meetings seemed mainly to lead to more meetings, as he reached out for more advice, more recommendations. "President Clinton uses the coagulation theory of decision-making," wryly confessed Robert Reich. "Listen to all perspectives, then let enough time pass so that all opposing views coagulate into something that is equally satisfying and dissatisfying to all." Clinton reversed Harry Truman's much quoted desk adage, "The buck stops here." Clinton bucked decisions back down to cabinet members, staff advisers, consultants, old friends.

Most of all, he consulted Gore and Rodham Clinton. He needed their decisiveness, steadiness, and absolute loyalty. They needed his enthusiasm, energy, and resilience.

Still, this complementary network of character traits suffered shortcomings. The troika found it difficult to convey the administration's achievements to Americans. Disappointment, or indifference, for instance, marked the public response to the August 1993 reconciliation bill, though it contained some solid achievements. Clinton felt that the Earned Income Tax Credit was a major boon to the working poor. Anyone putting in forty hours of work per week was guaranteed an income level above the poverty line through tax credits or payments by the government. That message did not seem to get through. Worse, a false message did. Polls showed that most people erroneously felt that the burden of taxes used to achieve deficit reduction fell on the middle class. Although the economy was recovering nicely—unemployment had reached an alarming 7.7 percent by the time Clinton assumed office—the President got little credit for it.

Angrily, the troika focused first on the White House communications staff and then on the press itself. Rodham Clinton complained again about the lack of a communications strategy. She also harbored hostility toward the press, prompting journalist Ann Compton to fume, "Hillary Clinton is the first First Lady to have a legitimate policy role in the administration, and she is the first one I have covered out of five who has totally ignored and avoided the White House press corps."

The President likewise went through a period of treating the press with contempt. "Heck," he noted, "half the time I watch the evening news, I wouldn't be for me either." Clinton briefly closed the corridor between the press briefing room and George Stephanopoulos's office and considered moving the press corps out of the White House entirely. He told correspondents he could "stiff" them on press conferences because talk shows like *Larry King Live* allowed him to speak directly to the public. He complained that the press dwelt on his defeats and ignored his accomplishments. As public confidence in his leadership waned, Clinton blamed the press for making him feel like, as a country song put it, "They Changed Everything but My Name."

Press criticism of the presidency was hardly new. Americans have always had a highly ambivalent relationship with their leaders. Journalists and historians questioned George Washington's expense accounts, his egalitarian instincts, and his military acumen. Lincoln has been accused of racism and mishandling law clients, as well as warmongering. Even one of Clinton's presidential heroes, Jefferson, suffered relentless hounding by the Virginia press throughout his lifetime.

But into the 1970s, the White House press corps had a partially protective relationship with the president; illnesses, extramarital affairs, and other foibles were generally well known, though not reported. In some cases, as in the portrayal of Franklin Roosevelt as a vigorous and healthy leader and the cover-up of extramarital adventures by Kennedy and Eisenhower, the press colluded in deceiving the public.

Persistent president-bashing is a phenomenon notably of the last two decades. Gone is the full honeymoon once accorded a new White House. Favorable White House stories far outnumbered the unfavorable ones during honeymoon years from the Eisenhower through the Carter administrations. Bill Clinton was denied virtually any kind of honeymoon at all. The Center for Media and Public Affairs, in an extensive study of media coverage from inauguration day to June 1994, concluded that "whatever his mistakes, Clinton has been unfairly portrayed as a failed president." Analyzing all media sources and eliminating partisan commentators, the study found that Clinton's honeymoon period drew far more coverage than did that of President Bush. Clinton made lots of news; in the first sixteen months, his administration was the subject of some 4,256 stories on network evening news. This was 44 percent higher than the coverage of the Bush presidency during the analogous period. But Clinton faced an average of five negative comments per night on nightly network news, with nearly 62 percent of all comments being negative.

In the early going, Hillary Rodham Clinton fared much better on the evening news than her husband, largely due to her savvy communications-trained chief of staff, Margaret Williams. During that time, she garnered better coverage than any other troika member—76 percent positive. But even Rodham Clinton's numbers would eventually plummet as the promise of health care eroded and Whitewater took its toll.

The bombardment of negative news accounts was only the beginning of the problems inflicted on the Clinton administration by the media. Another was the shift in the very nature of news reporting. Many reporters had turned into news analysts, with the emphasis on discovering and expounding upon problems. The line between reporting and commentary had become permeable, sometimes nonexistent. Many journalists would report a story, interpret it, and then tell readers how to think.

"Speaking truth to power" remains a noble undertaking in a democracy. But journalists since the Watergate era look to role models such as Bob Woodward and Carl Bernstein who not only reported, but took down leaders and authority figures. "Reporters have to have a 'take' and it has to be negative, or you are accused of being 'in the tank,'" Clinton consultant Paul Begala complained. Tom Rosenstiel, who conducted a content analysis of the *New York Times,* the *Washington Post,* and the *Los Angeles Times* during the Clinton honeymoon, saw an unseemly haste. His conclusion: "The speed with which journalists make these judgments has become breathtaking."

In a downward cycle, the press criticism creates an inflamed public, which in turn compels elected officials to waffle and evade, which in turn incites the press to attack, which begets still more evasion by political leaders and more distrust and disrespect by the public. This insidious cycle affected Clinton as he watched his negative media coverage drive down his presidential poll ratings, indeed his presidency.

The press has always had an ambivalent relationship with Bill Clinton, since his early Arkansas days. "He has always been an enigma to the press. They are naturally drawn to him but they are also very harsh if he doesn't meet their expectations. They held him to a high standard," said longtime Arkansas aide Mike Gauldin.

The effect of this high standard—in part a testament to the campaigning Clinton's ability to inspire hope—more often served to complicate than facilitate Clinton's governing. Voters mistrust Clinton in part because the media keeps telling them not to trust him, concluded *New York* magazine's Jacob Weisberg.

Against this backdrop of media harassment and public disregard or worse, Clinton launched the work of the presidency. He would accept blame for early stumbles, beg the press to relent during his on-the-job training. Gradually he recognized that force of will, his "staying power," even multiplied by the troika, was a poor match for the public projections he confronted.

Early in the Clinton presidency, Hillary Rodham Clinton urged senior strategists to "tell a story." It worked well in Arkansas, she reminded them, and it could work on the national level too. The administration should craft a strategy with a story line, depicting a long journey, with milestones along the way to mark the progress. We need to create a vision, she said, that connects with people, with characters and a plot, told from a moral point of view. With such a story, people would know where the country was going and how far it had come.

Rodham Clinton wasn't wrong and her advice was not new. Presidential stories and subtexts have a long history.

John Adams was perhaps the first president who complained about the need for an image. In his time, he grumbled, "a man must be his own trumpeter. He must write or dictate paragraphs of praise in the newspapers. . . . He must get his picture drawn, his statue made, and must hire all artists in his turn, to set about works to spread his name, make the mob stare and gape, and perpetuate his fame."

One of Clinton's presidential icons, Abraham Lincoln, embodied a homespun tale. But his son later denied Lincoln had lived in a log cabin; and his stepmother refused to affirm that "Honest Abe" read his schoolbooks by night by the fireplace. Still, presidential stories, true or not, endure.

Teddy "Rough Rider" Roosevelt was the master of presidential subtexts. Roosevelt was shrewd enough to recognize that his upper-crust upbringing needed to be "democratized," so he crafted his own "hero tales" for magazines and books. He set up frontier stages and scenes, always making sure his theatrics were photographed. "The climactic spectacle of Roosevelt's rise—and the one that became the centerpiece of the legend—was San Juan Hill," wrote political scientist Bruce Miroff. Roosevelt arranged with Scribner's editor Robert Bridges for the account of his combat in Cuba to appear first in magazine form, and later as a book to shore up its legitimacy as a permanent historical work. *Rough Riders* appeared in 1899. Within three years, the hero of San Juan Hill was in the White House. Never one to argue with success, one of his first acts was to establish the institution of the White House Press Corps.

Some presidents, such as Lincoln, Roosevelt, and Reagan, quickly established their own complimentary thematic subtexts; others, such as John Kennedy, benefited from history-minded widows to create their Camelots.

A few, such as Richard Nixon, forever branded as Tricky Dick, fall victim to the press and never escape. Would Clinton, who never managed to shake the stench of scandal, share Nixon's fate?

A politician's story has to be developed and sold relentlessly, or the press will find its own story. Reagan's team, which developed the "great communicator" image, may have been the most masterful and focused. Richard Wirthlin and the White House Communications Office worked out a symbolic presentation of the Reagan presidency and reinforced the message every day he was in office. Wirthlin's efforts in creating and sustaining Reagan's presidential image ultimately won him *Advertising Age*'s Advertising Man of the Year Award in 1989.

But in the absence of a carefully crafted image, the press is likely to substitute a superficial caricature. This "journalistic shorthand" has a deleterious impact on both candidates and on the process. "Anyone who glances at the headlines or the evening news comes to know the journalistic shorthand for players on the public stage," maintained Howard Kurtz of the *Washington Post*. "Bob Dole has a 'short fuse.' Bill Clinton is 'Slick Willie.' Al Gore is 'stiff as a cardboard cutout.' Let the buyer beware: each of these portrayals is a caricature, often exaggerated to the point of parody."

Most journalists embrace the conventional wisdom and, often with no personal experience of the candidate at all, perpetuate the subtext caricatures in lockstep. "It's possible for a candidate to go through a whole campaign," noted political biographer Richard Ben Cramer, "and never have one story written about him which is totally true."

Whether Clinton's negative subtexts were true in whole or in part, they became an entrenched representation of him. In his early years in office, five interrelated media subtexts emerged consistently with Clinton: he was a compromiser; he lacked a core set of beliefs to guide decisions; he was chaotic and disorganized; he was indecisive and avoided conflict; and he needed to be liked.

These shibboleths of the conventional journalistic wisdom came to dominate reporters' judgments. They are evident in the following phrases, drawn from assessments of Clinton by major journalists or presidential scholars:

". . . yet to establish in the minds of people the nature of his political core."

". . . no fixed views or beliefs."

". . . near terminal ambivalence."

". . . indecisive, emotionally needy, and congenitally disorganized."

". . . indiscipline and incoherence are the norm."

"His thriving on chaos and uncertainty . . ."

"He was energized by self-created chaos."

"... difficulty making decisions and sticking to them, that he dislikes conflict, that he loves to talk policy and think out loud ..."

"... caves in to pressure, tells people what they want to hear, reneges on promises and doesn't tell the whole truth ..."

"... vacillating, passive, nonconfrontational, unable to make up his mind, frozen into indecision ..."

"... undisciplined, indecisive, emotional, fragile man-child ..."

At the start of his administration, Clinton appeared trapped in a vast echo chamber where every sound bite bombarded him a hundredfold—an environment that only contributed to the widening gyre between citizens and leaders. "We've hit a point where the coverage is so nasty and there's so much of it that it's produced a qualitative difference in the way people feel about their president," concluded Robert Lichter in his report for the Center for Media and Public Affairs.

We asked Clinton shortly before his election what he would do if he faced this kind of hostile environment in his second or third year, and he replied, "Wear them out. I'm good at that. Keep at it. Roosevelt had that good mental energy to keep after it. I'm going to hang in there."

PROMISE KEEPING

With the budget in place, Clinton turned to other campaign pledges that could fit with fiscal realities. One of his highest priorities was an idea that promised to resonate well, both with his generation and the one coming after it. In his inaugural speech the President put out his call: "I challenge a new generation of young Americans to a season of service."

National service was helpful to those who would work in the program, useful for communities that would be served, and poetic in its potential. Kids from the suburbs would find themselves in the inner city teaching some tough teenagers how to wield construction tools. A young woman from a wealthy family in the Northeast would cross the Mason-Dixon line to help poor women start their own businesses. Citizens with the shared vision to give something to their country could earn college tuition vouchers while working directly on a range of social problems. AmeriCorps, as the program was called, was introduced on April 30, 1993, in the midst of the President's economic battles on Capitol Hill.

Clinton had not originated the national service idea. More than two hundred years earlier, Jefferson had written, "Each person owes a debt of national service to his country." A proposal for national civilian service was published as early as 1910. More recently, Congress had passed a demonstration program in 1990 with $22 million earmarked for eight projects. In its election manifesto to the new President, the Democratic Leadership Council picked up on Clinton's own work on the issue and recommended a national service program as "a new compact for opportunity and citizenship."

But Clinton embraced AmeriCorps with personal fervor. It allowed him to exercise "responsive leadership," giving the public what it wanted on an issue of particular passion in his own life. For Clinton, national service represented the most intimate link to his campaign theme of community, opportunity, and responsibility. It resonated of Kennedy's Peace Corps and was in fact referred to as a "domestic peace corps." For President Kennedy, the Peace Corps had become an example of transformational leadership, leadership that improves the lives of the people, much as the Tennessee Valley Authority was for Franklin Roosevelt. If there was to be an initiative for which Clinton would be remembered as a transformational leader, national service was a likely candidate. AmeriCorps evoked all the sentimentality of a small-town boy, who, through his community service, met a president and built on a dream. It was Clinton's signature program.

In the skillful hands of its future director, Eli Segal, national service was shepherded through rough congressional terrain. Critics attacked a new government-financed program in a time of retrenchment. They questioned whether those who worked in exchange for tuition vouchers and small stipends were volunteers at all. The critics reduced the President's request, but they could not kill it. The program was launched on a fall day in 1994, undeterred by the clearing of debris from a small plane that had crashed into the White House. Twenty thousand volunteers took an oath and then spread out to community projects around the country.

National service fit neatly into one early and recurring theme of the new President—enhancing education and training. Clinton made a number of substantial steps forward on this issue. Direct student loans were only one example. Another poorly publicized part of Clinton's perilously passed reconciliation bill, the loan program was a major long-term innovation. No longer would banks, guarantee agencies, and secondary markets control the financial future of students and families needing to finance higher education. Federally financed student loans would be less expensive and repaid according to income.

Another of Clinton's "human investment" initiatives was the establishment of national education standards. Passed after a year of work, the Goals 2000: Educate America Act set eight national education goals for elementary and secondary schools, but left state participation voluntary. It was shorn of the voucher provision for private schools that President Bush had tried to insert during his tenure. It was also shorn of major funding. Because of fiscal restraints, the bill had to be trimmed to fund only model projects. Lacking the teeth of enforcement, Goals 2000 was more gesture than genuine reform.

Closely tied to Goals 2000 was Clinton's initiative for Head Start. On this issue, the President enjoyed extraordinary bipartisan support, with Democratic and Republican leaders of the relevant committees as cosponsors. The bill expanded Head Start's reach and quality assurance. Hillary Rodham Clinton, a deeply committed advocate for children's rights, helped propel Head Start to the forefront of Clinton's domestic initiatives.

Toward the other end of the educational pipeline, another DLC-promoted idea had strong presidential support. Clinton signed a school-to-work bill in May 1994 giving non-college-bound students a boost in finding skilled work. Tied into national education standards and competitiveness, the plan was modeled on European apprenticeships giving on-site career training. It was one more link on the "lifelong learning" track that Clinton was constructing.

Education was a good middle-class issue, a good bipartisan issue. The Clintons were, moreover, comfortable with it. It was, in many respects, an attempt to replicate on the national level the winning strategy they had formulated in Arkansas, raising educational standards, supporting and challenging public schools, reaching children in need at the earliest possible age, and helping non-college-bound youth into jobs commensurate with their abilities.

Education was also an integral part of the vision that all three members of the troika shared for America. In the next century, they saw a country that thrived by creating, managing, and transmitting knowledge to an unprecedented degree. The information superhighway touted by Gore was part of that vision. So was the Clintons' commitment to lifelong learning. Still, the vision would never become a reality unless the people had the education to make it so.

But while expansion of Head Start and reformation of the student loan program were changes of some magnitude, Clinton's other educational reforms were whittled or watered down to an extent that denied him the leadership victory these initiatives initially promised.

Vice President Gore, meanwhile, carved out an important territory of his own, with the full support of the Clintons. Gore would be the force behind environmental policy, the reinvention of the government, the information superhighway and other new technologies.

Gore, like Clinton, was a member of the DLC. He was an adherent of the New Democrat philosophy that government should be "entrepreneurial," treating citizens as "customers." An October 1997 report, titled *Businesslike Government: Lessons Learned from America's Best Companies,* further invited comparisons between government and business. Reinventing government, or REGO, was based on the idea that streamlining and downsizing government and improving efficiency would lead to customer satisfaction. Moreover, Gore felt, though the Office of Management and Budget disagreed, that his streamlining ideas would save $108 billion.

The architects of REGO—the National Performance Review, later dubbed the National Partnership for Reinventing Government—could claim some substantive success. Government shrank by 350,000 jobs, 200 programs, and 16,000 pages of regulations. The White House operation and policy staff was smaller than that of President Bush, whose domestic agenda was feeble in comparison. Procurement rules were vastly simplified. Federal employees could make small purchases without reams of paperwork and bids. The personnel system was revamped. REGO made it easier for federal workers to replace leaky steam traps or to eliminate competitive bidding for lawn work at houses seized in drug raids by the U.S. Marshals Service. Federal employees were empowered to use "total quality management," be "customer-friendly," and work in teams. Agencies and programs were forced to contend with market forces and incentives. In the end the effort amounted to maintaining "current levels of government services at lower cost"—a useful but hardly inspiring outcome.

Did these few successes surprise some members of the Clinton administration? "Sure as hell did," chortled Roy Neel, Gore's former chief of staff. Neel recalled that giving Gore REGO was seen by some as "sort of like giving the third child the crumbs." Most Clinton aides "thought it was a throwaway issue. They didn't think there was much political juice in it. . . . But they just did not know how Al Gore takes on projects like that."

But were these changes any greater than the cyclical housecleaning of previous administrations?

Not if judgment was based on the criterion Gore and Clinton set for themselves: changing individual Americans' opinion about their government. In that respect, REGO was largely ineffectual. A 1998 Pew Research Center for the People and the Press poll found that 35 percent of Americans thought the number of people employed by the government had increased, when, in fact, payrolls had lightened. Gore and Clinton had hoped that getting government's house in order would "revolutionize the government itself so that the American people trust the decisions that are made." Despite a coordinated communication effort with well-scripted appearances by Gore, there was only modest warming in the public attitude toward government. Well into Clinton's second term, 56 percent of Americans described themselves as being frustrated by government; 12 percent confessed to being angry with government.

Change had proven, predictably, easier to promise than to deliver. There was, of course, a modest laundry list of items the President could tick off in response to critics. He had fought for and signed the Brady Bill, putting new restrictions on handgun sales. But that measure by no means ended the hail of bullets on American streets. The bill did succeed in unleashing the fury of the National Rifle Association's adherents on the President and supporters of gun control. But that was hardly the kind of change Clinton had promised.

Legislation to relax the off-duty restrictions on the political activities of federal workers and voter registration linked to getting a driver's license were worthy achievements, but they paled in comparison to the failure to enact any lobbying, campaign finance, or congressional reform.

What is striking about the first two years of the Clinton administration is the extraordinary burst of activity. The domestic agenda was more ambitious than at any time since Lyndon Johnson's presidency.

And in one sense, Clinton was LBJ-like. His position prevailed 86 percent of the time on congressional roll calls in 1993, presenting a striking contrast to George Bush in 1992, who emerged victorious a miserable 43 percent of the time, with a Democratic Congress. In 1994, Clinton's position also carried the day 86 percent of the time. This was a success rate rivaled in the last twenty-seven years only by Reagan's 82 percent in 1981. But Clinton paid a price. Several of the President's successes were by paper-thin margins and the result of intense pressure on targeted legislators in a majority Democratic Congress—and were foisted upon a disgruntled public.

The legislative success rate was also partly illusory. Some of the President's "wins" were holdovers from the previous Congress and had already garnered bipartisan support. This was the case with seven major bills in 1993. By 1994, the number of major bills had dwindled to three, the lowest for any post–World War II president.

Why the disparity in these two years? In part, the answer lay in Bill Clinton's Chinese-menu approach to the presidency—some policy initiatives from column A, some from column B, and some from column C. In a sense, Clinton's "strength becomes his weakness," noted former congressman Timothy Penny. "His strength is that he is very knowledgeable; he sees the interconnectedness of all of these issues. He's interested in promoting policies and programs that respond to all of these areas, but as a consequence, he comes across as someone without any firm agenda." From up close, the assessment was equally critical. Said Robert Reich of Clinton's decision-making style, "It's one of tactical process decisions, rather than irrevocable large decisions."

For former Clinton gubernatorial aide Steve Smith, Clinton was not exercising leadership as much as he was solving problems. "He's not trying to overpower anyone or outfox anyone, but [has the attitude of] 'Come, let us reason together and come up with a good policy based on the facts.'" Betsey Wright, another former aide, agreed that Clinton "likes nothing better than to help warring parties make peace and establish their own compromise. His leadership style very much is in bringing people together to achieve consensus."

Someone once asked Arnold Toynbee, author of a multivolume work on the history of civilization, what he had learned from a lifetime's study of history. He replied, "The urgent is so often the enemy of the important." This too seemed a fitting evaluation of the first two years of the Clinton presidency.

CHAPTER FIVE

The Tragedy of Health

Clinton chose health care reform as the first major work of his presidency. It was a choice driven as much by the political, social, and psychological moment as by the lifelong striving of a passionate believer in reform. "Jobs, education, health care—these are not just commitments from my lips; they are the work of my life," he proclaimed in his acceptance speech. It was a choice in favor of creating real change in the lives of millions of Americans.

Clinton's vision of a brave new world of health care reform meant individuals would find easy access to health care providers and have the insurance coverage to ensure care. No one would be left out. Not children, not the elderly, not the homeless, not those who now told shocking stories of being turned away from hospital emergency rooms for lack of an insurance card.

Health care change in Clinton's vision would usher in a social transition to a level of domestic security never known in America. But the change Clinton foresaw was ultimately misconstrued and misunderstood. Its tremendous importance and economic implications made it a large target for an organized, powerful opposition. The fault was partly Clinton's. His claim of health care as the work of his life had a disingenuous tinge. His terms as governor were marked by few initiatives related to the dire health needs of poor Arkansans. But now he was responding to a growing public dissatisfaction that had been pinpointed at the outset of the campaign by his chief strategist, James Carville.

Carville came to the Clinton camp fresh from a run as the campaign manager for Democrat Harris Wofford's U.S. Senate race in Pennsylvania. In 1991, an airplane crash that killed Republican senator John Heinz of Pennsylvania had led to an off-year Senate campaign putting health care front and center. Wofford won the seat in 1991 with an astute syllogism: "If criminals have a right to a lawyer," Wofford repeated across Pennsylvania, "working Americans should have a right to a doctor."

Less than a year after the Pennsylvania election Clinton announced his run for the presidency. He pledged to present a plan to Congress for affordable, quality health care for all Americans.

Health care had grown from a $60 billion crisis in 1970 to $800 billion by 1991. Americans were spending more per capita than any other nation, but felt they were getting less. The 1980s saw the ranks of the uninsured rise, up to 2 million more people per year in 1988, and then came the 1990–91 recession, bringing more hardship.

The nation's health care system had grown into a behemoth that consumed one-seventh of the total economy. It was bigness without balance. Overall costs were growing at a rate well in excess of inflation, and companies that provided health insurance to their employees complained that the cost was making them less competitive in world markets. Medicare spending on the elderly was the fastest-growing entitlement program in the federal budget. But few of the national indices of health and longevity were rising to match the expenditures. In a nation worried sick over the status quo, the system was ripe for new thinking and was a major issue in the 1992 campaign.

Clinton and his democratic rivals were riding a political wave that had washed in dozens of bills to stem the health care crisis. Candidates in the 1992 presidential election could not ignore health care. Nebraska senator Bob Kerrey, in particular, pushed forward on the health care issue. He put Clinton "under enormous pressure to create a health care plan," according to political columnist E. J. Dionne of the *Washington Post,* even though Clinton was worried that the plan he envisioned would be too complicated to put forward in the campaign.

Once elected, Clinton could not forget his oft-repeated, if loosely formed, promise to fix the system. He seemed to want to make his mark as the kind of president who does more than administer what was bequeathed by his predecessors. He wanted to be a president who changed the character of government and citizens' perception of it. Health care was to be the vehicle for that change.

The political moment for health care reform seemed promising as well in terms of people's needs. Not only were Americans losing coverage or feeling that their coverage was threatened, they were worried about health care costs. Large majorities of the public wanted reform and were willing to support cigarette and alcohol taxes to fund a rebuilt system. Voters were talking to political leaders through polls, and Clinton was listening as he stepped forward briskly with health care reform. It was his "full-scale effort at responsive leadership."

More critical for Clinton than any other circumstance was the psychological satisfaction health care reform provided. Ambitious and confident, Clinton loved immersion in large, complex policy actions. Motivated by his needs for validation and affirmation, Clinton saw a huge personal payoff to accomplishing a "vast social good." He gambled on health care reaping him major rewards early in his presidency. Clinton had faith in his remarkable talent for selling policies, but little understanding of the broader role of president as educator on policy. He was still the campaigner cajoling voters for a cause. But selling is not the same as building understanding and support among the electorate.

TASK FORCES, TOLLGATES, AND TIMING

Clinton's understanding of a health care fix had been slow in coming. Not until late in the 1992 campaign had he begun to specify what he meant. When he did, he staked out a prematurely centrist position, between the extremes of a program wholly financed and managed by the government and the laissez-faire market alternative of leaving people and their employers to make what arrangements they could. He spoke of "competition within a budget," a shorthand reference to a reform model called managed competition that was a hybrid of ideas from various sources. Clinton was trying to find an easy "middle way between market tendencies and government involvement." His rhetoric sounded "liberal to liberals and centrist to centrists." Setting off to achieve the greatest effort by government on behalf of its citizens in thirty years, Clinton chose compromise as his compass.

Once in office, he moved quickly to demonstrate what he had called "leadership committed to change." Dramatically elevating the profile of health care reform, the President appointed his wife to head the effort. Ira Magaziner, another Rhodes Scholar and highly successful business consultant, would be her chief aide and architect of much of the plan and process.

Why did the President put the First Lady in this unprecedented position of power and vulnerability? She, of course, displayed intellectual brilliance that rivaled his own. They had worked as a tag team of governor and wife in Arkansas, with Rodham Clinton carving out important policy turf as her own. Did Clinton truly believe that Rodham Clinton would serve best as the general of his main battle plan for domestic renewal? Or was there, as one former senior aide related, a dark side to Clinton's choice? Was he letting his wife take an enormous risk of reputation and stature with little hope of reward? Was this a passive-aggressive, possibly unconscious, familial attack by an angry husband, played out in a national arena? Clinton spoke with absolute faith, and no hint of irony, of his wife's ability for this enormous task. It was left to Washington and the nation to wonder and speculate about his remarkable, unorthodox choice for health care policy leader.

Magaziner was a policy intellectual. Though he had grown wealthy as a corporate consultant, his reputation in Clinton's governing elite sprang from the broad reform efforts he had led. Magaziner started with curricular reform in his student days at Brown University and went on to an effort to transform an old Massachusetts factory town into a model of social democracy. He was, *The New Republic* said in 1992, "a social planner with an unbounded faith in . . . grandiose systems."

From the outset, Magaziner had the unswerving support of the First Lady. He saw her as a clearheaded thinker, strong in her ability to "follow things through to a logical conclusion." She trusted Magaziner, seeing him as a creative force and custodian of the process to reach their mutual goal. Health and Human Services Secretary Donna Shalala, whose department might normally have been expected to draft a health care reform proposal, viewed the relationship with barely disguised envy, complaining that "Ira has mesmerized Hillary." Shalala was not alone in criticizing what many viewed as an inauspicious collaboration.

How could the President's wife expect candid, full-throated debate given her position? Why should Magaziner, a stranger to Congress and newcomer to health care, be trusted to mastermind the crucial plan? As the Task Force on Health Care was forming, these questions had already begun to roil the reform effort.

Magaziner and Rodham Clinton quickly set up a five-hundred-member task force to draft a reform bill. The members included experts from within the executive branch and the congressional committee staffs, along with some outside experts and scholars. The task force process was exhausting, intricate, and elaborate. The members worked almost continuously for the first five months of 1993, often staying at their desks past midnight. Magaziner broke them into "clusters" and "workgroups," sent them through "tollgates," and organized critiques of the work-in-progress by "contrarians" and "auditors."

But the process was not open. The task force sessions were closed to the press and public, despite Magaziner's protest. He was overruled by the White House communications team. Rodham Clinton felt maligned by the press and agreed to the closed process. Although some 572 different organizations met with the task force, several key groups, including the American Medical Association, had no representative on the task force itself.

This left bruised egos, in both the lobbying community and the media. Newspaper editors complained in frustration that their calls to the task force were always returned by low-level functionaries authorized only to parrot the official line of the day. As a communications strategy, this stonewalling was meant to protect against premature leaks that would confuse and frustrate the planning.

After more than six months of work, the task force finally produced a plan of staggering complexity. The untimely death of Rodham Clinton's father in April 1993 diverted her attention from the project, but the drafting churned ahead. The legislative proposal ran to 1,342 pages. Magaziner said there were "eight hundred movable parts." The overall health care reform initiative was to be the climactic final chapter in a decades-old campaign to guarantee citizens certain basic economic protections—a campaign that could be traced at least as far back as social security's introduction in the 1930s. No longer would children, the elderly, the homeless, the poor, or working poor be denied the basic right to health. But how would the public feel about such a grand scheme involving what promised to be enormous costs?

Under the administration's plan, companies bore most of the expense for their employees, while the federal government subsidized coverage for the poor and for small-business employees. The plan envisioned "health care alliances" in each state, quasi-governmental structures that would enroll citizens and manage their health care dollars, bargaining with hospitals and providers to keep costs low. Insurance premiums were capped.

In an era when ideological politics were reputedly passé, the plan bore Clinton's decidedly anti-ideological centrist stamp. It attempted to reach a liberal goal—immediate, universal coverage—without eliminating any of the major private actors in the existing system: doctors, hospitals, and insurance companies. In adopting that strategy, the Clintons bypassed other options. They did not seriously consider a Canadian-style, single-payer system, in which the government replaces private insurers, finances all health care, and imposes cost limits—even though such a plan had the virtue of relative simplicity and had some support in Congress. They decided against the "play or pay" proposals advanced by other Democratic legislators that would require employers either to provide insurance or pay into a fund for uninsured workers. Play or pay, however, would not cover the unemployed. And they decided against gradual approaches, plans that would either delay attaining universal coverage or limit the kinds of coverage that would be universally available.

Choosing the form the plan would take, recruiting and managing teams of experts to draft substance, weighing the interests of competing groups, this was the herculean effort shepherded by Magaziner and overseen by Rodham Clinton. Their hope was to move the bill quickly because, as Magaziner explained, "this was an issue that could easily become politicized in midterm elections." The fastest way to pass health care was as a rider to the President's economic package, known as the budget reconciliation bill. This bill required only a majority, and filibusters were not allowed. But this approach required bending parliamentary rules. Courtly, crusty Senator Robert Byrd, a venerable Democrat from West Virginia, was a stickler for keeping budget bills free of legislation properly left to the full process of committee consideration, floor debate, votes, and possible filibuster. The health care team's first approach to Congress was quickly rebuffed, even as the President's economic plan ran into rough terrain.

Rodham Clinton and Magaziner were bluntly informed by the President's economic advisers that the economic plan had to precede health care. Even worse, the task force was told to shut down, because leaks of parts of the health reform proposal were complicating the budget fight. At one point a proposal to use wine and spirit taxes in addition to tobacco taxes to pay for health care brought angry reactions from Democrats and Republicans. "Not only would they oppose the health care bill," Magaziner recalled, "but they would oppose the economic package if we did not assure them that that would be taken out. That's one example, but I could show you about forty examples of the same kind of thing. So we were forced to shut down the health care package process."

As budget wrangling continued through the summer, administration health reform advocates steered clear of Congress and the press and did little to educate the public on the plan. Meanwhile the President maneuvered and horse-traded for a deficit-reduction budget that would take eight months to pass, and would then succeed only with the help of the Vice President's tie-breaking vote. Thus, the President's first budget battle was a cliffhanging ride that pushed health care entirely off the track. The result was that "both health reform and the President himself lost credibility with the public and Congress."

The First Lady spent much of the summer of 1993 as a roving ambassador for health care reform. She visited a hair salon and talked with the owner, who was frustrated at being unable to afford health insurance for the salon's employees. She spoke with people who couldn't afford to leave jobs they hated because they would lose their health insurance. She talked with those who had no insurance at all.

Both Clintons went to Capitol Hill when the plan finally emerged, several months late, in the fall of 1993. The President rose superbly to the task of introducing the legislation. Despite a TelePrompTer cued up with the wrong text, Clinton delivered a moving, even passionate address. He spoke with conviction. The system, Clinton said, was "badly broken and it is time to fix it." The nation responded. Public opinion–poll support for the plan peaked in the immediate aftermath of Clinton's address.

Then it was Rodham Clinton's turn. She became the third first lady to testify before Congress (following Eleanor Roosevelt and Rosalynn Carter) and the first to take the role of leadoff witness on an issue of such major national importance.

Her performances before the major committees with pieces of jurisdiction over the proposal were widely hailed as brilliant. She had, noted the *Washington Post,* "an exceptional gift for mastering the head-breaking details of a hard subject and translating them into understandable English." She testified for four hours without once checking her notes or consulting with the entourage of nine staff assistants who sat behind her. Said Dan Rostenkowski, the chairman of the House Ways and Means Committee, "If there was any doubt about whether the President should have appointed her, there's no doubt about it any longer." The episode attracted the attention of some members of the Senate too, who watched and marveled. "Hillary," said former senator Harris Wofford, beaming, "is an extraordinarily powerful, effective, focused, disciplined, [and] determined person."

But the glow from the President's masterful presentation speech, the glitter from newscasts of the First Lady enthralling Congress's most powerful committees, quickly dissolved. Clinton called health care reform the work of his life, but the call of his presidency in the fall of 1993 was far from domestic concerns. American troops had been killed in Somalia. In Haiti, desperate refugees fled military rulers refusing to abide by an agreement to a political transition. And in Moscow, barely contained internal crises threatened Yeltsin's presidency. Then Clinton abruptly moved health care off the legislative radar screen with his decision to pass the North American Free Trade Agreement (NAFTA) at all costs.

After its portentous launch, indeed, the President devoted little time and attention to health care in the first year of his presidency. Those who thought Rodham Clinton's prominent role guaranteed health care priority on the President's agenda were puzzled. Some advisers saw the President's inattention as proof that Rodham Clinton was set up for failure, her husband handing her the policy as punishment for their personal troubles. Others, less cynical, saw a President whipsawed by the many diverse opinions he sought and overcommitted to a highly ambitious agenda. In his hurry to do everything, Clinton endangered his ability to bring his most important programs to fruition.

Magaziner remembered promises but no follow-through on support from the White House legislative team, the communications office, and Deputy Chief of Staff Harold Ickes. In frustration, he urged Rodham Clinton to pressure her husband to see the urgency of the health care agenda. But policy focus blurred in the whirl of events, and health care became a mired giant.

Slowly and agonizingly, the project fell apart. In his January 1994 State of the Union speech Clinton tried to jump-start health reform, but it was too late. The First Lady was beset with the emerging Whitewater controversy from Little Rock days. Opponents of health care reform were fully mobilized and funded. Key proponents such as labor were still boiling with anger over the President's victory on NAFTA. By the summer of 1994, Democratic congressional leaders informed Clinton that no sweeping overhaul of health care would emerge from the 103rd Congress.

Bill Clinton's first bid as a transforming leader had failed along with his chance to be "remembered as putting the last piece in the New Deal and Great Society panoply of social programs." Clinton recognized that "this kind of sweeping reform is rare in our country's history." He had gambled against the odds, betting on his "third" way that was not "liberal or conservative . . . a new kind of leadership . . . not mired in the politics of the past, not limited by old ideologies." His was an approach through the center of health care's rising storm of discontent. He emerged bruised and battered by the whirlwind of forces fighting against change.

WHAT WENT WRONG?

There was more than enough blame to go around.

The decision by Hillary Rodham Clinton and Ira Magaziner to close the task force meetings to the press and the lobbying community was, in retrospect, a mistake that started the effort with a burden of suspicion; one of the first things that beset the task force was a lawsuit brought by health care organizations and a public interest group, seeking to open the meetings. The decision for secrecy underestimated the importance of both the press and the lobbyists in the Washington process.

In an era when the "base of political leadership . . . is less and less belief and more and more communication," the task force leaders and the President failed to communicate on every level. Despite involvement of some congressional staff on the task force, there was continued rumbling throughout the spring and summer of 1993 by members of Congress and staff who felt ill informed about the task force process. Some could not understand why the President, who was clearly being guided by bills introduced by moderates in both parties, did not let the legislation emanate from the Hill with his input. The press made unfavorable comparisons to Jimmy Carter, the last Democratic president, who seemed to have contempt for his party's leaders in Congress.

The failure to recognize allies, to build alliances where needed, to understand the power of a wholly entrenched Democratic leadership in Congress, emerged as a fundamental leadership failure on the part of the President. Used to being his own lobbyist in the homey halls of the Arkansas legislature, Clinton was alternately active, intimidated, and aloof in his relations with congressional power brokers. While he had some key aides, notably George Stephanopoulos and Howard Paster, who had considerable experience on Capitol Hill, most of Clinton's closest advisers were as new to the ways of Washington power as their boss. Policy ideas floated with little connection to the leadership needed to bring those ideas to fruition.

The press resented the spoon-feeding of administration pablum on health care from low-level White House staff. Always on the lookout for "conflict and dissent rather than clarification of goals and searching for consensus," the press found little at either end and focused instead on personalities and rumor.

The Clintons' most egregious failure was in educating the public. Polls showing the public's support for changes in health care had disguised the uninformed nature of that support. There was little understanding among most Americans of how the health care system worked, or even of how they received their own health care if they had coverage. What "education" the administration eventually offered was too little and too late in the face of the flood of negative reaction from adversaries. Journalists offered scant aid in helping their audiences grapple with substance and issues, preferring instead to highlight personalities and the conflict of positions.

The public constituency for health care reform was there and willing to listen. While the task force looked inward, weighing and balancing the complexities of changing one-seventh of the economy, no one in the administration was tackling the equally enormous job of building informed support for the eventual plan. The Clintons failed to provide leadership "in the classic sense: that educates and informs rather than responds." Instead, the enemies of change took readily to the task of swaying the public mind to their side.

Curiously, in health care reform the Clintons balked at the kind of public relations opportunity that had been their forte in the campaign for president. Clinton, the consummate campaigner could not translate campaign governance to the higher level of true governance. Rodham Clinton said of the health care failure, "We just got outspent and outsmarted." But more than that, they got outcommunicated. The administration's health care effort ran on confusing slogans and catchphrases. There would be "universal coverage," "managed competition," "health security." Internal White House message memos warned, "Whatever you do, don't get caught up in the details of the policy." The President's advisers believed the public could not understand the plan, but would respond to focus-group-tested messages.

Building public support for health care reform became an administration sales job, rather than a project to educate "people to the merits and limitations of the alternatives chosen, and the rationale for having done so." Clinton's hubris was a failure to recognize that his "mastery and belief in his political and policy understandings is not the same as the public understanding." The Clintons were, in the words of correspondent Robin Toner, "politically tone deaf" on health care reform. They were also too ready to shift the prerogatives of leadership to self-appointed intermediaries for the public—the pollsters. The decision to reject the single-payer system and at the same time to eschew gradual steps toward universal coverage assured that the plan would be colossal, difficult to understand, potentially expensive, and still inadequate. Worse, it made it harder to rally public support.

The plan was perceived as bureaucratic and costly in an era when the Republicans had successfully implanted in the public mind a strong distaste for both government spending and government employees. This distaste had been reinforced by Clinton in his presidential campaign. After having run as the Washington outsider and making good on his antibureaucratic rhetoric by reducing the size of the White House staff and putting the Vice President in charge of a massive effort to "reinvent" the federal government, Clinton could hardly turn around and propose a health care plan that would enlarge government or appear to raise taxes. And Republicans seized on the message by calling the plan a "bureaucratic takeover by welfare-state liberals."

Clinton feared the *liberal* moniker. He fretted over perceptions of the government that he had come to lead. There existed a "basic public dilemma" in the lack of "public trust in public policy," so Clinton steered a circuitous course. Health care alliances, the redistribution of premiums, and employer mandates were devices designed to disguise and deflect from the government's role. At a time when the urban underclass of anxious workers saw government as "either indifferent or incompetent in assisting them through the immense structural changes in the American economy," Clinton had little faith in his ability to build public confidence in a government program that would effect powerful change in people's lives.

Six months after Rodham Clinton's public campaign for health care legislation began, a poll again showed that only 34 percent of the public had any understanding of what the White House was proposing. One-fourth of that group did not know that employers would bear the brunt of the costs. And it was hard to rouse enthusiasm for such a centrist plan. "There is no passion in the middle. There's only passion on the left and right," Louisiana senator John Breaux, a Democrat, observed.

But if the public was confused and indifferent, the interest groups were not. The Clinton proposal had something to gore every ox. Doctors worried about government intrusion into their relations with their patients. They feared that spending limits would affect their services. They felt the bill's reform of malpractice law did not go far enough. Insurance agents saw their jobs—and insurance companies saw their profits—disappearing in favor of bureaucrats in the new health alliance structure. Drug companies and hospitals predictably feared price controls. Cigarette companies rallied tobacco farmers and workers against the prospect of funding the plan, in part, through higher cigarette taxes.

The Clinton team failed to appreciate the strength of these interest groups until it was too late. The interests all had grassroots organizations that could and did apply pressure on Congress. "I get listened to on the Hill," said John Motley, a small-business-organization lobbyist who vehemently opposed the Clinton plan. "They know I have six hundred thousand small-business men behind me back home. The grass roots give me standing."

Reaching the grass roots was a growth industry in Washington. Whole companies had formed solely to assist corporate clients in finding and mobilizing public support. The American Medical Association, which opposed the Clinton bill's cost-control features, developed a brochure for 660,000 doctors and 48,000 medical students with ten questions and answers on the plan. There was a 1-800 number for those wishing further information.

Then there was the ubiquitous "Harry and Louise." The Health Insurance Association of America, an organization of small- and medium-sized insurance companies, spent $5.5 million to create and air a series of television advertisements featuring a fictitious middle-class couple who fretted over the complexity, cost, and lack of choice in Clinton's plan. The ads had been tested in focus groups and were aimed at educated women likely to communicate to Congress. Harry and Louise were the quintessential modern example of the "tools, techniques, and philosophy of modern campaigns corrupting policy-making." The ads generated more than 125,000 calls to the organization. Every caller got a brochure attacking the Clinton plan.

The White House, meanwhile, tried to make up for lost time on the public relations front. The First Lady, clearly in campaign mode, established a "war room" similar to the successful venue so named at campaign headquarters in Little Rock. She gave staffers pep talks that prompted one to describe her as "Carville in skirts." The tactic proved ill suited to the task. War room staffers were instructed by the pollsters and consultants to keep repeating simple messages that seemed to resonate in focus groups. The strategy was ineffective against the counteroffensive. "They introduced this very complex piece of legislation and then decided that all they would say were phrases that had been market-tested, like 'health care security,' " complained Democratic congressman Henry Waxman of California. Clinton would later admit that the "screwed-up part" was losing the "communications and the political war."

Hillary Rodham Clinton, for all her leadership abilities, proved less than an unalloyed asset to the health care effort. Her dual roles as both policy leader and First Lady proved difficult to blend. Inside the policy-making process, those who thought some of her ideas were mistaken or too expensive were often too intimidated to argue with her. Public perception of the health care plan became entangled with public perception of Rodham Clinton herself—and many people saw her as an ambitious woman, disdainful of women's traditional roles, wielding power she was not elected to hold. The lobbyists fighting the bill took to calling her "Big Sister." Then, both Bill and Hillary were tarnished by the Whitewater miniscandal, involving investments they had made back in Arkansas. By the closing months of the health care debate, in the summer of 1994, the First Lady was perceived by some as a liability. The unprecedented collaboration of leadership between the President and his spouse, on an issue of the greatest import, was never fully tested as Rodham Clinton unobtrusively retreated from the battle. The troika system had not withstood this test.

That left the President to carry the banner, and he too was badly weakened. The minor scandals, misjudgments, and horse-trading of the first eighteen months had sapped his power to cajole or coerce the Congress. By substituting regulations for revenues the Clinton team hoped to make the health plan palatable to the Congressional Budget Office (CBO), which had absolute authority to forecast the plan's cost. The tactic proved worse than useless. CBO's projections were far less optimistic than Clinton's, and the administration proposal with its numerous regulations was a perfect target for enemies of reform. The weakness of the plan bred further divisions among the Democrats.

Congress was atomized, a product of the same politics of personality that had produced the President. Many members of Congress felt, with Clinton leading the way, that they did not "need a party or an ideology. They have television." Representative Jim Cooper, a Democrat from Tennessee, introduced his own health care reorganization plan, which eliminated the employer mandate and drew potential votes away from Clinton's plan. Emboldened, Senator John Chafee, Republican of Rhode Island, presented a plan that promised universal coverage, but not for a decade. Jim McDermott, a liberal Democrat from Washington, introduced his version of the single-payer plan. It picked up ninety cosponsors in the House.

The President, attempting to save his proposal, tried melodrama in his 1994 State of the Union address. Brandishing a pen before the assembled legislators, he vowed to veto any health care plan that did not have universal coverage. The public found the gesture counterintuitive to its perception of Clinton as a waffler. The effect was minimal, and on the Hill his own first-year record betrayed him. Legislators saw the First Lady, whatever her failings, as the one who was tough, principled, and willing to fight to the last for what she believed in. The President was perceived as a man willing to bargain, a man who could be rolled.

Clinton had brought this on himself. In his first budget proposal, Clinton had gone to House members and asked them to go out on a limb for him by voting for a new tax, the so-called BTU tax, which would have been based on units of energy burned. Then, in negotiations with the Senate, he had quickly and abjectly abandoned the proposal, leaving those House members who had supported it alone to explain their votes to antitax constituents and Republican opponents. Now he was asking these same representatives to take another political risk for him by voting to force employers to pay for their employees' coverage. Many of them declined.

Nor did Clinton garner any Republican support. No GOP member of the House voted for the health care proposal in any major committee. Republicans, with an election coming up, sensed the advantage of leaving the Democrats to stew in their own disarray. "Why," asked Dick Armey, a vituperatively conservative Republican from Texas, "should we be enthusiastic about helping the Democrats pull their political fat out of the fire with our ideas?" Bill Kristol, a conservative intellectual who led the Project for the Republican Future, urged party members to "send them [Democrats] to the voters empty-handed."

Through the dog days of the summer of 1994, Clinton searched for a way to keep the health care plan alive. He signaled retreat on the pledge he had made in January, saying he would only insist on "functional universal coverage," which in the health care debate was defined as 95 percent of all Americans. But it was too late. Senator George Mitchell made one final try, before the 1994 election recess, to forge a compromise amenable to a coalition of Democrats and moderate Republicans. He failed. And when Congress returned, it would return with a new Republican majority.

In choosing comprehensive health care reform as the definitive effort of their first years in office, did the Clintons choose wisely? They can certainly be accused of attempting too much. They had, after all, only a 43 percent mandate. Fifty-seven percent of the voters had chosen either a candidate (George Bush) who was willing to ignore the problems of the health care system, or another (Ross Perot) who had campaigned on distrust of Washington and zealous opposition to the federal budget deficit. The political climate, therefore, was hardly propitious for a program that promised to create a bureaucracy in Washington at a cost that was hard to estimate.

Still, while the Clintons had made mistakes in the pursuit of their initiative, they were probably not as crucial as the changes that had occurred in the system since the days of the New Deal and the Great Society. Franklin Roosevelt did not have to cope with mass communications, sound-bite politics, and AstroTurf grass roots. Only a relative handful of lobbyists worked the Capitol in 1934. The Washington the Clintons faced had grown sclerotic through the influence of lobbyists and the media.

Health care was a noble failure, but a failure nonetheless. And it would have consequences far more costly than what Hillary Rodham Clinton and Ira Magaziner could have calculated in the heady early days of their task force.

THE COST OF FAILURE

The autumn of 1994 found Bill Clinton and his party demoralized and defensive. In mid-October, the President's approval rating was gauged by Gallup and *Wall Street Journal* polls as somewhere between 41 and 48 percent. This was an ominous indicator. A sitting president's party typically lost congressional seats during midterm elections, but it did worse when the president's approval was under 50 percent in the polls. Kennedy, Nixon, Carter, Reagan, and Bush had stood at 49 percent or better at midterm time and saw their party lose fifteen House seats or fewer. But Johnson, Nixon before his resignation in August 1974, and Reagan in 1982 were appreciably below 50 percent and lost 47, 48, and 26 seats respectively.

Had things gone according to plan, Democratic candidates would have faced their constituents with the boast that they had passed universal health care. But not a scrap of the Clintons' grand scheme was left to carry home. The President's crime bill, passed before the August recess, was a mixed blessing. Republicans had successfully tagged the bill as pork-laden, and it contained a ban on assault weapons. This was anathema in many districts where the Second Amendment to the Constitution was considered tantamount to the Eleventh Commandment. The National Rifle Association, its organizational structure firmly in the hands of gun extremists, spent millions of dollars for ads using the assault weapons ban against endangered Democrats in targeted districts.

The administration did have several major accomplishments—budget deficit reduction, AmeriCorps, NAFTA—but they were not the types of issues that would galvanize labor, minorities, the elderly, or other core constituencies. Primary turnout for the Democrats in the spring had been only 19 percent, suggesting that the party's voters had lapsed into apathy.

Democratic candidates knew their political history, and many clung to a strategy guaranteed to further divide a divided party. They ran hard away from their President, a tactic that had worked for southern Democrats for two generations. Don Sweitzer, the seasoned political director of the Democratic National Committee, had his ears soundly boxed by the White House for saying publicly what everyone was thinking in private. He advised Democratic candidates to distance themselves from the President if they needed to do so. Democrats desperately tried to keep their races local.

Republicans were busy nationalizing the election. Minority Leader Newt Gingrich, working with other conservatives and with carefully conducted polls of the electorate, crafted a manifesto for Republican candidates to run on. The Contract with America, as it was called, was a promise and a platform for American voters' evaluation and response. In reality, little attention was paid to it by the voters, but the Contract created cohesion among GOP candidates. They were energized by its vision, and Gingrich backed up his ideological blueprint with personal appearances and dollars from his own political fund, GOPAC. Republican candidates had a leader giving guidance, inspiration, and organizational support. Many Democrats preferred not to be led.

The Republicans' one-two campaign punch started with the positive message of the Contract and ended with relentless pounding on Bill Clinton, their best weapon against the Democrats. Tony Coelho, former congressman and master House political operative, was brought back to Washington to try to shore up the DNC. As he put it, "The whole Republican campaign is based on embarrassing Democrats because they are affiliated with Clinton."

While not an unusual tactic during midterm elections, the attacks on the President seemed intense by recent historical standards. Republican campaign commercials "morphed" Democratic candidates' images to that of Clinton. Democratic incumbents were attacked for their votes on Clinton's budget, which the public wrongly perceived as raising middle-class taxes. Gun control, in the form of the Brady bill and assault weapons ban, was next in the Republican arsenal, with abortion rights and gays in the military directed at receptive audiences.

The Democrats, Don Sweitzer said, "don't have a national emotional issue that moves our base." Voters viewed the President as a failure in delivering on his promises, and as part of partisanship and gridlock at the expense of change.

Ross Perot, the independent candidate for president in 1992, leaped into the GOP camp for the midterm balloting. Appearing on his favorite venue, CNN's *Larry King Live*, Perot called on his supporters to vote Republican and give the GOP a chance to run things.

Meanwhile, Democratic base voters were best described as confused, disappointed, and angry. Labor was upset with the President and congressional Democrats for their support of NAFTA. Unions had withdrawn their support and money from the National Health Care Coalition after the NAFTA fight, further weakening the already tepid field effort for the President's plan. The environmental community had had high expectations for the new administration, but felt seriously shortchanged. The reliable core Democratic constituencies of the elderly, blacks, women, and Jews were threatening to stay home. White House and party staff and surrogates begged the national organizations representing the Democratic base to concentrate on voter turnout. While the midterm election traditionally held little promise for the President's party, the 1994 election turned particularly sour for Democrats as the calendar edged closer to election day.

The White House tried to rationalize the Democrats' problems. The President wanted to probe the public psyche, suggesting that people feared change although they wanted it. That was why his efforts to reduce the deficit, increase trade, and rewrite foreign policy were hurting him in the short term. He admitted that the White House had failed to communicate successes, or to calm voters unsettled by global changes in economics that could affect their standard of living. He labeled the Republican Contract as nothing more than Reaganomics revisited. But the "abiding image of the 103rd Congress was institutional inaction," with the President personifying voters' frustrations. Scholar Robert Erikson said of the voters, "Half were upset because they didn't like [Clinton's] policies, and the other half were upset because he couldn't enact his policies."

In October the President's approval rating took a slight bump upward. He had successfully stood up to Saddam Hussein in Iraq, restored the presidency of Haiti to Jean-Bertrand Aristide, and found agreement with North Korea on nuclear weapons.

There was no stampede, but a few Democratic candidates asked their President to pay a campaign call. The week before the election, Clinton stood with Ted Kennedy's son in Rhode Island as young Patrick closed in on one of the few House seats that would go into the Democratic victory column. Clinton went to Pennsylvania, where his friend Harris Wofford was running to hold the Senate seat he had won in 1990 with the promise to work for health care reform in the Congress. Clinton stumped in Pittsburgh, near where a gun show had recently displayed a sign reading, "Happiness is Clinton's face on a milk carton." Then the President headed westward through the battleground states of Ohio and Michigan. But the campaigning did not help.

On November 8, 1994, all of the Senate seats that changed hands went to the Republicans, giving them control of the upper chamber. Thirty-six Democratic members of the House of Representatives were defeated. Not a single incumbent Republican running for the House, the Senate, or a governorship lost. For the first time in forty years, the GOP would reign as the majority in the House of Representatives. Newt Gingrich would be the Speaker of the House, ousting Thomas Foley of Washington. Foley would be remembered as the first sitting Speaker to lose his race for reelection since 1860. It was one of the most decisive midterm elections in the history of the republic.

The postmortems for the Democrats mixed fear of Republican majorities with a hope that the political system might now be so thoroughly shaken that real change would ensue.

William Greider of *Rolling Stone* viewed the results with a mixture of loathing and optimism. The House of Representatives would be led "by a world-class demagogue, a talented reactionary in the vengeful tradition of Governor George Wallace or Senator Joe McCarthy," he wrote. But the elections had "upended the decadent status quo of American politics," which might now finally start to "get real."

Michael Lind of *The New Republic* blamed "progressive liberals" for alienating once-Democratic, white, middle-class Americans who had been drifting for a generation between the two parties. During presidential election years, he said, these voters had often lived "in sin with the Republicans," but "on November 8, they married them." Clinton, said Lind, had tried, mostly superficially, to appeal to this "rightward-drifting center" with his affrontive comments about Sister Souljah, taken as a slap at black leader Jesse Jackson in the 1992 campaign, his call for boot camps for youthful offenders, his assault on labor over NAFTA, and his conversion to the cause of deficit reduction.

But Clinton's failure to deal with the uneasiness toward racial preferences and immigration were, in Lind's view, critical mistakes. They left the

Republicans to exploit these wedge issues and capture the center of the American electorate. The President's focus on the deficit, Greider concluded, had only proved once again "what George Bush discovered in 1992 about the politics of fiscal responsibility. Except for editorial writers and other elites, nobody rewards politicians for shrinking the deficit."

Vice President Gore had a slightly different explanation of the November debacle. He gave a muted endorsement to the complaints of the Democratic Leadership Council that Clinton had confused and failed the voters by straying from centrist policies. Using a metaphor close to the hearts of the purveyors of entrepreneurial government, Gore acknowledged that smart corporate managers keep a friend who tells "when you're messing up. This lesson applies to politics as well."

As shock settled in, a chastened President tried to regroup and plan for two more years of "trying to lead a cynical and angry electorate." The day after the election, he signaled his direction. "Most of the good ideas are ones that move us into the future, not to the left or right," he said. He asked Republicans to "join me in the center of the debate."

Soon after, the President suggested he might support Republican moves for prayer in the school. In mid-December he fired his surgeon general, Joycelyn Elders, much hated by social conservatives and the right wing, after she made some outspoken and impolitic comments on sex education. Bush cabinet member and sometime presidential candidate Jack Kemp found cause to proclaim, "We're dragging the Clinton administration to the center-right, where most of the people of this country are."

Kemp had a point. The setback for Democrats in the 1994 election came from angry center-right Democrats. Many white males with high school degrees and uncertain job futures switched their party allegiance to vote Republican. For the first time since Reconstruction, Republican candidates won the majority of the southern vote, by a margin of 55.9 to 44.1 percent.

The Democratic party was seen by swing voters as "seeking to redistribute income from workers to nonworkers." An economist affiliated with the Democratic Leadership Council (DLC) was more charitable. "We are not seeing the pauperization of the middle class. It just hasn't been a time of massive upward mobility."

But voters thought they had struck a better bargain when they elected Clinton in 1992. He had made a covenant to lead America as a different kind of Democrat. But faith in him as a leader, and the keeper of a new Democratic vision, was clearly ebbing.

He had not, according to his DLC colleagues, convinced voters that he had reformed the way government did business. This was, in DLC philosophy, the basic first step necessary for the construction of great change. To these voters, welfare reform had to precede health care reform. Clinton had

139

also been, in the minds of many, too accommodating to the entrenched Democratic leadership in the Congress. Matching the record of Millard Fillmore in the 32nd Congress of 1853, the President vetoed no bills during the entire 103rd congressional session.

Voters were left without a sense of national purpose, their increasing alienation heightened by their frustration with politics as usual. The measure of Clinton's failure was the call for new leadership voiced through the November election. As the President himself said, "They looked at us and said they want to see some more changes."

But what changes could the President hope to deliver with a Congress of the opposing party? Clinton's problems were compounded by congressional Democrats, now in the unfamiliar role of the minority, moving quickly to distance themselves even further from the White House. In December, House minority leader Richard Gephardt announced a plan for a tax cut two days before Clinton unveiled his own "middle-class bill of rights." Gephardt did not mince words when he said, "Our agenda will come from America's houses, not the White House."

Congressional Democrats blamed the President for their losses. The White House insisted that the congressmen had only themselves to blame, having failed to save themselves by reforming their institution while they were in power. By January, as the President's State of the Union address neared, "the estrangement [was] palpable. The White House used to send representatives to House Democratic caucuses, whip meetings, and the daily message meeting. Now White House officials show up infrequently."

Clinton's compass would swing widely in the twenty months leading to his reelection campaign. He would announce the prohibition of funding for fertility research on human embryos, increase the Pentagon budget by $25 billion, and submit a balanced budget plan so close to the Republican version it would be called GOP lite. But he stayed near the traditional Democratic line on affirmative action, gave labor an executive order against replacing striking workers on federal projects, and waved his veto pen threateningly toward Republican cuts in social programs.

The President still claimed to be a New Democrat. He implored Americans in a July 1995 speech to make good, informed decisions as the "board of directors of America." He asked them to listen, as he was, to those with differing views and to seek "common ground."

But the midterm elections suggested an ironic outcome for a President determined to renew faith among the citizenry in American government. Based on years of studying the electorate, Curtis Gans wrote, "What we are seeing is dealignment rather than realignment—a turning away from both major political parties. The future trend is toward disengagement and nonparticipation." Clinton had not only failed to mobilize a constituency for health care, he had turned many Democrats into disinterested observers.

In the end, after the plan's final gasp, "small steps" became the health effort's legacy. In 1996, legislation was passed helping workers and families keep their insurance coverage if they changed or lost their jobs, and requiring coverage for preexisting medical conditions. The law, cosponsored by Senators Edward Kennedy and Nancy Kassebaum, was a swipe at the insurance industry. Insurance companies, formerly in the practice of denying coverage to people with known or chronic illnesses, were now required to cover everyone.

The new law shone a small ray of light toward the kind of change Clinton had sought in 1993. But Clinton had pushed for comprehensive reform, taking aim at the whole system at once. His effort in 1993 was more than the craving of an overreaching, impatient leader. Without reforming the entire system, costs and benefits would bulge and shrink in all the wrong places. The new Kennedy-Kassebaum law exemplified this problem. Workers were assured of finding coverage, but no cost controls were imposed. The insurance companies could and did simply charge whatever they needed to cover their risk.

Similarly, the 1997 budget bill would contain language, again sponsored by Kennedy and conservative Republican senator Orrin Hatch, offering federal grants to states to cover children who are uninsured. Clinton kept his distance from the effort, but Kennedy and Hatch were a dogged team. The bill was aimed at children who fall in the coverage gaps between low- and high-income families. States could choose to cover children in families earning up to three times the poverty level, meaning some coverage would be given to those already covered through employer-paid plans.

These moves toward "bite-size" reform offered nothing in the way of controlling costs, which was the essence of Clinton's compromise of managed competition. "Clinton's 1994 plan was an effort to restrain health care spending by harnessing market forces. Incrementalism is an effort to restrain the market forces themselves." Ironically, these small reforms that followed the 1994 crash of Clinton's health care plan were more liberal and government-controlled than the President's original full-blown proposal.

By 1998, the President had jumped on the bandwagon pulled by powerful polling results. Americans were angrier with the insurance industry than they had ever been before. A popular movie of 1997 contained a line critical of health maintenance organizations. It garnered spontaneous applause in theaters across the country. Both parties introduced legislation to give patients guaranteed rights in dealing with their insurance companies. It became the most salient issue of the 1998 midterm elections, a welcome alternative focus for the President, beleaguered by personal scandal.

In some ways health care reform had come full circle. A complacent electorate fearful of changes to the status quo of health care delivery was once again up in arms. This time their target was not government but private greed and mismanagement. But amid the emerging troubles at home and abroad, Clinton had little strength left to take advantage of the public's new mood toward health care reform. This time he followed the lead of others and spared himself any chance of further policy humiliation.

PART III

THE WIDENING GYRE

CHAPTER SIX

Squarely in the Center

How could it happen that a politician known as Slick Willie, the practitioner of "pragmatic," transactional politics, could take a leading part in framing a long-run, thoughtful, and even analytical reassessment of American party strategy? How could he become the prime leader and beneficiary of that reassessment and establish himself as a rare president who consciously pursued a strategy of presidential leadership?

As a southern governor, Bill Clinton had become closely involved with self-styled "mainstream Democrats" who had long been frustrated by GOP victories caused by liberal Democrats stuck in their "old, worn-out ideological groove." The four Eisenhower and Nixon wins were bad enough, but the shocker was Ronald Reagan's triumph in 1980. Not only did he beat an incumbent, Jimmy Carter, but he led his party in taking control of the Senate and boosting Republican numbers in the House.

The mainstream Democrats appeared to be far angrier with the liberals in their own party than with the Reaganists. Indeed, they accused the liberals of being more out-of-date than Reaganism itself. Even worse, they complained, George McGovern, Walter Mondale, and Michael Dukakis had brought huge Democratic defeats. Mondale was the centrists' special target, since under his leadership, they charged, the Democratic party had sanctioned seven official caucuses of blacks, women, Hispanics, Asians, gays, liberals, and businesspersons/professionals. Centrists fumed that the Democratic party had been reduced to a factional interest-group morass.

What to do? The centrists had a role model—a Reagan Republican role model. They were much impressed by the brilliant tactics of the Republican right in gaining control of the GOP, repudiating the moderate leadership of the Dewey-Eisenhower-Rockefeller crowd, and electing a truly conservative president. They discovered that the success in 1980 of the old Taft-Goldwater wing was not due merely to choosing a candidate with Hollywood glitter and a pleasing personality. The takeover was more the product of focused political analysis. Unless conservatives realized "that massive public education must precede any hope of a presidential victory," William F. Buckley Jr. had written years before Reagan's win, "they will never have a president they can call their own." Centrists saw in this advice a lesson for themselves too.

Think tanks were founded for incubating ideas, and foundations for incubating think tanks. Serious journals such as *The Public Interest* were all the more influential for being temperate in tone and scholarly in format, with tables, charts, and footnotes. Right-wing strategists drew from a remarkable array of old and new conservatives: Friedrich von Hayek, Milton Friedman, Jeane Kirkpatrick, William E. Simon, and others less famous but influential in diverse ways.

Why could not the Democratic insurgents emulate this kind of analysis and self-confrontation, leading to a fusion of party doctrine and practical application, and in turn to a takeover of the Grand Old Democracy? mainstream Democrats asked. Why not indeed?

THE RISE OF CENTRISM

By the end of Bill Clinton's first term as president, a joke making its way around Washington, D.C., asked, "How do you stump a liberal?" The answer: Ask him or her whether President Clinton is one.

Like all jokes, this one resonated because the punch line tapped into widespread popular perceptions. Few were certain—at least, not for very long—what breed of political animal Bill Clinton was. It seemed that one could see in Bill Clinton what one wanted to see. He was a sort of political chameleon—the "protean president," charged journalist Thomas Byrne Edsall. Though Clinton donned the Democratic party garb, many of his positions and tactics were markedly different from the policies traditionally pursued by Democrats. For instance, Clinton vowed to "end welfare as we know it" after the 1994 midterm elections, long supported the death penalty, never was chummy with organized labor, and pushed for international trade accords such as NAFTA (North American Free Trade Agreement) and GATT (General Agreement on Tariffs and Trade)—all of which were more favored by Republicans than Democrats.

Conversely, Clinton's efforts during 1993 to dilute the military's ban on homosexuals and to overhaul the nation's health care system, if not eagerly received by voters, at least added to the image of liberal Democrats as knee-jerk promoters of minority rights and big government. So lay the makings of a conundrum for most Americans when they cast their ballot for Bill Clinton in 1996: Which Clinton were they getting this time? Wasn't presidential leadership about articulating a vision and then sticking to it, come hell or high water? Clinton's zigzagging appeared the antithesis of leadership.

The fence-straddling notwithstanding, voters still managed to size up the incumbent. On the eve of the 1996 election, after four years of close scrutiny, 43 percent of Americans branded Clinton a liberal. In 1992, 38 percent of voters had hung the *liberal* signpost around his neck. Against more politically adept and telegenic opponents in either year, Bill Clinton might have met a less sanguine fate on election day. Having to dodge the "liberal" arrows unleashed from the quivers of George Bush and Bob Dole consumed much energy and demanded considerable dexterity, but Clinton had ample quantities of both. He needed them too. If the Bush or Dole arrows had found their quarry—and the *liberal* moniker had stuck—Clinton would have been politically wounded, perhaps mortally. At the end of the twentieth century, being branded *liberal* was about as popular with some Americans as banning professional baseball.

Why all the brouhaha surrounding the L-word? How is it that John F. Kennedy, whom Clinton admired openly, could refer in 1960 to "a liberal, responsible Democratic party that believes in the people" and still get elected, yet Clinton was compelled in the months leading up to the 1992 election—and then again in 1996—to abandon the term *liberal* in favor of more ambiguous language advocating a "New Choice" for voters, especially those in the middle class? In part, the answer lies in one of the great metamorphoses of political terminology. Whereas *liberalism* once connoted freedom from authority, it had by the end of the twentieth century come to be associated with authority itself, or at least with government and its expansion.

The English word *liberal* traces its etymological origins to the Latin term *liber*, or "free." Ancient Roman writers regarded generosity, or "liberality," as one of the hallmarks of a gentleman. As a full-fledged philosophical movement, "liberalism" cohered in the late seventeenth century with the writings of the Englishman John Locke. In his *Second Treatise of Government* (1690), Locke defended the precepts of parliamentary supremacy and constitutional monarchy, so recently established in the Glorious Revolution of 1688. "The natural liberty of man," Locke wrote, "is to be free from any superior power on earth. . . . The liberty of man, in society, is to be under no other legislative power, but that established, by consent, in the common-wealth; nor under the dominion of any will, or restraint of any law, but what that legislature shall enact, according to the trust put in it."

A century and a half later, on the eve of the American Civil War, another Englishman mused on the topic of liberalism. In 1859, John Stuart Mill, probably the most influential British philosopher of the 1800s, published *On Liberty*. In it, he explored many of the themes advanced by Locke. Particularly worrisome to Mill was the possibility that government might run roughshod over minority voices and suppress individuality. The "most cogent reason for restricting the interference of government," he wrote, "is the great evil of adding unnecessarily to its power." To that end, maintaining free trade was important: ". . . both the cheapness and the good quality of commodities are most effectually provided for by leaving the producers and sellers perfectly free." Finally, Mill warned that "the mischief [of government involvement in the lives of its citizens] begins when, instead of calling forth the activity and powers of individuals and bodies, it substitutes its own activity for theirs; when, instead of informing, advising, and, upon occasion, denouncing, it makes them work in fetters, or bids them stand aside and does their work instead of them."

Closely tied to English culture and politics, Americans paid attention to these debates on the proper role of government. Locke's work influenced Thomas Jefferson and James Madison as they labored on the Declaration of Independence and the Constitution; Abraham Lincoln turned to Mill's writings for insight and perspective in the months preceding the attack on Fort Sumter that started the American Civil War. But with few exceptions—such as policies to aid the economically downtrodden of the type devised under the late-nineteenth-century British prime minister William Gladstone, and his Liberal Party—*liberal* in the United States meant something quite different from *liberal* in England and, for that matter, in the rest of the world. Only in the twentieth-century United States does *liberalism* refer to a political philosophy that advocates more government. In a grand historical flip-flop, the nineteenth-century conception of liberalism—free trade and minimal government interference—became by the 1920s the hallmarks of American conservatism.

Bill Clinton understood this change firsthand. Having been branded a liberal of the twentieth-century variety, he had suffered that devastating gubernatorial reelection loss in 1980. Voters protested that he and his staff were too out of touch with Arkansans and too bent on promoting bigger government as the solution to the state's woes.

Clinton took the defeat personally—perhaps a bit too personally, for the loss was symptomatic of widespread voter disenchantment with liberalism. In the 1980 elections, President Jimmy Carter pulled down only 41 percent of the popular vote to challenger Ronald Reagan's 51 percent, while Republicans gained twelve seats in the Senate and thirty-three in the House of Representatives. To be sure, as a first-term governor, Clinton had violated one of the cardinal rules of leadership—communicate with followers often enough to ensure there are people willing to be led—but his basic problem was that most voters simply were not buying what he was selling.

Faced with the unsettling prospect of having his best years behind him at the age of thirty-four, Clinton turned introspective. "He literally felt his life was over," remembered Clinton friend Harold Ickes Jr., son and namesake of Franklin Roosevelt's interior secretary. "He would come to New York and we would have dinner. This boy was down in the dumps—as they say in contemporary phraseology—'big time.' " The loss "had a profound, profound, profound, profound effect on him."

But Clinton was no quitter. He soon managed to climb out of his funk, of course. Perhaps helpful during his convalescence were remarks he had made at the 1980 Democratic convention. Only now, after the sting of a defeat, the words must have seemed more apropos, even soothing. "We were brought up to believe, uncritically, without thinking about it," said Clinton, "that our system broke down in the Great Depression, was reconstructed by Franklin Roosevelt through the New Deal and World War II, and would never break again. And that all we had to do was try to reach out and extend the benefits of America to those who had been dispossessed: minorities and women, the elderly, the handicapped, and children in need. But the hard truth is that for ten long years through Democratic and Republican administrations alike, this economic system has been breaking down. We have seen high inflation, high unemployment, large government deficits, the loss of our competitive edge. In response to these developments, a dangerous and growing number of people are simply opting out of our system. Another dangerous and growing number are opting for special-interest and single-interest group politics, which threatens to take every last drop of blood out of our political system."

Clinton was right to sense that voters were clamoring for something new in their politics. Problem was, an actor-turned-pol sensed it a bit sooner. Ronald Reagan anticipated the shifting political tide and managed to rally Americans around his government-which-governs-best-governs-least cry in 1980 and 1984. Voters preferred this optimistic note to Jimmy Carter's talk of the country's malaise.

Within his own party, Clinton knew there had been talk of devising "more creative and realistic" solutions to national problems since George McGovern's loss in 1972. Watergate and then the Carter victory in 1976 had forestalled some of the Democrats' self-analysis. Republican presidential triumphs in 1980 and 1984 reinvigorated the discussions.

Nearly any examination of leadership—political, presidential, business, or otherwise—concedes that vision is a critical element. What knave follows someone without first buying into his or her vision for how things should be? Charisma, articulateness, personal affability, empathy, and other leadership characteristics are for naught if they fail to undergird a vision that motivates followers. Even more, leaders in various fields seldom have consistently innovative minds. Political leaders are intelligent, but not usually original thinkers. Recall, for instance, the detractors of Warren Harding, who likened his mind to stellar space—a huge void filled with a few wandering clichés; or cartoonist Garry Trudeau's sketch of an explorer making his way through the innermost contours of Ronald Reagan's brain to determine how—or whether—it worked. Rather, leaders' strength often lies in their ability to implement ideas, woo would-be opponents, and rally support for changes. On those criteria at least, Reagan performed admirably.

For presidents in the twentieth century, this practice of presenting fresh ideas to voters has become commonplace, even an expectation. At their disposal, presidents still have what Theodore Roosevelt dubbed the bully pulpit: an exalted position from which to goad the nation, the Congress, the world, to right a wrong or improve living conditions. Addressing a Cleveland, Ohio, audience in 1992, candidate Bill Clinton agreed: "A president's words can move a nation, but talk must be backed up with action, or we risk diminishing the bully pulpit into a pulpit of bull."

His actions may have been inconsistent and his ideas may have inspired disagreement, but Bill Clinton was unquestionably a man of both word and deed. He doted too long on ideas and solutions; he frustrated aides who yearned for a clear directive and final decision—but it was because the nuances and range of possibilities genuinely intrigued him and not always because he was action-averse. He was that rare political leader, that rare president, who was equally at home in the universe of philosophical thought and in the world of concrete plans.

Concrete plans and fresh ideas were what Democrats had gotten with Franklin Roosevelt's presidency in 1933: a try-anything-and-let's-see-what-works approach that stood in marked contrast to the hands-off stasis of most of Herbert Hoover's tenure. Similarly, fresh programs and heady optimism characterized Lyndon Johnson's Great Society. By Jimmy Carter's years in office, the idea well seemed to have run dry for Democrats. "Government cannot solve our problems," warned a disillusioned Carter. "It can't set our goals. It cannot define our vision. Government cannot eliminate poverty or provide a bountiful economy or reduce inflation or save our cities." Carter's premise was accurate—government has limited resources to solve problems—but his rhetoric was too dire. Americans may have needed to hear that government was no panacea, but they hardly needed, or wanted, to hear their president reciting a litany of things he could not do. Honest talk is one thing; doom and gloom quite another.

Carter's words were a consequence of the dreary economic events of the mid- and late 1970s: high unemployment, rising mortgage rates, soaring inflation, and skyrocketing interest rates. Probably too his election-year comments were designed to offer congressional Democrats some cover from voters' complaints come November; lowered expectations of government in January might save Democratic seats in the House and Senate. This was not the sort of talk Americans wanted from their president. Surely, there was more than Carter's lowest-common-denominator leadership?

There was. And Democrats well before Carter's ascendancy to the White House were laboring to exercise it. One month before the 1968 presidential election, some two hundred Democrats, many from the failed Eugene McCarthy campaign, had convened in Minneapolis to discuss reforming the Democratic party. Referring to themselves as the New Democratic Coalition (NDC), the attendees sought to make the party more responsive to the "will of the voters." NDC members warned that the "present liberalism of the Democratic party is stale and irrelevant" and concluded that the NDC had to labor to transform the party from "a machine to get people elected to an instrument of public service."

The reform spirit swept through Democratic ranks. Nixon's victories in 1968 and 1972, seeming to fulfill journalist Kevin Phillips's prophecy of an "emerging Republican majority," served up more evidence to some of the party faithful that Democrats needed to retool their message. They wasted no time. Barely one month after the McGovern debacle, Democratic National Committee chairwoman Jean Westwood of Utah bowed to pressure to resign. Her successor, Texas lawyer and businessman Robert Strauss, immediately pledged his intent to move the Democrats in a new direction. "I am a centrist, a worker, a doer, a putter-together, and those talents belong to you," Strauss vowed on the day of his election.

To keep Strauss honest and faithful to his pragmatism, but even more to offer an alternative strategy, the Coalition for a Democratic Majority (CDM) was formed. CDM attracted many erstwhile Hubert Humphrey and Henry "Scoop" Jackson supporters, such as journalist Ben J. Wattenberg and such neoconservatives as Norman Podhoretz and Midge Decter. Other notables who joined CDM were Max M. Kampleman, former head of the American delegation to the Conference on Security and Cooperation, erstwhile Arms Control and Disarmament Agency director Eugene Rostow, Reagan-era U.S. ambassador to the United Nations Jeane Kirkpatrick, and U.S. senator Daniel Patrick Moynihan. CDM adherents urged Democrats to take stronger stands on national security matters and to move to the political center on social issues such as crime and busing.

But CDMers remained an ephemeral bunch, even losing some members over the years to the Republicans—part of the "Reagan Democrats" phenomenon. "We're a funny organization," former CDM chairman Ben Wattenberg admitted in 1983. "We kind of self-destruct and self-resuscitate as conditions demand. Maybe we're a state of mind rather than a movement, a state of mind quite consistent, we believe, with mainstream Democrats." Ephemeral or not, though, Wattenberg was committed to this "state of mind." He had toiled since the late 1960s to limit the influence of "the cause groups"—labor unionists, blacks, feminists, gays/lesbians, government workers, environmentalists, and other activists—within the party, even coauthoring in 1970 *The Real Majority* to urge Democrats to adopt more moderate policy positions.

Wattenberg and his cohorts knew that winning the nomination required Democratic candidates to appeal to these liberal groups. Yet to win the White House, a candidate had to appeal to a broader array of groups, notably evangelicals, southern whites, and western independents. Because conservative and moderate voters dominated in the general election, the Democratic candidates, who had to be liberal to win the Democratic nomination, often lost in November. For Democrats hoping to win presidential elections, it was a vicious, even near-predictable, cycle—or so the centrists alleged.

Despite McGovern's loss, though, not all Democrats were willing to give up on liberalism. Michael Harrington, author of *The Other America,* which documented the grim poverty in which millions of Americans still lived, sought to flank the CDM on the left to reach the Democratic party's soul. In the weeks following the 1968 election, Harrington helped lead the Democratic Socialist Organizing Committee, a group committed to shoring up support for liberal initiatives within the party.

For some elected Democrats, Wattenberg's moderation versus Harrington's liberalism represented false choices. New York congressman and NDC member Herman Badillo was sour on the possibility of finding any central purpose to the Democratic party. "There really is no Democratic party," complained a bitter Badillo in 1973. "I don't see any likelihood that there will be any attempt to have a Democratic party in Congress that will seek to provide an alternative to the Republican party in domestic and foreign policy." In a phrase that would sound eerily familiar to some voters in the late 1990s who saw not a dime's worth of difference between the two major parties, Badillo then concluded that "most of the Democrats and [Republican] Nixon are really on the same side." In 1998, Badillo announced his switch to the Republican party.

Partisan wrangling was, of course, nothing new to Democrats. During the so-called Age of Jackson, factions within Old Hickory's party seceded over President Jackson's antagonism toward the Second Bank of the United States and other issues. The dissidents formed the Whig Party, which defeated Democrat Martin Van Buren in the 1840 White House contest. Not long thereafter, with war clouds gathering, the Democrats' fissure widened even further over slavery. Southern Democrats backed John Breckinridge in the 1860 election, behind a platform permitting slavery in newly acquired western territories. Northern Democrats nominated Stephen A. Douglas, who vaguely endorsed popular sovereignty and proposed that the Supreme Court resolve questions of slavery in the territories. The party rupture paved the way for Republican Abraham Lincoln's victory.

In the twentieth century, the squabbles were no less acrimonious. Republicans won all three presidential elections in the 1920s, in part because of Democratic feuding between rural prohibitionists and urban "wets." Then in 1937, conservative southern Democrats opposed FDR's plan to pack the Supreme Court with pro–New Deal justices. Roosevelt retaliated by campaigning against some sitting members of his own party in 1938, but he succeeded only in allying many southern Democrats with Republicans. Thus began the slow erosion of the once "solid," pro-Democratic South.

This kind of infighting had led Will Rogers to make his famous gibe: "I belong to no organized political party. I am a Democrat."

By the mid-1980s, the spats were no less intense, though they had become more expected, even bureaucratized. After 1980, for instance, Democratic National Committee chairman Charles Manatt formed the Democratic Strategy Council to serve as a debate forum for elected officials. The Council met intermittently between 1981 and 1983, then sank. Its demise was almost predictable, given the recent aversion of both national party chairs to policy development as too controversial.

Congressional Democrats had better luck at creating a sustainable organization, largely due to the efforts of Congressman Gillis Long of Louisiana. As chair of the House Democratic Caucus, Long assembled the House Democratic Caucus Committee on Party Effectiveness (CPE) in 1981 to debate privately Democratic positions on specific issues such as the economy, housing, crime, and national security. By 1984, it was clear that CPE's work was partly constrained by Long's need to maintain ideological balance: CPE was, after all, an arm of the House Democratic Caucus. Such equilibrium diluted CPE's output, though, and glossed over rifts between party liberals and moderates.

Walter Mondale's 1984 loss and four more years of Republican White House rule prompted Democrats to search for a new road map for 1988. "Your leaders are out of touch," said Arizona governor Bruce Babbitt in late November 1984. "Tell them to get outside of Washington and rediscover America. The dogmas of the past may not be adequate to the present and the future."

An effort to repudiate Shakespeare's observation that "what is past is prologue" gave rise to the Democratic Leadership Council, or DLC, in the months following the Mondale-Ferraro whipping. DLCers had a prescription for the Democrats' schizophrenia: forgo liberalism and move to the center of the political spectrum. Though the so-called remedy had been perched in the Democrats' medicine cabinet for years—beginning at least with the Coalition for a Democratic Majority in 1972—the recent string of Republican victories gave Dr. DLC lots of referrals. Young Democrats and up-and-coming heavyweights such as Richard Gephardt, Sam Nunn, Charles Robb, Lawton Chiles, and Bruce Babbitt soon joined the organization. Al Gore and Joseph Biden also participated in DLC activities. Alvin From, former aide to Gillis Long and executive director of the House Democratic Caucus, agreed to serve as the DLC's executive director. The DLC's formation was formally announced in January 1985.

The DLC made an immediate splash. It soon helped create a new prize in the Democratic presidential-primary sweepstakes: "Super Tuesday." This bit of election ingenuity pushed to a single date the primary elections of many Southern states, with the intent of helping a moderate or conservative

Democrat gain the party's nomination. The strategy proved impotent in 1988 with Michael Dukakis. But with Bill Clinton's victory in 1992, the DLC had its payoff.

The DLC was audacious in its centrism. Its agenda for 1985 was to change the public image of the Democratic party from liberal extremism to moderation. Indeed, during its first four years of existence, DLCers worried more about selling this image than about crafting specific policy proposals. After Dukakis's loss in '88, the DLC's image-versus-substance equation was less one-sided. "The Democrats' 1988 defeat clarified the DLC's purpose," wrote political scientist Jon F. Hale. "Henceforth, the DLC would become less of a benign forum for Democrats of all ideological stripes to discuss issues and less of a political image-maker for moderates wanting to use it for personal publicity and would be more of an ideas-based movement focused on shaping a specific mainstream alternative identity for the party."

To generate those ideas, the DLC spawned an affiliated think tank in 1989. The Progressive Policy Institute (PPI) explored innovative ideas and policy proposals that were, in turn, often nabbed by DLC politicians. Three fundamental principles guided New Democrats' message, said Al From. "First, that growth, not redistribution, is the key to increased opportunity, and that the private sector, not government, is the primary engine for economic growth; second, that the values most Americans share—liberty of conscience, individual responsibility, work, faith, family, and community— should be embodied in the policies of our government; and third, that there is a role for activist government that equips people to solve problems, but not big government that does it for them." More succinctly put, the New Democrat message championed opportunity, responsibility, community, and a government that empowers.

Nice platitudes. But what did New Democrats propose by way of specific policy pursuits for this activist government? The ideas ranged from expanded trade to school choice to progressive taxation to welfare reform to tough "deadbeat dad" penalties. And the strategic thinking behind these policies was as important as the policies themselves.

New Democrats likened their efforts to devise political innovations to FDR's toils in the 1930s. "Just as the New Deal shaped the political order for the industrial age, the new politics can define a political order in the information age," according to Al From. New Democrats believed America was at a crossroads. Democrats and Republicans were clinging to obsolete political visions; New Democrats were bent on dislodging what they saw as a perennial political logjam. They were content to do so within the existing political system, eschewing efforts to organize a third party. Foes within the Democratic party would welcome their departure, though, seeing New Democrats as divisive.

Of course, the Republicans continued to be the main adversary. Like their ideological kinfolk in the Democratic party, New Democrats scolded the GOP as the party of privilege. They claimed that above others this was the essence of Republicanism, making it, willy-nilly, averse to needed change. "Extending property to the propertyless, using government to help create opportunities, can never overcome the need to freeze class relations as the [Republican] party's basic mission," argued PPI's Joel Kotkin.

The New Democrats' critique of the Democratic party was equally unforgiving, charging that Democrats "are as reactionary as Republicans—they simply seek to preserve a different version of the past." What kind of past? One epitomized by large bureaucratic structures and one that still sees large corporations—as opposed to the small- and medium-sized companies that account for much job growth and wealth creation—as the nation's economic lifeblood. "In health reform, in regulatory policy, and in tax policy," proclaimed a New Democrat in 1993, "the voice of many so-called progressives today is essentially the flip side of Republican reaction; it seeks, by government fiat, to create a corporate universe frozen in time and technology."

Democrats also came under fire from their New Democratic cousins for pursuing equality of results rather than equality of opportunity. This risked transforming the American economy "into a second-rate system, much like those of the former Soviet bloc." Perhaps even more to the point for election-minded politicians, New Democrats alleged that this approach by Democrats "virtually invites a Republican resurgence among middle- and working-class Americans."

With Clinton's 1992 victory, making use as he did of many DLC-inspired ideas, New Democrats had convinced themselves they were the future of the Democratic party. Nothing succeeds like success. Or does it? Was the DLC phenomenon bringing about a bold new realignment within the Democratic party? Were old FDR-LBJ-style liberals now consigned to the periphery? And was this a good thing for the party? For American democracy?

CLINTON AND HIS CENTRISTS

The Democratic Leadership Council's growing appeal was evident as early as 1990 when Bill Clinton, a politician from somewhere besides Washington, was elected as its chair. Clinton's DLC involvement was a natural step for someone who had railed against New Deal liberalism at the 1980 Democratic National Convention. With the DLC, Clinton found a way to deliver a mainstream message with a southern twang. The DLC was Clinton's new way, his middle way, his third way, and, as it turned out, his way to the presidency.

Bill Clinton "operates better in a bipartisan atmosphere than he does in a pulverized partisan atmosphere," DLC head Al From observed. He remembered, back in the '92 campaign days, Clinton saying, "I can get just as mad as Tom Harkin or I could get red in the face" and give tough speeches, "but it's not going to help convince anybody to vote Democratic because we've got to give people a reason to vote for us and not just a reason to vote against them." But From granted that Clinton had run not only as a New Democrat but also as an "old" one: "the truth is with Clinton he was running as a little of both," and, "you pay for it."

Instructively, Clinton's active involvement with the DLC dated to the aftermath of the 1988 elections, a period when he was carefully eyeing the Oval Office. But this was also the period when the DLC was beginning to crank out moderate policy proposals. Ideas appealed to Bill Clinton, and ideas were what the DLC was supplying.

From Democratic moderates' perspective, these were the very ideas that had been in short supply—or short circulation—since at least 1980. Still, if liberalism would not define the Democratic party, then what would? For nearly a decade, Democratic middle-of-the-roaders had been relegated to nipping at the heels of Republicans or shouting "Me too!" in support of Republican proposals. "We're obsessed with our process, we're compulsive tinkerers, because there's such a vacuum on policy," complained Bruce Babbitt in 1984. Later, a disconsolate Daniel Patrick Moynihan sized up the strength of ideas within the Democratic party: "We're about at the level of bereft." Clinton and the DLCers disagreed, believing that with the Progressive Policy Institute they had the ideas to wean the Democratic Party away from mere identity politics. Thus unshackled and equipped with ideas, the Democrats could fairly compete with Republicans for the presidency.

Conservative Republicans had led the way. Since the mid-1970s, right-wing think tanks had been a rich source of ideas for Republicans. The Cato Institute and the Heritage Foundation, for instance, supplied the Reagan administration with policy proposals on scores of public issues. With PPI, moderate Democrats now had a potentially fertile field of ideas too. "We are more akin to the conservative movement in the Republican Party after the 1964 Goldwater defeat," maintained Al From. "They put a lot of effort into developing ideas and changing the nature of the political debate."

But, as Reagan knew and as Clinton was to discover, it cuts both ways. Once Clinton began to pick fruit from the DLC-PPI idea tree, the DLC became yet another constituency that would hold Clinton's feet to the fire regarding promises made as a "New Democrat." On matters such as health care reform and Clinton's initial approach to gays in the military, New Democrats pulled few punches in telling the President how mistaken he was. A month after the 1994 election, then-DLC chairman Representative Dave McCurdy of Oklahoma castigated Clinton as a "transitional figure" who had won the 1992 election as a "moderate Democrat, a new Democrat, a DLC Democrat," and was now evidently both a turncoat and a failure.

Where was the Vice President in this party and policy fracas? Gore turned the other cheek. He admitted that the White House had "not been 100 percent faithful" to the DLC's centrist agenda. Although Clinton and Gore had continued to be accessible to DLC executive director From in their early White House years, there was no mercy now for possible apostates. There were even warnings that the DLC might pull out of the Democratic party. While this struck some as a bit like Napoleon threatening to retreat from Moscow, at the very least it indicated that sometimes there is nothing so immoderate as a moderate.

Through the DLC, Clinton managed to articulate and then refine his political message before he was even officially a candidate for president. The long-term wisdom of Clinton's centrism aside, his foresight on this score was a key event in the annals of presidential campaign history.

Clinton often appeared chary, even coy, when it came to describing his political ideology. "The change I seek and the change that we all must seek isn't liberal or conservative. It's different and it's both." Some of his closest aides agreed. The old terms "don't work anymore and they do not apply to Bill Clinton," insisted Betsey Wright, Clinton's chief of staff during many of his years in the Arkansas governor's mansion. "He is not conservative, he is not liberal. I'm very comfortable with calling him a progressive." Former White House counsel Jack Quinn echoed Wright: "I think that the President is a progressive Democrat who does not believe that truth lies at the extremes of ideological argument. . . . I think that he would, in philosophical terms, be in the school of American pragmatism of [John] Dewey and [Charles Sanders] Peirce."

And where did the First Lady fit into this? She was a balancing force to Clinton's—and Gore's—centrism. "I think Hillary is an old-fashioned liberal for the most part," said old friend Ann Wexler. In part, Rodham Clinton retained her youthful restlessness—a restlessness that had led to that polite rebuke of Senator Brooke at her 1969 college commencement: "[W]e feel that for too long our leaders have used politics as the art of the possible. And the challenge now is to practice politics as the art of making what appears to be impossible, possible." But the First Lady could not move too far to the left if she was to remain a working partner in the White House. Indeed, she talked at times like a centrist; when David Gergen told her that some people—presumably including himself—felt that she kept pulling her husband to the left and thus helping cause his zigzagging image, she contended that she had taken many centrist positions in Arkansas and in fact was a pragmatist.

It was not that simple, though. If Clinton and Gore were centrists who often made rhetorical and policy concessions to the left, Rodham Clinton in most respects was a liberal Democrat who knew that even the great progressive presidents, such as FDR and LBJ, had had to negotiate across the political spectrum. It was this anomaly that helped shape Rodham Clinton's strategy—and thus her defeat—on her major undertaking of the health bill.

In his insightful 1988 book *Laboratories of Democracy,* David Osborne discussed an emerging political paradigm that eschewed the old labels. "To boil it down to a slogan," wrote Osborne, "if the thesis was government as solution and the antithesis was government as problem, the synthesis is government as partner." Even then, four years before the 1992 election, Osborne specifically cited governors such as Bruce Babbitt, Bill Clinton, and Chuck Robb—DLC stalwarts—as championing this new model. Osborne continued, "Within this new paradigm there is a left, a right, and a center, but they have little to do with the left, right, and center to which we are accustomed. They have less to do with questions of spending and taxing, for instance, than with how aggressive government should be in reshaping the marketplace, and whose interests should be protected in the process. . . . Clinton [and others] have moved right on some issues, compared to a Mondale or a Kennedy, but they have moved left on others. More to the point, they have moved to different issues altogether."

But there were limits to this moderate, or third way, approach. "Leaders of the 'third way,'" noted political scientist Stephen Skowronek, "are neither great repudiators nor orthodox-innovators. . . . Theirs is an unabashedly mongrel politics, an aggressive critique of prevailing political categories, and a bold celebration of new mixtures."

Another difficulty, of course, with centrist politics or with this supposed new paradigm was that most voters continued to think in liberal-conservative terms. Politicians who embraced the middle path could, therefore, seem squishy, inconsistent, core-less. Campaign adviser Drexel Sprecher counseled candidate Clinton in 1992, "Our approaches to issues do not have to be based on the either/or thinking of the left/right debate. Many of your proposals and plans embody aspects of a new political philosophy. Yet these remain fragmented and implicit rather than coherent and explicit. . . . Your synthesis is a new developmental stage in political philosophy, more advanced than either left or right. And the heart of it is recognition that we are all connected. Individual, community, society, and nature are linked in complex and dynamic interdependence."

The DLC had itself reached similar conclusions a full six months before Bill Clinton even announced his candidacy for the presidency. Significantly, with its May 1991 issue—at a time when Bill Clinton was its national chairman—the DLC changed the name of its official magazine from *The Mainstream Democrat* to *The New Democrat.* The reason, editors readily confessed on the inside cover, was because too many people misunderstood their mission. "We're not trying to move the Democratic party to the center," they reasoned. "We want to move it forward." Reaffirming their commitment to "rouse, inspire, goad, provoke, and incite Democrats to chart a new course for our party and the country," editors then made plain their impatience with compromise between the old ideologies of left and right. "We see no point in fighting for the middle of the wrong road." But this defense still left the DLC's critics wondering, Was the organization implicitly suggesting it would fight for the middle of some other road? And did all this talk of middleness belie the DLC's insistence on its newness? What was so new about being in the middle, anyway?

So who was this Bill Clinton who was so wedded to centrism? His resistance to the old labels and search for a new way had led him to the DLC. In the DLC, Clinton the pragmatic politician and Clinton the programmatic Democrat united. The DLC trimmed the edges on many of the most contentious policy matters, yet did so under the rubric of "Democrat," thus permitting Clinton to remain true to some of the liberal heritage that had originally compelled him to work for George McGovern back in 1972. But because that same liberalism, in part, cost Clinton his governor's seat in 1980, he could not openly embrace it—at least not for long. "The left has been the conscience, the core, of the Democratic party," admitted DLC chairman Roy Romer in 1997. "But the business of politics is getting votes . . ." Clinton understood that as well as anyone.

The DLC was also particularly appealing to Clinton because of his southern roots. In the South, wrote historian Richard K. Scher, "'liberal' and 'conservative' have had meanings different from those they have had elsewhere in the nation. Liberal ideologies have scarcely existed at all [in the South], and much of political ideology has been variants on a fundamentally conservative view of the role of government in human affairs." Not surprisingly, a significant number of founding DLCers were from the South, home to conservative Democrats. To stem the rising Republican tide and save their own leaky boats, Democrats had to identify themselves with moderation, and not the liberalism that dominated the party's northeastern wing.

Finally, consensus rather than conflict appealed viscerally to Clinton the person, not just Clinton the pol. As a youngster, "I was a peacemaker, and I hated conflicts," recalled Clinton. "It was a source of great pain in my childhood. One of the biggest problems I had in fully maturing was learning how to deal with conflict, and express conflict and express disagreement without being disagreeable, without thinking the world would come to an end, without feeling I would kind of lose my footing in life."

The moderate message championed by the DLC grew organically from within the Capitol's walls too. The New Democrat Coalition, for instance, formed shortly after the 1996 election as a haven for moderate to conservative House Democrats. Many of its members hail from the West, particularly California. Slightly older were the so-called Blue Dog Democrats, formed in early 1995 among chiefly moderate to conservative congressmen from the South. In their original incarnation, Blue Dogs were likely to be out of favor with the Democratic leadership. Their name was a play on the sobriquet "yellow-dog Democrat," a faithful Democrat who would sooner vote for a yellow dog than a Republican. But why *blue*? Because these Democrats claimed they were occasionally squeezed until they turned blue by fellow Democrats for not toeing the—often liberal—party line.

Some Republicans, even, embraced a more centrist path. In early 1997, Indiana senator Dan Coats unveiled the Renewal Alliance, a group of some two dozen Senate and House Republicans endorsing ideas like a charitable tax credit and more flextime for working parents. In the spring of 1997, another group of moderate Republicans debuted. Calling itself the Main Street Coalition, it hoped to nudge Republicans back toward the political center, but by late 1997, its lone staff member conceded, "We've spent a lot of our time contemplating our navels." Not all the GOP faithful were clamoring for membership cards to these organizations, though. "At some point," insisted Congressman John Kasich of Ohio, "you can't compromise anymore because then it starts to erode the values and you lose the good policy that we need to save this great, precious nation of ours."

Democrats understood this, as not all of them rallied around their party's effort at moderation, the DLC. The Reverend Jesse Jackson, one of the few remaining highly visible, if unelected, liberal Democrats, once complained that DLC stood for Democrats for the Leisure Class. In 1986, Michael Harrington, who nearly two decades earlier had labored on the Democratic Socialist Organizing Committee, again sought to influence the Democrats' future by convening the New Directions conference with its slogan "Because One Republican Party Is More Than Enough." Harrington complained that the Democratic party had been "miserable, ideologically bankrupt, unprincipled, and almost nonexistent" in the face of Reaganism.

Conservative politics in the 1980s also aroused the ire of U.S. senator Howard Metzenbaum, who in 1990 organized the Coalition for Democratic Values (CDV) to reassert the Democratic party's liberal roots in the face of the DLC's moderation. An indignant Metzenbaum complained of DLC executive director Al From in 1992, "He doesn't know shit from Shinola." Early CDV supporters included Senators Tom Daschle, Christopher Dodd, and Paul Simon. All wanted to show fellow party members that "the future of the Democratic party does not lie in the fine-tuning of Reaganism."

George McGovern got in a few shots at moderation too, after Clinton had been bruised by Republicans in the 1994 midterm elections. "My conviction," wrote McGovern, "is that the Democratic party has lost the confidence of the American people, not because it is too liberal, but because it has neither kept faith with the historic values of liberalism nor defended those values to the public." Offering a perspective worthy of his doctorate in history, the former South Dakota senator concluded, "It is, in fact, the creative tension between conservatism and liberalism that is the genius of American democracy. The nation suffers when either of those traditions is denigrated or undefended, as is now the fate of liberalism."

Well into Clinton's second term, Vermont congressman Bernard Sanders, the lone independent elected to Congress, kept the liberal flame burning. A Democratic Socialist, Sanders led and regularly convened a Progressive Caucus of House members to champion left-wing issues.

Even House Minority Leader Dick Gephardt, inaugural chairman of the DLC, had by the end of Clinton's fifth year in office grown uncomfortable with the President's brand of leadership from the center. At a December 1997 speech at Harvard University, which drew a stinging response from the White House, Gephardt distanced himself from "some who now label themselves as New Democrats, but who set their compass only off the direction of others. Who talk about the political center, but fail to understand that if it is only defined by others, it lacks core values."

Beyond the Washington Beltway, former Texas agriculture commissioner turned talk-show host Jim Hightower likewise chided DLCers. "There's nothing in the middle of the road," proclaimed the title of his 1997 book, "but yellow stripes and dead armadillos."

Moderation was just tinkering, liberals concluded; it was not leadership. "If fainthearted Democrats think that fidelity to convictions is politically suicidal," wrote Arthur Schlesinger Jr. in 1986, "they might remember that Ronald Reagan got where he is today not by me-tooing the opposition when it was in power but by insisting on his beliefs . . . and in doing so in bad times as well as good."

CENTRISTS AND IDEOLOGUES

"The best lack all conviction, while the worst are full of passionate intensity," wrote William Butler Yeats in two of the most memorable lines of "The Second Coming." Seventy-five years later, most Americans seemed politically irresolute, uncommitted, unimpassioned, bored. Surveys showed a heavy grouping of attitudes around the middle of the ideological spectrum. An August 1997 poll found no evidence that "Americans long for the good old days of partisan wrangling and sharp left-right choices."

People were ambivalent about their leaders too. Tracked in the polls throughout their months in the White House, Clinton, Rodham Clinton, and Gore ended up in one mid-1994 survey as they often were: bunched together at midpoint or just below—47 percent approval rating for the President, 48 percent for Rodham Clinton, a little higher for Gore. Near 1995's end, Clinton's overall rating had breached the 50 percent mark, but less than half of Americans thought he was doing a good job handling either

Bosnia or the economy. Even a mock November 1995 national urban presidential primary that turned out some 225,000 voters in seventeen cities gave Clinton a modest 43 percent victory margin over the likes of Bob Dole and Phil Gramm.

In glaring contrast to such moderate endorsements was the passionate intensity of private militias, fanatical patriot groups, homicidal right-to-life activists, and zealous Christian fundamentalists somewhere on the far right; and ideologically vocal but politically diminished radical populists on the far left. But were these dismal alternatives the only ones?

The 1994 midterm elections had reflected all the ambivalences and imbalances, particularly in the virtual dead heat between many Democratic and Republican candidates for Congress. But among the Republicans especially were scores of men—and a few women—of truly passionate intensity. They came to Washington ready to declare war on the Democratic establishment, to drastically cut back on entitlements, and to reverse a half century of New Deal and Fair Deal programs. Without embarrassment, they called themselves revolutionaries. Newt Gingrich led their charge.

How can a president deal with such a mixture of ideology and passivity? Franklin Roosevelt faced a comparable situation in 1935 when he had to represent mainstream Democrats but also contend with the extremists of his day—Father Charles Coughlin denouncing bankers and Jews, Huey Long attacking financiers and fat cats, Dr. Charles Townsend arousing old folks to near fanaticism. But FDR had a solid base in a victorious Democratic party and long-honed skill at appealing to their zealous supporters without confronting Coughlin, Long, & Co. personally and frontally.

Bill Clinton had neither advantage. And, far more than Roosevelt, he was a victim of his earlier centrism. He had played to, and played up, the mainstream forces, often at the expense of the traditional Democratic labor, urban, women, consumer, and African-American constituencies. Election results proved he had not mobilized a true "constituency of the middle," partly because these elements were unorganized, uncommitted, and lacking in any conviction except for a mood of "agin the government." How could the head of the government mobilize *them*?

At least, during all the recrimination Clinton had plenty of advice. With something of an I-told-you-so attitude, DLC centrists proclaimed that Clinton had lost the 1994 midterm election by running as a mainstream New Democrat and then failing to govern as one. He must now steer clear of gay extremists, the ACLU, NOW, SANE-Freeze, the Rainbow Coalition, and some of the more leftist union elements. The DLC centrists were not abashed by the fact that many mainstream and conservative Democrats also lost in 1994 while some Ted Kennedy–style candidates survived.

Conservative Democrats in Congress urged the President to leap over the mainstream and embrace a right-of-center strategy. Gingrich-style

Republicans had moved so much farther to the right that such a move would still leave a significant gap between the parties. This was the Grover Cleveland strategy of outflanking the GOP on the right—and Cleveland was the original comeback kid, winning back the presidency from Benjamin Harrison in 1892. But the strategy had serious flaws. Cleveland had also lost the presidency earlier, key conservative Democrats in 1995 were already shifting to the Republican party, and politics had changed a bit in a century.

Why not instead join with the Republicans in an honest and forthright bipartisan coalition? This, pundits proposed, would be a transforming act that would solve the problem of divided government. They noted that Clinton shared many ethical values with conservative Republicans. He had concluded a talk to California Democrats in April 1995 by quoting some of the ideals that schoolchildren had listed: "Cooperation, Respect, Patience, Caring, Sense of Humor, Common Sense, Friendship, Responsibility, Flexibility, Effort, Creativity, Initiative, Communication Problem-Solving, Integrity, Perseverance." These could have been chapter headings, columnist Fred Barnes observed, from William Bennett's *Book of Virtues.*

"Old-fashioned liberals" observed all these alternatives with alarm. Their advice to Clinton was predictable: return to the progressive principles of the FDR-Truman-JFK-LBJ presidencies. Shun compromise with the Gingrich Republicans because you will only compromise your own principles. Don't seek "middle ground" with an opposition whose only motive is to beat you in the next election. Work closely with the Kennedy and Gephardt liberals in Congress. Confront Republican pro-corporate policies in health, environmental, labor, tax, and all the other key issues. Fight for the working class as well as the middle class. In short, go for broke.

For Clinton, this array of alternatives, from right to left, boiled down to a choice between centrist tactics of accommodation and bipartisanship and a left-of-center strategy of opposition and confrontation. What could a beleaguered president do? What Clinton did was to display an extraordinary brand of leadership-by-followership as he shifted from one tactic to another during the better part of 1995 and 1996.

Baffled and chagrined by the 1994 election results, he appeared for a time uncertain as to what course to follow, aside from the usual obligatory remarks about working with the winners for the betterment of all. He told a DLC meeting that government could be made leaner without becoming meaner and challenged the GOP's new avatar, Gingrich, to friendly debates. A few weeks later, as Clinton listened to the GOP's rhetorical onslaught against some of his favorite health and environmental policies and governmental reforms, he threatened to veto anti-administration measures, but added, "I was not elected president to pile up a stack of vetoes."

Still later, he conducted in New Hampshire what reporters described as a virtual "love-in" with Gingrich. Only a month after that, he criticized Gingrich for not living up to a promise to work with him in setting up a commission to consider lobbying and campaign finance reform. Soon Clinton was hotly defending Medicare against alleged GOP threats and making a ringing reaffirmation of the goals of affirmative action.

Clinton was shifting back and forth between accommodation and confrontation for a simple reason. Neither was working.

Dealing with the House Republicans did not work because they did not make deals. Gingrich might offer pleasantries, shake hands over a vague agreement, offer a concession here and there, but this was only a show of politesse. Even if Gingrich wanted to deal, it was impossible for him. He was both the leader and agent of the most ideologically disciplined and unified faction of congressmen that the House had seen in decades. Any show of "weakness" on his part would endanger his leadership.

Nothing in Clinton's experience had prepared him to deal effectively with ideologues. His legislative leadership in Arkansas had required only melding together a disparate array of Democrats and brokering with some of the more amenable Republicans. During his first two years in the White House, he had held the support of most of the congressional Democrats. When he needed more votes, he and Gore had negotiated with conservative Democrats and moderate Republicans, picking up support through ad hoc, one-on-one pressure and deals. Usually, the most resentful or rebellious of Democrats could be tempted back onto the reservation by a judicious mixture of praise, promises, and patronage.

Not so the House Republicans after their November 1994 triumph. Of course, the new GOP Senate, priding itself on being more moderate and deliberate, was ready to exercise the upper chamber's ancient privilege of trimming and modifying the impulsive actions of the House. But under the circumstances of the upcoming 1996 GOP presidential contest, Clinton could not deal effectively even with the slightly more centrist Senate. Bob Dole and Phil Gramm were vying for support from the most conservative and fundamentalist voters. They were far more fearful of alienating Gingrich—always a possible last-minute candidate himself—than the President of the United States. At best, the Senate Republicans were too divided and factional to provide assured votes to the White House even if heavily pressured.

The alternative tactic of confronting and defying the GOP was equally unrealistic. The veto power had its limitations. Occasionally congressional Republicans could overcome the vetoes by combining their own disciplined numbers with enough recalcitrant Democrats. In most cases, the presidential veto would be sustained—but these would be only Pyrrhic victories, for they would leave Clinton in the worst political posture of all—as a generator of gridlock. Historically, when Congress and the president are deadlocked, voters tend to turn their frustration against the White House. Amid all the mutual finger-pointing, one thing is clear to the voters—the yes-or-no presidential veto. Presidents can avoid blame only by clearly and dramatically putting the onus on Congress, as Harry Truman did in 1948.

Why not then imitate "Give 'em hell Harry," who in the face of what seemed overwhelming odds struck out against the Republican "obstructionists" and pulled off his "miracle victory" against Tom Dewey? In 1996, there were tempting parallels to 1948. Truman had lost his Democratic majorities in the Senate and House to hard-core conservatives; their leaders were Robert A. Taft and Joseph W. Martin rather than Dole and Gingrich. The victorious Republicans sought to repeal much of the New Deal just as the Republicans of 1995–96, even of 1997–98, proposed to undo key legislation passed during the Kennedy, Johnson, and Carter administrations. Truman shrewdly made the "do-nothing" Republican congressional leadership the target, rather than the moderate Governor Dewey.

Could 1996 have repeated 1948? The simple answer is that Bill Clinton was no Harry Truman; he lacked the temperament for slash-and-burn campaigning. Nor is today's Democratic party much like the Democrats of 1948. The Truman Democrats could remobilize the great Roosevelt armies of the 1940s; Clinton inherited only the tattered Democratic battalions of the 1990s. He would be hard put, too, to define the Republicans as do-nothing naysayers; under Gingrich's leadership they had become a positive force for their ideology.

If there was no political solution to Clinton's dilemma, was there an institutional one? In Britain and other parliamentary democracies, a leader as repudiated as Clinton appeared to have been in 1994 could appeal to the country for a direct and final vote on his or her leadership. But the American presidential system offered no such machinery for resolution. Despite the dramatizing of their "reinventing government" program, neither Clinton nor Gore had shown much interest publicly in major institutional restructuring, in part on the reasonable assumption that tampering with the venerable checks and balances in any major way was unmanageable and virtually un-American. But even Lyndon Johnson, not noted for proposing institutional change, recommended a constitutional amendment that would lengthen representatives' terms from two to four years, concurrent with the presidential. But this moderate reform never had a chance.

As it was, Clinton faced a classic dilemma of leadership-followership. More than two centuries ago, Englishman Edmund Burke succinctly presented the issue: "Your representative owes you, not his industry only, but his judgment; and he betrays instead of serving you if he sacrifices it to your opinion." American politicians are called on to be leaders, pointing the way ahead and taking bold and even unpopular positions, at the same time that they are supposed to be democrats, following the "will of the people." Poking fun at politicians who poll the voters before taking stands, Russell Baker wrote: "Since we are being followed, not led, our followers—whom we call 'leaders'—stagger along like blind drunks, trying not to bump headfirst into the lampposts."

Could Clinton solve this conundrum? How?

The least likely solution was making some kind of strategic change as the 1996 campaign season approached. Given all the uncertainties, he would probably continue to follow a wavering line, between centrism and somewhere left of center. He would continue to follow the polls avidly, knowing full well how treacherous they could be—that "presidents who carry the latest polls in their pockets are more likely to govern with an eye toward what is popular rather than what is sound," in political scientist Herbert B. Asher's warning. And if Clinton doubted the results, he could always change his pollsters.

He would continue to be the tactical president, the transactional leader, conciliating, brokering, seeking the center. He had his own concept of progress. "If you think about our most successful periods of reform," he told a Dallas audience in 1995, initiatives "have been shaped by presidents who incorporated what was good, smoothed out what was rough, and discarded what would hurt. That was the role of Theodore Roosevelt and Woodrow Wilson in the aftermath of the populist era. That was the role of Franklin Roosevelt in the aftermath of the La Follette progressive movement." It was a revealing summary of presidential history, shrinking previous White House "greats" down to Clinton's size.

As preacher-in-chief, the President would continue to emphasize values well into his second term, but they would be the values and processes of transactional leadership—compromise, flexibility, reciprocity, adaptability. He would also speak out politically on the "safe" values, ranging from a crusade against teenage pregnancy to tougher national standards for collecting child support to "stopping kids from smoking" to environmental programs to public broadcasting to family medical leaves to lower interest rates for student loans.

Still, "safe" values were not always safe. When the President endorsed more school prayer, within closely constricted guidelines, the *New York Times* editorialized that his emphasis on the permissive rather than the protective aspects of the First Amendment was "troubling and dangerous." Seeking the middle way, Clinton found it full of potholes.

As he continued to alternate between accommodation and confrontation late in his first term and early into his second, the President's thinking seemed to be undergoing a sea change. Observers continued to speculate about the "two Clintons": the divided Clinton, the indecisive Clinton. But perhaps it was less a matter of ambivalence than that a visionary president was hoping to break through the endless restraints on presidential action and rise above the day-to-day brokerage of the White House. Clinton still seemed to have a vision of the president he would like to be—not only talking about change but delivering it, not only proclaiming his ideals but carrying them to the people.

No president in American history had sought more often than Clinton to physically escape from the White House. All presidents had fled the Executive Mansion—but some mainly to play golf or poker, despite their protests that they wanted to get "closer to the people." Day after day Clinton hurried out of the besieged White House to face crowds, grab hands, and hug old friends. His motive was mainly political—votes. But it was also psychological—he needed the feeling of connection as well as the applause.

THE CASE FOR CENTRISM

Most noteworthy about the rise of the Democratic Leadership Council was that, from its very start, it attracted politicians of national stature. Sam Nunn, Dick Gephardt, Al Gore, and Bill Clinton were no young upstarts. Well, young, yes. Upstarts, no. By the mid-1980s, they had each held public office—and been reelected several times over. So why would they saddle up on a new breed of Democratic mule? Had their political identity not been sufficiently formed? Had they not already found their ideological niche and managed to convey it adequately to voters? What exactly is it about centrist doctrine that appeals to elected officials, especially those who have been in the game for some time?

To many of these politicians, centrism seems safe, sensible, comfortable. It provides a political and intellectual haven between the tendentiousness of left and right. It responds to the yearning for civic virtue, citizenship, community; for unity, harmony, togetherness. If it had anything so strident as a slogan, it would be, "Let's all sit around the table and iron out our differences."

Centrism is policy-friendly. Typically a potpourri of items borrowed from liberal and conservative programs, the centrist agenda can pick up the death penalty and welfare reform from the right and education and national service from the left. If pressed from the right, centrists can add boosted defense and school choice; from the left, more public investment and job training. Coherence among the policies is not a major consideration—only quick and easy flexibility in the name of moderation—even though the grab-bag approach drives the public perception of Bill Clinton as a political opportunist with no core convictions.

Centrism is nonpartisan or bipartisan or antipartisan. At a time of political and ideological polarization, the middle way between parties offers a way to rise above the raucous voices of right and left, to transcend the bickering and pettiness of "pols." Thus centrism can readily be taken for lofty statesmanship. Ours is a system in which the noblest practitioners of foreign policy have advocated letting politics stop at the water's edge. Franklin Roosevelt was an adept practitioner of this stratagem. More recently, centrists and others have called for suspending party debate and conflict over fiscal policy, education, the environment, civil rights, welfare policy, immigration, even farm policy.

Centrism plays particularly well to the talents of expedient, entrepreneurial politicians. It enables them to range widely across the political spectrum, looking for targets of opportunity, making deals, catering to "special interests" with diverse memberships. "He Seen His Opportunities, and He Took 'Em," Tammany Hall's Boss Plunkitt once proposed for his own epitaph. With the decline of the old machines like Plunkitt's, political entrepreneurship now operates best in an environment without strong ideological or party moorings that might—and once did—exercise some control over politicos, protecting the movement or party from the taint of pandering to special interests.

Above all, centrism is "practical." Americans "have not been much interested in the grammar of politics," wrote historian Daniel J. Boorstin in the early years of the cold war, at the height of what is sometimes dubbed the consensus school of United States history. "We have been more interested in the way it works than in the theory behind it." In the face of a complex, often deadlocked system, centrism strives to get things done. It does not call for transcending commitment or high moral leadership. It merely requires splitting the difference between liberals and conservatives, Democrats and Republicans. It moves slowly, a step or two ahead, then a step backward or sideways, but it gets there in the end.

For Clinton, centrism seemed the best strategy for coping with the GOP right. But the Republicans' leadership and discipline and sheer force contrasted mightily with the President's mongrelized moderation. And GOPers didn't just talk change; they voted change, as they dismantled liberal laws and agencies. They had no fear of conflict—they loved the fight.

The Republicans wanted conservative ideology. The liberals still wanted liberalism. Clinton could have the center.

CHAPTER SEVEN

The Intrusion of Foreign Affairs

A president was dead. Washington, indeed the whole world, was astir with the news. Not since Harry Truman and Lyndon Johnson died within one month of each other, in December 1972 and January 1973, had America mourned a former chief executive. And not since those years had the nation collectively engaged in the intense retrospection, reassessment, rethinking—and even rejuvenation—of a president's legacy that often accompanies such passings.

The weekend of Richard Nixon's death in the spring of 1994, Bill Clinton was hosting several Arkansas friends at the White House. The breakfast conversation was lively and wide-ranging. Arkansas politics. Health care. Democratic fund-raiser Pamela Harriman. And, of course, Richard Nixon. Out of the blue, Clinton stunned Joe Purvis, a former assistant from his Arkansas attorney general days, by inquiring after his brother, Tom, whom Clinton had not seen in ten years. Was he still living in El Dorado, Arkansas, the President wanted to know? Clinton's memory for people and details, Purvis recalled later, "literally blows you away."

A phone call interrupted the reminiscing. It was National Security Adviser Anthony Lake, with news for the President about Bosnia. Yes, Bosnia—that "quagmire," as Clinton had called it, of Eastern Europe. It was an unwelcome reminder that the postcommunist world would not necessarily be any less bloody or less complicated than the cold war era.

That was the way Clinton often seemed to handle foreign policy in his presidency—as an unwelcome, unpleasant intrusion on the affairs that truly engaged him. In a White House where staff jockeyed with one another for Clinton's time—and where, early on, the President was given to surrendering far too much of it—foreign affairs issues simply were not regular contenders. During his first term, the President might start the day with a briefing from Lake, but Secretary of State Warren Christopher and the defense secretaries, Les Aspin and William Perry, saw him less often. It was not unusual for foreign policy meetings to be dropped from the President's schedule altogether when domestic matters seemed more pressing. Indeed, Lake and Christopher well understood that their primary task was to keep foreign policy issues from diverting the President's attention away from domestic concerns.

Of course, this was, to some degree, the kind of government the Clinton troika had promised to the electorate when they vowed that they would focus on the economy "like a laser beam." Through the early years of the Clinton presidency, an occasionally fickle voting public proved remarkably consistent too. Less than one month before the 1994 midterm elections, one poll found that crime, unemployment, and health insurance continued to cap voters' list of national problems. Not foreign policy.

Such lack of interest in events beyond America's shores explained, in part, why Republicans lost the White House in 1992. Voters did not have "foreign policy expertise" high on their presidential wish list. Here was a clear affirmation that much of leadership is in the timing. George Bush's background was not as impressive as it might have been in another era.

Voters' snapshot opinions notwithstanding, foreign policy deserved to be a more pronounced election issue than it was in either 1992 or 1996. "A great president," wrote Henry Kissinger, "must be an educator, bridging the gap between his people's future and its experience." A bold and visionary presidential candidate needed to disregard for once those tempting opinion polls and make foreign policy a central consideration. But George Bush and Bob Dole lacked the leadership skill to bring the issue to the forefront; Bill Clinton had just the right amount of dexterity to relegate the issue to second-rate status.

What would this relative inattention to foreign affairs mean for America's standing in the world under Clinton's watch? Entering the White House, Clinton could not claim nearly the foreign policy experience of his predecessor Bush, the erstwhile CIA director and U.S. ambassador to the United Nations. Indeed, Clinton's résumé on this score was more akin to that of Jimmy Carter, another southern governor who had made his way to the Oval Office. But then, as president, Carter had helped broker the seminal Camp David Accords between Israel and Egypt. For a time, Americans held out for a comparable achievement from the Arkansan. In NAFTA and, later, in Northern Ireland, they were pleased. More often, they were disappointed. Clinton's shilly-shallying in foreign affairs bred an erosion of confidence in his abilities that America the superpower could ill afford.

WHO KNOWS THE NEW RULES?

Around the end of 1918, a few weeks after the close of the most wanton and needless bloodletting in a century, Irishman William Butler Yeats conjured up a millennial, apocalyptic vision in a magnificent lyric, "The Second Coming," that foreshadowed the harrowing decades ahead. A philosopher and theosophist, he had mused on perennial topics: on the rise and fall of great civilizations; on the alternation of chance and choice and of chaos and order; on millennial decay and destruction followed by rebirth. In his gloom over the continuing tumult and bloodshed in Eastern Europe and Russia and elsewhere, the poet saw a new god, rising out of desert sands, bestial and monstrous, intent on banishing chaos—but at what price?

The poem could as well have been written in the 1990s. Since the armistice of 1918, the blood-dimmed tide had swept on to unimaginable extremes. Out of desert sands, but also out of inflamed cities and regions around the globe, preachers and practitioners of violence were arising. The Four Horsemen of the Apocalypse were riding again. People numbering in the hundreds of millions were being born in poverty and ignorance; expanding populations were bursting or fighting their way across fragile national borders; environmental pollution was proliferating; murderous regional conflict and "ethnic cleansing" scarred the globe; horrendous violence was rearing up where least expected, as in Oklahoma City and Littleton, Colorado. It was a time to test not only men's souls but also their hearts and minds—and especially those of world and national leaders.

With both hubris and honesty, every generation sees itself as standing at a crossroads. Presidents are no different. It is their election, they often maintain, that will determine the nation's fate for years to come. But in truth, only history reveals the genuine turning points. Woodrow Wilson and Harry Truman, holding office in the immediate aftermath of this century's world wars, presided over two of those decisive periods. Bill Clinton assumed the presidency at the genesis of a similarly confusing, yet immensely promising, time.

Clinton, Gore, and Rodham Clinton grew up in a world beset by conflict. They governed in a world beset by conflict. Things are the same, yet they are different. Challenges to democracy remain, but they now arise in the form of independent-minded rogues, as opposed to the grand design of an "evil empire." The United States has always sought to secure its economic hegemony over other nations, but the absence of a communist threat in the 1990s compelled the President and the Congress to be more forthright about economic initiatives as opposed to military ventures. The two could no longer so easily be conflated. Cold war presidents from Truman to Bush instinctively dipped their rhetorical ladle into communism's well whenever they wanted a scoop of justification for military action. Clinton had no such resource.

"Today is not a time for big ideas," warned political scientist Stanley Hoffmann. "Foreign policy paradigms today are a lot like French fashion. They are launched with lots of fireworks, but we move on so quickly, nothing can be resolved." And the traditional making and breaking of alliances must now share the foreign policy stage with truly global concerns such as overpopulation, pollution, deforestation, and other environmental matters.

Confronted with a full plate of issues, Clinton resolved early to delegate significant authority to Al Gore. Part of the style was by design, part by default. Clinton was accustomed to such limelight-sharing with Rodham Clinton from their Arkansas years. Indeed, Clinton had never held elected office without Rodham Clinton by his side. He routinely sought her collaboration. She was, and remains, his most trusted adviser. Hers was a role that Gore could never expect to equal, much less surpass—but the Vice President closely emulated her. Gore's experience in the Congress on domestic and particularly on foreign policy issues rendered him invaluable to the President. Secretary of State Warren Christopher admitted that Gore "is relied on more heavily than any vice president has ever been in the past."

Gore was prepared to rise to the challenge, but was the rest of the world? Foreign leaders might see Clinton's willingness to offer Gore a prominent foreign-policy-making role as evidence of the President's own disinterest in matters beyond America's shores. Worse, Gore's visibility in global affairs could signal Clinton's weakness and indecisiveness—and what anti-American aggression would that provoke?

And what of that campaign theme—"change"? What application did it have in the foreign affairs arena? Administration policies toward Haiti and Bosnia—and even, perhaps especially, regarding NAFTA and GATT—were largely extensions of Bush's positions. What had "changed" on the foreign policy front in the early years of the Clinton presidency was not so much the direction of that policy as it was a decided shift in the President's willingness to conduct it. On the international scene, the troika did not so much foment change as preside over it.

Clinton understood well the challenges of the post–cold war world. The question lay in how much attention he was willing to give those challenges—and how much political capital he would risk to meet them.

The world would offer new tests of leadership, candidate Clinton told the Los Angeles World Affairs Council in August 1992: "The first is to grasp how the world we live in has changed. The second is to assert a new vision of our role in this dynamic world. The third is to summon all of our strength, our economic power, our values, and, when necessary, our military might in the service of our new vision. . . . In a world of change, security flows from initiative, not from inertia."

Such platitudes were fine, as far as they went. But Clinton had a few more specific notions as well. In the same Los Angeles speech, he spoke of the need for "a fresh assessment of the new dangers that could threaten our interests and potentially require the use of force, including the risk of new threats from former Soviet republics should democracy fail, especially before all the nuclear weapons have been dismantled." He also spoke of international affairs as an extension of his domestic agenda: "My first foreign policy priority will be to restore America's economic vitality."

The world of the 1990s, alas, would not permit such simple priorities. In Eastern Europe, the President would have to help manage the transition from the disintegrated Soviet Union to some new security and economic arrangements. This would include maintaining control of the thousands of Soviet nuclear weapons, some of which had been inherited by the new states of Ukraine, Kazakhstan, and Belarus. It would mean helping Russia establish democratic institutions, a market economy, and a new world role, lest it slide back into some form of aggressive authoritarianism. It would mean shoring up the sovereignty of the new states in the region and helping to give meaning to their independence. It would mean creating new security arrangements that would prevent the former Warsaw Pact countries of Eastern and Central Europe from again becoming a battleground for Russia and Germany.

Other flash points cried out for attention too. The end of the cold war had done nothing to end conflicts and crises in places like Somalia, Haiti, and the former Yugoslavia. In some cases, the elimination of the Soviet Union and the communist system was like pulling a blanket off a bed of embers. Fires that had been suppressed burst into flame again. None of these conflicts threatened the United States as directly and powerfully as had the Soviet bloc. But they often seemed to jeopardize American interests or, at least, to engage Americans' humanitarian sympathies.

And that, in turn, posed a difficult question. Under what circumstances, in the new order of things, could or should the United States use force abroad? Should it take unilateral responsibility for ending the massive suffering and bloodshed caused by conflicts in places like the Sudan, Rwanda, and Bosnia? Or should it rely on international institutions such as the United Nations? If the answer was neither of the above, and nothing was done, what would the consequences be?

And then there was the complex of issues posed by the rapid decline of state sovereignty in the economic sphere. Clinton had promised a foreign policy that protected American employment and American wages in a global marketplace. But what did that mean?

The complex nature of foreign relations demanded more than ever a steady set of hands to ensure that Clinton bespoke a strong nation to the world. The United States needed political leaders who could ensure that the international tide ebbed and flowed with predictability; it could do without leaders whose inexperience or indecisiveness in overseas imbroglios might, to borrow from Yeats, bring about a tide dimmed with Yankee blood.

THE USE OF FORCE

As Clinton took office, American forces were already operating abroad, in Somalia. President Bush, while a lame duck, had sent them there. Their mission was to protect the international famine-relief effort from attacks by bands of armed thugs and paramilitaries that answered to no recognized government. Somalia had disintegrated into chaos, and people were starving.

Quickly, Somalia taught the new administration some hard lessons in international politics. A phenomenon known as mission creep set in. In addition to relieving the famine, the forces were given the job of trying to track down and arrest the local warlords deemed guilty of preying on the population. This proved an exacting assignment for which the troops were ill prepared. Firefights erupted, and on one calamitous day American soldiers were ambushed and killed. Crowds dragged the body of one fallen soldier through the streets. This spectacle was filmed, photographed, and disseminated widely around the United States.

The horrified American reaction suggested one of the realities of the post-Vietnam world. American tolerance for casualties in foreign operations had become exceedingly low. A total of thirty soldiers died in Somalia—significant, yes, but a number smaller than might be killed on American highways during a holiday weekend. Their deaths created enormous pressure to bring the troops home, which Clinton did by the end of 1993.

Many believed that such casualties resulted in part from an overall mission whose aim to begin with was at once ambitious, ill defined, and of little benefit to U.S. strategic interests. Fixing roads, disarming paramilitary groups, and other "nation building" pursuits were well intended, but were not—and probably could not reasonably have been—well executed under the circumstances. Admitted Defense Secretary Les Aspin, "What is very difficult and very dangerous is to take an eighteen-year-old and cross-train him or her to be both a soldier and a policeman. What is even more dangerous is then leaving it up to the eighteen-year-old to decide whether he or she is a policeman or a soldier."

Ultimately, whatever the military's role and wherever it was carried out, the news media was sure to televise and photograph it for public consumption. A post–cold war president who wished to send troops into harm's way would have to convince voters that vital American interests required it.

This was a lesson that the troika, children of the Vietnam era, absorbed quickly, and it was to prove extremely influential in the crises to come. One of the first involved the hermitic state of North Korea.

Clinton's North Korean problem had had a long germination. Under pressure from the Soviet Union, North Korea had agreed in 1985 to sign the Nuclear Non-Proliferation Treaty, renouncing nuclear weapons and submitting to International Atomic Energy Agency (IAEA) inspections designed to assure that its civilian nuclear operations were not clandestine weapons programs. In 1993, shortly after IAEA inspections began, North Korea withdrew from the treaty; it was the first signatory to do so.

By the spring of 1994, Kim Il Sung, North Korea's "Great Leader," denied IAEA inspectors access to suspected plutonium production sites. His communist government defiantly noted that it would "never allow" its nuclear plans to be derailed. International officials then left the country, declaring their mission a failure. North Korea, it was clear, was bent on making a bomb. Were it to succeed, the entire structure of Asian security, guaranteed by the United States throughout the cold war, would be imperiled.

Clinton was in a fix. His predicament was a direct consequence of Washington's long and still-unresolved conflict with North Korea. The tension was as old as the cold war itself. Mindful of the mood of a nation that had just emerged from a worldwide conflict, President Truman had sent troops to the region in 1950 to engage in a "police action"—but not a "war." The stalemate that followed was America's second concession to communism in the post-1945 era; the first had been acquiescing in the USSR's occupation of Berlin. As Korea ultimately divided into a communist North and a pro-democratic South, American presidents over the next half century sought to maintain cordial relations with the former but still court the latter.

Clinton adopted a similar strategy, but his most immediate predecessor hadn't helped matters much. Bush had let Korea simmer. Korea was proof of a presidential paradox: presidents inherited both successes as well as failures. The trick was to wring out every last drop of political capital from one, and to minimize the negative effects of the other.

It did not appear that Clinton was doing well in this highly visible highwire act. He had not picked the Korea issue. Like Bosnia, Haiti, and Somalia, it had picked him. This was the price he paid for relegating foreign policy matters to the periphery of his administration. "We had hoped," an administration official confessed late in 1993, "to keep foreign policy submerged." But when Secretary of State Christopher, National Security Adviser Anthony Lake, and others could not manage matters, Clinton was forced to wrestle with them while the world watched and editorialized.

Though American forces were stationed in Korea, Clinton did not seriously consider unilateral action. He spoke of United Nations sanctions against the North Koreans. But China, Russia, Japan, and South Korea all demurred. Into this breach stepped former president Jimmy Carter. Since leaving the White House in 1981, Carter had developed an impressive career as a freelance peacemaker. He was invited to visit Pyongyang as early as 1991, but when the Bush administration opposed the trip, preferring to handle Korean diplomacy itself, Carter yielded.

The new Korean crisis gave Carter a fresh opportunity to offer his services. He checked with his contacts and determined that he would still be welcome in North Korea. He consulted the White House and found support there, as well. Clinton arranged for briefers to fly to Carter's Georgia home to bring him up to date on the situation. Carter then told Gore he was "strongly inclined" to accept the North Korean invitation. Gore spoke to Clinton, who approved Carter's plans.

The White House calculation was simple. Carter might well have gone to Korea without its blessing. If his trip proved successful, Clinton would share the credit. If it failed, Carter would shoulder most of the blame. The risk seemed low.

But that calculation did not adequately account for two factors. One was Carter's unwillingness to be bound by the policies of the administration of the moment. In 1991, for instance, when President Bush asked the United Nations Security Council for a resolution permitting armed action against Iraq, Carter had written to the leaders of most Security Council members and asked them to vote against the request. (He did not send a letter to Margaret Thatcher, deeming it "a waste of a stamp.")

The second factor was the impossibility of maintaining the notion that Carter was merely a private citizen. As an ex-president, traveling with the blessing of the White House, his actions and statements would inevitably become at least partly the responsibility of the administration.

Carter flew to Pyongyang and met with Kim Il Sung. In mid-June 1994, he appeared on CNN and announced a "breakthrough." North Korea would hold a summit meeting with South Korea over its nuclear program.

Some of the statements Carter made directly rebuked the administration. He criticized the strategy of trying to bully North Korea into complying with the IAEA inspections. He reasoned that the United Nations sanctions sought by Clinton would have placed the United States in an untenable position. Moreover, he said, "the declaration of sanctions by the UN would be regarded as an insult by [North Korea], branding it as an outlaw country."

That was precisely what many people thought North Korea was. But, Carter said, he was in no position to judge Kim's past record of tyranny and broken promises. Instead, he praised the doddering dictator as "vigorous, intelligent, [and] surprisingly well-informed." (A few weeks later, Kim died.)

Carter had gone beyond his brief. He had assured Kim that the United States would drop its pursuit of sanctions, well before the Clinton administration agreed to do so. An administration amply criticized for flip-flopping on both domestic and foreign issues now had to explain why its public stances were being tweaked on the fly by someone who was not officially part of the government. Though Clinton had vowed in November 1993 to be "very firm" with the North Koreans, and not to hold face-to-face talks until Pyongyang revealed all plutonium diversions, he was now confronted with a situation where talks had been promised and the sanctions threat dropped, in return for little more than a North Korean pledge to do what it had previously agreed to do under the Non-Proliferation Treaty.

Clinton chose to put the most positive spin he could on the story. At a news conference, he called Carter a "distinguished American private citizen," who had gone to North Korea "to communicate the position of our administration." In fact, it would have been closer to the truth to say that Carter had gone to North Korea to formulate a new position and then communicate it *post facto* to Clinton. It seemed more a case of Clinton catching up than leading.

When formal talks between the United States and North Korea convened in October 1994, there were more American concessions. Critics of the agreement gibed that it was hard to tell who the offender was. North Korea agreed to freeze weapons-connected work and eventually to dismantle all related facilities. In exchange, the United States pledged to improve its political and economic ties with the rogue state and to ensure that North Korea received two new Western-style nuclear reactors and several hundred thousand metric tons of heating oil. Despite the CIA's conclusion that the nuclear research complex at Yongbyon was a weapons development site, the accord declared that site off-limits to IAEA inspectors for five years. And despite the administration's initial assurance that the accord would cost the United States little, it soon became apparent that the bill would run into tens of millions of dollars.

"While it was not unconditional surrender [on the part of the U.S.]," huffed former secretary of energy James Schlesinger, "it was a negotiated surrender."

The Korean crisis was the sort of event that made presidents "mice" or "men." It was also the sort of episode that, during the cold war, might have produced an exercise in brinksmanship and a risk of armed conflict. Americans could not forget how John F. Kennedy had resorted to an act of war—a naval quarantine—in 1962 over the issue of Soviet nuclear weapons in Cuba. Nor could they forget the agonizing wait to the outcome of the Kennedy-Khrushchev staring match.

In 1994, Bill Clinton was neither willing nor able to resort to what the North Koreans had deemed would be an act of war, the imposition of UN sanctions. Instead, Clinton accepted from Carter and the North Koreans what he could get. It was consistent with his career-long predilection to compromise and take a centrist position. The danger lay in whether the North Koreans would interpret such compromise as weakness and in the coming months and years defy once again the international community.

Clinton's handling of the crisis reflected how much both the international and domestic climates had changed—much for the better—since Kennedy and Khrushchev and Cuba and 1962. The doctrines of containment and brinksmanship had been buried with the cold war. Kennedy had operated in a political milieu that punished Democrats seen as soft on communism. Clinton was approaching midterm elections in a country intolerant of even minimal American casualties abroad. And the President was notably unwilling to expend his political capital on attempts to reverse this prevailing attitude.

Moreover, Kennedy had at least the tacit backing of the NATO allies in 1962. With both China and Japan—presumably the countries most vulnerable to a North Korean bomb—complaining in 1994 that imposing sanctions was inappropriate, Clinton faced the possibility of acting alone. Clinton was also facing the prospect of sending troops to Haiti. One crisis at a time, thank you.

In light of those factors, Clinton probably got a moderately successful deal that defused the immediate crisis. Some leading members of Congress begrudgingly admitted as much. But it was gained more by fortune than by design. And it had two serious flaws. First, it did not guarantee that North Korea's pursuit of nuclear weapons would end. This was particularly worrisome, not just for the sake of stability in Asia, but also for peace in the Middle East, given North Korea's record as the biggest supplier of missiles to Iran, Syria, and Pakistan. "The failure to deal with the problem of nuclear proliferation in North Korea will inevitably lead to a nuclear arms race in the North Pacific," predicted former UN ambassador Jeane Kirkpatrick. By mid-1998, Kirkpatrick's words seemed prophetic. U.S. intelligence analysts discovered that North Korea was digging an underground cavern, probably designed to house a nuclear reactor or reprocessing plant. To boot, North Korea brazenly test-fired a medium-range ballistic missile over Japan in late summer 1998. Both actions jeopardized an already tenuous agreement.

Even more, Clinton undermined his own international credibility. By threatening sanctions and then backing off and accepting Carter's deal, he suggested that American warnings need not be taken at face value. Firm rhetoric followed by quick side- and back-stepping was no way to go about global leadership.

"In a crisis," Richard Nixon chortled to an aide as he watched George Bush in the early months of the Persian Gulf imbroglio, "a good leader should always say, 'No comment. We haven't ruled out any possibility.' Keep them guessing. That's the only way to do it. Uncertainty—that is the key to getting the advantage, particularly early on in a crisis." At times, Clinton was only too willing to comment.

George Bush's success at coalition-building for the Persian Gulf War turned out to be Bill Clinton's undoing in the Korean nuclear episode. In part, the Bush model blinded the President. It suggested to Clinton that the American course of action against a defiant nation should be to seek friends and stand tall, rather than to just stand tall. As was clear by North Korea's continued obstinance in 1998, such alliance-making did not necessarily resolve foreign affairs dilemmas—it merely prolonged them. Clinton's concessions in 1994 considerably complicated his own future interaction with the country—and quite likely his successors' relationship too. In a new world order where rogue nations were given to intermittent challenges to the lone remaining superpower, that was a legacy the President—and the country—could do without.

UPSTAGED ON THE WORLD STAGE . . . AGAIN

Shortly after the battle of Antietam in the American Civil War, an exasperated President Lincoln sent a terse message to General George McClellan, commander of the Army of the Potomac. The President was irked by McClellan's refusal to pursue Robert E. Lee's retreating rebels in the days and weeks immediately following their September 1862 engagement in the Maryland countryside. It was a lost opportunity, Lincoln thought, that the North could ill afford. So Lincoln wrote the general, who had complained that his horses were tired, "Will you pardon me for asking what the horses of your army have done since the battle of Antietam that fatigue anything?"

Soon thereafter, Lincoln relieved McClellan of his command. The President had grown weary of sticking "sharp sticks under McClellan's ribs" to compel him to pursue the enemy, and tired of haggling with a soldier who fought like "a stationary engine."

That was leadership. Lincoln kept his eye on the objective and had little tolerance for those who he believed clouded his mission and prolonged the war. In all, he changed commanders of the Army of the Potomac some half-dozen times before finally settling on Ulysses Grant. Lincoln's house had been divided long enough, and he was resolved to unite it for good.

Bill Clinton faced no American civil war in the 1990s, but he did encounter the same challenge that had plagued Lincoln and all other Oval Office occupants before and since: how and when to use military force. North Korea had provided him with one set of lessons; the crisis in Haiti presented a different balance of arguments. In both, the specter of Jimmy Carter loomed large, accentuating Clinton's inexperience and indecision.

American troops had been in Haiti long before Clinton, Rodham Clinton, and Gore were born. The two Roosevelts, Wilson, and Hoover had all dickered with a military presence on the Caribbean island. During the cold war, the United States tolerated the Duvalier dictatorship. The family may have been thugs and thieves, but they were noncommunist thugs and thieves, and therefore preferable to the dictatorship in neighboring Cuba.

With the cold war now in history's dustbin, though, the American calculus in Haiti had changed. The Bush administration helped bring about free elections, which resulted in the installation of Jean-Bertrand Aristide as president. Aristide, however, was overthrown by Haiti's military in 1991 and fled to the United States. So did thousands of desperately poor Haitians, who took to the sea in rickety boats, risking the journey to Florida for a chance to seek asylum. The Bush administration concluded that admitting these boat people would only stimulate the flight of thousands more, far more than the United States could absorb and more than the voters of Florida would tolerate. The administration began turning the refugees back, leaving them little alternative but to retreat to Haiti.

The forced repatriation of the Haitians incensed many Americans, and candidate Bill Clinton responded to their anger. Combining his own political astuteness with the luxury of making bold promises that accompanies nonincumbents, Clinton pledged to permit the boat people to enter the United States. If he were president, he maintained, he "wouldn't be shipping those poor people back."

It was the kind of campaign rhetoric that did not wear well under the pressure of governing. Once in office, the Clinton team came to many of the same conclusions their predecessors had reached. Granting asylum to Haitian boat people would only produce more boat people; any administration that did so would lose Florida's electoral votes; and any truly stable solution in Haiti would ultimately require the acquiescence of the military and business elite that had felt threatened by Aristide. So Clinton, while insisting that he would find a way to restore Aristide to power, continued the Bush policy of turning the boat people away. In this instance, the "change" that candidate Clinton had pledged to foment fell by the wayside.

"I don't suppose you'd want anybody to keep a campaign promise if it was a very unsound policy," reasoned Secretary of State Warren Christopher.

Not surprisingly, some took Clinton's campaign promises more seriously than the secretary of state, including members of the congressional Black Caucus and many human rights activists. One of them was Randall Robinson, head of TransAfrica, a foreign affairs lobbying group. Robinson declared a hunger strike, which lasted for twenty-seven days and drew much sympathetic attention from the media.

In the face of this pressure, Clinton changed course again. He openly endorsed Robinson's protest and conceded in May 1994, "We ought to change our policy." What was this? Had Clinton forgotten that as president he controlled policy and had the authority to change it? Admitting misjudgments and granting that others might possess a better solution had long been admirable components of Clinton's leadership. But his choice of words—"we ought to change" as opposed to "we will change"—was hardly inspiring confidence in his steadfastness.

Predictably, Clinton's decision to reconsider asylum requests from boat people only stimulated more boatbuilding in Haiti. Other measures were suggested, tried, and discarded. UN sanctions were imposed and then suspended. The USS *Harlan County*, sent to Haiti in October 1993 as a show of force, turned around and steamed out of the harbor at Port-au-Prince after the Haitian military arranged for a riot on the pier.

Clinton's lack of consistency made a solution more difficult than it might otherwise have been. In frustration, Clinton's special adviser on Haiti, foreign service officer Lawrence A. Pezzullo, resigned in April 1994. He complained that the National Security Council had not coordinated Haitian policy and the State Department had not exerted leadership. At the rate things were going, Pezzullo wrote to Warren Christopher, he was gravely concerned that "we are heading irrevocably down a path toward unilateral military intervention in Haiti."

Pezzullo, it turned out, was right. In late July 1994, the administration obtained from the UN Security Council a resolution permitting a multinational force "to use all necessary means" to force the Haitian military leaders from power. Approaching that international body was fast becoming a staple of American post–cold war foreign policy. The U.S. had sought similar authorization in the months before the Gulf War and, more recently, with respect to North Korea and Somalia. America the military superpower was loath to act on its own; its economic backside and positive international image first had to be protected, or at least not unreasonably sullied.

Administration tough talk grew tougher in August and early September 1994. But the stern messages had little effect on the Haitian military junta of Lieutenant General Raoul Cedras, Brigadier General Philippe Biamby, and Lieutanant Colonel Michel Francois, since they had always survived American threats.

Perhaps the junta sensed that, internally, the administration was still divided over the use of force. Defense Secretary William Perry, whom Al Gore had talked into replacing Aspin in January 1994, opposed an invasion. He and some of the uniformed military leaders believed that military intervention in Haiti posed "too much of a Mogadishu possibility." They recalled that, not a year earlier, eighteen American soldiers had been killed, seventy-four wounded, and one captured in a bloody firefight in the streets of the Somalian capital. After securing the UN's support, then, the administration reverted to threats and bluster. The stern messages had little effect on the Haitian military junta.

But by the end of August, Clinton's assessment of the risk of using force had shifted. The Korean crisis was cooling down, eliminating the prospect of fighting two conflicts at once. Nonintervention carried palpable costs: to his own credibility; to his support among African-Americans; and to his chances of carrying Florida in 1996. Although polls showed that about two-thirds of the voters opposed a Haitian invasion, Vice President Gore pointed out the importance of demonstrating that force would be used when the circumstances demanded it.

Gore was not skittish about deploying America's military resources, having been one of the few Senate Democrats who backed President Bush's use of force in the Persian Gulf in 1991. Gore also knew that Clinton particularly looked to him for advice on foreign policy issues. "In meetings, when a lot of people talk, you'll see the President looking around the room," said a White House aide. "When Gore talks, the President is absolutely riveted." Both Clinton and Gore telephoned world leaders to muster support for America's actions in Haiti. Gore was often on the phone with Aristide.

On August 26, the President approved an intervention plan the military had spent months crafting. U.S. troops were to be prepared to storm Haiti's coasts in late September. They would restore Aristide to power. Somalia's lesson was that doing any more was too costly, both militarily and politically. With Aristide returned, the United States would have no moral obligation to accept Haitian refugees.

But Clinton still hoped to make the intervention bloodless. He announced his intentions to the nation in a September 15 television broadcast directed as much to the Haitian coup leaders as to the domestic audience. With nearly twenty U.S. warships already poised off Haiti's shores, the President announced sternly, "The message of the United States to the Haitian dictators is clear. Your time is up. Leave now or we will force you from power."

This was an uncharacteristically bold move for a President who often sought consensus and public support for any action—foreign or domestic.

True to form, though, Clinton was working both sides of the fence. Minutes after the cameras blinked off, Clinton huddled with Gore and other advisers in the private study just off the Oval Office. His national comments apparently left the Haitian junta no alternative but to leave. Yet the President had another card to play. In his study he communicated that he wanted Jimmy Carter, U.S. senator Sam Nunn, and General Colin Powell to be prepared to broker a last-minute deal.

There was some debate over whether Carter should be included. Finding themselves on opposite sides of an issue just as they had in the Korean ordeal, Gore and Christopher offered the President their differing opinions. Gore favored using Carter; Christopher expressed strong reservations. The final decision to send him was consistent with a by-now understood White House phenomenon: Clinton's tendency to take his Vice President's advice.

When the White House received word that the Haitian rulers might receive a last-minute delegation, the trip was on. Still, remembering how Carter had undercut him during the Korean crisis, Clinton admonished the trio that they must not offer either delay or cancellation of the impending invasion. They flew to Port-au-Prince on September 17 and met not only with members of the ruling junta, but with business leaders and parliamentarians.

General Powell seemed to impress the Haitian officers more than diplomats had been able to do. His words were blunt and, coming from the leader of the rout of Iraq, credible. "You have no idea," he told them, "of the firepower we have."

Still, the Haitian generals resisted and dithered. As the appointed hour for the invasion approached, Clinton nearly lost patience. He wanted the emissaries out of Haiti before the firing started. "We've been friends for a long time," he told Carter by telephone. "But I'm going to order you out of there in thirty minutes. You've got to get out." It was well into the eleventh hour before Powell called and informed Clinton that a deal had been struck.

The settlement made a few minor concessions to the junta leaders. They were allowed to stay until October 15. Though Clinton had denounced them as thugs guilty of murder, they were granted amnesty. But the important thing was that the next day, two thousand American troops landed in Haiti without opposition, and the junta members had no choice but to depart by the agreed date. Aristide returned to power soon afterward, and reasonably free parliamentary elections soon followed.

In a test of wills and resolve, Clinton had finally won. The President, said Republican senator William Cohen, "deserves credit for seeking a diplomatic solution and achieving one without bloodshed." There could be no guarantees that Haiti would not revert to its chaotic and repressive past. But for the moment, the administration could boast of an accomplishment. "Let it be noted," one White House official crowed, "that we have done what we said we would do."

There were at least two lessons in Haiti. One was that Clinton could mold public opinion; he could lead. Fifty-seven percent of Americans disapproved of U.S. troops' presence on the island in late September 1994, but only 39 percent felt that way by mid-October. This was welcome news for a President who more often found himself responding to voters and espousing "change," rather than educating voters and creating it.

Haiti's second lesson was more complicated and the depth of its import not as obvious. Clinton was again the benefactor of good fortune. Illinois congressman Henry J. Hyde acknowledged that the President "has survived another tough situation. He is a very fortunate man." With public opinion and congressional sentiment stacked against him, it is doubtful that Clinton, in the wake of the Somalia failure, could have maintained support for a Haiti invasion if that action had produced significant American casualties. The President unnecessarily placed—and allowed to be placed—too much emphasis on the return of Aristide to power. He needlessly backed himself into a corner over a largely domestic crisis in a foreign nation. He had to make good on threats or lose face. Was that the way to conduct foreign policy?

Clinton had not been the first president to demonstrate American military power. His immediate predecessors had done as much in Grenada and Panama. But the difference between Clinton's handling of Haiti and Reagan's and Bush's handling of other Latin American hot spots lay in decisiveness. Clinton dillydallied far more than the others. He spent most of the first two years of his presidency speaking of what he would do in Haiti rather than talking of what he did do.

For a man who rushed to accomplish things on the domestic front, Clinton was generally of a slow and deliberate mind on international fronts, such as North Korea and Haiti. These are often laudable qualities in foreign policy, but Clinton's own lack of interest in conducting such policy only exacerbated his timid nature and gave way to confusion and idle threats. When swift and decisive steps were taken on the international front, they were either "safe," such as the June 1993 bombing of Baghdad in the wake of news of a plot to assassinate former president Bush, or they were steps made by Carter or Gore.

Too often, Clinton had to be pushed and then pushed again into making hard decisions—decisions that could have been considerably less complicated and dangerous had he not vacillated from earlier positions. No other president in recent memory had asked so much of advisers. His undergraduate degree in international relations aside, no other president had asked for such clarification upon clarification of policy positions, either. But then, perhaps such honing of issues was a consequence of his academic training. Perhaps the President's intelligence occasionally impeded his ability to lead instead of accentuating it.

MARKETPLACE LEADERSHIP

In the midst of the contentious 1993 congressional fight over the North American Free Trade Agreement (NAFTA), House Minority Leader Robert Michel of Illinois pleaded for his colleagues' assent. Voting for the measure, he acknowledged, might be difficult, but it would be a courageous indication to the rest of the world that the United States was prepared for the economic demands of the twenty-first century.

Michel railed against NAFTA's opponents, who he said wanted "to define our time as the age of anxiety, in which our only response to the challenges of global competition is to retreat, whine, and whimper."

The "age of anxiety"? Time—and historians—would reveal whether this characterization, forged in the crucible of a legislative fire, was well suited. But for now it was at least intriguing. It comported with a host of other titles bestowed upon previous decades, half-centuries, and centuries—designations like the Age of Discovery, the Age of Revolution, the Age of Empire, the Age of Reform, the Age of Money, the Age of Extremes, and so on.

NAFTA was a prickly issue among Democrats and Republicans. Some congressmen, Michel among them, argued that the trade agreement would foster jobs and be of significant benefit to American workers. Others, equally as well-intentioned, marched determinedly to the rhetorical battlefield armed with statistics predicting just the opposite.

Congressional approval of the North American Free Trade Agreement was one of the key legislative successes of the entire Clinton administration. Sure, the President had signed the Family Leave Act into law and had managed to noticeably improve the college loan program, but those met with little opposition and hardly rivaled NAFTA in scope. No other measure of that first year so boldly promised to perpetuate America's economic strength. The troika could point to NAFTA—and the subsequent passage of the General Agreement on Tariffs and Trade (GATT)—as evidence that they were working hard toward fulfilling their principal pledge to voters during the 1992 campaign. Here was evidence of change. Real change.

And not only could these trade agreements be dubbed legislative triumphs. They could equally, and properly, be touted as bona fide foreign policy accomplishments.

Well into his second term, President Clinton continued to regard a strong economy as central to America's future. Complimenting Franklin Roosevelt on his involvement in the creation of the International Monetary Fund and the World Bank, Clinton quoted approvingly of FDR in October 1998 that such financial institutions "spell the difference between a world caught again in the maelstrom of panic and economic warfare or a world in which nations strive for a better life through mutual trust, cooperation, and assistance."

Of course, economic security was hardly a novel concept. Worldwide expansion of American trade and investment had long been a component of international relations. The Marshall Plan, which helped to rebuild a devastated Europe after World War II, was born of American financial self-interest at least as much as any moral obligation to assist former Allies. But now, a half-century later, communism's demise, capitalism's growth, and increasing technological innovation and proliferation engendered more concern over American economic stability and expansion than ever before. Here was an arena that cried out not just for presidential assurances, but for presidential leadership.

In truth, no president wields as much control over the economy as voters believe. But this hardly dissuades them from demanding much of him on that front. In recent years—and for the foreseeable future—a president's economic plan has comprised the core of his campaign platform. At least as much as Republicans George Bush and Ronald Reagan before him, Clinton understood that *both* foreign and domestic presidential leadership demanded discussing and actively encouraging job growth, trade surpluses, and the like. It is hardly surprising, then, that some of Clinton's biggest foreign policy triumphs came on those very issues.

The President discovered via troubles in Haiti, North Korea, and other locales that traditional, strategic concerns endured despite the cold war's end—even if the solutions weren't cold war vintage. Long before arriving in the White House, he and Gore understood that those matters must share an ever-increasing portion of the foreign policy stage with other, newly emerging issues. In the arena of international economics, Clinton showed his New Democrat stripes.

Clinton had fumbled over NAFTA as a presidential candidate. His own campaign camp was divided on the issue; some endorsed it, others opposed it, and still others advised him to avoid it whenever possible. The resolution, in the end, was wholly Clintonesque. He announced his support for the pact, but did so without much vigor, leaving room to change his mind later.

By the first fall of his presidency, though, the President had decided to stand firm. An admitted policy wonk, he had studied NAFTA in detail, sought more advice, and finally resolved that it was good for the country. Other practical considerations likely fueled his backing too. Every living former president—from Richard Nixon to George Bush—supported the treaty. Bush had, in fact, taken many steps toward NAFTA's passage before he was bounced from office. Moreover, Clinton may have believed that the Democratic support he received in Congress during the summer of 1993's budget battle would again work on his behalf these few months later. Finally, looking ahead to 1994, he must have concluded that a NAFTA victory would provide him with much-needed political capital and credibility for the forthcoming health care debate.

Though the President was generally loath to tackle foreign affairs issues, NAFTA's concurrent implications in the domestic arena were clear-cut. To boot, enough old-fashioned politicking was involved in NAFTA to get Clinton's juices flowing and to command his attention—eventually.

Much was riding on NAFTA. No president since World War II had ever lost a trade agreement in Congress. NAFTA might well determine if the Clinton presidency—already limping from some ill-chosen issues, sex scandals, and bungled foreign policies—could exert effective leadership. If NAFTA bombed, Clinton was in danger of becoming a strange spectacle indeed: a virtual lame-duck president before the end of his first year in office.

NAFTA aimed to create the world's largest free trade zone among Canada, Mexico, and the United States. Proponents—including economists, CEOs, and foreign policy experts—proudly proclaimed that it would extend from "Yukon to the Yucatan" and that America would profit considerably. Labor unions fought vehemently against the pact on the grounds that not every American would profit; they maintained that it would cost American workers jobs. They, and others such as the comical alliances of Ross Perot with Ralph Nader or Jesse Jackson with Patrick Buchanan, were convinced that American businesses would move to Mexico, where they might significantly reduce their operating costs.

The publicity that NAFTA garnered belied its real impact. By itself, the agreement promised neither to substantially enhance nor cripple the American economy. Supporters contended that the trade pact would create some 200,000 jobs. Opponents charged that anywhere from 5,400 to 550,000 jobs might be lost. Statistically, these figures meant little in an economy in which some 120 million Americans went to work every day. Opinion polls even demonstrated that voters were unlikely to oust their representatives on this issue alone. NAFTA was clearly important, but the symbolism of Americans either losing or gaining jobs was what attracted the real public attention. NAFTA represented, in many respects, isolationist versus internationalist tensions and raised substantively for the first time the question of America's economic role in the cold war's wake.

Clinton knew in NAFTA he had his work cut out. In July, House Speaker Tom Foley had admitted that he believed the pact to be dead and that there was nothing Clinton "or anyone on the planet" could do to breathe life into it. Those were ominous words from the leader of the majority party, who presumably knew better than anyone else the pulse of his chamber. A few weeks later a presidential aide conceded that most senior administration officials privately thought the President should let the agreement die. Still, Clinton was undeterred.

The White House began the NAFTA fight in earnest on Tuesday, September 14, 1993. Only the day before, Clinton had presided over the signing of an Israeli-PLO peace agreement on the South Lawn. The President had actually had little to do with bringing the two rivals to this point. Norway had brokered the agreement, but both Israeli prime minister Yitzhak Rabin and Palestine Liberation Organization chairman Yasser Arafat wanted the official ceremony to be in Washington, D.C. American noninvolvement notwithstanding, the event was grand. Clinton's speech was eloquent. Guests roared when the two adversaries shook hands. Clinton hoped he might be able to tout the agreement as a much-needed foreign policy achievement.

If NAFTA passed the House a bit later in the fall—its Senate passage was virtually guaranteed—then Clinton's approval ratings might rise again, the President calculated. His image in international affairs might become one of a president who had hit his stride. Nine months into his tenure, he "had leaped from ice floe to ice floe and was still standing, but he hadn't become a commanding leader. The Oval Office seemed to have become a vise for him rather than a liberator of his talents." As September turned into October, with the embarrassing specter of an American warship retreating from Haiti at the sight of an angry mob, Clinton understood that this trade pact increasingly meant more and more to his administration.

The Middle East peace signing brought former presidents Carter and Bush to their old stomping ground, and Clinton took advantage of their presence. The day after the South Lawn event, he launched a pro-NAFTA rally in the White House East Room. Joined by Gerald Ford, each of the men spoke and each lauded the trade pact's merits. The President's speech particularly impressed Senate Minority Leader Dole. "Clinton," he said afterward, "hit it out of the ballpark."

They were preaching to the converted, but that mattered little. Business leaders, congressmen, and others who had long praised the agreement in the absence of the President's support now knew they had it.

They also knew they had a fight looming in coming weeks. The day after the President's East Room remarks, only 65 out of 258 House Democrats were willing to vote for NAFTA. Clinton and his team went to work.

Every Tuesday or Wednesday, for several weeks in October, the President met in the White House's Roosevelt Room with a handful of undecided House members. Clinton pressed both Democrats and Republicans, as he recognized that to gain passage he would have to construct another unwieldy and unlikely coalition—just as he had done for his summer 1993 budget battle.

True to his collective approach to governing, the President also actively enlisted the support of others. While he met with fence-sitting legislators, Vice President Gore, Treasury Secretary Lloyd Bentsen, trade representative Mickey Kantor, and economic adviser Robert Rubin assembled once a week to cajole some one hundred businessmen and other community leaders. The recipients of this lavish attention were often selected by those same House members whom the President was lobbying. And, to ensure they did not feel slighted by Clinton's absence, he sent each a follow-up note and directed that someone from the NAFTA "war room" call them.

Occasionally, high-ranking officials were even dispatched to the offices of individual lawmakers—or beyond. Bentsen might personally soothe a congressperson's fears over NAFTA's economic impact. Similarly, Interior Secretary Bruce Babbitt or Environmental Protection Agency director Carol Browner might be called upon to reassure another member about the pact's environmental effects.

If a bit more indirect but still potent strategy was needed, officials took their show on the road. Transportation Secretary Federico Peña traveled to Baltimore, Maryland, and spoke of the benefits that awaited a dredging-equipment company if NAFTA passed. Council of Economic Advisers chairman Laura D'Andrea Tyson flew to Atlanta and spoke to business leaders. Not coincidentally, in both instances, the congressional representatives in those districts had yet to decide how they would vote.

From mid-September through the House's vote two months later on NAFTA, freshman congresswoman Anna G. Eshoo of California journeyed three times to the White House, dined once at the Vice President's residence, and spoke frequently with other high-ranking administration officials. In all, since his East Room kickoff speech, the President had embarked on eighteen public events, meetings with 150 lawmakers, and countless hours of telephone lobbying.

Clinton also called upon his predecessors one more time. The day before the House vote, Richard Nixon, Gerald Ford, Jimmy Carter, Ronald Reagan, and George Bush sent a letter by Express Mail to every House member. It was the first time all their signatures had ever appeared on the same document. Drafted by Carter aides, the letter reported that "NAFTA represents a turning point for America. If you vote against it, the role of the United States as a world leader will be severely damaged, and the prosperity of the United States and the international economy will be endangered." The mailing acknowledged "the loneliness of making difficult decisions," but pleaded with the lawmakers to approve the pact, thereby signing their names "on the right side of America's history."

In basketball terms, all of this amounted to a full-court press. These were offensive moves. And the White House cared little about disguising its strategy from the opposition. If the White House were to lose the NAFTA effort, Clinton resolved that it would not be for lack of effort.

Central to the highlight reel of the NAFTA contest, aside from the President's strong September endorsement of the pact to start the game clock ticking, was Al Gore's appearance on CNN to debate Ross Perot. Newt Gingrich had made it clear to the White House that one way to obtain more votes from House freshmen was to step on Ross Perot. His persistence and his potentially powerful United We Stand America organization threatened the reelection prospects of lawmakers who did not want to be on the wrong side of an issue so early in their Washington careers.

Broadcast on *Larry King Live* on November 9, 1993, the much-ballyhooed contest featured an articulate Vice President and a petulant Ross Perot. Clinton had advised his partner, "Relax, be loose, but don't let the other side get the emotional edge. Make it clear we're on the side of the worker." Gore did all of that and more. At one point in the verbal volleys, Gore let go with a bomb: he knew of no other corporation in recent years that had lobbied Congress as heavily as Perot's. The Vice President had won the match, hands down.

Gore was a hero. For some time, aides joked with him by bowing before him and flailing their arms in exaggerated praise. In truth, the Vice President surprised no White House officials or former congressional colleagues, who knew full well of his talents.

Clinton and Gore could not have anticipated this particular development in their administration, but it was surely the sort of thing that made the President pleased to have the Tennessean on his team. Clinton had complete confidence in Gore's abilities. "I cannot imagine," said White House aide George Stephanopoulos, "the President making a major decision before talking it through with the Vice President."

Gore's former chief of staff Roy Neel agreed. Neel admitted that senior staff members who were no longer in the White House, or who were there

189

but powerless, were those who failed to understand from the beginning that if they wanted the President behind their plan, they needed to get both Rodham Clinton's and Gore's support too.

Clinton was known to put lawmakers on the Oval Office speakerphone when Gore was around. They lunched together privately once a week. They often exited meetings together side by side, discussing what had just happened. Gore was so connected, maintained Neel, that he and Clinton had "achieved what I call gestalt," alluding to a psychological term signifying properties that exist only in a unified whole, as opposed to their individual parts.

Gore was a team player. He and aides were repeatedly confronted with questions about whether and how he was sheltering himself from the political fallout of Clinton's mistakes in order to someday run for president on his own. He and his aides just as repeatedly dismissed those rumors. The Vice President confessed early in 1995, "Everything I do is according to one simple game plan: how can I best help President Clinton be the best president he can possibly be."

That philosophy was clearly evident on the Perot page of the NAFTA saga. Gore had jumped at the prospect of sparring with the Texas billionaire, even pushing at one point for three debates. Rather than needing to be pumped up for the challenge, he had to be calmed down.

Gore's triumph lent the administration's efforts a welcome lift. But their struggle was not over. One of the more painful aspects of the NAFTA fight was Clinton's break with organized labor. Long a financial backer of Democratic candidates in general and of Clinton in particular in his Arkansas days, labor organizations made no effort to conceal their disapproval of the President's support of NAFTA. The most powerful and numerous labor organization, the AFL-CIO, led the opposition.

What doubtless made Clinton's NAFTA backing a particularly bitter pill for labor to swallow was the President's duplicity. During the 1992 campaign, candidate Clinton had pledged to AFL-CIO president Lane Kirkland that he would not support the trade pact without certain modifications to benefit workers. Hearing this, Kirkland had then announced to state labor presidents that they should proceed with formal endorsements of Clinton. But the President did not keep his word, according to Kirkland. In a news conference after NAFTA's passage, he announced that Clinton had "stiffed" working people and that "there was not one word [in the agreement] about the rights of workers on both sides of the border to obtain decent wages and safe working conditions or to defend themselves from gross exploitation." Kirkland then predicted that his and other unions would retaliate at the polls in November 1994.

Kirkland had even threatened ballot-box revenge several weeks before the NAFTA vote, prompting Clinton to shoot back with some stern comments of his own. In an early November 1993 airing of *Meet the Press*, the President complained that labor was engaging in "real roughshod, muscle-bound tactics" when it contemplated withdrawing contributions for lawmakers who voted for NAFTA. He then quickly sent AFL-CIO president Lane Kirkland a note pleading, "I hope my remarks didn't ruin your Sunday." Clinton made similar efforts to heal wounds with Kirkland after NAFTA's passage. The President had stood firm, but moved to close the gap as quickly as possible.

The organized labor rift was not the only sore spot for the President, either. He had likewise broken ranks with many in his own party. Two of the top three ranking House Democrats, Majority Leader Dick Gephardt and Majority Whip Dave Bonior, worked against Clinton and Gore. This was dangerous business. The President would need those men and the votes they might round up for the First Lady's forthcoming health care initiative. No matter what his cozy relationship with Republicans on NAFTA, he would not always be so chummy with them. If angering Democrats on some issues and warming to GOPers on others would be the fate of a president committed to centrism, then indeed this first term would be exhausting. On NAFTA, Clinton was uncharacteristically pushing the proverbial envelope—but at least he was pushing something with vigor.

The final tally sheet was convincing: in a 234–200 NAFTA victory, 132 Republicans and 102 Democrats defeated 43 Republicans, 156 Democrats, and one independent. Most landmark legislative successes of this century—social security, Medicare/Medicaid, the Civil Rights Act of 1965—had attracted a sizable percentage of Republicans, but those measures also enjoyed the support of members of the President's own party. With NAFTA, three-fifths of Democrats opposed Clinton.

Still, a squeaker it wasn't. The "Great Showdown," noted one report, became the "Great Steamroll."

Compromise is either the great equalizer or the great bane of the American political system—and it is frequently both. There had been a flurry of compromising in the weeks and days—even hours—preceding the House's NAFTA vote. The White House made it known that it was ready to deal in order to secure votes. Commented one administration official, "Is the bazaar open? Absolutely." Predictably, reactions were mixed. Legislators whose requests were accommodated maintained that they were serving their constituents' interests. Others thought Clinton had given away the farm without at least first trying to sell it.

Among the White House deals were agreements to limit the amount of Canadian peanut butter and wheat shipped into the United States, to ensure that Australian and New Zealand beef did not enter the United States tariff-free via Mexico, and to temporarily raise duties on Mexican vegetables such as tomatoes if those products achieved too large a market share. Nearly $33 million was promised to some members of the House's Florida delegation to construct an agricultural research station; $10 million was pledged to raise a Center for the Study of Western Hemispheric Trade in Texas.

These and other concessions were, of course, aimed at attracting specific lawmakers. When the administration shelled out $15 million to hire 136 new customs agents for the textile and apparel industries, it garnered the attention of two Georgia Democrats. Notably named Nathan Deal and George "Buddy" Darden, both lawmakers ultimately sided with the President on the trade pact. Their colleague Esteban Torres of California—along with other Hispanic members of Congress—was the target of an even bigger financial outlay: the binational North American Development Bank. The estimated cost of this U.S.-Mexico venture? Two hundred million dollars. But Torres voted for NAFTA.

Texas congresswoman Eddie Bernice Johnson reportedly hit the biggest jackpot with the NAFTA issue. A *Journal of Commerce* story revealed that an administration official pledged to her that the Pentagon would purchase two new $1.4 billion C-17 cargo planes from the Vought Aircraft factory in her district. Johnson denied she voted for the trade agreement on this basis.

All told, the White House spent at least a cool $300 million in taxpayers' money. Some sources announced that it was far more. Ralph Nader's *Public Citizen* estimated the deals cost $4.4 billion, and *The Nation* magazine put the figure in the $50 billion range. By contrast, it was projected that the anti-NAFTA forces, including Ross Perot and labor unions, forked out a paltry $10 million.

Clinton's oft-mentioned buzzword *change* was not an entirely appropriate description of NAFTA. If the trade agreement promised to be a step in the right economic direction, it was hardly achieved with the new methods candidate Clinton had espoused. In accepting his party's nod for president in July 1992, Clinton had lamented special interests and horse-trading. "For too long," he maintained amid cheers, "those who play by the rules and keep the faith have gotten the shaft. And those who cut corners and cut deals have been rewarded." Barely a year later, fuming over the White House's NAFTA deals, Charles Lewis of the Center for Public Integrity wrote that "those who kept the faith that Clinton might change the way politics is done in Washington were the ones who got the shaft."

Had the President not waited so long before announcing his support for NAFTA, he might have secured the measure's passage with less bargaining. As it was, he permitted his opponents to prance around the battlefield for too long trumpeting their message without much opposition. Clinton simply had too much ground to cover by mid-September to survive without making deals.

The frenzied scene of last-minute scrambling was old hat to seasoned

Clinton-watchers. A former gubernatorial aide to Clinton, Bobby Roberts, conceded that NAFTA was "classic Bill Clinton. . . . He waits too long to get started on trying to get his point across and then he realizes that he's behind the curve, and then he works his own rear end off . . . and then pulls a [victory] right out of the jaws of defeat. I mean that's personal Bill Clinton. That's not his staff."

An itinerant White House adviser agreed. The President's modus operandi, he charged, was "the adult version of the all-nighter in college. You screw around, party too much, cut classes, and then you pull an all-nighter and pass. It's government by pass-fail."

If this was how the President was given to operating, some said, then he was sure to exhaust his staff—and cost taxpayers millions. That brand of leadership exacted too high a price.

Clinton seemed to be mistaking capitulation for power. The presidency had many privileges, but this president was making excessive use of the wrong ones. Whatever happened to moral suasion or good old-fashioned arm-twisting of the Lyndon Johnson variety? Clinton had the right idea of working for votes, but he had his process backward. Instead of giving away projects and money, why did he not simply threaten to withhold those same projects and money?

Representative Louise Slaughter of New York foresaw the perils of the Clinton way. She admitted, "I can't tell you how many people I've talked to who have said, 'Now I know the game. You don't commit on your vote until you see what you can get for it.'" In words that must have made the President perk up, she then said, "I think it's going to be harder to pass health care. . . . Buying votes every time we put something up here is not a good idea in my opinion."

Clinton revealed a curious mix of both pragmatism and principle. Most political leaders purport to possess such qualities. Their success or failure is often explained by what dose of which quality they administer to which cause. Clinton's pragmatism, said a former aide, comes from an understanding of the political process. "I think he does see politics for what it is," noted the aide, "which is a process of compromise, of shifting positions within some acceptable parameter. . . . That is, to me, just inherent in the political system and he likes that part of it."

Aides agreed that Hillary Rodham Clinton was a good balance for the President's altruism. She realized that "people had their own agendas and you had better be willing to use power and influence." Clinton was not always comfortable with the grittiness of power—the pressure on lawmakers, the threats, and the like. But he had come to grips with it, in part because of his wife's counsel and in part by dint of his own missteps. His understanding of power, though—especially if he regarded his massive trades as evidence of that power—still needed some seasoning.

Consistent with the attention NAFTA was garnering in the media, the House was itself an exciting scene during the floor debate on Wednesday, November 17, 1993. The vote was deliberately slated to take place immediately before a meeting of the Asian-Pacific Cooperation Forum, so that the White House might argue that the President should not be rebuked by Congress before such a significant meeting. Nothing was left to chance.

Technically, the House was not deliberating the agreement itself that evening. President Bush had already brokered the deal. Rather, House members were deciding whether to approve appropriate changes in American law so that the pact might go into effect. Befitting a hot issue that divided many lawmakers, special accommodations were made. Instead of granting half the eight-hour debate time to opponents and half to proponents as was the usual practice, time was split into fourths, so that Republican and Democratic supporters and detractors might each make their pleas.

A staged interruption by environmental protesters in the House visitors' gallery notwithstanding, the show went on as planned. Lawmakers who had spent weeks either being courted by the White House or avoiding the administration's advances could at last get on with it. Some weren't content with mere rabble-rousing, though, and used the pre-NAFTA buildup to plan something more. Freshman representative Donald Manzullo of Illinois argued for the pact's passage, flanked by two constituents and props that included an oil gasket, sliced Swiss cheese, and frozen corn.

By contrast, Democratic opponents Dick Gephardt and Dave Bonior stuck with a tried-and-true staple crop: an impassioned speech. Majority Leader Gephardt reminded his colleagues, "This country's greatness was not built on cheap labor." Majority Whip Bonior was equally as charged. "The work of America," he noted, "is still done by people who pack a lunch, punch a clock, and pour their heart and soul into every paycheck. And we can't afford to leave them behind."

Of concern to lawmakers and lobbyists opposed to NAFTA was less the accord's impact on U.S.-Canadian trade and more its impact on U.S.-Mexican trade. Indeed, Canada was America's largest trading partner, and the two countries had already negotiated a Free Trade Agreement, which took effect on January 1, 1989. NAFTA promised only to expand on it. Mexico was the sticking point. There were fears that too many of NAFTA's benefits were tilted in one direction: south of the border.

Clinton's thirty-four-vote margin of victory was impressive, given his late decision to push for NAFTA. He and Gore grinned wide as they entered the White House's Grand Foyer to comment on their triumph. Before the year's end, the Senate had given its assent to the pact, but it was anticlimactic. The real battle had been in the other chamber, and for once the administration came out on top.

Or did it? Critics gibed that America's economic future would be bleak if

NAFTA passed—that, in Ross Perot's terms, there'd be a "giant sucking sound" of jobs flowing south to Mexico. That wasn't entirely true, although some workers were displaced. Near the end of 1994, after almost a full year of NAFTA's implementation, the Department of Labor's NAFTA Adjustment Assistance Program listed approximately 12,000 persons who were unemployed as a consequence of the trade pact.

Other statistics were more upbeat. Despite those 12,000 lost jobs, in the economy as a whole, some 3.5 million more Americans held jobs in October 1994 than in December 1993. Moreover, the Department of Commerce estimated that some 130,000 fewer jobs would have existed in the third quarter of 1994 without the NAFTA-induced surge of exports to Mexico. From January to September 1994, U.S. exports to Mexico were up 21.7 percent from the previous year, totaling a nine-month record $37.5 billion. Much the same was true for Canadian exports too. In the same nine-month span, exports to the north stood at $83 billion—up 11.4 percent from the same period in 1993. A snapshot of one industry, automobile manufacturing, indicated that over 22,000 passenger vehicles were shipped to Mexico in the first eight months of 1994. This was more than twice the 11,000 units shipped to the country in all of 1993.

Overall, trade among the three NAFTA partners in 1994 rose 17 percent, or $50 billion. As for the trade deficit, official statistics revealed that the pact accounted for 9 percent of the U.S. merchandise trade deficit, but 29 percent of the total U.S. goods trade.

By early 1995, the Department of Commerce conceded that NAFTA would not likely figure as prominently in U.S. export growth for the coming year. The peso's depreciation and lower Mexican incomes were cited as reasons for decreased demand for American goods. But, as the Mexican economy adjusted over the next one to two years, it was believed that Yankee exports would again rise. Real change appeared on the way. NAFTA was looking like a success.

In NAFTA, the President had at last committed himself to a legislative initiative and fought hard for it. Shoot first and talk later. Surely, he did not relish the prospect of antagonizing organized labor or of rebuffing most of his own party, but he was clearly willing to take several steps in that direction. Here was Clinton fighting, communicating, persuading. Here was Clinton leading.

Even more, here was Clinton learning. The path to victory was strewn, in fact, with elements of the lessons learned from the President's other legislative missteps. "The intensity came from the budget struggles; the focus came from the fallout over the gays-in-the-military policy; and the politics of the head count came from the determination not to leave another supporter out to dry like the White House did when it forced Representative Marjorie Margolies-Mezvinsky, a Pennsylvania Democrat with a precarious hold on her job, to cast the decisive vote for the higher taxes in the budget bill."

On NAFTA—as well as on other economic initiatives such as GATT, the Summit of the Americas, the Asia-Pacific Economic Cooperation Forum, the World Trade Organization, and the Group of Seven (later the Group of Eight, with Russia's membership)—Bill Clinton exhibited real leadership. Those efforts toward international economic connectedness and cooperation promised genuine change, and the President convincingly and consistently articulated as much.

Yet, as was often the case with Clinton, both the good and the bad surfaced in his struggle. NAFTA may have been transactional leadership at its best, but it also exposed the limits of that form of leadership. In pushing for NAFTA, Clinton waited too long and consequently doled out too much. His dealings imperiled his presidency's overall capacity to foment enduring change. Distributing legislative perks en masse to dislodge legislative logjams could not be an approach taken with every bill of consequence; eventually, the gift well would run dry. The mass bartering on NAFTA was a strategy that only compromised the political viability of other initiatives with transforming possibilities, such as health care reform.

"Until NAFTA," wrote one observer, "Clinton had appeared stale, partisan, unprincipled, and weak. NAFTA fixed what was broken." Not quite. It was still evident after the trade pact—and particularly after the 1994 midterm elections—that Clinton was weak, given to saying what needed to be said at the moment his polls instructed him to say it. But NAFTA would be tucked in his holster and in the minds of still-hopeful Clintonites as evidence of what the troika *could* do.

Considerable questions remained, though, especially in the foreign policy arena, as to what they *would* do.

Les Aspin did not make it easy for President Clinton to relieve him of his duties as defense secretary in late 1993. Aspin's ties with the military were prickly, his relationship with Secretary of State Christopher and National Security Adviser Lake strained, and his style too informal. By the end of his first year in office, Clinton had heard enough such complaints that he resolved to dump Aspin—though with as little ignominy as possible. The secretary protested, offering a litany of achievements from his brief tenure.

What really resonated with the President was Aspin's unexpected criticism of Clinton's leadership. Clinton was unhappy with Aspin's leadership, but his consequent decision—to replace Aspin so suddenly—was itself poor leadership. Good leaders, urged Aspin, identify shortcomings and then permit subordinates to change. Clinton was ousting his secretary on virtually a moment's notice, without giving him time to modify his approach to his job. The charge stung Clinton, who himself knew well of second chances and often counted on them. Always one to consult, the President plaintively asked his advisers, "Are you sure we're doing the right thing?" The episode revealed much about Clinton's ambivalence in matters of foreign affairs, and his particular proclivity in that arena to defer to the opinions of others. *Caution,* rather than *change,* seemed the apt description of Clinton's foreign policy.

Considering the whole of his foreign policy from 1993 through 1996, it was apparent that where Bill Clinton had opportunities to change public opinion, enlist other leaders, mold a new consensus, or take the country in a new direction, he often passed. Clinton permitted an ex-president to refashion American policy toward North Korea, then acceded to a treaty that allowed the rogue state to continue developing its nuclear technology. He intervened militarily in situations where the political costs of inaction were becoming intolerable (as in Haiti) or the role of U.S. troops was ambiguously defined (as in Somalia). Even the NAFTA experience, for all of the import of economic globalization, revealed an administration willing to bargain haphazardly and with scant consideration for how its "y'all come" strategy might adversely impact future legislation.

By the end of 1995, Bosnia had become—quite unexpectedly and, it turned out, only fleetingly—the strange exception to all of this. After months of lofty platitudes and empty rhetorical posturing, Clinton worked to try to rally the public to stop the bloodshed in the Balkans. It was an agreeable turnabout to see a President who appeared to believe firmly in a mission and who was willing to justify his actions on something other than opinion polls.

Yet in Bosnia, too, Clinton soon stumbled. His persuasive efforts often lacked prescriptions for the future as to when or under what conditions the American military might play a role in ethnic and humanitarian crises around the world. He also was relatively silent on the reasons behind the downsizing of the military, if Eastern Europe, North Korea, and the Middle East apparently remained so unstable.

"What is astonishing about Bill Clinton," said Newt Gingrich, "is he does care about race, international trade, and the U.S. position in the world—but he has no consistency in fighting for anything."

Clinton nurtured an ideal conception of presidential leadership in foreign affairs. He too often craved information at the expense of decisions. Seldom do fixed solutions exist in any presidential arena, and almost never do they emerge in global matters. If they did, Americans might better select academics, bureaucrats, or technocrats to four-year Oval Office terms. Clinton wanted absolutes where his foreign-policy-making was concerned, but an effective leader relies on probabilities and possibilities, and on his own ability to convert one into the other.

Clinton's general passivity in foreign affairs in his first term may have rescued him from some risks. But then, presidents do not become leaders, much less great leaders, by hedging bets and sidestepping issues.

PART IV

THINGS FALL APART

CHAPTER EIGHT

Forward, About-Face, March

Jim Malloy could be garrulous, talking with the working-class growl reminiscent of his Buffalo, New York, upbringing. Now he sat silently, viewing the Washington Monument from his office in the heart of the Capitol and recollecting how far he had come. Malloy ushered presidents to the floor of the House of Representatives for the State of the Union and other important speeches. To him fell the task of loudly calling out the traditional announcement, "Ladies and gentlemen, the President of the United States." Malloy reveled in this aspect of his role as doorkeeper to the House of Representatives, even aside from the prerogatives and privileges he had amassed after twenty-one years in the job. He would gladly have carried on, but it was November 2, 1994, and he knew the end of his run was near. For he was a Democrat.

The doorkeeper's office had represented the prerogative of a deeply entrenched majority. Now history, legacy, and institutional memory were about to face a hostile new regime.

As the midyear election results rolled across the two television sets in the main room of the doorkeeper's offices, Malloy emerged briefly. The room was crowded with the young, fresh-faced men Malloy employed as well as the labor lobbyists who had long enjoyed the privilege of gathering in his inner sanctum. They spoke glumly about the stunning turn of events. It had been thought nearly inconceivable that Republicans could win the forty seats necessary to gain the majority in the House. Clinton had brilliantly won the presidency two years before, but now his party and his aides reeled with shock and disorientation.

From statehouses and legislatures to the Congress, the midterm elections of 1994 were remarkable for the sheer number of seats that shifted from Democrat to Republican. In the House of Representatives, Democrats saw 35 incumbents defeated out of 225 running for reelection. Out of 31 open seats vacated by Democrats, 21 moved into Republican control. No Republican incumbent was defeated for reelection. After four decades in the minority the Republicans took over the House with 230 seats. A slimmer victory brought Republicans to the majority in the Senate with 52 seats to the Democrats' 48.

To some, it felt as if the Capitol dome had fallen on the democracy. The

President, an astute student of political history, was well aware that midterm elections go against the party holding the White House. Clinton had been expecting the worst, while hoping that the House at least would stay in Democratic hands. As the election approached, Clinton flew to Democratic candidates who would have him by their side. Many had turned the other way, anxious to distance themselves from Clinton's shrunken popularity.

Democrats were running, but they were having trouble hiding from their standard-bearer. An uptick in the President's popularity the week before the election generated a short flurry of appearances. It was too little too late, as a Republican tide had risen across the country.

At the state level Democrats started at a disadvantage. More Democratic governors were up for reelection than Republicans. A total of five Democratic incumbents lost, including such stars of the Democratic party as Mario Cuomo of New York and Ann Richards of Texas. Republican governors were now ensconced in thirty statehouses compared to the nineteen they had held prior to the election. It was the first Republican gubernatorial majority since 1970. "Not since 1867—before the readmission of ten of the eleven ex-Confederate states to the Union—had Republican gubernatorial candidates done this well."

Republicans reveled in a victory that reached right down to statehouse doors. By the morning after the election, Republicans were in control of seventeen more legislative chambers, having "won more than 100 state Senate seats and about 370 House seats." Republicans went from control of less than a third of the ninety-eight partisan state legislative chambers to control of one more than the Democrats, and a tie for the majority in three states.

On election day, director of communications Mark Gearan had done a poll in the White House. Not a single aide predicted the imminent takeover of the House of Representatives by Republicans. Now, despondent Democrats were turning on their political leader as the likely scapegoat.

The President could not fathom his rejection by the voters just two years after entering office. Why did the public have so little conception of his good works? He had lowered middle-class taxes in the 1993 budget bill, passed a sweeping crime bill, established freer trade to build the economy, banned handguns, and put family values in the forefront with the Family Leave bill. If he had misstepped, it was out of exuberance for change. Failure to pass health care reform should not, in Clinton's mind, have overshadowed that it was a good and necessary effort. Why didn't the public recognize the recalcitrance, the outright obstruction, of the Republicans? As the President agonized, his party splintered.

Accounts of the last transition of the House of Representatives from one party to another existed in press reports that were four decades old. Who would know what to do?

Jim Malloy understood quickly what few had grasped that evening. The new Congress, soon to be defined as the Gingrich Congress, would be utterly different from the old. The leadership and committee systems would change, new members would be given unheard-of power, and government would be attacked from within. And, alas, one of the first symbols to fall was the office of the doorkeeper, eliminated just days after Newt Gingrich was sworn in as the first Republican Speaker of the House in four decades. In striking contrast to Clinton's transition in 1992, Newt Gingrich had planned his takeover with precision. The victors moved into prime offices, and the evicted Democrats scrambled for the best space they could find. Gingrich settled into the grand office of the Speaker, with its imposing view down the length of the Mall to the Washington Monument.

On the other side of the Capitol, Senator Bob Dole of Kansas once again took up the role of Majority Leader. Republicans had briefly held the majority in that body from 1980 to 1986. Dole, looking forward to running for president in 1996, was pleased to have such a visible perch from which to launch his campaign.

Meanwhile, official Washington and the press speculated about the country's future as a new year began with the American government divided in a way that few had ever witnessed.

UNDER THE EYES OF FREEDOM

The West Front of the Capitol faces toward the Washington Monument and Lincoln Memorial, the real estate of national remembrance and commemoration. Grand sculptures to presidents and soldiers share space with treasures housed in the museums flanking the Mall's broad lawn.

On September 27, 1994, 367 Republican incumbents and challengers had gathered around House Minority Leader Newt Gingrich as he stood on the West Front steps, under the refurbished statue called *Freedom* that graced the Capitol's dome. Gingrich was about to defy the conventional wisdom of opposition parties in midterm elections. Attacking the President and his party, savaging their two-year record, was the historical precedent Gingrich, a former history professor, knew well. It was "an age-old way to conduct midterm elections: talk retrospective and make vague promises." But the "Had enough?" campaign of Republicans against President Truman, inspired in 1946 by the work of an advertising agency, was not Gingrich's model.

Rather, he sought to reclaim majority status for Republicans in the House of Representatives with a "party and a movement that is based on ideas." Gingrich was out to show the press corps and the country that "a brain-dead Congress is a bad Congress," and that Republicans offered a real alternative.

Gingrich and his allies constructed a platform that was both a campaign theme and the focus for the first one hundred days of legislative work. It was a strategy rooted in Gingrich's 1980 campaign, when he proposed a "covenant" of five steps to improve the quality of American life. Reagan had watered down that effort. Not so for the resurrected covenant in 1994.

Those gathered on the esplanade of the Capitol had signed a document called the Contract with America. The ten numbered provisions of the Contract carried the biblical overtone of ten items of faith. A balanced budget and line-item veto; middle-class tax cuts; capital gains cuts; an anticrime package. Under the Contract, the federal government would chase down errant parents for child support, give more aid to senior citizens, and step up to the issue of legal reform, at the same time shifting responsibility to the states in a major restructuring of welfare policy.

Increased funding for national security and a vow to prohibit UN command of U.S. troops predictably held a spot in the Contract. The last provision, reflecting the perspective of the new "citizen-legislators," placed term limits on members of the House.

Unspoken was the extent to which the Republican program "was a political mirror image of Clinton's 1992 program. In effect, the Republicans were trying to recapture both the electoral and the intellectual ground they had lost to Clinton (and Perot) two years earlier." Aimed at voters disgruntled with government and fearful of "moral decline . . . the Republicans' 1994 program worked as well as Clinton's had two years earlier." Part of their success lay in the same fertile territory for new initiatives that had animated many of the President's proposals.

Crafted to enhance solidarity, the Contract did not take a position on abortion or school prayer. But the "subordination of social to fiscal issues" would prove impossible to maintain. Immediate strategy for the Contract left little to chance, not even the weather. Months before the event Gingrich consulted a weather forecaster friend to be sure the sun would shine for the momentous day. It did.

Republican leaders were united in believing that the party should clearly "stand for something." The President's reputation as an indecisive and non-ideological leader made him an inviting target for Republicans seeking the high ground. GOP conference chair Dick Armey proclaimed with the bluster of newly acquired power that "running solely against an unpopular president would only deepen the public cynicism. . . . It's time for the Republican Party to accept the role of leadership the American people are demanding." While Democrats seemed to be "caught in an issueless fog," *Washington Post* editorial writer E. J. Dionne observed, "the intellectual energy had again shifted back to the right." A president with the intellectual imagination of Bill Clinton could not help seeing the irony of ceding the territory of ideas to his adversaries.

Meanwhile, Gingrich, the political general who had won the forty years' war to oust the Democrats from the House majority, enjoyed tidal waves of fan letters and media coverage after the election. *Time* magazine dubbed him "King of the Hill," anointing him the "preeminent political leader in America" as the New Year began. Gingrich helped the attention along by opening his daily briefing to television.

But Gingrich's disapproval ratings began rising shortly after the election. A December 1994 poll showed 32 percent of Americans did not think Gingrich had good ideas for the country, and only 29 percent thought he did. In answer to the question "Is Gingrich a leader you can trust?" 52 percent answered no and 19 percent answered yes. Perceived as dogmatic and arrogant, Gingrich added to his poor public perception with early missteps and ethical problems.

Gingrich's testy, petulant nature seemed at times uncontrollable. He lashed out at the press despite his awareness of the role they had played in advancing his cause. Just days after the election he characterized some of the Washington press coverage as verging on "the bizarre." In the same breath that he talked about "the established order's ability to thwart things," he pointed only to the media as examples.

Some of Gingrich's remarks came across as even more bizarre. During his first year as Speaker, he called for a return to orphanages and blamed a hideous murder in Chicago on welfare turpitude, saying, "What has gone wrong is a welfare system which subsidized people for doing nothing, a criminal system which tolerated drug dealers, an educational system which allows kids to not learn and which rewards tenured teachers who can't teach while destroying poor children who are trapped in a process with no hope." He carped over being seated at the back of the presidential plane on the flight to Israel for the funeral of the prime minister. By April 7, 1995, an NBC News/*Wall Street Journal* poll showed only 27 percent of those surveyed viewed Gingrich favorably, against 39 percent who did not.

Yet popularity was only one factor in Gingrich's strategy of leadership. He calculated on creating a legislative branch that would dominate the executive. Republican priorities would not only drive the electoral victory in 1994, they would drive an agenda for a seismic shift in policy. Historical comparisons, the stuff on which Gingrich thrived, were compelling.

Thus he knew that President James Madison, the "master builder of the Constitution," saw the legislative branch grab dominance with the election of the "War Hawks" in 1810, during his first midterm. Led by freshman Henry Clay as Speaker, the new Congress put forward an agenda of "nationalism, aggressive expansionism, economic development, and, in the short term, war against England. They got much of what they wanted." A half century later another aggressive group of reformers seized the midterm opportunity.

The tumultuous events that propelled Andrew Johnson to the presidency in 1865 left him scant time before he attempted to short-circuit the radical Republicans in the midterm of 1866. Frustrated by Johnson's indulgent policies toward his native South, including the restoration of civil government in the Confederacy and the refusal to grant equal civil rights to freed slaves, the radical Republican Thaddeus Stevens took leadership of a special session of the 40th Congress. Historian Gingrich was mindful of the power partisan victory had brought to his predecessors.

More than half of the Republican freshmen and freshwomen who entered the 104th Congress had never previously won elected office. They called themselves citizen campaigners, believed ardently in term limits, and possessed the unshakable confidence of the self-righteous. Government would be delivered back to the people, and the new nonpoliticians would deliver themselves back home when their work was done.

First, however, a remarkable experiment in leadership was being tested by the new Speaker, who gave new Republican members of the House unprecedented prestige and power. Seven of the eleven open slots on the powerful Appropriations Committee, and three of ten spots on the Ways and Means Committee, went to freshmen. Gingrich angered senior members of his own party by his break with committee convention. Demonstrating an approach both staunchly ideological and astutely political, he raised two Republican freshmen to the dizzying height of subcommittee chairmen. Gingrich proudly and accurately declared that committees with the newest Republican members would have the responsibility for passing most of the Contract in the first hundred days.

Gingrich simultaneously consolidated his power and delegated authority. He and his followers were determined to act within the confines of House rules. The result revealed a party with roll-call cohesion unmatched since the nineteenth century.

New members spoke glowingly of the Speaker's ability to listen, of the attention he paid them. It was a time when Gingrich, perhaps the most leadership-conscious politician in the country, could glory in the results of decades of planning.

Even Vice President Gore recognized that Gingrich had a unique capacity to combine history and action. Gingrich harked back to "original principles," and Gore believed this ability to put "present battles into historical context" raised the public stakes, even if the rhetoric was insincere. Gore, notoriously stiff and scripted in his public speaking, grudgingly admired the grand, if undisciplined, sweep of Gingrich's speeches as leader of the conquering conservatives. Gingrich's style of "leading by including, and . . . giving authority from the bottom up instead of just from the top down," echoed in the Vice President's own reinventing-government project.

To Gingrich, leadership constituted an explicit process expressed in a mantra he often repeated: "Listen, learn, help, and lead." The formulation was founded on followers. They were the ones to be listened to and learned from. If a leader after listening and learning can help, then the people will want to be led.

On the great question of "Leadership for what purpose?" Gingrich eschewed being coy. Leadership will bring change that is "very deep and very bold" from leaders demonstrating "grand partisanship." In his inauguration speech Gingrich expanded on his expectation for change. "We should not be happy just with the language of politicians and the language of legislation. We should insist that our success for America is felt in the neighborhoods, in the communities, is felt by real people living real lives who can say, 'Yes, we are safer, we are healthier, we are better educated, America succeeds.'" These grand ideas sat atop careful planning and implementation.

Gingrich gave a paper to the incoming Republican members describing the role of a leader. First a leader must "set and create a focus; second, be a symbol—go places where the simple act of being there communicates. . . . Three, gather resources in the society at large. Four, using the resources of the federal government, govern." His unlikely hero was Franklin Delano Roosevelt, who he believed had done all four jobs. To Gingrich, "he's the greatest leader we ever had."

While Gingrich enjoyed the limelight, his counterpart on the Senate side, Robert Dole of Kansas, had a more complicated path to navigate. He clearly coveted the party nomination for president in 1996 and was positioning himself to thwart likely competitors in the Senate. Dole and Gingrich were not factionally allied, yet the Gingrich wing of the party loomed as a powerful force of delegates at the Republican convention. Anxious to negotiate an independent agenda from that of the House, Dole, nevertheless, quickly became captive to Gingrich's well-planned transition to power.

Early indicators of the future for House-Senate relations were not encouraging. Gingrich succeeded in seeing his former House ally Trent Lott of Mississippi elected as Senate majority whip over Dole's choice, the more moderate Alan Simpson. Lott was typical of the group of House Republicans who had moved to the Senate, energizing more conservative activism on that side of the Hill. Dole, long known as a centrist or moderate Republican, shifted between competing factions in his party and a determined Democratic minority.

Dole's main Senate rival for the presidential nomination was Phil Gramm of Texas, who was aggressive in finding opportunities to attack Dole's leadership. By July, several items of the Contract were stalled in the Senate. The Texan sent a fund-raising letter directly attacking Dole's leadership as inferior to Gingrich's. That same month, Dole, thrice thwarted by a Democratic filibuster over applying risk assessments to regulatory reform, complained to a Republican meeting that if they wanted he could "be another Ronald Reagan." The contradiction and irony were not lost on his Senate colleagues. Ronald Reagan seldom acted like a weather vane.

The first workday of the 104th Congress was, as Gingrich had promised, prodigiously long. In the next ninety-two days the House voted on every Contract provision, passing all but the constitutional amendment for congressional term limits.

Democrats displayed varying degrees of disdain and derision as the unusual convergence of party unity and growing Republican conservatism fueled the new agenda. According to political scientists, changes in House rules "were intended to strengthen the role of political parties by strengthening House leadership." In turn, the terms of debate were increasingly partisan. The former Democratic committee chairs, especially the so-called cardinals, who headed the most powerful committees, were particularly stunned and disgruntled. One Republican freshman referred to Commerce Committee Democrats, who had been led by a powerful chairman, John Dingell of Michigan, as "heavily sedated and deep in therapy." The metaphor seemed apt for both ends of Pennsylvania Avenue.

On April 7, 1995, Newt Gingrich became the first House Speaker in history to ask for airtime on national television. True to his admiration for FDR, Gingrich used the historic one hundred days mark as the occasion for his speech. The Contract with America had been delivered, he said, if not passed into law.

Yet even as Gingrich radiated the confidence of his accomplishment and position, unexpected White House maneuvers began to weaken his power. The President seemed to stir to life as he offered a strategy that turned the 1995 budget fight into a titanic struggle for the public's head and heart. Clinton, according to one policy aide, "discovered his center of gravity, which was pretty close to the center of gravity of the country, and that's where he stayed." The resulting reversal of Gingrich's personal fortunes was nearly as stunning as his ascension to Speaker.

A DARK MOOD IN THE WHITE HOUSE

The secret of government in 1994 rested in those oft-touted but little read documents that established and guide the constitutional system. Presidents hold as much constitutional power as divided government allows, and two hundred years teach that this is often a limited amount, especially if the President approaches the Congress with the lack of assurance that Clinton displayed in his first fateful year.

Not since his 1980 defeat in his reelection bid for governor of Arkansas had Clinton felt as devastated as on the night of November 8, 1994. Comparing the aftermath of the 1994 election to Clinton's darkest days on the primary campaign trail, one close policy aide said he sank "almost as far down . . . as he was . . . in New Hampshire." According to Deputy Chief of

Staff Harold Ickes Jr., Clinton was rattling around the near-empty White House during the 1994 Christmas holiday period. The President engaged in long laments, almost soliloquies, about what the election meant and where the country was going.

Nineteen ninety-four had been a punishing legislative year. The President's boldest initiative, reform of the national system of health care, had ignominiously departed the legislative stage. His own party, in control of both houses of Congress, never took a vote on any version of the plan. Weeks before the election, Democrats were desperate for good news to carry home on campaign rounds.

Worried thoughts of a historical parallel to 1946 began to creep into Democratic minds. In that year Republicans swept into the majority of both houses of Congress, took a majority of state governorships, and vanquished Democratic machines from Chicago to New York. President Truman was mortified by the defeat in Kansas City of his handpicked candidate for Congress, who lost by six thousand votes.

Truman accepted the recommendation that he not make campaign appearances or political speeches. His campaigning partisans "resorted to playing old recordings of Roosevelt speeches to boost their chances" and avoided even mentioning the President's name. But the miracle of modern politics did not afford Clinton Democrats the same cover. In 1994, from television commercials to old-fashioned campaign mailings, Republicans used every medium to tie congressional Democrats to their President.

Clinton, unlike Truman, was anxious to go on the stump. He determinedly, almost compulsively, tried to tout the administration's victories. But rather than hitting the broader themes that his position allowed, Clinton "would run forty-five minutes at a minimum and often an hour five to an hour and ten minutes, and they would be this mind-numbing litany of accomplishments. It was painful to listen to." The President was certain that "we'd beat their ass" if he could tell everyone in American what big changes he had made.

Extensive public opinion surveys confirmed Clinton's despair over the failure to reach the public with his message of optimism and change. Skepticism about the viability of government programs, about politicians' concern for ordinary people and their sympathy for the poor, had grown dramatically since 1987. Asked to agree or disagree with the statement that "most elected officials care what people like me think," nearly 65 percent disagreed in 1994 as compared with less than 50 percent in 1987. Fewer than half of all Americans believed that "government is really run for the benefit of all people." A healthy majority wanted new people in Washington, "even if they were not as effective as experienced politicians."

Remarkable coherence in Republican ranks was a hallmark of the 1994 election. Many of the Republicans' close victories resulted from a high degree of loyalty from voters who had previously switched party allegiance from one election to the next. Perot voters gave Republicans about 2 million votes. Non-college-educated white men, and to a lesser degree women, abandoned the Democrats in 1994. In contrast to Republican vigor in getting their voters to the polls, certain groups of "demoralized Democrats" stayed home. Notably, turnout among African-Americans rose and among women and low-income voters remained unchanged from 1990 to 1994. Well-educated women, in particular, continued to fear losing abortion rights and other civil rights advances. But "mostly younger, non-college-educated voters who leaned strongly Democratic but who remained disengaged, largely because of their ambivalence about the President," stayed home. Republicans had secured a core that political scientist Walter Dean Burnham dubbed the "Great Protestant White Middle." Another commentator noted that after a long period of effort the "southernization of the GOP" had finally come to pass.

Part of the remarkable Republican success lay in the strategy devised to deal with the most conservative wing of the party. Christian conservatives, who emphasized highly divisive issues including abortion and religion in public life, could not be ignored. They formed too large a piece of the core Republican electorate. The key lay in convincing them that "rather than urge massive new forms of government intervention on behalf of conservative values . . . the best thing that could be done for traditional ideas and institutions was to tear down federal programs and union-dominated city bureaucracies." This election tactic turned out to be brilliant.

For Democrats to retain their majority they needed the voters who were turned off, tuned out, and unwilling to make the effort for party or President. Democratic voters may or may not have wanted what their party was selling, but "they weren't even getting into the car to go to the store." Those who stay home often decide midterm elections. Too many Democrats exercised their right to the nonvote vote.

Amid the hand-wringing and dislocation of defeat, some Democrats began to wonder whether the future was even bleaker than the present. Had a wholesale realignment occurred? Was 1994 a "critical election" in which one party system gives way to the continuing success of another? Such realignments are historically the result of "major political or social disruptions which the previous party system seems incapable of resolving."

The House Republican majority held control with a narrow margin of twenty-six votes. The Senate was not filibuster-proof, and Republicans were well schooled in the debilitating effects of a determined minority in that chamber. At the least, it appeared that Republicans had succeeded in throwing the country into the "midst of a historic period of party realignment." Where it would lead after the shouts of victory faded depended on the political skills of the only Democratic leader left in charge of his domain.

GRABBING FOR THE RUDDER

The President, surveying the bleak landscape now thinly populated by his partisans, tried to plan his political future. The words that had followed Harry Truman after the Congress moved to Republican control in 1946 could aptly be applied nearly five decades later to the brooding Clinton: "Probably no President since Andrew Johnson had run out of prestige and leadership more thoroughly." Congressional Democrats were regrouping as if there were no executive branch. Senate Democrats were intent on talking among themselves "about the importance of a number of pieces of legislation." No one appeared anxious to include the President, who seemed to accept the responsibility for the election disaster that his own party heaped on him.

Clinton showed a remarkable, almost empathetic, ability to take the blame. The day after the election he acknowledged that "with the Democrats in control of both the White House and the Congress, we were held accountable yesterday, and I accept my share of the responsibility in the result of the elections." Sounding much like the man who had led the charge against him, Clinton pronounced, "It must be possible for us to give our people a government that is smaller, that is more effective, that reflects both our interests and our values."

Speaking about the core of the Republicans' plan, Clinton allowed that "there are some things in that Contract that I like." The line-item veto, a technique for presidential budget-cutting that any executive would love, was first on Clinton's list of accords. He wanted to reform welfare, move aggressively to reduce federal spending, cut income tax rates, and enact campaign reform. Sounding as if he and Gingrich were sharing speechwriters, Clinton spoke for a strong country with "strong families, better education, safer streets, more high-paying jobs, a government that reflects their values and the interests of the American people."

The President struggled with a reporter's question on what he would say to Democrats in the House who were considering switching parties. "Let me say," Clinton declared, "that if we can have a bipartisan coalition, then we can be both nonpolitical and more centrist. I ran for president saying that we should not be governed by either Republicans or Democrats who are pushed too far in either direction. That most of the good ideas are ideas that take us into the future not push us left or right." By spring, the President began moving back toward a middle-course strategy that pushed straight up the center.

The concept of "triangulation" was the vehicle behind Clinton's transformation, and Dick Morris was the driver. Political consultant Morris was a longtime strategic adviser to both Clinton and Republican politicians. Critics regarded him as a smarmy Svengali, but both Clintons felt attached to Morris.

An early skirmish with the new Congress helped Clinton and his team realize that his approach to leadership and governance faced radical change in 1995. Republicans showed derisive contempt for the program most dear to the President's heart. The National Service Corporation, modeled on the Peace Corps but directed to domestic concerns, received intense scrutiny and criticism from GOP lawmakers convinced that it was another liberal entitlement scheme. They jeered at the notion that the program claimed to be voluntary since AmeriCorps workers, as they were called, received monetary stipends.

Shortly after his first visit to the White House as Speaker, Gingrich came out with a blistering attack on national service. In a speech in Denver on Martin Luther King's birthday, Clinton took the opportunity to fire back. At the White House a press conference quickly formed with national service workers standing in the spotlight. Chief of Staff Leon Panetta took note of the favorable press coverage for the White House and concluded "drawing the line on Congress would give us momentum." Now the trick was figuring out where to draw other lines.

Journalist Elizabeth Drew dubbed this period of Clinton's presidency the "second transition." But rather than focusing on the infrastructure of cabinet and White House staff, the second transition focused on strategy, philosophy, and style. Could the President recast this defeat as an educational experience? A way to grow as a leader? Advisers thought Clinton recognized that the people wanted a commander in chief as President. As presidential media consultant Frank Greer put it, "They don't want a legislator in chief and they don't want a campaigner in chief."

The moderate strategy that emerged to deal with defeat brought Clinton no nearer to the media he now treated as enemies. He knew he needed the press, now more than ever. Harold Ickes pressed the President to spend some of his volubility on a select group of reporters. But Clinton kept his distance, and the price of his recalcitrance would grow three years later as he faced the midterm of 1998.

The contrast between Clinton's State of the Union speeches of 1994 and 1995 reveal the beginnings of a changed leader. Many remembered an emphatic President in 1994, waving a pen as a prop for his vow to veto any health care bill that did not provide universal coverage. That speech was tightly crafted by Clinton standards, only sixty-four minutes long and limited to eight initiatives as priorities for the year.

Now, in 1995, as he entered the House chamber for his address to the nation, the President acted anything but bold. He harked back to the "new covenant" of his presidential campaign, made a plea for comity, and appeared generally on the defensive. He spoke for one hour and twenty minutes and succeeded only in revealing his uncertainty on where and how to lead.

Clinton struggled with finding a new way, but he did not struggle alone. He spent many hours in the White House residence with his wife and Al Gore planning his reemergence as leader. The Vice President served as an integral part of the team, seeing his political life "every bit as much on the line as Clinton's." Gore brooded over the political setback to reinventing government that resulted from the health care bill's agonizing death in 1994.

One of the key initiatives that Gore had undertaken was administrative change designed to alter government service in several agencies. But the health care battle had overshadowed the "reinvention" of government.

At the fifty-day mark of the new Congress, the President arrived on Capitol Hill to meet with House Democrats. Inside the Capitol, with its vaulted ceilings graced by magnificent artistic renderings of history and myth, Clinton entered one of the warrens of windowless rooms in the cavelike basement. It was the best venue Republicans cared to offer, and less than two-thirds of the decimated Democratic ranks filled the folding chairs.

The President reprised his lament that the public simply did not understand what the administration had done for them. The members were restless, anxious to leave. Clinton fielded questions with no apparent recognition of his audience's discomfort. "Why couldn't he leave before everyone got tired?" one member wondered. "You lose your majesty and power and importance through incidents like that. When he makes a call, we want to be intimidated by it." Another wondered simply why the President had bothered to come at all.

It was June 1994 and a new ABC News/*Washington Post* poll showed an unchanging public attitude toward Congress. When asked if they approved or disapproved of the way Congress was doing its job, six out of ten respondents disapproved. Two years before the results were virtually the same. President Clinton fared little better in a *Los Angeles Times* poll in July. Voters thought he lacked common sense and was unaccountable.

Many politicians began to think the same could be said for the voters. Hadn't they turned on President Bush despite the extraordinary public favor he had received after the Gulf War? Despite his hope to conclude a sixteen-year reign of Republican hegemony in the White House, Bush was ousted in favor of youthful vigor, a focus on the domestic concerns of the nation, and most of all on change. Now, it seemed, public expectations were unreasonably high, and Clinton was on the receiving end.

During Reagan's midterm in 1982 the public was disgruntled as well. High unemployment and the worst economic decline since the Depression turned the election into a referendum on the President. The Republican National Committee ran advertisements pleading with the public, "For gosh sakes, let's give the guy a chance." Reagan implored the country to "stay the course," and they did. Republicans kept the majority in the Senate they had won just two years earlier. Party losses in the House were "just over half the number the President's party had lost in the out-party landslides of 1958, 1966, and 1974." Would a Reagan-type appeal have worked for Bill Clinton in 1994?

The President faced a public sourer and less tolerant than did Reagan. The steady climb of disapproval for government might have left the "Great Communicator" floundering by 1994. But Clinton also lacked the ace in the hole of deficit spending that Reagan had skillfully played. All Clinton drew from Reagan was a debilitating legacy of debt and deficit spending.

Eisenhower had faced a similar problem with a New Deal Congress saddled to his presidency. But working with Lyndon B. Johnson as Senate leader, Ike got credit for massive highway building, expansion of social security, and a dollar-per-hour increase in the minimum wage. He won a huge reelection majority.

Clinton did tout his aggressive legislative agenda. But his campaign book, *Putting People First,* had suffered a figurative burning when the President discovered that his domestic agenda had fallen hostage to a higher than anticipated deficit. Cost cutting was not what Clinton or the Congress had had in mind when they celebrated victory in 1992. The legislative agenda twisted in the knots of tight money. The first legislation Clinton passed, the Family and Medical Leave Act, promised, in the parlance of the day, to be revenue neutral.

In the President's eager enthusiasm to govern he had failed to understand the limits of his ability as an executive hoping to legislate. Despite having a Democratic Congress with a considerable majority, Clinton still believed he had to be chief salesman to the people. Being "a better educator than a legislator," according to one aide, Clinton built relationships in the hinterlands. But at home, few members of Congress knew him well, and he had no cadre he could rely upon.

For their part, congressional Democrats showed little patience for an administration that stumbled as it reached the front door. Although the leadership knew their fates were, as far as the public was concerned, inextricably intertwined, the habits and arrogance of single-party rule were self-defeating.

SEARCHING FOR THE DYNAMIC CENTER

Blamed and scolded for failing as political leader in 1994, Clinton faced a greater challenge in 1995. How would he recapture the leadership needed to govern? Faced now with an opposition party in control of both houses of Congress, could he find the power, the moral and constitutional authority, to prevail with his own agenda?

Now Clinton faced the "off off-year," the year without federal-level elections. There was nowhere to politic, nowhere to campaign. In 1995 the President gazed out toward a year of governing that looked as bleak as a fire-ravaged forest in the Ozark Mountains of his home state. He seemed unsure where to retrench, how to lead. He needed to revive not only his programs and policy, but also his ailing spirit. For once Bill Clinton's indefatigable optimism appeared to flag. The White House mood had sunk so low that the early strategy for dealing with the new Congress was a nonstrategy. Democrats would sit back and wait. The President would be patient, incremental, and nonconfrontational. Republicans would surely, eventually, fall victim to their unbridled hubris. They were overreaching, and the parlance of the day dictated that their parsimonious proposals would "come back to bite them" in the end.

But was this the kind of leader Clinton wanted to be? Restrained, reactive, praying for Republican missteps and self-destruction? These were odd ambitions for the self-proclaimed "man from Hope." He had fared unspectacularly with his own party controlling the congressional gavels. Could he possibly hope to do better, create real change or leave a legacy under the new regime? And the demands of reelection would soon be bearing down on the White House. Little did either side realize the drama of changed circumstances that would envelope them all during the next three years.

Throughout the raging budget fight of 1995, Bill Clinton strained to capture the flag of the center. Invoking the resurgently popular words of Ireland's greatest poet, he proclaimed, "Our mission is to show that the center can hold." How ironic then that victory over the Republicans slowly emerged from a strategy of extremes. By New Year's, 1996, Republicans were in disorderly retreat, and Clinton seemed steadfast with conviction. The Armageddon over government's role continued between America's two dominant parties. But the President had recaptured important ground in some early conflicts.

The first day of the 104th Congress saw Republicans take center stage on the reordered floors of the House and Senate. They immediately began maneuvering toward shrinking the federal government's role in American life.

The possibilities seemed endless and various. Some members were determined to eliminate departments, most notably Education, Commerce, and Energy. Others wanted to return money to the American people through a tax cut that would demonstrate Republican sincerity about remolding federal priorities. Democrats, after all, were just tax-and-spenders. And how in the name of Thomas Jefferson had so many programs fallen under the power of the federal bureaucracy? State governments and local control were the place for all those schemes to raise up the poor and relieve the wretched that had steadily evolved during forty years of Democrats dominating the Congress.

Under Republican authority, Democrats charged, the Great Society meant devolving government to the level of a local social club.

States' rights was a sword that Republicans thrust forward—and at times tripped over. The temptation to wield federal power, by directing and redirecting revenue streams, often proved too great for even the most committed federal downsizers. Christopher Shays, a moderate Republican from Connecticut, observed early in the year that "as a party . . . we have some conflicting interests and we want block granting and freedom for local and state governments when it fits into our agenda and we want restrictions when that fits our agenda. We make contradictory arguments."

Republicans, strongly encouraged by the National Rifle Association, planned to pass six crime bills to dismantle Clinton victories on the Brady Bill and assault weapons ban. But caught in the reformist tide were long-stifled Republican schemes. Republicans offered money for prison construction as long as states gave violent offenders more prison time. The quids and quos between the new wielders of Washington power and their state counterparts were continually being negotiated.

Meanwhile the first days of Congress saw Republicans speaking in sonorous tones at congressional microphones, while behaving like kids at the candy store. Words like *revolution* were used freely and often. Change aroused great expectations. Gingrich joyfully announced the sale of a House office building. Eliminating the jobs of congressional elevator operators, allowing members to sleep in their offices to trim expenses, poking at old perks and prodding the institution into a new culture, served the leadership's purpose of making a drama and show of change.

Changes for future policy were quickly implemented. Committee structure and leadership were reorganized giving individual members and the Speaker more clout. Funding for the mostly Democratic caucuses of common-interest groups, including women and blacks, was cut off. Proxy votes in committee were banned. Most disturbing to many Democrats and a good number of moderate Republicans was a requirement of a three-fifths vote to raise income taxes. But in the spirit of Republican unity even this potential hammer-hold over tax making was passed. Completing one hundred driven, whirlwind days of legislating in the House, the Speaker mounted his media pulpit in the spring of 1995 to announce his next changes.

Change of the magnitude Gingrich had in mind was not unprecedented. But the "welfare state" that he endlessly ridiculed was nevertheless a benefit given to people. The Speaker's proposals appeared as direct retractions of benefits citizens had taken for granted for decades. The sine qua non of Republican doctrine, a balanced budget, was unachievable without cutting federal dollars from direct service programs. Gingrich had declared at the beginning of the year that he was "prepared to stake everything to get to a balanced budget."

The problem lay not with the still-disciplined troops in the "lower" chamber, but with the powerful brake on House leadership, the Senate. In Latin, Senate means a "council of old men," and in ancient Rome it consisted of representatives elected by the patricians. The United States Senate aptly reflected the origins of its name. Only a handful of women held seats in the U.S. Senate in 1995. The rest of the Senate was mainly older men, and all were white. Although elected popularly, the Senate reflected its patrician heritage. Distinguished, deliberative, and struggling with internal political one-upmanship, the Senate under leader Bob Dole was far less enamored of change than its congressional counterpart.

Now Dole was forced to contend with a conservative mantra, a bill for a constitutional amendment to balance the budget that had been passed in the House with votes to spare. Receiving the bill in early February, Dole knew he faced a situation barely within his control. The Kansan faced a class of Senate freshmen equal in their activism to their compatriots in the House. Dole had the added problem of his own quest for the presidency, and the possible competition for that prize by those who served side by side with him in the Senate—Phil Gramm of Texas, Richard Lugar of Indiana, and Arlen Specter of Pennsylvania. Defeat of the Balanced Budget Amendment would open the door to attacks on Dole's leadership and his fitness to challenge Clinton the following year.

Despite efforts that were at times unseemly and at least extraordinary, Dole could not deliver the budget amendment. In the branch of Congress notorious for its independent membership, and the power of the minority, Dole was undone by one of his own party. The amendment was meant by conservatives to act as the automatic brake on social spending, restricting liberals far into the future. But the impassable obstacle to expansion of government rousted a liberal Republican senator from Oregon into solid opposition. Mark Hatfield saw the amendment as too great a threat to social programs.

Hatfield, a political institution in his own state, infuriated his party and frustrated the leadership by steadfastly refusing to vote for the amendment. Younger members called for Hatfield to be stripped of the chairmanship of the Appropriations Committee. But Dole did not harbor the radical drive for retrenchments that now governed the House. Hatfield would retire from the upper chamber at year's end, months after casting the one vote that made Dole's early leadership trial an ignominious failure.

Just how would the Republicans now manage to balance the budget? Where would the cuts be made? Democrats were counting on the belief that the underbelly of fiscal restraint would not be a pretty sight for citizens to see.

Republicans proposed budget balancing by 2002. Among the most vulnerable programs, Democrats focused their attack on the one area that seemed a certain "third rail" in the GOP's economics. Medicare carried a $176 billion price tag as the health care program for the elderly. Clinton's State of the Union speech had contained a line swearing protection for Medicare as a source of revenue for Republican tax cuts.

Then Gingrich threw a curve at his own team, telling a conservative seniors' meeting that Medicare could be put aside, separated from consideration of the budget. It made no sense. Social security and interest on the debt were already off the table. The Republican Conference chairman said, "We were doing fine until Newt stumbled." The seed of a Democratic strategy began to grow.

The field grew more open for Democrats to attack Republicans for plain meanness—meanness to children, meanness to the elderly, meanness to the poor. Gingrich worked feverishly on a primer for his majority as they left for the spring recess. They needed to talk with one voice about the large cuts to come, about the need to tame the budget beast and the prosperity this would bring.

Gingrich saw himself as the visionary leader among his colleagues. Tactical but impatient, strategic but unpredictable, Gingrich's unflinchingly loyal troops were soon forced to reckon with the appearance of their Speaker's clay feet.

MODERN ANTI-FEDERALISTS

Hand-sitting was an art Bill Clinton cared little about. He craved action, political maneuvering along with attending to mind-numbing details. "This man needs to have spontaneity like he needs to have oxygen," quipped former aide Betsey Wright. "He should answer the [White House] switchboard an hour a day."

Lyndon Johnson, who lost his first election by taking a supposedly solidly Democratic district for granted, vowed never to make the same mistake again. He would have admired Clinton's leave-nothing-to-chance approach. But the giant prism through which Clinton viewed and reviewed his options too often turned into a kaleidoscope of choices.

Visitors petitioning for a cause felt well listened to by the President. They often left feeling he leaned to their side or had even promised full support. Only later would they bitterly reassess their impressions, as the President's follow-up failed to materialize.

To the voting public Clinton defied ideological typecasting. What to make of this sincere, earnest ex-governor who supported abortion rights and the death penalty? Who stood up for gay rights and nationalizing of health care from the start of his presidency, at the same time that he succumbed to the pressure of Wall Street and the bond market? As William

Galston, one of his close economic-policy aides, framed it, "Was he the fiscally restrained free-trade centrist? Or was he a New Deal, Great Society Democrat trying to push national health care? Or was he a George McGovern 1972 Democrat trying to insert gays into the military?"

As Clinton entered the second half of his first term, he uneasily cast about for direction. He had tried big government with the health care plan and failed. Democrats were still being cast as big taxers and spenders, poster children for the governmental colossus that Republicans were determined to beat into submission. Clinton "basically vowed," according to his former deputy chief of staff, "that he was never going to get caught in that big-government, big-this, big-that trap again."

Now, paradoxically, Clinton had something more valuable in American politics than money or message. He had decisive, clear-cut opponents facing him not in the electoral arena, but in the vast and complex theater of governing. With his eye always on reelection, Clinton began to evaluate the possibilities for turning a menacing juggernaut into the force that would propel him to another four-year term.

After he and Rodham Clinton spent the first cold month of the new year intently listening to "personal growth" and "peak performance" coaches at Camp David, the First Lady granted an interview with gossip and feature writers. The supposedly off-the-record session instead found Rodham Clinton being quoted as saying that she had been "naive and dumb" when considering the politics of health care.

It seemed as if nothing could go right in the White House. Henry Foster, President Clinton's nominee for surgeon general, faced withering replays of the controversies surrounding other ill-vetted appointees. One revelation barely reasoned away was that Foster had sterilized women with mental retardation, for "hygienic" reasons.

In early April 1995, Clinton traveled to Dallas for a speech before the American Society of Newspaper Editors. Clinton claimed to have had a "clear mission . . . to grow the middle class, shrink the underclass, and speed up the opportunities for entrepreneurs," during his first two years in office. He emphasized his commitment to education, a strong turn in direction that followed the 1994 elections, and seemed to be offering a conciliatory path for the "second one hundred days." Partisanship would be put aside because "the old labels of liberal and conservative, spender and cutter, even Democrat and Republican, are not what matter most anymore." His approach would be "practical" and "pragmatic." Clinton intended to smooth out the roughness of radicalism, preserve the good, and root out the bad. He understood his job for "the next one hundred days and for all the days I serve as President."

As the President began to break free of his cocoon of doubt and hesitation, the First Lady displayed signs of a new direction as well. The day before Clinton's Dallas speech the *New York Times* had carried the front-page headline: "Hillary Clinton, a Traditional First Lady Now." Hillary Rodham Clinton, and first daughter Chelsea, had taken a spectacular trip to South Asia. Visiting India, Pakistan, Bangladesh, Nepal, and Sri Lanka, they were treated to all the exotic flavor and fabulous photographic opportunities that the romantic journey could offer, including a trip to the Taj Mahal.

Just prior to leaving for the trip Rodham Clinton had held her first live televised interview since the November election. Her attention, she declared, had turned to a policy haven from the past, women and children. In March, the First Lady made speeches to United Nations conferences on social and women's issues and wrote about the need to put more money toward education and children. But was she the policy powerhouse many considered her to be just twenty months earlier?

Eleanor Roosevelt, of course, had cared deeply about many liberal causes, and had pressed for them with FDR throughout their political life. According to biographer Blanche Wiesen Cook, even as governor of New York FDR was "only occasionally willing to include in his program and actually fight for" many of the liberal positions taken by Eleanor Roosevelt. For her part, Eleanor Roosevelt considered it "impossible for husband and wife both to have political careers." More than sixty years later Hillary Rodham Clinton seemed to be proving this harsh rule. She had stepped too close to the flames of political fires with her leadership on health care.

Still, she invoked the spirit of Eleanor Roosevelt when she spoke at a United Nations conference. Like the woman she so admired, Hillary Rodham Clinton implored the UN to "play a leadership role . . . [for] women, as they raise their children, manage their households, or work at their jobs."

Acting as an icon was one thing. Acting like a leader was another, and Hillary Rodham Clinton would forswear any claim to the latter. The White House policy staff had been roiled by a debate between fiscal conservatives and those pushing for more government investment in social policy. Asked at her live interview if she had opposed aides in the White House calling for deeper deficit reduction at the expense of the President's proposed tax deductions for education and tax credits for families with children, Rodham Clinton demurred, "I was not involved in most of the work that was done on the budget." The wording sounded like a mild dodge. What part of the work had involved the First Lady? And how much influence did her more liberal views toward social spending have on the President? In the first spring of divided government the White House carefully avoided any answers.

By May, the First Lady had a "mammogram campaign" and was speaking out strongly on behalf of veterans suffering from Gulf War syndrome. Tying the two together, she enjoyed using the line, "If we can send missiles down chimneys from thousands of miles away, we ought to be able to do a better job of detecting lumps in women's breasts." Taking a direct shot at Republicans, and the Speaker's dismissive linkage of cultural elites with the arts,

Rodham Clinton devoted a June opinion editorial to saving the National Endowment for the Arts (NEA). The NEA had helped "transform whole communities by bringing the arts and artists to millions who otherwise might never have had the opportunity to explore firsthand our shared artistic heritage." She grounded her argument in the benefits to children.

Was Rodham Clinton sticking close to the safe issues? Going for the easy victories and winning photo ops, as many critics disdainfully proclaimed? In front of a safe audience of unionized service employees she argued a bit more forcefully that the reaction to the President in November was because of his actions in trying to change twelve years of Reagan-Bush economic policies, and the inability of the administration to get its message heard. "But we must," she said with a hint of anger, "let our views be known."

Still, Rodham Clinton's public persona had turned decidedly noncontroversial. The contrast to her tenure as health care impresario was stark, and her explanations reflected an underlying ambivalence: "I can't be worried about what people say . . . I do what I'm interested in doing." To some she sounded "a bit weary, if resigned, about the ongoing analysis of her motives."

Perhaps Rodham Clinton felt freer to step forward again because she and the President had once again enlisted the help of a man who had gotten them out of the mire before. Dick Morris made many White House staffers uncomfortable, if not outraged. But the President and his wife appeared to treat Morris like a guide in the wilderness, and true to form he set them on a path of his own making.

It had started after the November election with Morris's help on the President's first postdebacle speech. Morris dreamed up "triangulation," the three-pointed strategy of placing "the orthodox views of the two parties at each end of the base and his views at the apex." Triangulation created "a way to change, not abandon, the Democratic party. . . . A president can step out ahead of his party and articulate a new position."

Clinton's first effort to triangulate followed Morris's formula of blending the best views of the party but also transcending "them to constitute a third force in the debate." The idea of a middle-class tax cut rested on the triangle base of the traditional Democratic party fear of cutting taxes, because its effect would be to shrink the already thin resources for social programs, and the Republican party support for tax cuts, but which always aimed to favor the wealthiest Americans. Clinton's third way focused on class divisions and helping those who were trying to help themselves.

According to Morris, the decisive turning point in Clinton's move to the center was an April 5 strategy meeting in which Panetta on one side and Morris on the other argued their respective positions. Clinton and Gore listened as Panetta contended that Clinton should stick close to party leaders, make April education month, and keep betting on the boomerang of Republican extremism. Morris argued for a "triangulated third way." The President turned to Gore for his opinion. Gore was for coming out of the "shadows" and "articulating what we will accept and what we will not in a clear and independent way." The President agreed, much to Panetta's chagrin, and the battle went on. The President scheduled his coming-out address for the same hundred-day anniversary on which Gingrich had planned his own speech and celebration.

In one of the ugly ironies of politics, an unspeakable tragedy gave the President his first chance to be presidential after months of feeling, by his own public admission, irrelevant. The date was April 19, the anniversary of a deadly federal raid on an enclave of antigovernment militants in Waco, Texas. A government building in Oklahoma City, Oklahoma, housing employees of several federal agencies, and a day-care center to accommodate workers, crumbled under the impact of a car bomb. Blame quickly moved toward foreign terrorists, but as the victims were slowly pulled out from under tons of debris, Americans were shocked to learn that the Oklahoma City bombing was as homegrown as the surrounding fields of wheat.

All the heartfelt sympathy of a nation flowed through the President's words and deeds. If he was anything, Bill Clinton was the great comforter. He carefully avoided politicizing his reaction. Together with Hillary he reached out to survivors and victims' families. By the end of May his average favorability rating had inched up to 51 percent.

To members of his own party Clinton's triangulation strategy simply meant "an alarming tendency to abandon party principles in the service of political expediency." Stuck in a pattern of two steps forward, one back, Clinton appeared before an audience of wealthy business leaders in Texas in October to blame Congress for making him raise their taxes too much. Stunned Democrats in Washington complained bitterly of the President's inconstancy. By December, Clinton seemed less the apex of Morris's geometric construct than a foot soldier in the Republican guard. Within less than twelve months he had gone from accepting deficits to a ten-year balanced-budget plan, to a seven-year plan that mimicked the proposal put forward by Republican leaders.

But the President now accomplished two remarkable political feats, nearly simultaneously. He moved steadily further toward a conservative view of deficit reduction and budget balancing, but he had shown uncharacteristic resolve in standing up to the trimming and cutting of social programs. The latter brought him closer to his own party and its leaders, while the former broke the Democratic mold. Was this an example of centrism, a visionary new approach to governing outside conventional wisdom, or a demonstration of trying to be all things to all concerned? More fundamentally, was Clinton leading or following as he struggled to raise his public standing with the presidential election year approaching?

With a Morris-orchestrated media blitz in targeted Republican congressional districts, the Democrats attacked Republican stinginess by denouncing the GOP assault on Medicare, Medicaid, education, and the environment. The Medicare issue became, in the words of Gingrich, "a great public relations opportunity for Bill Clinton." Seniors were worried, and middle-class voters didn't like the Republican proposals to cut back student loan programs and loosen environmental controls. By the autumn of 1995, as Clinton's attack on the GOP mounted, the Republicans unwittingly called their own bluff by shutting down the federal government.

Constitutionally, technically, as a matter of record the executive and legislative branches shared responsibility for the shutdown. Congress sent the President bills to sign for funding various federal departments, and Clinton began piling up the very stack of vetoes he had vowed at the beginning of the year to avoid. But as national parks closed and federal workers went on furlough, public opinion mounted on the side of the Democrats. The President grew more resolute. From the Roosevelt Room of the White House, in late October he declared, "Hear this, before or after a veto, I am not prepared to discuss the destruction of Medicare and Medicaid, the gutting of our commitment to education, the ravaging of our environment, or raising taxes on working people."

The capital city erupted in a swirl of meetings, rumors, and uncertainty. A continuing resolution got the government going again, only to see another shutdown just as Christmas approached. Now government workers were telling tales of missed mortgage payments and no toys under the tree, and the grinch-stole-Christmas stories became irresistible fodder for the media. But Clinton had his foil: "a very fat punching bag in the person of Newt Gingrich," noted Senator Bill Bradley. Fallout rained on Republicans, who had their seven-year balanced budget at a price they had never expected to pay.

In his remarkably candid account of his first year as Speaker, Gingrich admitted that the Republicans underestimated Clinton, believing him to be a "weak President who would ultimately feel required to sign an agreement with us for a balanced budget with tax cuts," and failing to recognize how advantageous the Medicare media campaign would be. The damage to Republicans throughout the country gave some heart to congressional Democrats, still adjusting to the role of minority. Maybe there existed a chance to keep the presidency after all, perhaps even win back the House or Senate.

But Democrats became divided too. By 1996, the President's party was glimpsing the self-protective nature of Bill Clinton's political leadership. The President focused with great intensity on his own campaign, as he gathered all the resources possible for his own political survival.

Democrats were "dropping out like flies." In early October 1995, the *New York Times* carried a front-page story, "Democrats Fleeing to GOP

Remake Political Landscape." A graphic map of the United States dramatized the flight. From Texas to North Carolina, straight across the South,
Democratic members of Congress and state legislators had made dramatic
shifts to the GOP. From Clinton's election in1992 through October 1995,
137 Democratic officeholders nationwide had left their party. It was "probably the greatest one-way exodus we've ever seen," according to one
Republican.

Was this further evidence of realignment? The defectors claimed they
found less and less room for their conservative viewpoint in the Democratic
party. Analyst Charles E. Cook Jr. summed it up: Democrats were "a party
under siege."

And what of the leader of the party? How had the President, an acknowledged master of the political game, allowed his own party to fall into such
disarray? Bill Clinton proclaimed himself a proud, lifelong Democrat. Party
loyalty coursed through his blood, or so it seemed as he retold stories of his
family's fealty to the party of Franklin Roosevelt. But for Clinton, political
expediency had always been more compelling than party loyalty or tradition. In the go-it-alone politics of the 1990s, the President was his own political entrepreneur. So it happened that when Dick Morris commanded a
king's ransom for television advertising in 1995, few thoughts of the consequences for congressional challengers and incumbents crossed the strategists' minds. Money drained out of donors and into the hands of consultants
for a media blitz that left the President well positioned and reborn as 1996
began.

If the President treated his party cohorts as if they were an unfamiliar
band of little consequence, his actions had some rational base. In a way, Clinton had formed his own party of one. Perhaps he could call it the "centrist"
party or the "triangularist" party. He stood as the one adherent, proselytizer,
and intellectual force. Even the DLC types were somewhat outside the
main party dogma that Clinton seemed to make up as he went along. Democrats for their part put forward few proposals to counter either Republicans
or the President. If Clinton's programmatic meandering left many in the public confused, the Democrats just seemed absent from the debate.

Clinton had demonstrated a leadership resiliency that defied labels and conventional wisdom. In January 1995 he was pictured as a sure loser for a second term, an early lame duck. His peculiar combination of left-right leadership
was now seen as inadequate against a disciplined GOP Congress.

CHAPTER NINE

Welfare and Illfare

For the fifth time as President, Bill Clinton enjoyed the labors of generations of White House gardeners. It was spring 1997. From his living room
window in the White House residence, Clinton could see that the north
lawn and, beyond, Lafayette Square were small forests of the palest greens.
A new planting of tulips graced the square's spring beds, set off by wrought-
iron fences and crisscrossing walkways.

From the Oval Office looking south, the magnificent formal grounds
began their season-long procession of color and form. Washington's glorious
spring would move the most jaded and callous leader, and Bill Clinton was
neither. He seemed delighted by new experiences, by letters from admiring
citizens and by pleasures as prosaic as a Big Mac. Early in his presidency he
admitted to being "humbled to find out how hard it is sometimes to translate
convictions into policy and into people's lives," but found it "exhilarating to
have the opportunity and the obligation to try every day."

In the first year of his second term he was resolutely optimistic. Deputy
Chief of Staff Harold Ickes Jr. said the President was one of the most optimistic people he had ever known. Clinton was still questing for good works,
still affectingly empathetic. Spring was the time of hope and change. In
1997, Clinton believed he would achieve a fair measure of both.

In one area few would question Clinton's claim of having made change.
The previous summer Clinton had signed the most sweeping transformation of New Deal policy since Franklin Roosevelt's famous pledge of change
to himself and his nation. Clinton's own bill to reform welfare had died a
silent death two years before. Now, after eighteen months of congressional
squabbling and two presidential vetoes, Clinton had signed a bill in August
1996, drawn largely from the House Republicans' manifesto, the Contract
with America.

The change was undeniable and inexorable. The federal guarantee of
welfare help to needy mothers and children was ended. After six decades
and for the first time in U.S. history, a major federal entitlement program
was transformed into block grants to the states. Food stamps and supplemental security income were denied to legal immigrants. Food stamp

spending overall was reduced by 13 percent over five years. Cash assistance for the poor who were aged, blind, and disabled was cut by 12 percent. Within two years of receiving aid, adults on welfare had to find work, and no federal dollars would go to anyone receiving welfare for more than a total of five years.

Clinton had signed on to a change of enormous institutional, personal, and political importance. But was it the kind of change he had envisioned in his many musings on the accomplishments of presidents? How would this reform be measured? Who would be hurt, who helped?

These were the questions Clinton pondered as he struggled with dissension among his top advisers prior to signing the legislation. Rumors spread that his liberal, well-respected secretary of Health and Human Services, Donna Shalala, would resign over the bill. Clinton's political advisers, particularly the ever-calculating Dick Morris, were urging the President to sign. Substance struggled with perception as Clinton considered the stark risks of shredding the worn but intact safety net of welfare entitlements.

Poverty and its solutions were an intractable problem for every leader in the world. In the wealthiest nation on earth Clinton had often witnessed the devastation of those submerged in economic quicksand. The unskilled, the uneducated, the second and third generations of the poor, were desperately hard to bring into permanent economic stability. But Clinton's natural empathy and honest compassion were hard-pressed by the demands of a conservative opposition Congress and an electorate divided and on edge over work and wealth.

As he prepared to announce his decision to sign the reform bill, Clinton's head echoed with the vitriol of his friends and the attacks of his enemies. Republican conference chairman John Kasich took credit for convincing the President that welfare reform was "a bill that America wants and America needs." Children's Defense Fund president Marian Wright Edelman, long-time friend of both Clintons, angrily prophesied that the bill would "leave a moral blot on his presidency and on our nation."

The untenable status quo of the welfare state drove the President, for reasons of politics, promises, and pressure, to a hostile crossroad. Vetoing welfare reform for the third time could kindle his presidential rival's smoldering fire and cost his party a chance to regain the majority in Congress. Signing the bill meant turning his back on dear friends, political compatriots, and his own conscience. Yet the box he had built for himself on reforming welfare rested solidly on the slogan "opportunity and responsibility." Cleverly, and with a hint of irony, Republicans titled their welfare reform bill the Personal Responsibility and Work Opportunity Act.

In the end, Clinton's announcement on welfare reflected his heavy heart. Even before signing the bill he admitted parts of it were "wrong" and there were "serious flaws." He talked of coming "a long way" in the welfare debate, of fifteen years of work on the issue as governor and president. It was a weary, backhanded announcement tinged with an unmistakable sense of resignation. "Today, we have a historic opportunity to make welfare what it was meant to be: a second chance, not a way of life. . . . I will sign this bill, first and foremost, because the current system is broken."

A FEARSOME ASSUMPTION

The President and the First Lady often measured achievement by the conditions of children. The First Lady had published a well-received book, *It Takes a Village*, speaking from her heart on children's issues. But as welfare reform entered its first full year of implementation, the despair promised by opponents of the reform effort was starkly evident. Reality belied good words and intentions by the White House.

During heated public debate over the bill, the head of the National Urban League, Hugh Price, asserted that "Washington has decided to end the War on Poverty and begin a war on children." Only blocks from the White House, in the spring of 1997, that war was being fought. An ambulance rushed three-year old Tyrone Temoney to the hospital from a day-care center in the District of Columbia. The child had been found in a laundry room lying dazed in a pool of Pine Sol. As part of the President's welfare reform bill, Tyrone's mother received a certified day-care subsidy to enable her to work. But child-care choices for the poor were limited at best, perilous at worst. The day-care center where Tyrone was injured was the only one with space available when a job came through for his mother. After the incident Michelle Temoney returned to welfare rather than take any more chances with her child.

The President's empathy for poor parents was noted by the *Washington Post*: "You cannot ask somebody on welfare to go to work if they're going to neglect their children in doing it." But the *Post* observed, day-care "deficiencies cloud the . . . forecast for welfare reform."

The forecast for children affected by the reform bill was disastrous. Senator Edward Kennedy, who voted against the bill, described its provisions as "legislative child abuse." The President protested to the contrary, but children's advocates were adamant that his proposal was devastating to the young. Representative Charles Rangel, representing a Manhattan district hard hit by the welfare cuts, openly denounced Clinton: "My President will boldly throw one million into poverty." On the Senate side, the senior senator from New York, Daniel Patrick Moynihan, spoke from the experience of welfare reform fights of years past. As protesters were removed from the Senate gallery for shouting "Shame, shame," Moynihan echoed their anger. The legislation was based on the idea, he said, that "the behavior of certain adults can be changed by making the lives of their children as wretched as possible. This is a fearsome assumption."

Particularly galling were the changes affecting the most helpless of the young. Publicly, the program for low-income children with only one parent in the home was well known as AFDC, or Aid to Families with Dependent Children. AFDC is welfare, but other benefits unrelated to AFDC were reduced or eliminated by the reform legislation as well. Peter Edelman, the Clinton-appointed assistant secretary at the Department of Health and Human Services, saw many of the bill's provisions as "just mean, with no good policy justification . . . and benefit reductions unrelated to welfare." Edelman resigned over the President's acceptance of a bill Edelman saw not as reform, but as cuts to "programs for the poor other than welfare," many of them affecting working families.

One such program, less well known than AFDC, but of nearly equal size in the federal budget, was assistance for children with disabilities who live in one- or two-parent households. Known as Supplemental Security Income, the program had grown threefold in the 1990s thanks to vigorous advocacy, a favorable Supreme Court ruling, and administrative decisions. By the middle of the 1990s the program cost $5 billion a year.

Critics alleged abuse of the system. Republicans in Congress, joined by a few Democrats, called for a major reordering of rules for eligibility. Children who may have been needy, but who were not truly eligible as disabled, had to be stopped from "gaming" the system. An issue of such emotional power, perfectly suited to the rhetorical heft legislators relish, was not destined for sharp congressional line-drawing. A bipartisan group of senators, neatly sidestepping more draconian House proposals, produced language open to a broad regulatory range.

Inexplicably, Clinton's regulators chose standards that resulted in nearly two-thirds of the 260,000 cases in dispute being dropped from the rolls. Tens of thousands of children who would have been eligible for disability had they been adults lost their benefits. Multiply impaired children were disqualified because no single disability met the new criteria.

People like Vanessa Cooke, whose nine-year-old daughter suffered from brittle diabetes, called the disability cuts "a nightmare." Cooke was drawing her daughter's blood and giving her injections at least seven times each day. She echoed the despair of many parents caught in an unforeseen change, saying, "I can't just jump up and get a job. The problem is being able to stay for eight hours a day. . . . When I say, 'I have to leave, my daughter's sick,' what's the chances of them keeping me?" A year after the welfare reform law was passed, Cooke was told her daughter no longer qualified for disability.

How had Clinton, who included care for children in every address on welfare reform, let his reform lead to such misery for the weakest of the weak? In late summer of 1997, no response could be heard from the White

House amid the crowing over shrinking welfare rolls. Indeed, one year after the reforms were passed, more than one million people had left the system. Most were skilled and easily placed in jobs in a strong economy. States had not, as predicted, reduced spending levels precipitously and were trying to provide support to get people working. And Clinton had succeeded in restoring some of the harsher cuts from the 1996 bill. Supplemental security income for about half a million elderly and disabled legal immigrants was restored. But few leaders in Washington agreed with the President when he declared that "the [welfare] debate is over." The ban on food stamps to legal immigrants was just taking effect. The foreign-born—some disabled, some refugees—found themselves without money to buy food for their children.

Reductions in supplemental security income and food stamps were dire setbacks for many people under the new law. Other changes were more obvious and immediate. Poor parents who still received AFDC faced hard choices between work and care for their children. In addition, child-nutrition programs were reduced by nearly $3 billion over six years. Marian Wright Edelman carried on her crusade against the reform with the credibility of her Children's Defense Fund as backdrop. Her rift with the Clintons was still deep one year after passage of the bill, as states began to implement the new law.

For a President who avowed parenting was a more important job than his own, criticism over welfare was an embarrassing attack on his leadership. He had always hoped to do good. Now, the most far-reaching change of his administration badly threatened those he had seemed most intent upon protecting.

Nevertheless, one year after passage of the bill, Clinton was able to stand before an audience of job trainees and business leaders and announce, "We now know that welfare reform works." Clinton pointed to welfare rolls reduced by 1.45 million. The total number of welfare recipients in the country was down to 10.7 million. At no time in the country's history had people moved off welfare as steadily and precipitously.

The President's message was met with more skepticism than relief, however, even from his own cabinet. Donna Shalala said "the real test" was ahead. A study by the White House Council of Economic Advisers showed that the strong economy accounted for about 40 percent of the decline, with another 31 percent attributable to states getting federal permission to implement policy changes. Shalala understood it was easier to find people a job than to keep them there. Cautiously she said, "Ask me two or three years from now where people are."

In Clinton's own state of Arkansas, the governor's welfare-reform czar was surprised by a higher drop in welfare than anticipated. "The people with skills found jobs quickly, and a certain number of the people who had been getting assistance may have been just gaming the system . . . [and] just decided to stop getting their checks." Even Arkansas was enjoying the general economic well-being blanketing the country.

States were so flush with cash they were delightedly debating tax rebates and buildups of capital funds. But if the economic engine slowed, who, welfare advocates asked, would be thrown off the train? Without federal protection, many feared it would be those least skilled and most in need.

Clinton had ended a well-hated welfare system, but he ignited a debate that raised fundamental questions of rights, morality, responsibility, and justice. This may have been the inevitable result of an avowed social liberal adopting a conservative plan. With welfare Clinton compromised both policy and principle. He produced change for which few in his own party felt conviction. The welfareless future looked fragile and dangerous. The possibility that the bill would ultimately lead to more pain than renewal left some wondering how the President, after vetoing two previous Republican bills, had succumbed to this harsh reform. The explanation lay in nearly two decades of struggle for Bill Clinton with one of the most intractable issues for any nation.

A BROKEN SYSTEM

Bill Clinton knew about struggles of work and family. His was no silver-spoon childhood. Often and with repeated eloquence Clinton had laced his campaign speeches with stories of his mother. Widowed before her first son was born, Virginia Cassidy Blythe worked hard to stay ahead of dependency on family or government. Two-year-old Bill lived with his grandparents in Arkansas while his mother traveled to New Orleans to study nursing. Over the next two years, her leave-takings were difficult disruptions in the life of her small son and herself.

Virginia's father owned a grocery store on the edge of the black neighborhood in Hope, which had its share of the poor in an already dirt-poor state. In Eldridge Cassidy's grocery store, the next generation growing up in poverty were freely extended credit by the man Clinton called "the kindest person" he ever knew. Twenty-six years later Clinton was elected the youngest governor in the United States in forty years. Carrying the memories of his grandfather's compassion, Clinton surveyed his state. Arkansas ranked among the top ten in the percentage of the population living in poverty. He set out with vigor to bring a backward state forward.

As part of his ambitious first term, Clinton began to build the box that would confine his choices on welfare nearly two decades later. Poverty was a problem Clinton's fertile, complex intellect could devour. He was anxious to find a bold, new solution. The idealistic thirty-two-year-old governor could hardly imagine that as President he would change the spirit, process, and intent of assistance to the poor for generations to come.

Still, Clinton's ignominious defeat for reelection had also left little achievement on the welfare front. But by 1984, Clinton had won back the governor's mansion. More and more his eye was focusing on the national stage. He was anxious for national visibility. One vehicle for that visibility was the National Governors' Association. It was the perfect forum to roll out program ideas around his new-Democrat concepts. "In the aftermath of Mondale's defeat," Clinton biographer David Maraniss wrote, "Clinton began to place his programs into a broader philosophy of opportunity and responsibility, which he saw as a theme that could lead to change without alienating the middle class." Welfare reform perfectly suited the opportunity/responsibility theme. The poor would get workfare, training, and child care in exchange for eventually finding permanent jobs and ending their dependency.

Clinton's immersion in welfare had a long background. In 1986, two months before he became chairman of the National Governors' Association (NGA), Clinton traveled to Memphis, Tennessee, for a hearing held by a House Ways and Means subcommittee. Congress was looking at the persistent and disproportionately large problem of poverty in the South. People on welfare would rather work, Clinton told the committee. "You should have work programs in every state and require welfare recipients to participate." He spoke of the need to keep young people in school, reduce teen pregnancy, and train the unskilled.

Eight months later Clinton was in Washington speaking at a National Press Club luncheon just before the NGA convened its annual meeting. Clinton urged his fellow governors to support a "comprehensive bipartisan welfare reform policy, which represents a considerable departure from the present system," and from what President Reagan had proposed. Clinton wanted to transform the system from a primarily "payments" system to a jobs program. Every welfare recipient, except those with children under three years old, would work. The cost was a steep $2 billion, and he criticized the Reagan administration for an emerging plan that shifted current expenditures to the states to administer.

Clinton, the "education governor," told the press that chairing the governors' group led him to realize that education reform was not enough to make America work. With his usual empathy, Clinton spoke of the "rural heartland" of the country. "I come from a state," he said, "full of broken farmers, idle factory workers, and aching poor people."

Clinton's proposal placed him on one side of the philosophical divide that characterized the history of the welfare system. For its first fifty years, welfare was almost exclusively viewed as a program to provide money for poor people. By the 1980s the goal had shifted to ending dependency by getting poor people self-sufficient and working.

231

Doug Besharov of the American Enterprise Institute described a historical shift in values toward the poor. The welfare system has been viewed as either "a program of social control or social rectitude" for citizens who are morally lacking, or simply a way to help ordinary Americans who need money. The latter was the attitude through the 1960s and 1970s, but before the 1960s welfare workers acted as "moral enforcers" of the system. Clinton reflected the shift back to pre-1960s social control.

In 1988, Congress passed a celebrated welfare law that was to bring revolutionary change to the system. The Family Support Act was, according to Senator Daniel Patrick Moynihan, a proponent, a new social contract that emphasized mutual obligations between government and the poor. The law required every state to run an education, training, or work program for parents on welfare and provided up to $1 billion in federal matching money. It was meant to encourage state experimentation with moving welfare recipients into jobs. The law was a compromise for Democrats, who gave in on work requirements in exchange for Republicans agreeing to federal funding for job training, placement activities, child care, and health coverage.

Governor Clinton had been actively involved in the debates that led to the Family Support Act. The bill would form the basis for his own federal welfare reform attempt in 1994. In Arkansas he had started Project Success. The program offered schooling, job training, and work experience for those on welfare.

Alas, as a test of Clinton's welfare philosophy, Project Success had poor results. Between 1989 and 1992, six thousand people came off the welfare rolls in Arkansas, but many returned. Caseloads grew at the rate of other states, with the recession adding to the tight job market for welfare mothers. The governor was accused of living up to his growing reputation for having great ideas but not devoting the time or administrative direction to carrying them out. According to a local citizen activist, Brownie Ledbetter, "he gathered a bunch of people together and said, 'Go do it,' and then disappeared." Another problem was political. Rather than targeting limited resources, Clinton decided to give something to all seventy-five counties in Arkansas. He did not want anyone feeling left out.

Project Success was the beginning of a decade where Clinton would approach welfare by mixing politics and program. Clinton sincerely cared about the poor, and he sincerely cared about holding public office. For a time he had been the most visible governor in the country, heading the bipartisan organization of his fellow state leaders. He had traveled to Washington to argue for a new, reciprocal approach to ending poverty, yet Clinton spoke with conviction about the plight of the poor, and in the late eighties his proposals appeared innovative. After twelve years with Clinton as their governor, however, Arkansans' economic woes were little changed. Poverty's staying power as a social problem followed Clinton to the White

House. Defying remedy, it haunted him throughout his first presidential term.

LEAVENED BY THE HISTORICAL MOMENT

As the race for president in 1996 got under way, certain issues stood out like giant billboards on the road to the presidency. "Ending welfare as we know it" was a rallying cry from the earliest days of Clinton's first presidential campaign. Clinton still carried his gubernatorial notions about welfare. Fundamental restructuring meant giving states more control, devolving federal authority for welfare dollars. To Clinton, this approach would lead to local programs to end welfare dependency. With the large hand of the federal government out of state poverty efforts, welfare had to change. Governors would see that, for innovation and initiative were supposed to be at the state level. These were articles of faith for a five-term governor who had paid close attention to his colleagues around the country.

Clinton trusted governors, trusted state control. Given the chance, he believed, the states would solve the most intractable problem in the life of the nation. The current system of welfare would be ended in favor of a locally grown hybrid in which government gave, not to maintain the status quo, but to receive real change for the poor.

Sloganeering to end welfare was also part of a deft political strategy. Part of the New Democrat platform Clinton embraced, welfare reform was both an olive branch and a powerful symbol of Clinton's "third way." Rather than a real attempt to alleviate poverty, however, Clinton used welfare, in the words of two prominent antipoverty activists, "as an opportunity to gain support by inciting popular indignation at welfare."

Less affluent whites, especially white males in the South, felt betrayed by both liberals and the Democratic party. The poor, particularly poor black Americans, were the central focus of reform throughout the 1960s and 1970s. Joe Duffey, who knew Clinton as a young campaign worker in Duffey's 1970 race for the U.S. Senate in Connecticut, understood that "most liberals and reformers have acted as if there were only two major problems in America, race and poverty. Many of our policies have been formulated as if there were only two groups—the affluent and the welfare poor. But somewhere between affluence and grinding poverty stand the majority of American families."

This well of resentment was particularly deep in the South. Also, in that region the demonization of the First Lady seemed most intense. The intersection of problems around income inequality, race relations, and poverty turned Americans against one another in a rapidly changing, complex economy. In an interview midway through the first term, Hillary Rodham Clinton said, "People are not really often reacting to me so much as they are reacting to their own lives and the transitions they are going through." A real estate agent in Florida gave voice to the First Lady's point: "I think his wife is running the White House. . . . I think he's forgotten that there aren't just black people in the world, that there are also white people. The silent majority has no say in what's going on anymore. It's just the noisy minorities." With welfare reform Clinton hoped to make peace with middle-class white voters.

Clinton had also made a promise repeated so often it sounded like a mantra. Aides referred to the "end welfare as we know it" line with the acronym EWAWKI, because Clinton said it so often. Not only a promise grown from his centrist roots in the Democratic Leadership Council, Clinton's promise to end welfare resonated among some of his closest policy advisers and in the country at large. Poll numbers regarding welfare showed historic distaste for public assistance in a country rooted in a culture of personal independence and individualism.

The year AFDC was created in the Social Security Act, the Gallup organization included the first welfare question in their polling history. In 1935, 60 percent of Americans agreed that the government was spending too much for "relief" or government work projects. Only 31 percent thought the amount spent was about right. By the 1950s, antipathy to handouts had lessened for very targeted assistance, such as help for unmarried mothers. Yet, in the 1990s, Americans continued to stand in sad contrast to citizens of Germany, France, England, and Spain, where the majority believed it is government's responsibility to take care of the very poor who cannot take care of themselves.

Clinton's promise was propelled by more than two hundred years of American leaders' struggles with poverty and reflected controversy over welfare programs that dated back to the English poor laws in the fourteenth century. In the 1760s, James Madison wrote that he had "nothing to brag of as to the state and liberty of my country. Poverty and luxury prevail among all sorts." In the early nineteenth century, more than one-third of the U.S. population was destitute. Cholera and typhoid epidemics in overcrowded cities brought death to the poor in 1832, 1837, and 1842, even as the wealthy fled. By the late nineteenth century, "the same government that had not a dollar for the indigent [poverty being a matter best left to private charity] gave 21 million acres of land and $51 million in government bonds to the few railroad financiers." By the late 1920s a study showed that almost 60 percent of U.S. families did not receive enough income for basic necessities. And Franklin Delano Roosevelt's ambivalence about relief was evident even as he wove in the 1930s the safety net that would take sixty years to rend. Worrying about the effects of government assistance given too freely, he said, "Continued dependence upon relief induces a spiritual and moral disintegration fundamentally destructive to the national fiber."

Clinton was in good company as he struggled with a promise propelled by politics and national sentiment. As his 1996 reelection campaign accelerated, Clinton felt more pressure to fulfill his explicit guarantee on welfare. Memories were fresh of George Bush and his fateful reversal on taxes after the "read my lips" pledge. Having vetoed two previous Republican welfare bills, could Clinton risk a third veto just months before the election? Could this bill, admittedly of Republican origin, be altered enough to tolerate, enough to try?

The President's advisers were again divided between campaign types and policy stalwarts. The welfare bill had noxious elements. It was unfair in its treatment of legal immigrants, harsh to children, punitive to parents. This was the view of Cabinet Secretary Shalala and her most senior policy staff, including Mary Jo Bane and Peter Edelman. Chief of Staff Leon Panetta, Deputy Chief of Staff Harold Ickes, and George Stephanopoulos opposed the bill. Chief welfare strategist Bruce Reed, Commerce Secretary Mickey Kantor, and political consultant Dick Morris were on the other side. One administration official, refusing to be identified, said, "War is going on in the White House."

The day before announcing he would sign the bill, Clinton gathered more than a dozen senior aides and cabinet officers for two and a half hours of intense, searching debate. Panetta and Vice President Gore, leaders of the opposing sides, sat quietly as the President questioned the group, which included Treasury Secretary Robert Rubin, Housing Secretary Henry Cisneros, Labor Secretary Robert Reich, and the head of the National Economic Council, Laura D'Andrea Tyson. Maggie Williams, Hillary Rodham Clinton's chief of staff and former chief of staff at the Children's Defense Fund, was uncharacteristically absent. The First Lady, former chair of the Children's Defense Fund board, was at the Olympics.

The Vice President wanted Clinton to sign. Polls showed overwhelming public desire to see welfare changed. Gore wanted no chances taken with the President's reelection. Panetta believed the President could hold out, win the upcoming election, and then push for better legislation. Shalala spoke most forcefully against the measure, although there was a growing sense that the President would sign. Not in attendance was presidential political guru Dick Morris, whose dire prediction that a veto would mean political catastrophe hung like acrid smoke in the room.

Clinton's biggest reservations centered around Republican cuts. His original plan for welfare reform, introduced in 1994, included no spending cuts. Through cost shifting he intended to add about $10 billion for spending on the poor. That original effort, the product of two intensive years of behind-the-scenes policy work in the administration, had four key elements that built on the Family Support Act Clinton had championed years before.

First, making work pay—by expanding the Earned Income Tax Credit

(EITC), ensuring universal health care coverage, and providing help with child-care costs—was an essential element of Clinton's vision for moving people off welfare. At least one part of the plan worked. The EITC was greatly expanded in Clinton's first budget. Health care reform, however, the pivotal structural element for changing welfare, was never enacted. Clinton had made a small move toward making work pay, but it was not nearly enough to entice people off the welfare rolls.

Second, getting people into jobs quickly. "Two years and you work" was the operative phrase for administration policy-makers, even if the jobs had to be subsidized. Third, the policy planners sought to beef up child support enforcement, and fourth, to fight teen pregnancy with innovative new programs. Many of the ideas in the original Clinton bill were being put into effect by states that had applied for waivers from federal rules. These state efforts had the ironic result of promoting the idea that state control of welfare dollars was a positive change. Clinton's grip on a federal solution was noiselessly slipping away. Inadvertently Clinton was also fueling later Republican demands for time-limited benefits.

Clinton's four-point plan went nowhere in 1994. *The New Republic* trumpeted the headline, "They Blew It," saying the policy was right but the timing was wrong. The Democratic Leadership Council (DLC) smirked, having pushed vociferously for welfare reform to precede health care. Indeed, the health care effort so overshadowed welfare reform that one crafter of the welfare policy said, "I doubt most Americans are even aware that we introduced a welfare reform bill."

Meanwhile, Republicans had regrouped from their post-1994 election grandstanding. Clinton and the Democrats had successfully pilloried the Speaker and the Republicans for their talk of bringing back orphanages and putting school lunch programs into block grants. Yet Clinton was silent on other measures in the Republican bill as wrangling roiled the House and Senate. Hill Democrats, welfare advocates, and his policy-makers in and outside the White House waited vainly for Clinton to take the Republicans on. But he was silent on block grants, silent on time limits, both of which were contained in a Senate bill only slightly more moderate than the House version. Just prior to the Senate vote on September 19, 1995, Senate Democrats swarmed to the majority as Clinton signaled his approval. But the version of the bill sent for presidential signature contained provisions on food stamps, disabled children, and foster care that Clinton would not approve. Next, Republicans sent a bill moving Medicaid into block grants as well, combining it with welfare reform. Although he had shown some willingness to consider Medicaid block grants, by the spring of 1996, Clinton was firmly opposed. Another veto was penned, and many thought the issue was permanently deadlocked.

Not yet. Inside the White House, presidential advisers Rahm Emanuel and Bruce Reed were convinced that welfare was a political must for the election year. House Republicans, previously content to embarrass Clinton by forcing vetoes, were becoming concerned over their own fortunes. Bob Dole looked lackluster throughout 1996, and Republicans were worried about the ticket in their own districts. Separating welfare from Medicaid, they finally agreed to a bill with the most draconian sections from the previous fall removed.

Clinton now agonized over a plan that contained $42 billion in welfare cuts, and provisions he had never dreamed of introducing in his initial attempt to fulfill his welfare pledge. People would be forced off the rolls with no health care guarantee. Child-care support and nutrition programs were being cut. Once again, Clinton was caught between principle and pragmatism. Most Americans hated the system. Clinton believed this feeling extended to welfare recipients as well, fueling anger and resentment.

As critics inveighed against Clinton, Jeff Jacoby, conservative columnist for the *Boston Globe,* defended moving away from an old liberal program that was fraught with dire consequences. "Over the past 3½ decades," he wrote, "the percentage of American children on AFDC has rocketed from 3.5 percent to 13 percent. The great majority of black children, more than 70 percent, spend at least part of their childhood on welfare. The rate of births to unmarried teenagers has tripled, from 15 per 1,000 in 1960 to 45 per 1,000 today. The growth of welfare has not ended child poverty, it has fueled it: In 1970, 10.4 million children lived in households with earnings below the poverty line. By 1993, the number was more than 15.7 million. . . . The welfare state hasn't cured poverty; it has incubated it." Maybe welfare change, even painfully questionable change, was better than doing nothing at all.

In the end Clinton opted to do something. He picked up a rock and tossed it into the dark, still waters of the welfare system. He had made a pledge when the Congress was in Democratic hands. Now, after the health care debacle, he had to deal with the harsh reality of a Republican Congress. He believed, said one aide opposed to the bill, that the "stars don't align that often, and we were going to lose the opportunity." George Stephanopoulos insisted that the President was thinking of history, not politics, when he signed the bill. "I think everybody was leavened by the sense of historical moment. Everybody knew how big this was."

The enormity of social change wrought by welfare reform was deeply felt by all sides. Al From, from his perch at the DLC, praised the President for redeeming the most prominent pledge of his 1992 campaign. Congress's leading authority on these matters, Senator Daniel Patrick Moynihan, condemned the Clinton defection from the New Deal standard to the New Democrat's sliding scale. Had Clinton compromised and collaborated for the country's good? Was welfare change for change's sake? Or was it politically motivated out of desperation with the status quo?

Clinton's pledge sounded like conviction. He had a history with poverty issues. He spoke with feeling of raising people to economic independence. Fundamentally changing the seemingly intractable process for combating poverty was part of Clinton's grander scheme of leadership, as it had been for leaders of the past. But he wanted to "revolutionize" the system. Welfare would be "a second chance, not a way of life." The transformation was not liberal or conservative. It was "change"—and this Bill Clinton claimed as his own vision. It was also a doubtful legacy he would come to witness with apprehension.

Having acquiesced with silence at crucial moments in congressional deliberations, the President confused his party and confounded his advisers. He seemed to think like a governor while having to govern as the President. Now his historical fortunes were in the hands of governors and state legislatures, both of which had turned decidedly more Republican during Clinton's terms as President. Welfare promised to be a bold change for the country, but a tenuous legacy for the President who professed to feeling others' pain.

ENTITLEMENT TO TOUGH LOVE

Two years after welfare reform swept out of Washington, D.C., into the states, the reviews of its impact were mixed, although the statistics were not. Huge numbers of people had left the world of welfare checks and entered the world of work. In the healthiest economy in decades, jobs were plentiful, especially at the bottom where most welfare-to-workers were entering the labor pool. The numbers were worth touting and the administration held well-publicized events to do just that. Between January 1994 and September 1997, welfare caseloads decreased by 30 percent. The decrease accelerated each year during that period, with more than two-thirds of the decrease occurring since January 1996.

The statistics seemed to be almost miraculous news. Had the President really ended welfare as Americans had known it? What would the new world of work without handouts look like? Could training and placement, but no net to catch failures, be a viable alternative to a government program that had faltered from its own expansiveness? These were the unanswerable questions that the administration swept behind a curtain of good cheer and credit-taking.

Some officials in the states called welfare reduction a "tough-love program." The real change came from states moving from the idea of entitlement to the imperative of self-sufficiency. And it was in every state's financial interest to get people off the rolls. No longer would welfare recipients sign up to simply receive assistance alone. Job placement was tied to requests for assistance as tightly as states could manage, and sanctions for nonparticipation were strengthened. Those unwilling to participate in the new push toward work were left without benefits or voluntarily came off the rolls.

The President took the occasion of the first anniversary of the new welfare law to crow anew about its success. More single parents were moving into the workforce, the percentage of citizens on welfare was at its lowest point in twenty-nine years. States were spending more for welfare-to-work than in the previous two years, and job training, placement, child care, and job retention were part of the new state focus. Meanwhile, the administration's trusted friend Eli Segal had started a welfare-to-work initiative among corporations. The idea was to encourage the hiring of welfare recipients by businesses across the country.

All of the publicity and self-congratulations failed to mask one critical point. No one knew what was happening to families after they left welfare. How were their children faring? What was their economic stability should there be a downturn, and what if someone became too sick to work? Although those on welfare were now truly shifting into the workforce, the jobs they were taking were the lowest paid and most sensitive to economic slips and slides.

In early 1999, the state of Wisconsin issued a report on the "leavers," those former welfare recipients who had left the system since Wisconsin began one of the first state reform programs. Most leavers had been employed at some point since leaving welfare; a majority worked more than forty hours per week with the typical wage being higher than the minimum wage by $1.50 per hour. A third of the leavers had not worked at all, mostly because they couldn't find work. Welfare caseloads had plunged in Wisconsin at the same time that critics charged that those on welfare were struggling with access to education, training, child care, and the receipt of other federal entitlements.

As the stock market grumbled over disruptions in foreign economies and markets, the months leading toward the spring of 1999 threatened a new turn in the welfare saga. Americans who were feeling secure with the economy were startled to hear the whispering of possible troubles from other shores. Would the good American economy be rocked out of complacency by the turbulence abroad? What then would be the fate for those weaving their way through the new welfare world? But Republicans scoffed at the idea that welfare rolls would be sensitive to changes in the economy. "Changing values and expectations, not a bull market, are moving former welfare recipients to work," Representative Bill Archer, the chair of the House Ways and Means Committee, had declared the previous summer. If Archer was right, the President had found the transformational change he had cast about in so many policy areas attempting to achieve. But changing the lives of the poor with small carrots and large sticks was a transformation filled with irony for Bill Clinton.

CHAPTER TEN

True North

Often in the life of leaders, an early event has transformed them forever. It can temper ambition with purpose and challenge teachings of the past. It holds a mirror up and demands "Who are you?" and "What do you stand for?" For some it was Selma and Birmingham; for others it was looking down a rifle in Vietnam or at Wounded Knee. For Bill Clinton, it was the Little Rock Nine.

In 1957, shortly after the Supreme Court ruled to dismantle segregation in *Brown v. Board of Education,* nine black teenagers walked silently to the door of Central High School in Little Rock. The televised event mesmerized the eleven-year-old Clinton, who attended Ramble Elementary, a segregated school fifty miles away in Hot Springs.

He watched as Governor Orval Faubus dramatically summoned the National Guard to prevent them from entering the school. He watched as President Eisenhower then ordered the Army's 101st Airborne Division to the state capital. He watched as the teenagers were escorted through angry mobs to the front door by soldiers with gleaming bayonets drawn, for all the world to see on the nightly news. "It was Little Rock that made racial equality a driving obsession in my life," he later admitted.

A decade later, in July 1969, Clinton himself, in a little-noted event, would lead a group of seventy-five young people, mostly black, on a march on the Hot Springs whites-only swimming pool. It was unseasonably hot and his hometown had only one swimming pool.

He was twenty-two, back from Oxford, waiting on the draft board. He was oversize with long hair and ragged clothes. He exuded wildly conflicting energy—raw, full, and florid. The times were raw too. "There was a lot of racial tension in the community. And there had been some racial incidents—shots fired into black stores at night and curfews imposed," he recalled.

Young Clinton wrestled with the situation in late-night rap sessions with Glen Mahone, a local activist, and a close group of friends, black and white. They talked about the South's "peculiar institution" and about how little had actually changed since nine black teenagers desegregated Central High

School. They talked about their hero, Martin Luther King Jr., assassinated the spring of the year before. But what could they do?

The answer was just down the hill and below the Boys Club—the only pool in town sparkling and shimmering in the wavy heat of July. Robert Kissire remembered the summer and how in Mississippi they had integrated the public pool. First it was whites-only hour, then the blacks-only hour, then they drained the entire pool of water and filled it up again for whites-only hour.

Actions like this had enraged Clinton and his friends. They marched to the Hot Springs pool, black and white mixed together. "We're here to swim," Clinton, towel in hand, proclaimed as the group's spokesperson. No immediate change resulted. No police. No fire hoses. No barking dogs. They were turned away at the gate and the pool was immediately shut down.

But over the next few weeks Clinton and a handful of the activists began a series of quiet negotiations with city officials and business leaders that soon led to the integration of the facility. It was a telling victory for the future president. And it presaged one of his enduring reactions to conflict— quiet persistence.

DEEP SOUTH

Bill Clinton came of age during a time that historians remember as the civil rights era. Growing up in a segregated Jim Crow South, he was ultimately called upon to confront W. E. B. Du Bois's "problem of the twentieth century": the color line.

One of the words most often used to describe Clinton is *pragmatic*. Some argue that he has no constancy or core—no values or ideals that are not up for trade. But if values can be described as core beliefs arising from the essence of individual character, then deep in his heart Bill Clinton always had a passionate desire for justice and equality, particularly for black Americans. That desire he would not moderate or ignore. It was etched in his soul, his music, his friendships, his marriage, and his early life experiences.

Since his earliest childhood days, he had been committed to equality. "My entire public life has been dominated by three things: economics, education, and race. It is a part of who I am and what I've done," he said. Hillary Rodham Clinton too would note in 1998 that racial justice was her husband's deepest conviction. Harold Ickes, a veteran of the civil rights movement in the South and former White House deputy chief of staff, agreed: "If there is a true north to Bill Clinton, it is race."

Raised by grandparents who ran their color-blind store in the black part of town, Clinton never knew how his grandfather Eldridge Cassidy had come by his strong convictions. Cassidy had only a sixth-grade education from a tiny rural school, but he taught young Clinton by words and example that "we are all equal—with a right to live in dignity." The year Cassidy died was the year Little Rock's Central High School became one of the touchstones of the civil rights movement. Young Clinton's friends remember him arguing that integration was the only moral outcome. The Little Rock Nine changed—and sensitized—him forever.

As a young delegate from Arkansas to Boys Nation, Clinton was one of only three or four southerners who voted for its civil rights plank. President Kennedy cited their courage in that now-famous Rose Garden ceremony, referring approvingly to the boys' statement in the *Washington Post* that morning that "racism was like a cancerous disease."

Like so many young people of his generation, Clinton was deeply moved later that same summer by Martin Luther King Jr. "I was in my living room in Hot Springs," he said later. "I sat and watched on national television the great March on Washington unfold. I remember weeping uncontrollably during King's speech, and I remember thinking when it was over, my country would never be the same and neither would I." He memorized King's "I Have a Dream" speech.

As a college student in Washington, D.C., during the race riots when the city burned in the spring of 1968, he drove to the inner city to help. Still in his twenties, the young Rhodes Scholar organized and took part in mixed-race dialogues and dances and led acts of civil disobedience in his hometown, like that integration of the Hot Springs swimming pool. Later the following year, as a young Yale Law School student, he routinely sat at the "black table" in the school cafeteria, with Bill Coleman, Lani Guinier, and others. He identified with the black students, particularly the southerners, and shared a beach house with Coleman.

As a maverick young attorney general in Arkansas in the mid-1970s, Clinton brought a wave of young attorneys to the state, many of them blacks and women. As governor, he appointed more blacks to state boards and commissions than all the other governors in the state's history combined, and he appointed the first black to the Arkansas Supreme Court. His commitment was not token: he and his wife would send their only child to the predominantly black Horace Mann School in Little Rock.

Longtime Clinton observer and reporter John Brummett credited Clinton's gubernatorial tenure as showing, above all, his "uncanny ability to connect and empathize with all people, especially blacks."

When, on a bright autumn day in October 1991, Clinton stood with his family by his side on the steps of the Old State House and announced his intention to run for the presidency, he mentioned the issue of race once—by acknowledging that southerners had been "divided by race too long."

On the corner outside the statehouse that morning, an aging Orval Faubus, Clinton's predecessor and the Little Rock Nine's protagonist, had assembled a makeshift vendor's booth to sell one of his books. The contrast between the two men and their two eras was as stark as the candidacy of a young southerner, deeply committed to ideals of racial equality, who nevertheless was about to embrace the Southern Strategy.

THE SOUTHERN STRATEGIST

A dangerously polarizing tactic had emerged in the latter half of the twentieth century. First identified by Stan Greenberg in 1985, so-called wedge issues and wedge politics have divided the Democratic party, motivating a large number of working-class whites to vote Republican. But the "racism wedge" as such—exploiting the fault line of race and racism in politics— was not especially new. It operated virulently under slavery, flourished in the populist era, and created problems in FDR's New Deal coalition.

Racial issues have created some of the most effective political wedges, particularly in the South. Manifestations of racism have devolved from slavery to lynching to segregation to code words, but the pervasiveness of its effects have helped to shape one of the most entrenched and notorious of presidential campaign strategies—the Southern Strategy.

Fifty years before Clinton's era, Strom Thurmond, then governor of South Carolina, launched a campaign against incumbent President Truman, first on the Democrats' convention floor in 1948, and later as an independent candidate of the States' Rights Party. Thurmond's "Dixiecrats" coalesced around a number of issues, but perpetuation of racial segregation was the core. Their dander was up over Truman's efforts at equality, notably his move to integrate the armed forces. The Dixiecrats won four states in the '48 general election, all in the Deep South, marking the beginning of the shift in voting patterns among white southerners. For the next thirty years, a series of Republican and independent candidates from George Wallace to David Duke crafted overtly racist campaigns aimed at conservative white southern voters.

Party realignment, after a century of steady Democratic victories, has given Republican presidential candidates a powerful base of support in the South. When Eisenhower won the Oval Office, 85 percent of white southerners were Democrats. By 1998, Republicans held a slight majority among registered voters in the region. Richard Nixon helped usher in this metamorphosis. In an effort to gain the GOP's presidential nomination in 1968, he forged the so-called Southern Strategy to counter the potential loss of right-of-center white southern voters to Alabama's George Wallace.

Sensing the shifts in the South, Nixon made a tactical decision not to spend money on the black vote, there or elsewhere, but to spend considerable time and money reminding voters that the Democratic party was the party of black

Americans. He cleverly aligned himself with southern segregationists of both parties, chiefly Thurmond and Mississippi senators James Eastland and John Stennis. "Here was the birth of the Southern strategy," wrote political journalists Rowland Evans and Robert Novak, "conceived in necessity . . . and gradually taking on the trappings of grand political doctrine."

During his 1968 campaign Nixon appealed to southern whites by calling for a "reinterpretation" with "all deliberate speed" of the *Brown v. Board of Education* mandate to integrate schools. Fending off Nixon, the Wallace forces won forty-six electoral votes and almost 10 million popular votes, nearly all in southern states. Wallace's campaign also brought Ku Klux Klansmen, neo-Nazis, and far-right activists into electoral politics for the first time. In 1972, again deploying the Southern Strategy, Nixon trounced George Wallace with a more nuanced "law and order" message.

In the post-civil-rights era, overt racism went underground, but it was no less pervasive. Politicians mastered the use of racial code words such as Nixon's *law and order,* along with others such as *welfare queens, inner city, at-risk, poverty, crime,* and *quotas.* Even *color-blind* had become a code for assaults on affirmative action.

To black Americans, these subtextual code words and symbols were like oil on fire. Justice Department nominee Lani Guinier suggested that they were loaded with racial innuendo and resentment. In an age of political correctness, sociologist Jerry Himelstein called these phrases "rhetorical winks," in that they communicate the message but allow the speaker to disavow the interpretation. Nobel Prize–winning author Toni Morrison went even further, defining these racial symbols as having no meaning "other than pressing African-Americans to the lowest level of the racial hierarchy."

Jimmy Carter, the only winning Democrat to confront the Southern Strategy before Clinton, was attuned to the coded language of race. Having grown up in a mixed-race environment, he did not race-bait during his presidential campaign. His campaign manifesto, *Why Not the Best?,* included numerous accounts of his personal and political efforts to alleviate racism in Georgia's Jim Crow days. He rounded up southern black leaders, including Martin Luther King Sr., Coretta Scott King, and Andrew Young to visibly support his candidacy.

But Carter did not commit himself during his presidential campaign to alleviating injustices, reasoning that he was positioning himself to do something during his administration. Despite his unfortunate use of the term *ethnic purity* to describe white-ethnic enclaves in neighborhood schools—calculated, some say, to gain the Wallace vote in Texas, Missouri, and Georgia—black voters delivered the margin of victory to the Georgian in 1976 in twelve states. Most white voters that year again came out for the Republicans and Gerry Ford.

Reagan in 1980 extended the Southern Strategy by urging working- and middle-class whites to abandon their black counterparts and align themselves with upper-middle-class whites. Strategists carefully built on a nascent feeling among working-class whites that the real enemies of Democrats were no longer big business and the very rich, but rather big government and the very poor. During the Reagan years, Republicans selectively targeted federal spending on vulnerable programs such as Aid to Families with Dependent Children. In 1984, Reagan won every southern state by a margin of at least 15 percent against Walter Mondale.

The Southern Strategy again showed its perennial staying power when, in the spring of 1988, Lee Atwater, a Strom Thurmond protégé and George Bush's campaign manager, asked campaign researcher Jim Pinkerton to come up with a short list of issues to portray Michael Dukakis as outside the mainstream. Pinkerton came up with five items: Dukakis vetoed a bill supporting the Pledge of Allegiance in public schools; he was a member of the ACLU; Boston Harbor was polluted; he favored gun control. But the fifth item was to become the sharp wedge Atwater needed to portray Dukakis in a damning light: Willie Horton. Black and a murderer, Horton won a weekend furlough from a Massachusetts jail and brutally raped a white woman and beat her fiancé. For campaign purposes, this event was silhouetted against a backdrop of skyrocketing crime rates in the cities. Atwater later claimed that his job was to "convince Americans that Horton was Dukakis's running mate."

The Southern Strategy, now consolidating the "Reagan Democrats," steadily chipped away at the Democratic New Deal coalition by siphoning off crucial white male voters. Over the past thirty years, the Republicans have insistently, if sometimes clandestinely, portrayed the Democrats as a party of undesirables: the poor, foreigners, homosexuals, and blacks. So much so that, according to some scholars, virtually all progressive symbols and themes had been redefined in racial and pejorative terms.

In 1992, Clinton deliberately sidestepped the issues of race, class, and abortion that had divided the Democratic party since 1964. Seeking protective cover, Clinton and his advisers looked for issues that would not split their traditional base and would halt their eroding numbers among white southerners. They knew that in states with the largest black populations they needed only 30 to 35 percent of the white vote to win, because they could count on 90 percent of the black vote. But it was also true that in such states, the white vote was much harder to secure: states with a greater proportion of blacks seemed to produce more hard-core white conservatives. Even Jesse Jackson's share of the white vote in 1988 was greater in states with the fewest African-Americans.

Thus, at the same time as white Democratic voters waned, black voters became crucial in Democratic primaries and general elections. Blacks were consistently more liberal than their white counterparts. Indeed, as political scientist Ronald Walters has documented, the Democratic party would have lost every presidential election from 1968 to the present if only whites had voted.

But the need to hold on to black voters presented a vexing problem to Clinton's centrist strategy: no group in the United States is more consistently liberal than African-Americans. Since the early 1950s, blacks have held mainly progressive views on most issues. Blacks' liberalism is greater than that of any other group in America.

And the leftward movement of the black population has occurred "not only on the issues of central importance to blacks—school integration and increased attention to black problems—but on issues of foreign policy and scope of government as well. Thus, while black voters have become increasing liberal, all other populations except Jews have become increasingly more conservative," noted Walters. The need to address policy concerns of African-Americans pushed the Democrats more leftward and, to some degree, Republicans more rightward.

The Clinton campaign needed to walk a tightrope, holding on to its black base without any concrete promises and at the same time attempting to attract southern voters who had been steadily Republicanized. Thus the white vote in the Deep South became a test of masterful manipulation of subtextual messages. Clinton, the passionate believer in and defender of equality and racial justice, felt forced to adopt a pragmatic stance with respect to race during the campaign. Like Carter, Clinton rounded up the early support of all the moderate black southern politicians—Mike Epsy of Mississippi, John Lewis of Georgia, William J. Jefferson of Louisiana.

Clinton was appalled by Stanley Greenberg's earlier study of Democratic party defectors in Macomb County, Michigan, once a stalwart base of Democratic votes. What united Macomb's residents, suffering from a downturn in the automobile industry, was a "distaste for blacks," Greenberg found. Whites felt that "blacks constitute the explanation for their [whites'] vulnerability and for almost everything that has gone wrong in their lives; not being black is what constitutes middle class; not living with blacks is what makes a neighborhood a decent place to live." Dick Morris, also examining Macomb, concluded that "Democrats were hurt because they were perceived as too close to minorities."

Morris and Greenberg warned of the danger Clinton faced by aligning himself too specifically with blacks. The candidate heeded their advice. Judged from the primaries onward, racial issues were virtually absent from the 1992 campaign discourse. The Clinton/Gore campaign platform in book form, *Putting People First,* detailed thirty-one "crucial issues" in alphabetical order from "Agriculture" to "Women." "Race" failed to make the list. The "Civil Rights" section gave more ink to "sexual preference" and "physical disabilities" than to racism. The only campaign promise articulated under "Civil Rights" was to "oppose racial quotas."

So, as race disappeared from Clinton's campaign agenda, the threat of the Southern Strategy on other issues still had to be contended with forcefully. Clinton's advisers and consultants believed he had to walk a very thin line to demonstrate that he was not soft on welfare or crime. The Clintonites seized upon several events that might "send a message" to southern voters.

During the period in the primaries when his campaign was struck hard with allegations about Gennifer Flowers, Clinton left New Hampshire to fly back to Arkansas to preside over the execution of Rickey Rector, a black brain-injured cop-killer. Having commuted the death sentences of thirty-eight first-degree murderers in his first term as governor, Clinton did not now want to be seen as soft on crime. After winning back the governorship in 1982, he set execution days for twenty-four death-row inmates. "Poor ole Rickey Rector's timing just happened to be real bad," said a defense attorney.

And one wonders how Clinton the idealist must have felt on March 2, the day before three primaries, when Clinton the pragmatist posed for press photographers with Georgia senator Sam Nunn at the Stone Mountain Correctional Facility. It was not lost on some southerners that Stone Mountain, Georgia, is the birthplace of the Ku Klux Klan. In the background stood a formation of mostly black prisoners. "Two white men and forty black prisoners, what's he saying?" asked Jerry Brown. "He's saying, we got 'em under control folks, don't worry." Was golfing at a segregated country club two weeks later a lapse in values or a stealth message under the radar screen to white Americans?

As the campaign heated up, Clinton then deployed a tactic he had deftly used in Arkansas—counterscheduling. "He was a genius at counterscheduling," said longtime Arkansas reporter John Brummett. The tactic involved picking a fight with a friendly audience to send a broader message to people who don't care for the politics of that audience.

Clinton's speech supporting NAFTA to the AFL-CIO convention was a counterscheduling opportunity. More notable was his attack on Sister Souljah in a speech to Jesse Jackson's Rainbow Coalition. Rapper Souljah had been quoted in the *Washington Post* as saying, "If black people kill black people every day, why not have a week and kill white people?" Clinton rebuked Souljah and equated her racism with David Duke's. His message, widely viewed as disrespectful of Jesse Jackson and the Coalition, was of course aimed at the television audience, not the Rainbow Coalition members at the conference. While not acknowledging that the Souljah attack was intentional, James Carville admitted that the "campaign had wanted to bait a prominent African-American." And their timing was not accidental; Clinton's other rare appearances at black events were intentionally scheduled to be too late for the evening news or otherwise subsumed by larger events.

As the campaign rolled to a close, Clinton's approach proved to be effective—at least in securing the White House. He had beaten the Republicans at their own game, and few could plausibly deny it was a tactical and strategic victory. He had zigged and zagged through the subliminal bog of American consciousness and bigotry and had won.

At the end of the election season, Clinton acknowledged that he had run a "foxlike campaign, but he planned to be a lionlike president." In many ways he was forced into positions and strategies that were not his doing. The Democratic party had been edging rightward since early 1977 when Carter made balancing the budget his top priority and social programs, job training, and welfare spending were drastically cut. Now, in 1992, Clinton had to patch together the northern Democrats and the southern Blue Dogs. Now he had to transform his carefully calculated electoral coalition into a governing coalition.

THE INHERITANCE

Not long after Bill Clinton's election and his subsequent default on her nomination to a high-ranking Justice Department post, Lani Guinier published a revealing opinion editorial in the *New York Times*. In it, she forgave the sins of the Southern Strategy by reasoning, "Perhaps election campaigns are not the best opportunity to turn the nation's attention back to the unfinished agenda of race relations."

But she stopped short of letting the President off the hook: "What is missing from public discourse is a vision of the future in which society commits itself to working through, rather than running from, our racial history and racial present. What is missing is leadership."

Leadership. Part of the test of great presidents since at least Abraham Lincoln has been the capacity to exercise bold leadership in confronting America's racial history. At the outset of his administration, the once pragmatic Lincoln was to some degree an apologist for slavery. He spoke of the "physical differences" between the races and opposed social and political equality for whites and blacks. He also opposed black-white intermarriages, black service on juries, black public-office-holding, black citizenship, and black suffrage. He supported colonization of Liberia by freed slaves and at times sought an end to slavery simply to destroy the Confederacy's workforce and boost northern morale and troop strength.

But in the throes of the "fiery conflict" he came to see the great "sin of slavery," and in his second inaugural address he declared that if it were "God's will . . . every drop of blood drawn from the lash shall be paid for another drawn by the sword." First and foremost, he wanted to preserve the Union, but he also sensed that his moral act of ending slavery would in the end mark his presidency. "If my name ever goes into history," he confided to the cabinet members and officials gathered around him as he signed the Emancipation Proclamation, "it will be for this act." Lincoln was later to say that creating a sense of national unity, a unity including the newly freed slaves, was America's "unfinished work."

For a quarter century after the Civil War, some presidents followed Lincoln's example and exercised leadership on the slavery issue, seeking to ease the new citizens' transition to freedom. In his 1881 inaugural address, President Garfield, himself a veteran of the Civil War, envisioned, "Fifty years hence our children will . . . surely bless their fathers and their fathers' God that . . . slavery was overthrown and that both races were made equal before the law." He used his inaugural address to send a tough message to white supremacists that there would be no compromise between slavery and equal citizenship, and that the nation would "permit no permanently disfranchised peasantry."

The abandonment of Reconstruction, however, brought a half century of presidential reticence, as presidents from Rutherford Hayes to FDR either avoided racial issues or indulged in high-sounding shibboleths.

True, Franklin Roosevelt did set up the Fair Employment Practice Committee, but only as a response to a threatened march on Washington by black leaders. And certainly Eleanor Roosevelt served as a back channel and advocate to the President for civil rights. She took her own public moral stands too, resigning from the Daughters of the American Revolution over their denial of the use of Constitution Hall to singer Marian Anderson, writing a *My Day* column about it, and later joining Anderson at her Lincoln Memorial performance. Though American blacks had turned Lincoln's portrait to the wall and flocked to the Democratic party in the 1930s, they were not fully dealt into the New Deal. Roosevelt's deference to powerful southern senators kept him from effective leadership.

It took Roosevelt's successor, Harry Truman, to belatedly bring issues of race to the twentieth century. At the outset, though, Truman's civil rights credentials were viewed with suspicion. During the 1944 campaign, a leading black journal had even accused the Missourian of being a Klan member. He was to prove everyone wrong by his leadership and action in the area of civil rights. Speaking in 1947 at the Lincoln Memorial to the National Association for the Advancement of Colored People (NAACP), Truman early on championed antilynching laws. The first president ever to address the NAACP, he spoke in typically Trumanesque, blunt terms. "When I say all Americans, I mean all Americans. Many of our people still suffer the indignity of insult, the harrowing dread of intimidation, and I regret to say, the threat of physical and mob violence."

Truman was not simply a rhetorical president; he acted. He oversaw efforts to desegregate the army and appointed the first presidential blue-ribbon task force on civil rights. The task force findings so enraged segregationists that thirty-five delegates from the Deep South bolted from the 1948 Democratic presidential convention to form the States' Rights Party.

During the ensuing Eisenhower administration, the Supreme Court struck down segregated schools in *Brown v. Board of Education*, a case submitted in 1952 by Truman's Justice Department. Hardly supporting this carryover from his predecessor, Ike resented the intrusion of the Truman agenda and instructed his attorney general to write a brief that "took no position on segregation, pro or con." Eisenhower had of course used federal troops to force integration in Little Rock's Central High School, but he hardly embraced or advocated better race relations. He took no action in the Montgomery bus boycott in 1955, nor in the University of Alabama desegregation fight, claiming "in some things, I am more of a states' righter." He was silent on the lynching of Emmett Till, the Rodney King of the 1950s.

John F. Kennedy, vowing a fresh approach to discrimination, took on George Wallace in Alabama schools, finding that civil rights "was a moral issue . . . as old as the Scriptures and as clear as the Constitution." Calling upon the moral authority of the presidency, he condemned racism in all its forms and wielded his executive power to dismantle discrimination in voting, the federal civil service, public facilities, private-sector employment, and housing. He introduced to the Congress the most important civil rights legislation in a century. Still, Kennedy benefited from Mohandas Gandhi's style of "leading by following," for much of civil rights reform was accomplished by a strong grassroots movement from outside Washington.

A week before his first presidential election, Bill Clinton was asked to name his presidential heroes. "Lincoln, the Roosevelts, Truman, and Kennedy," he responded. How would he approach the deep chasm of race in this country? Would he feel constrained, as FDR did, by the powerful forces of the status quo? Or would he be transformed, as Lincoln was, by his experience as president and grasp some elusive truth and make the country whole again? Or take to the bully pulpit, as Teddy Roosevelt did, and educate and cajole citizens back to that greatest of American values, equality. Or perhaps he had in mind the example of Truman, who would slowly but sure-footedly heal the brutal practices of the past? Time would tell.

In her book *The Tyranny of the Majority*, Lani Guinier complimented Lyndon Johnson for his legacy of leadership for black Americans. When she pleaded for more leadership from Clinton in healing the racial divide, she might have suggested he turn to Johnson, another southerner, as his exemplar. Although not in Clinton's pantheon of presidential heroes, Johnson did more for black America than any other president since Lincoln. Seizing the moral capital in the wake of the Kennedy assassination and negotiating with King and others for their support, LBJ kept his part of the bargain and pushed forward on the civil rights agenda from the first days of his presidency.

Johnson did not have to wait for the polls or the focus groups. Not long after JFK's death, he met with six major civil rights leaders—Roy Wilkins, Martin Luther King Jr., A. Philip Randolph, Andrew Young, John Lewis, and James Farmer. Johnson wanted not only to talk about getting a civil rights bill through Congress, but also to work with them throughout his term. In March of 1965, putting his political capital at risk and alienating many representatives from the South, he addressed a joint session of Congress and urged members to pass the Voting Rights Act of 1965. Signaling his own identification with civil rights protesters, he ended his speech with words from the most famous refrain from that era—a fiery "and we shall overcome. We shall overcome." He personally championed the ultimately successful 1965 legislation, and later he took on the Jury Selection and Service Act of 1968 and wrote the executive order creating the Equal Employment Opportunity Commission (EEOC). He pushed through the War on Poverty and ultimately his Great Society through sheer force of will, backed by both a Democratic majority in Congress and a strong civil rights movement. His actions had their transactional features, but there was little doubt of their ultimate force. Johnson's efforts were acts of transforming leadership—clear, intended, planned change that would produce measurable results for decades to come.

THE LEGACY

On September 18, 1998, a little noted but still remarkable report was released to the public. For fifty-two years the President's Council of Economic Advisers has delivered its Economic Report to the President. Ordinarily dry and analytical, it is read closely by bond traders, Wall Street analysts, and by scholars trying to decipher the causes of income inequality.

This edition of the report was astonishing because for the first time it included a new chapter assessing the extent of income inequality among racial and ethnic groups. Commissioned to provide reliable data to the President's Initiative on Race, it struck a blow at conservatives, notably Stephan and Abigail Thernstrom. The Thernstroms had insisted in a recent book that contrary to the liberal view, the gap between blacks and whites had closed and the country should be focusing on celebrating its accomplishments with respect to race.

The report documented the rise in black earnings from 1965 to 1975—credited to Johnson's civil rights legislation, and certainly cause for celebration. But in the years since 1975, the income of black families made no substantial increase compared to white families. In 1998, almost one-third of all black Americans lived in poverty, a figure triple the rate of whites. While during the Clinton administration the unemployment rate for blacks reached an all-time low, it still remained twice as high as that for whites. And the racial disparity was evident in every indicator: in education, in infant mortality, in heart disease, and housing. It was a litany as remarkable as it was painful. What had Clinton done about it?

In part, he wielded his power of appointment. Naming nonwhites to prominent administration posts would be one way to visibly demonstrate that African-Americans, Hispanic-Americans, and others were capable of making positive contributions and of leading.

Clinton had hit the ground running in late 1992 and early 1993 on his pledge for a government that "looks like America." One of his first acts as President-elect was to appoint Vernon Jordan, Madeline Kunin, and Warren Christopher to coordinate the White House transition. They in turn set up multiracial cluster teams to conduct interdepartmental reviews of the executive agencies. Clinton insisted that the directors of these cluster teams reflect gender and racial diversity, and he accomplished his aims: there were seven men and three women, including six whites, three blacks, and one Hispanic.

The cabinet selection process was tightly held, however, and no person of color sat in the inner circle of those deciding. Still, five black cabinet secretaries were nominated. Two of these, at Commerce and Agriculture, were first-evers.

Bruce Lindsey, Clinton's longtime friend, took charge of the next round of political appointments and managed to diversify these top positions. In the first six months of the administration, 34 percent of the top appointments went to women, 15 percent to blacks, 8 percent to Hispanics, and 2 percent to Asians. A solid 13 percent of all of Clinton's initial presidential appointments were black. At the beginning of his second term, the commitment to diversity still endured: there were three black cabinet secretaries, and the acting surgeon general, Audrey Manley, was black. Hispanics Federico Peña and Bill Richardson also held prominent posts—Peña at Energy and Richardson as U.S. ambassador to the United Nations.

The first-term appointments to the White House staff, by contrast, were almost exclusively white, especially in the West Wing. Eleven of the sixteen top positions went to white males, although the next level reflected considerable diversity. Harvard Law professor Christopher Edley Jr. noted that within the Office of the National Economic Council, the Domestic Policy Council, the National Security Council, the Office of Management and Budget, the Office of Science and Technology Policy, and the Council on Environmental Quality there were nearly 750 staffers, yet not one of these appointees was an African-American or Hispanic-American, and only one was Asian-American.

Still, all in all, with the notable exception of the White House staff, the administration made good on Clinton's promise of diverse leadership. He appointed more African-Americans, Hispanic-Americans, Asian-Americans, and Native Americans to cabinet positions and other high posts than any of his forty-one predecessors.

Less visible, but significant in its long-term impact, Clinton transformed the federal judiciary by appointing more women and minorities to the federal bench than any other president—and more than the last two presidents combined. Criticized as window dressing, his judicial appointments received from the American Bar Association a higher rating than any other administration's.

Clinton, the president who sought image and symbol, appeared to begin his new administration with a vigorous commitment to including nonwhite Americans, particularly black Americans, symbolically and substantively. Examining his two White House terms, however, his executive and legislative record puzzled civil rights advocates and to some degree contradicted his remarkable appointment record. His presidential performance on race was perplexing from a left-right perspective. A centrist, he spanned the political spectrum with no identifiable philosophical or ideological moorings. Where was true north?

Early on in his White House stint, Clinton raised the minimum wage, a standard test of liberal leanings. He increased tax credits for the "working poor" through the Earned Income Tax Credit Act. Head Start funding, an old liberal stalwart, was to some extent pitched to blacks. But Clinton's crime and welfare reform bills were centrist Democratic Leadership Council ideas lifted from the Republicans and appealed most directly to whites. This back-and-forth string of legislation kept the congressional Black Caucus from solidifying its own legislative agenda. A protracted effort on the part of the administration to woo votes for the welfare-to-work bill yielded only two from the thirty-nine African-American members of Congress.

The congressional schism spilled out into the ring of think tanks and advocacy groups circling the Capitol. The welfare reform bill of Clinton's first term was publicly and sharply criticized by Clinton's close friend Marian Wright Edelman of the Children's Defense Fund, on the grounds that it would "leave poor minority children out in the dust." To many, Clinton's was an appalling act of cowardice. But he took the criticism in stride, commenting that Edelman "was sincere and honest in her position and I'm sincere and honest in mine. And time will see who was right."

But what *exactly* was his position? There was considerable evidence that though personally and empathetically attuned to black Americans, Clinton was more aligned politically with a neoliberal approach to race. Philosophically he supported class-based criteria for social policy rather than race-based ones. Growing up in the South, Clinton knew too many poor white southerners in the Ozarks and elsewhere to buy into the prevailing stereotype that poverty was predominately a black problem.

A class-based approach to inequality too would explain the lack of explicit reference to race or civil rights in his campaign documents. His campaign pronouncements about the "truly disadvantaged" and the "working poor" were a seductive chimera to the civil rights generation, but in truth were indicative of his class-based predisposition. Yes, at times on the campaign trail he was more forthright about his philosophy, as when he told a reporter, "This country has to be healed. We're divided. It's not just white and black and brown—it's middle class and upper class and poor." But the interview was published in a southern newspaper, shortly before Super Tuesday, 1992, and was entirely consistent with his Southern Strategy.

Nor did his class-based approach change during his presidential tenure. Sociologist Nathan Glazer reflected that it was surprising that a fierce national debate over affirmative action not only persisted but intensified during the Clinton years. Yet, Clinton almost certainly opposed the premise of affirmative action, if not the politics of it. Clinton's view had always been color-blind, or as he said, "race-neutral."

The neoliberal approach, however, while having obvious strategic and possibly ideological advantages, did not attend to deep-seated structural racial conflicts in the United States. Many objected to a purely class-based agenda, as it failed to adequately address continued racism, racial hostility, segregation, institutional discrimination, and white privilege.

Perhaps Clinton was ahead of his time and of himself. "Can political will be summoned to pursue a strategy of making skin color less relevant in public life?" importuned scholar and presidential friend William Julius Wilson. Historians of the future may see Clinton as a neoliberal, neo-civil-rights radical, taking up Martin Luther King Jr.'s unfinished work toward an economic justice that transcends race. At the time of his assassination, King "was organizing a multiracial Poor People's Campaign around economic and peace issues—jobs and economic justice at home and peace abroad in Vietnam," noted Jesse Jackson. Clinton's approach to race as President, seen from this perspective, was at least a powerful attempt at the first White House transracial agenda on poverty since the enactment of 1960s civil rights legislation.

But while strong presidential leadership could potentially have created coalitions and bridges across the racial divide, no such coalition—not even Jackson's Rainbow—had ever been sustained in the past. Such a coalition would take an act of transforming leadership on the order of the New Deal. It would take political capital, moral standing, and the political will of Lincoln. Did Clinton have the will? The answer appeared to be no.

The priorities of presidents are reflected in their budgets. To what ends would Bill Clinton allocate the nation's financial resources? To talk about priorities was one thing; to budget for them quite another. Budgets in Clinton's first term included a number of proposals that impacted black Americans, but they existed under the rubric of "urban," "empowerment," and other class-based strategies. Clinton and his team knew full well of research that race-targeted programs were not the best way to gain support from white Americans. They had mastered the "don't ask, don't tell" strategy of racial empowerment.

Not until Clinton's second term did he frame issues in specifically racial terms. His plan on this score included six broad goals, all related to race, and all earning a position in the White House budget: policy action, constructive dialogue, highlighting promising practices, recruiting leaders, establishing an advisory board, and producing a report on race. When a summary of the accomplishments of the plan in each of the six areas was released in November 1998, the silhouette that emerged was one of tinkering rather than transforming.

The policy action successes, for instance, included increases in funding in civil rights enforcement to a multitude of federal agencies, as well as increases in block grants for child care and after-school programs. Some twenty-seven other items, exuberantly itemized as "High Hopes for America's Youth," "Opportunity Areas for Out of School Youth," "Expanded Youthbuild," and "Play-by-the-Rules Home Ownership Initiative," sprinkled money in an array of actions, all destined to deliver incremental assistance.

The money, for the most part, was funneled to enforcement efforts of existing programs. Unlike under LBJ, there were no legislative milestones or executive acts creating entities to address racial disparities or inequities. No Great Societies or Wars on Poverty. No Voting Rights Acts or Equal Employment Opportunity Commissions.

In his second term, Clinton's most publicized efforts at healing the racial divide assumed the form of the President's Initiative on Race, a series of meetings and venues structured around an idea originally proposed by Lani Guinier in her plea to him for "more leadership."

Launched in June of 1997 and described in media accounts as an effort to lead the country in a national conversation about race, the Initiative on Race was initially viewed with suspicion by all sides. Some claimed that all the Initiative members were supporters of affirmative action. A group of prominent conservative activists and scholars countered by announcing their own panel on race relations, chaired by Ward Connerly, architect of California's Proposition 209, an effort to turn back the clock on affirmative action.

Some felt that action and not talk was needed. Others complained that the Initiative focused too much on black-white issues, to the exclusion of Hispanic-Americans' or Asian-Americans' concerns. Still others predicted that the work itself would create divisiveness, for according to Roper polls, the state of race relations was a central concern for African-Americans but not for most whites. Indeed, the effort almost disintegrated into a morass of intergroup and political problems at the outset, but recovered some of its footing under the direction of its chair, historian John Hope Franklin.

In these forums, the President used his platform to paint a picture of the future, attempting to prepare citizens for the demographic and social changes they would encounter in the decades ahead. "I think we ought to be thinking about this not only today," he intoned in late 1997, "but what we're going to look like over the next thirty or forty years. Most Americans have not come to grips with the fact that within fifty years at the outside, there will be no single racial or ethnic group that will be in a majority in the United States."

He was right. Most Americans had not only not come to grips with the future, few knew the facts about the present. Despite decades of studies, reports, and media stories documenting disparities between whites and blacks, a great deal of misinformation persisted. More than four in ten white Americans still believed, incorrectly, that the average African-American was at least as well off as the average white. Forty-five percent believed, also incorrectly, that more poor people in the United States were black than white. And 58 percent of whites believed, again incorrectly, that more recipients of public assistance were black than white.

Perhaps the most important aspect of the President's Initiative on Race was Clinton's own willingness to explore the issue from a "white" point of view. But even this was no epiphany for him. Shortly after the 1992 election, at a secret Camp David retreat of senior staff members, the question came up about the southern, white, male, blue-collar voters who were so problematic in the election. Rodham Clinton was the first to speak, sharply arguing, "Screw them. Let's move on." But Clinton disagreed and prevailed: "Those bubbas, I grew up with them. I understand them. I know what they're going through. We can't win this thing unless the bubbas are respected too."

What was new was the President's willingness to discuss race so often and so publicly. According to Clinton, "Whites were not racist to say that a culture of welfare, illegitimacy, and absentee fathers cannot be broken by social programs unless there is first a more personal responsibility. Nor were they racist to shun neighborhoods where thugs carry guns like Old West desperadoes."

It was a laudable and herculean task, one the President took on vigorously but too late. A race initiative launched in his first term, when he had a Democratic Congress and the goodwill of the country, might have set the stage to mobilize Americans around the issue of racial reconciliation. As it was, in the second term, the nation's conversation about race was barely heard above the fussings of the Republican Congress and the squalling of the Monica S. Lewinsky imbroglio. The President lost the ability and credibility to move his race agenda forward in the media or the grass roots.

If his legislative leadership on race seemed sparse, it was probably because Clinton fundamentally did not see legislation as the best approach to changing deeply held beliefs. Racial problems, he asserted, "demand an individual, not a governmental solution."

In a major speech on affirmative action at the National Archives, the President hit hard with his view that laws do not change society, that "old habits and thinking patterns" are to blame, and that "this is work that has to be done by every single one of you."

But if Clinton had closely examined LBJ's efforts on race, he might have discovered data suggesting that behaviors do create new attitudes, not the reverse. Before Johnson's time, the black poverty rate was an unconscionable 87 percent. Sixty-four percent of black women worked as domestic servants. Yet only 45 percent of whites thought that African-Americans should "have as good a chance as white people to get any kind of job." Less than one-half thought blacks were "as intelligent as white people."

After Johnson's time, in the wake of the Great Society's antipoverty and pro-civil-rights initiatives, 97 percent of whites said they believed blacks should have equal opportunities to get a job and 80 percent of whites believed blacks were of equal intelligence. This seemed a prescription for more presidential action and exhortations, not less.

Since Teddy Roosevelt's time, the rhetorical and symbolic aspects of presidential leadership have gained importance, partly because of the vast expansion of the media and partly because of the failure of bipartisan legislative leadership. The president, Roosevelt said, should be the "steward of the people." Woodrow Wilson extended the rhetorical role by establishing the presidency as the "guiding force of the nation." If race were indeed the country's deepest chasm, then why couldn't Bill Clinton, this son of the South, be such a force, the repairer of the breach?

His background—seeing his grandfather operate a color-blind store, protesting the whites-only swimming pool in Hot Springs, driving through riot-torn Washington, D.C., in the wake of King's assassination—sensitized him to issues of race and enabled him to talk intelligently and emotionally to both blacks and whites. He had lived through, and participated in, some of the greatest struggles of his generation.

Strong leaders are guided by moral and ideological compasses. They know where true north lies and how to find it when the night is dark, the way treacherous, and the enemies plentiful. The great divides of the past called for and were addressed not just by legal and legislative action, but by strong exhortations and appeals to conscience and justice, many emanating from the White House itself. The Johnson era delivered economic and political empowerment for blacks—and over time public attitudes on race changed for the better.

The work of racial reconciliation is no easy task, and no president can be expected to undo four hundred years of inequality in eight White House years. "I expect this to be a central part of my work in the next two years and a central part of the work I do for the rest of my life," Clinton noted in 1998.

Through his cabinet appointments, his clandestine budget maneuvers, and perhaps most of all through his Initiative on Race, Clinton sought to address racism and racial inequality more than any other president in the past twenty-five years. He did not have to appoint so many blacks or Hispanics to his cabinet. He was reelected in 1996 long before announcing his race initiative. And blacks appeared likely to continue to support him. "Black Americans know that Clinton is the only thing that stands between them and Newt—or worse," noted scholar Ronald Walters. So to tackle these issues in the first place took courage.

But in tossing his hat into the race ring, Clinton failed to capitalize on two important lessons that had emerged from the civil rights battles of his youth. First, that transformational change can come about, even when it confronts violent and vocal resistance—as from the whites of the South who fought racial integration. And second, that leadership efforts benefit from good timing. Part of the success of the civil rights movement of Clinton's generation was due to the cold war and America's need—in the face of that global confrontation with communism and a world that watched keenly—to make good on democracy's promises of equality.

Clinton had also misjudged Americans' relationship to their elected leaders. Again, as the sixties made plain, Americans would tolerate change—radical change—if leaders articulated values and visions consistently and succeeded in conveying a sense of urgency. Clinton did neither. His pursuit of racial justice was itself centrist.

In the end, Clinton was content to tinker, when he had had a genuine opportunity to transform.

PART V

THE SECOND COMING?

CHAPTER ELEVEN

God and Second Chances

In the pantheon of political ego boosts, few are more heady than winning a presidential election. Perhaps the rush is trumped only by reelection. Like the runner who defends her marathon title or the baseball team that beats back all challenges to its league title, so do presidents enjoy particular satisfaction in triumphing a second time after all gun sights and typewriters have been trained on them for four long years. Upon winning an unprecedented fourth term in 1944 over New York's Thomas Dewey, Franklin D. Roosevelt joked, "The first twelve years are the hardest." Other presidents would relish the opportunity to make such complaints.

As the 1996 election season began, Bill Clinton and Al Gore's prospects for another stint in the White House were bright—and a far sight better than anyone would have prophesied in November 1994. Following the midterm elections that month, the President's approval ratings dipped into the 40 percent range, and with the Republicans assuming control of the House for the first time in two generations, Clinton seemed to be afflicted with the same disease that had struck fellow Democrat Jimmy Carter: one-term-itis. Though the losses initially set Clinton into a deep funk, he recovered. In his new nemesis at the other end of Pennsylvania Avenue, the President found not only a wily tactician but an unexpectedly cautious one. Newt Gingrich noted soberly in the wake of November's "Republican Revolution" that "in terms of World War II, we are at 1942. We have begun to mobilize the forces. We have begun to launch bridgeheads. We are a long way from D day."

As events in 1995 unfolded, though, the anticipated landing at Omaha Beach was more like spring break at Daytona Beach. The Republicans did not so much storm Congress as wade through the treacherous political tides that come with being in power. Nonetheless, the GOP resurgence forced Clinton to shift his governing approach away from the occasional left-leaning tendencies of his first two years and steer the ship of state more resolutely toward the middle of the electoral ocean. Not for the first time in his political career would he be criticized for following the consensus rather than leading the fight to forge one.

Nor for the first time in his political life would Bill Clinton's wife figure prominently into the election equation. The Whitewater scandal continued to percolate, raising questions about Hillary Rodham Clinton's sincerity and prompting *New York Times* columnist William Safire to label her a "congenital liar." Rodham Clinton's own approval rating in January 1996 was a paltry 54 percent, giving her the dubious distinction of being the most unpopular First Lady in history. How would this play out on the campaign trail?

What Clinton sought to do in 1996 was no simple feat. If he won, he would be the first Democrat since FDR to gain consecutive presidential terms and only the third since fellow southerner Andrew Jackson did it in 1832. But momentum—even aside from the economy and the lackluster Republican nominee—played to the President's advantage. Clinton had not lost an election in nearly two decades, not since the 1980 Arkansas gubernatorial bout. Voters in states like New Hampshire saw his doggedness in 1992 in the aftermath of the military-draft and adultery charges. "If you'll give me this election back," he then pleaded, "I won't be like George Bush. If you give me a second chance, I'll be there until the last dog dies." Clinton's political resurrection since November 1994 intimated that he would fight equally as hard for a second term in 1996. "The God I believe in," he confessed, "is the God of second chances." Few other phrases better captured the President's modus operandi. But the question for voters in 1996 remained whether Clinton's political religiosity would compel him to sacrifice genuine change efforts on the altar of the here and now. Would a second term for Bill Clinton—a second chance to hold an office to which he could not be reelected—affect him significantly? Would he exercise bolder, more visionary, and less incremental leadership?

ADULT LEADERSHIP

Presidential primaries are not unlike high school junior proms. Knowing there's a bigger event looming, participants still toil tirelessly to make a name for themselves. This is the "show," at least for now, so they reason to make the most of it. Yet they dare not incite too much of a stir for fear of what others will think in Monday morning's algebra class and for fear of seeing their stock plummet. The idea is to be popular, perhaps even mildly intriguing or quixotic. But certainly not notorious.

By January 1996, a number of Republican candidates were vying for the prom king title—and the right to boogie with Bill Clinton at the big dance in November. For his part, the President wasn't much impressed with the competition. Surveying the Republican primary field, Clinton confided to press secretary Mike McCurry, "Look at the bunch of nitwits they've got running. Dole's the only one that's got any capability to do the job. . . . I want to have some confidence in the person I turn the keys over to."

If Dole's GOP rivals had anything to say about it, Clinton would not be turning over the keys to Dole anyway, but to them. And incurring the President's disdain as a "bunch of nitwits" was closer to compliment than criticism.

The Republican lineup offered voters several options on various policy fronts—from big-business stalwarts to corporation-bashers; from pro-lifers to abortion proponents; from affirmative-action foes to semi-supporters. But the candidates' differences were less evident in the charisma category: with perhaps the lone exception of Patrick Buchanan, no one in the field was likely to moonlight successfully as a rabble-rousing speaker at evangelical revival meetings.

"Ideology" buzzed in the Buchanan camp, but it often sounded closer to a murmur under the tent of odds-on favorite Robert J. Dole. The Kansan's three and a half decades in Washington had shaped a deal-maker, not a demagogue. Dole was acutely uncomfortable with the primary-engendered need to make strident attacks and paint issues as black-and-white. Owing to his long service in the deliberative Senate, he was more accustomed to reasoned debate than rapid sound-bite fusillades. During the federal government shutdown in late December 1995 and early January 1996, the Senate majority leader's condescending call for "adult leadership"—leadership that eschewed petty personality conflicts and sophomoric games of political chicken—earned him some supporters. But when governmental activity resumed and Dole's presidential hide was at stake in the primaries, he apparently concluded that he had too long hungered for the Oval Office to avoid playing the game as others did. When in Rome . . .

Dole and his rivals knew he was the candidate to beat. Dole and his rivals also knew New Hampshire's importance in securing or shaking his front-runner status. When king-of-the-Democratic-hill Edmund Muskie stumbled in the New Hampshire primary in 1972, his campaign eventually collapsed. Dole hoped to avoid a similar fate, but remained mindful of lukewarm comments about his candidacy, even by those who had endorsed him. Said a Republican congressman not long before the 1996 New Hampshire primary, "There's nobody else. [Dole's] support is a mile wide and an eighth of an inch deep, and I'm still hoping there will be somebody else." Momentum coming out of New Hampshire could spell more contributions, more volunteers, and more media coverage. Sputtering out of the blocks there could spell a long winter and an early seat on the bench.

New Hampshire nail-biting was made all the more fierce for the Doleites in the aftermath of the February 1996 Iowa caucuses. There, 23 percent of Iowans cast their vote for Pat Buchanan, putting him a close second to Dole, with 27 percent. Former Tennessee governor Lamar Alexander followed with 18 percent of the tally, and magazine mogul Malcolm Stevenson Forbes Jr. tumbled into fourth with 10 percent. Phil Gramm finished fifth, behind Forbes, prompting him soon thereafter to quit the race altogether.

The combination of Buchanan's surprise performance and Gramm's hasty exit afforded Dole good cause to both crack a smile and wear a frown. The good news was that Dole might manage to woo Gramm's supporters. The bad news was that no Republican had ever won the nomination after losing New Hampshire. Never.

To boot, Buchanan's fiery rhetoric and penchant for corporation- and foreign-country-bashing had the potential to play well in the upcoming New Hampshire bout. Though the Granite State enjoyed a low unemployment rate and an export-oriented economy, voters reading daily newspapers about corporate layoffs remained uneasy.

In his eleventh-floor suite at the Manchester Holiday Inn, Bob Dole struggled with some uneasiness of his own. Before the results were known on election eve, a melancholy Dole complained to aide Mari Will, "You know, if I finish third, I will drop out." The gloomy comment was uncharacteristic of Dole, yet it revealed his gnawing fear that New Hampshire–ites would again deny him victory, as they had in the 1980 and 1988 primaries.

Shortly before 8:30 P.M., the networks were crowning Buchanan the winner, beating Dole by two thousand votes. "Nothing as significant as this has happened within my lifetime," crowed Buchanan. "All the forces of the old order are going to rally against us," he continued, gesturing wildly with his hands. "The establishment is coming together. You can hear them now. The fax machines and the phones are buzzing in Washington, D.C. Do not wait for orders from headquarters. Mount up and ride to the sound of the guns!"

Back at the Dole ranch, the mood was less cowboyish. The Kansan had lost, but he had at least avoided third place. Alexander suffered that fate with 23 percent of the vote. Forbes managed a distant 12 percent.

Dole consoled himself with the fact that he had beaten Buchanan in Iowa. Quid pro quo. Dole would do better in the primaries to come, he reasoned.

Voters in Delaware didn't help matters, though. On February 24, Dole again lost—this time to Forbes by a margin of 33 percent to 27 percent of the vote. But the state's three electoral votes were so few that Dole had decided not to campaign there at all, thus providing an easy explanation for the poor showing.

Excuses notwithstanding, the Dole bloodletting had the Republican political establishment in a tizzy. Two days after Delaware, Dole stalwart Pete Domenici of New Mexico quickly convened a meeting of nine fellow senators who had pledged their support to the majority leader. What the hell was happening? How had Buchanan and Forbes managed to land such blows on Dole's chin? What would come of the GOP if either of these two outsiders actually won the nomination?

The hastily called strategy session concluded with Senator Robert Bennett of Utah agreeing to accompany Dole on campaign swings. Less syco-

phantic than campaign staffers, Bennett could engage Dole as a peer, supplying unfiltered, no-bullshit reactions to the candidate's speeches. For the
time being, this course of action satisfied the majority leader's followers in
the Senate.

The plan was no panacea, though. Dole again placed behind Forbes in
the February 27 Arizona primary. If New Hampshire had knocked Dole off
balance, the one-two combination of Delaware and Arizona put him on the
ropes, toiling to stand upright. But Dole's swig of water and cut man were
not long delayed: on the same night he lost Arizona, the Kansan picked up
both Dakotas. Still, two months into '96, Dole faced the prospect of going
more rounds than he—and perhaps even Buchanan or Forbes—might have
predicted.

Party primaries are publicly ritualized infighting sessions. Part personality conflict, part ego display, and part ideological debate, primaries offer regular glimpses of the internal convulsions besetting Democrats and Republicans. On one level, these are healthy episodes: they give rise to disparate
voices, compel party leaders to recognize areas of dissent, and assure the rank
and file that avenues to register their concerns remain unclogged. But on
another level, party faithful fear that primary season is too akin to hunting season—and the hunted are members of one's own political family. "In 1984, they
had us killing each other for months, and then they delivered me, the
cadaver," remembered Walter Mondale. "It looks like the Republicans have
the same strategy." Democrats looked gleefully upon the fracas, hoping that
the name-calling and tattle-telling would so taint the image of the eventual
GOP nominee that Bill Clinton and Al Gore would waltz to a second term.

As the race evolved into a Buchanan-Dole-Forbes contest, it crystallized
three distinct clusters within the Republican party of the late 1990s: the
Buchanan-led cluster of economic isolationism and staunch moral conservatism; the Forbes cluster of global-minded free-tradism and libertarian-
esque policy positions; and the centrism cluster of Bob Dole, who split the
difference on issues such as free trade, where he offered qualified support
to NAFTA and GATT, in contrast to Buchanan's opposition and Forbes's full
endorsement. Keeping these disparate elements moving in the same direction, said Virginia governor George Allen, was "kind of like keeping the
reins on sixteen wild horses."

Where the pin-the-tail-on-the-elephant game would end was anyone's
guess in the wake of New Hampshire, Delaware, and Arizona. Less open to
conjecture was the dire effect that the Forbes candidacy, in particular, might
exert on the general election. The millionaire publisher certainly had pockets deep enough to run as an independent in the fall, thus threatening to
siphon off votes from the GOP headliners. Perhaps even more than Forbes's
potential to earn the nomination outright, this possibility gave the willies to
Republican standard-bearers such as House Speaker Newt Gingrich and

party chairman Haley Barbour. It foretold a three-way race of the sort that had booted George Bush from office in 1992. Forbes needed to be handled deftly.

In this regard, Dole complicated matters. Swinging wildly at Forbes-the-Foe, Dole's jabs were occasionally so wide-ranging that they threatened to alienate party bigwigs who supported some of Forbes's ideas. Dole's denunciation of Forbes's tax plan as "snake oil," for instance, put him at odds with House Majority Leader Richard Armey, who boldly pronounced, "The flat tax is the future of the Republican party."

Former congressman and secretary of housing and urban development Jack Kemp also was enamored of the flat tax. "In the great tradition of President Reagan," he calmly advised in February, "I strongly urge all Republicans seeking the presidential nomination to speak no ill of thy fellow Republicans' efforts to reform the tax code." This appeared a nonconfrontational way to urge Dole to temper his rhetoric. But despite such comments and despite a face-to-face meeting between Dole and Kemp in early '96 in which the candidate importuned the former Buffalo Bills quarterback's endorsement, Kemp remained cool on Dole. Then in March, just before the New York primary in which some one hundred delegates were at stake, Kemp committed the heresy. He officially lent his backing to Forbes.

The news hit hard because Dole's campaign manager, Scott Reed, had once served as Kemp's chief of staff. The Dole-ites, Reed not the least among them, had thought that while Kemp might shilly-shally for a bit, he would in the end pitch his tent with the majority leader. When he did not, Reed and Kemp exchanged fire over the phone. "I'm not in this for politics," Kemp insisted. "I'm in this for policy. This was the most difficult decision I made. Newt Gingrich told me I was done with the party. I'm done."

As it turned out, it was Forbes—and Alan Keyes and Robert Dornan and the other GOP hopefuls—who were done. Dole racked up victory after victory, beginning with South Carolina in early March and continuing through to the Super Tuesday primaries in midmonth. Kemp's apostasy notwithstanding, Dole prevailed. Now, Lamar Alexander and Richard Lugar were conceding the race and tossing their support to the Kansan. Forbes too surrendered, after having sunk a hefty $30 million into the venture. Dole even picked up the endorsement of the man who had sent him packing in 1988, George Bush. In a statement that began strong but then withered away into banal generalizations, the transplanted Texan called Dole a "great leader, a great friend with great credentials for president of the United States, mature leadership and character, and things of that sort." The "things of that sort" phrase reminded some of Bush's 1992 campaign-induced longing for what he called the "vision thing." Apparently, the former president still longed for specifics and energizing rhetoric. Would Dole too suffer from those same political ailments?

MAKE ROOM IN THE MIDDLE

During the federal government shutdown in January 1996, President Clinton phoned Majority Leader Dole with reconciliation on his mind. "Let's you and I fly off to Florida," Clinton urged, "and we can settle this thing." Eyeing the GOP primaries over the next several weeks must have convinced the President that if jetting to the Sunshine State was one way to resolve the budget impasse, it most certainly was not the best way to defeat candidate Dole in November's election. A more prudent plan seemed to sit tight and allow Dole and his GOP rivals to chew on each other.

Not only would the media spectacle likely impugn the image of the eventual Republican nominee, but Democrats might even eke out some positive publicity in the process. When Steve Forbes, for instance, made an unexpected surge in the primary race, his rivals quickly reminded voters that in a 1993 column Forbes had urged the President to appoint Hillary Rodham Clinton to a cabinet position or to the head of a federal agency. Such stories tickled Democrats: here were Republicans spending Republican money to remind voters that a leading Republican presidential candidate supported the Democratic First Lady. Even Richard Nixon's "dirty tricks" team would have been impressed.

Unlike Dole, who had to worry over a half-dozen committed rivals—as well as, for several weeks, the looming possibility that Colin Powell or Newt Gingrich might enter the fray—Bill Clinton and Al Gore escaped a nomination challenge from within their party ranks in 1996. Neither Richard Gephardt nor Sam Nunn nor Bill Bradley nor any other high-profile Democratic politicians believed the Clinton-Gore team to be sufficiently vulnerable. Democrats thus avoided a repeat performance of 1980, when a protracted primary struggle between President Jimmy Carter and Senator Edward Kennedy crippled Carter in the general election fight against Ronald Reagan. Perhaps the second presidential term that had eluded Democrats since FDR's day had at last arrived.

Still, if Clinton's tearfully devastating 1980 gubernatorial loss had taught him anything, it taught that reelections are not freely given. And they certainly don't come to pass with self-righteousness and overconfidence.

That's why pollster Stanley Greenberg's July 1995 memo—penned nearly a full eighteen months before Clinton's reelection—struck a chord with the President. The confidential missive worried over Clinton's second-term prospects, in the wake of polling data showing "the defection and disillusionment of working-class and noncollege white voters" from the Democratic party. "The President is fundamentally mispositioned for 1996," charged Greenberg. Voters without college degrees who were not doing well economically feared that Clinton did not identify with them or understand their struggles. These "doom and gloom" Americans were more

269

likely to vote after contemplating the present size of their bank accounts. Well-educated voters were comparatively more future-oriented: they were predisposed to compare the policy positions of candidates and make judgments about what might come to pass. Doom and gloomers had helped the GOP win the House in 1994; several months later, they remained similarly aligned, overwhelmingly supporting Bob Dole. Greenberg's memo ended bleakly: "As must be evident, we are walking into a potential storm."

Like all the constitutionally generated, four-year-cycle storms before it, this one would intensify after Labor Day, 1996. By mid-March, though, at least the Clinton-ites knew this particular twister would assume the form of Kansan Bob Dole. They did not need to wait to plot their strategy.

The White House tactics began to cohere by April. And the President was intimately involved. "There is no one," recalled Clinton's former gubernatorial chief of staff Betsey Wright, "who can write a poll question better . . . write an ad better . . . [or] come up with the perspective to put an opponent's votes into [any] better than Bill Clinton." As much as possible, Clinton and White House aides such as Harold Ickes, Dick Morris, and George Stephanopoulos agreed to paint Bob Dole as Washington, D.C., incarnate. Dole's thirty-five years in Congress would be noted at every turn, his service interpreted as desensitizing him to Middle America's concerns. To boot, inconsistencies in the majority leader's voting record would be trumpeted— he had some 12,500 roll-call votes that could be picked apart—along with his early opposition to the food stamp program and Medicare. The President and his team hoped to depict the majority leader as being mired in the legislative minutiae of the Senate, while Clinton was decidedly more "presidential" and above petty interparty catfighting. Clinton, not Dole, exercised capable leadership from his Pennsylvania Avenue perch—or so the President and his team labored to convey.

As the summer of 1996 approached, the White House also became increasingly convinced that efforts to associate Dole with House Speaker Gingrich might bear fruit. The once-heralded Contract with America had been devalued in the minds of many Americans as a Contract on America, and the guns of the "Republican Revolution" longed for ammunition. To the extent that Dole could be successfully linked with Gingrich-the-Extremist, whose poll approval ratings seemed to dip daily, Clinton could remain sanguine about his reelection prospects.

Dole, though, grew grumpy. By late May, his campaign car had stalled. The string of primary victories that had pushed him ahead of his Republican rivals seemed distant both to him and, more importantly, to voters. The Unabomber story, the Oklahoma City bomb trial, and the tragic death of Commerce Secretary Ron Brown commanded media headlines. The presidential campaign appeared destined not to perk up until the party conventions later in the summer. This mattered less to Clinton than to Dole because the President continued to enjoy a lead in the polls. Dole concluded that he needed to give his candidacy some juice. "The worst sin in politics," counseled Richard Nixon, "is being boring." Nixon devotee Pat Buchanan connected the dots for Dole: "Bob's sooo boring." Someone once jokingly asked, "What's the difference between mobster John Gotti and President George Bush?" The answer: Gotti has at least one conviction. Candidate Dole in 1996 could just as easily have been the butt of the joke. To a reporter in the months leading up to the Republican primaries, Dole fumbled through an explanation of why he sought the Oval Office: "Yeah, I guess this time I've really got to say why I want the thing, you know. I mean, what I'd do with it, right? Got to get some new ideas and flesh 'em out. Not all at once. You can't do it in one big sermon. It'll come." It'll come? Surely, that line would not send Americans to the voting booth in droves.

Dole's bold move to revive his breathless campaign was an intensely personal, secret—and ultimately emotional—venture. Few would have predicted that the Kansan, after three and a half decades in Congress and after having secured the powerful Senate majority leader post, would forgo it all for a shot at the digs on Pennsylvania Avenue. But then few understood how deeply the losses in 1980 and 1988 haunted Dole. This was his last shot at the presidency, and the man who had so often traveled the conservative footpath was now prepared to let loose a bit and traverse the weeds.

Dole's decision to quit the Senate had been brewing for at least a month before he made the unexpectedly moving announcement. An April conference call with some of the Republican National Committee's top money-tree shakers had started Dole thinking in earnest. There, the candidate's lame attempts to articulate what he stood for had provoked a critical response from one of the donors. The majority leader soon got his motor going again, but again the rainmaker interrupted and chided Dole for his poor ability to note clearly why he wanted to be president. Banal answers like because "every country needs a president" were hardly motivating. A long silence followed the Dole rebuke. "It was horrible," recalled an intimate, "just horrible."

The exchange tugged at Dole. If he was going to run for the presidency, he told himself, then he really needed to run for the presidency. Few pols got one shot at the Oval Office; this was his third. Be damned if he wouldn't make the most of it. So on May 15, 1996, surrounded by colleagues, staffers, wife Elizabeth, daughter Robin, and miniature schnauzer Leader, Robert J. Dole stood in his Hart Building office and resigned from the U.S. Senate.

"I will seek the presidency with nothing to fall back on but the judgment of the people and nowhere to go but the White House or home," said a wet-eyed Dole. Novelist Mark Helprin helped with the wordsmithery of the speech, which included a reference to the Greek mythological figure Antaeus, who renewed his strength by touching the ground. "It is in touching the ground in moments of difficulty," Dole confessed, "that I've always found my strength. I have been there before. I have done it the hard way, and I will do it the hard way once again."

It may have been the hard way, but for a few fleeting days after his resignation it also seemed like the right way to win the presidency. In the speech's immediate aftermath, Dole's approval rating shot from 43 percent to 51 percent. That was the good news. The bad was that Bill Clinton still clung to a 22 percent lead over the former majority leader, with most voters admitting that Dole's departure would little affect their November vote one way or the other. By the end of June, Bill Kristol's candor in the immediate wake of Dole's resignation seemed prophetic. "If a month from now nothing's changed," cracked Kristol, "then you just have a seventy-two-year-old ex-senator without a message instead of a seventy-two-year-old senator without a message." That's the sort of reproach that Dole hoped to avoid. Had he gone all out for bells and whistles, only to remain poverty-stricken when it came to substance and conviction and vision and message?

But then, hard-edged conviction had never really been Dole's mantra, anyway—at least not for years. Two decades earlier, the Kansan had been pegged as Richard Nixon's water boy. When he became Gerald Ford's vice-presidential running mate in 1976, Dole's bromides against Democrats helped portray him as a man who saw the world in black-and-white, but the attacks also ossified others' regard for him as a "hatchet man." The formula had worked well in the Nixon-Agnew years—President takes the high road, Vice President throws the punches—so it seemed a logical strategy.

Yet the loss to Carter and Dole's own senatorial campaign in 1974—in which he hammered his obstetrician opponent for performing abortions—exacted a price. Dole soon recoiled at his reputation as obdurate, and began using his mounting political seniority to craft a more supple image. Dole became difficult to pigeonhole. "His convictions are for very prudent fiscal policy," observed Senator Warren Rudman. "But he has a lot of compassion for people who are poor, who are disabled, who need help from the government." Dole's lifetime rating from the American Conservative Union (ACU) was an above-average 82 out of 100, yet in some years that rating sank to 53. Why the disparity? In part because, in 1975, for instance, Dole voted against trimming $25 billion from the deficit and for a consumer-advocacy agency's creation.

Not surprisingly, in 1994, Dole's ACU rating boomed to 100. Contemplating a run for the White House, he knew he needed to veer right to appeal to Republican voters in the primary elections. A strong voting record in support of recent conservative initiatives would help shore up support and immunize him from monikers like "Senator Straddle" that rival George Bush used so successfully in the 1988 primaries. In 1995, Dole supported a GOP-backed budget that sliced $72 million from domestic violence programs; voted for a budget reconciliation bill although it gutted $500 million from the school lunch program he had once endorsed; and promised the National Rifle Association a vote to repeal the ban on assault weapons.

Still, Dole's relationship with Newt Gingrich and the 1994 House Republicans proved tenuous. They were revolutionaries; he was reasonable. They were seventy-three Oliver Cromwells; he was Charles I. "I don't have any risky ideas," Dole purred during the primaries. His chief of staff, Sheila Burke, concurred: "He instinctively believes in reaching across the aisle. He is reluctant to look at extremes." But this was not all bad, for even some GOP lawmakers in the House had tired of the revolutionaries' obstinance. Said Congressman Peter King of New York, "It's a southern, anti-union attitude that appeals to the mentality of hillbillies at revival meetings." Lauding Dole's abilities as captain of the USS *Senate,* colleague Alan Simpson said of Dole, "His obsession is to stop gassing and make the damn thing work."

So for all of the hoopla about differences between Clinton and Dole—age, education, war experience, character—the political trajectory of both revealed a similar concern with getting things done. Action over ideology. And for both men, losing bids for office early in their career after assuming firm ideological positions—witness Clinton's gubernatorial loss in 1980 and Dole's vice-presidential loss in 1976—sowed the seeds of centrism. Both craved power and leadership positions. Neither would yield the reins easily. In part, this truism explained Dole's decision to resign from the Senate. "Psychologically," said a former aide, "Dole could never take walking out on the Senate floor as a mere senator. He had it in him to resign but not to take a demotion."

Where the looming 1996 general election was concerned, these political predispositions meant that by early summer both Clinton and Dole were jockeying for the middle of the political spectrum. Dole had to move to the right to win his party's primary during the first months of the year. Now, his instincts reported, he needed to inch back toward the middle to win the general election. One problem, though. Someone named Bill Clinton had staked out that terrain as his own.

Late spring and summer of 1996 found the President trumpeting one initiative after another in a rapid succession of White House policy concerts. "It ain't the New Deal," press secretary Mike McCurry reasoned, "but it ain't bad." Not the New Deal, indeed. FDR's remedies to ameliorate the Great Depression were bold initiatives enlisting billions of "real" dollars and creating new federal agencies; and though Congress acquiesced at nearly every turn, the proposed solutions still necessitated legislative approval. Not so with Clinton-the-Lesser. Many of his policy ideas in the months prior to the '96 election deliberately dipped below the congressional radar screen.

The strategy was twofold. First, the President's pro-family ventures—

273

from new federal meat inspection guidelines to stay-in-school schemes to computer programs aimed at tracing the sales of guns to kids to pleas for three hours of educational television programming per week to antismoking and antidrug speeches—all sought to milk Clinton's I-feel-your-pain image. Though many joked about this wear-your-heart-on-your-sleeve emotionality, it played well in contrast to Gingrich-the-Grinch and his Republican sourpusses, whom Americans increasingly viewed as too extreme.

Second, the flurry of White House activity projected a staying-busy President, earnestly attending to the people's business. The more Clinton could steer clear of seeking congressional approval—through bully-pulpit speeches, presidential directives, memoranda to agencies, or executive orders—the greater his opportunity to avoid partisan wrangling and to exercise leadership.

But then, was it really leading to avoid the fight altogether? The tussle of opposing viewpoints is the central dynamic of leadership. Leaders are forged in the crucible of conflict. In neglecting to throw a pitch down Pennsylvania Avenue for GOPers to swing at, Clinton eschewed the essential precondition for leadership: disagreement. The President wanted all of the appearance of leadership, but none of the antagonism. This was Clinton leading by fiat as opposed to the force of persuasion. This was Clinton using his constitutional prerogatives as President to push noncontroversal policies; less often was he advancing ideas that truly pushed the envelope. This was Clinton touting a litany of relatively minor "achievements" with little apparent regard for whether pursuing such itty-bitty initiatives in the first place was the best way to flex his presidential muscle. This was not transformational leadership.

The scope of the President's executive orders paled in comparison to the occasional grandeur of such orders over the past half century. Whereas Clinton pushed for school uniforms and mailed to sixteen thousand school districts a how-to manual, Harry Truman decreed the end to segregation in the U.S. Army in 1948. Whereas Clinton pushed for teen curfews, Dwight Eisenhower directed troops to Arkansas in 1957 to integrate a high school. In fact, technically, most of Clinton's efforts were not executive orders at all, but rather the less weighty "memoranda to agencies"—a president's way of instructing bureaucrats to take some specified action. Noted historian Michael Beschloss, "Clinton is the first president to use executive action the way a painter uses a brush: to slowly, carefully fill in parts of his own public image."

After nearly four years in office, the President's public image had a few blemishes too. Americans had come to expect that in the Clinton White House positive momentum seldom went unaccompanied by wheel-spinning or the taint of scandal. And events in late spring and early summer 1996 did not disappoint. First, two Clinton partners in the bungled Whitewater land deal, along with Arkansas governor Jim Guy Tucker, were convicted of misusing $3 million in federally backed loans. Then, a long-simmering story broke about several hundred summaries of FBI background files—mainly of Republicans, including the likes of former secretary of state James A. Baker III—being sent to the White House security office. As even fellow Democrats dubbed the gaffe "offensive" and an "abuse of power," Clinton apologized and saw to the resignation of a responsible White House official. Clinton aides began to wonder if Whitewater and the so-called Filegate uproar would dog their boss the way Gennifer Flowers and Vietnam had done four years earlier.

Dole, of course, relished news of the President's woes, remarking for instance that the FBI file brouhaha "smells to high heaven." The Kansan likewise announced to the nation that his opponent was an intellectual pickpocket. Frustrated by the "commander in thief" 's purloining of traditional Republican themes—on issues such as welfare reform, affirmative action, and homosexual marriages—a rankled Dole concluded in late May, "If this keeps up, Bill Clinton won't have to make speeches anymore. All he'll have to do is find out my stand on an issue and say, 'Me too.' " The President had so ensconced himself in the political center, in fact, that the GOP had little to campaign on, save taxes and character. And, disappointingly for other White House aspirants, even those issues allowed for little headway against the wily Clinton. In accepting the Green party's presidential nomination, consumer activist Ralph Nader charged, "President Clinton is too unprincipled ever to lose to Senator Dole. He will never let Dole turn his right flank."

Clinton's metamorphosis was evident in tag lines from his 1993 and 1996 State of the Union addresses. In 1993, fresh out of the starting blocks, a chipper Clinton counseled, "Tonight I want to talk to you about what government can do because I believe government must do more." Three years later, after the painful '94 purging of the Democratic battalions in the House, the President confirmed, "The era of big government is over." Bill Clinton the Democrat had become a Nelson Rockefeller Republican, a liberal Republican, even Newt Gingrich lite. "The good news is that we may elect a Republican president this year," mocked GOP consultant Alex Castellanos. "The bad news is that it may be Bill Clinton."

And so it fell to Bob Dole, once again, to gas up his ailing campaign jalopy. His Senate retirement in May had given him an ephemeral lift in the polls. By mid-August, he needed to ease into the political pumping station in search of higher octane fuel. If the car sputtered on the side of the road, the '96 election might prove as dull as some claimed the '92 contest was. When asked at that time what would make that Bush-Clinton bout interesting, one political scientist blurted, "Bush could die. That's about it."

Of course, dying and Dole's age in general were also aspects of the 1996 matchup not lost on late-night comics. Recounting a Dole anecdote to his television studio audience, Bill Maher noted, "At one point Dole said, 'If I were a senior citizen, I'd be a little fed up.'" Maher then teased, "If Dole were any more of a senior citizen, he'd be fed intravenously."

Dole's campaign lift came in his naming of a vice-presidential running mate, just before his party's nominating convention in August in San Diego. Wryly predicting a Dole upswing, the candidate's communications chief opined, "There is nothing wrong with Bob Dole's campaign that a good economic plan, a good veep choice, a good convention speech, and seventy-four million dollars won't cure."

Though General Colin Powell was, according to one senior Dole aide, "our first five choices" for vice president, Dole settled on Jack Kemp in the end.

Dole-Kemp was an uneasy and occasionally awkward alliance, no less so because of Kemp's frequent criticism of Dole and endorsement of rival Steve Forbes only five months earlier during the primaries. But the match nonetheless played to Dole's advantage. Kemp was upbeat and articulate, even motivating, on the campaign stump; applauded in Republican-scarce locales such as union halls and NAACP conventions; palatable to the GOP's pro-life wing; and popular in electoral-vote-rich states such as California, where Dole trailed Clinton by a horrendous twenty-five points.

Nationally, the President's lead was nearly as hefty—twenty points and climbing, in the glow of his own party's nominating fest in Chicago in late August. It was not lost on some that the Democrats again selected Clinton and Gore in a Windy City venue dubbed the United Center. United, because, having avoided the nastiness of party primaries for the first time in decades, Democrats were not bruised and bandaged as they piled onto the convention floor. Center, because that's the spot in the political medicine cabinet where Dr. Clinton had located the painkiller prescription for his party's presidential woes. Not all party delegates were wholly enamored of the President, yet for the smell of another victory they were willing to suffer a few other whiffs downwind.

The real skunk at the family picnic proved not to be a distant-relative delegate, but rather a presidential intimate: Dick Morris. Longtime adviser to Clinton, dating back to his Arkansas days, Morris had been summoned—some would say he summoned himself—to Washington to coagulate the Democratic bloodletting after November 1994. The President's move to the center in the wake of the Republican Revolution was partly Morris's handiwork, which, he once famously quipped, "requires the ability of an academic and the canniness of a drug pusher." Now, on the very morning of Clinton's triumphant acceptance speech at the 1996 convention, Morris had unwittingly stolen the headlines from his boss. Papers began reporting on Morris's yearlong affair with a $200-an-hour call girl named Sherry Rowlands.

The two tangoed almost weekly in the Jefferson Hotel in Washington, where, in between nibbling on *her* ear, Morris, compelled by his ego, bragged about how he had the President's ear on matters large and small. Morris promptly resigned, but the episode muddied Clinton's references to families and children in his convention acceptance speech. Bob Dole said simply, "It says something about who you surround yourself with, doesn't it?"

But perhaps aside from Hillary Rodham Clinton, Morris understood the President like almost no one else. And Morris held one card that trumped even the First Lady: he, like Bill Clinton, fundamentally enjoyed the rough-and-tumble, late-night-pizza-and-beer-strategizing element of politics. Though she endured them and occasionally participated in such sessions, the First Lady had less appetite for those shenanigans. Policy, not politics, was her preferred bailiwick.

Beyond politicking, Morris too paid attention to the President's ideological fussings. Clinton, he determined, is "the end product of the debate between Democrats and Republicans this century." The President was the Great Synthesizer, according to Morris, conflating traditionally Democratic ideas with stereotypically Republican ideas.

Synthesizer, yes. Great, no. Clinton's knee-jerk political instinct was survival first, principles second. Same for Bob Dole. Neither man was without principles, as was often suggested—consider, for instance, Clinton's NAFTA fight or his refusal to blink in the government-shutdown staring match of early 1996; and Dole's risky efforts in 1985 to push through the Senate a curb on cost-of-living adjustments for social security recipients. But seldom did either man knowingly risk office for principle. They were pols first.

Voters in the fall of 1996 were thus treated not just to the antics of the customary Democratic mule and Republican elephant. Joining the political-circus lineup were the fox and hedgehog. "The fox," wrote the ancient Greek poet Archilochus, "knows many things, but the hedgehog knows one big thing." In 1953, British philosopher Isaiah Berlin applied that distinction to Russian writers: Dostoyevsky was a hedgehog because he related everything to a single, unifying principle; Tolstoy was a fox because he felt less of this compulsion. To Berlin, the difference in worldview was profound, separating writers, thinkers, and politicians. Four decades later, the conceit remained instructive. Though the Dole-ites touted their candidate as playing a Republican hedgehog to Bill Clinton's Democratic fox, more accurately both nominees were foxlike. Both candidates were willing to shift course—to "triangulate," in Dick Morris's term—to accommodate the electorate and secure public office. Clinton simply boasted more backslapping campaigning skill and staked out more aggressively the political middle than foe Dole.

To Dole's frustration, even before the Monica S. Lewinsky story raised anew questions about Clinton's morality, few voters placed "character" as high on the presidential wish list as the Kansan would have liked. A summer

1996 poll determined that 67 percent of voters thought that a politician could suffer from "substantial flaws in personal character" but still govern effectively. In the same poll, 70 percent of respondents regarded Dole as "moral"; a paltry 41 percent thought the characterization befitting of Clinton. Still, among voters admitting to a presidential preference in the fall contest, Clinton ran a full 13 points ahead of his Republican opponent.

So what was the bottom line for voters? If not morality or character, what quality did they seek above all others in Oval Office aspirants? Leadership. Among five factors identified in a voter poll as desirable traits of presidential candidates—competence, empathy, integrity, leadership, and negativity—leadership was tops. Evidently Americans had, at least in the Age of Clinton, surrendered the ideal of the president as moral role model, unless they defined leadership itself as moral. The bottom line—action, action, action—ruled. If that constituted "leadership" to voters, then Clinton indeed fit the bill.

The problem was defining "leadership." A squishy quality of the I'll-know-it-when-I-see-it variety, leadership to some voters could apparently be divorced from ethical or moral contexts. To others, though, leadership was inextricably connected to morality. "Leadership for what?" they would ask. If Clinton's personal and, via episodes such as Whitewater, professional conduct were suspect, then could he genuinely lead as President? His "leadership" among these skeptics might better be described as "managing" or "brokering" because those terms connoted no moral underpinning. Or, they might concede that Clinton's leadership was transactional. Fleeting, ephemeral. And it was light-years from being transforming. Clinton may have mastered American politics, but not the American presidency.

As sobered voters trekked to the polls on election day, 1996, they harbored few idealized images of the candidates. Actor Mel Gibson complained, "It's like trying to decide whether you want to be kicked or gouged." Former Democratic presidential candidate George McGovern was equally disgruntled: "I think that [Clinton] has speaking skills and personality qualities and intelligence and [an] educational background that should have enabled him to do better than he has." And Newt Gingrich offered this assessment: "Bill Clinton has all of FDR's skills, but none of his iron."

Throughout the day, pundits sang the same song forecasting the President's reelection. Some Dole stalwarts still harbored hope. Taking a cue from Clinton's "Comeback Kid" nickname burnished in the '92 New Hampshire primary, Republican adviser Ken Duberstein dubbed Bob Dole the "Comeback Adult." But the damage had been done; no amount of wishful thinking, hand-holding, or cute nicknames would save the election for the ex–Senate majority leader. Voters returned the President to office by a margin of thirty-one states plus the District of Columbia to Dole's nineteen. Americans "preferred the middle way of Bill Clinton to the hard way of Bob Dole," wrote political scientist David M. Shribman. Though he garnered only 49 percent of the vote instead of the 50 percent he sought, Clinton claimed that his 379–159 electoral college victory was "an enormous consolation prize." Still, for the second time in two tries, Clinton's sub-50 percent showing saddled him with the "minority president" stigma. He was the first such president since Richard Nixon scooted into office in the same way in 1968, and only the third president—after Cleveland and Wilson—to have won both terms with less than half of all votes cast going to him.

In the 1996 bout, Texas billionaire Henry Ross Perot pulled in third with 8 percent of the popular vote, a pale comparison to the nearly 19 percent he had captured in 1992. As for the incoming 105th Congress, Republicans still held the reins in both chambers, swelling their Senate ranks to fifty-five, a Republican number not seen there since 1929.

Though, as one scholar noted, the 1996 contest was "so dull to journalists, so unremarkable to the voters, so odious to the practitioners themselves," a close look at the numbers still proves intriguing. Noticeably more than in 1992, the historical legs of the Democratic party supported Bill Clinton for reelection. Eighty percent of nonwhites voted for him in 1996, versus 76 percent in 1992; 54 percent of Catholics tipped their hat to him in '96 as opposed to 42 percent the first time around; and 60 percent of labor-affiliated Americans pulled the lever for Clinton in '96, while only 56 percent did so four years earlier. So for all of his moves toward the political center and his "New Democrat" sermons, Clinton still appealed to the core Democratic coalition—if only because they had no alternative in 1996.

To some, this trend's implications for the Democratic party's future seemed plain: moving to the left was the way to woo voters and win elections. But as the early months of the second Clinton-Gore administration revealed, the President read the road map differently. He saw the signs as pointing to more of the same—to more centrism. Clinton continued to pursue what to many appeared an ideological grab-bag approach to governing, which, because of its inchoate nature, likewise appeared something less than leading.

THE SECOND ERA OF GOOD FEELINGS

A second marriage, noted Samuel Johnson, is the triumph of hope over experience. In politics, though, second terms tend to be awarded more for the latter than the former. Unlike the I'm-for-change mantra that often dominates on the debut album, presidents' sophomore efforts croon, "I'm for more of me."

And so it was with Bill Clinton as he delivered his second inaugural address in January 1997, overlooking a sea of Americans from the Capitol's west lip. But characteristically, Clinton tried to have it both ways. He was for more change, but that, conveniently, meant more of him. "When we last gathered," said the President, referring to his '92 inauguration, "our march to this new future seemed less certain than it does today. We vowed then to set a clear course, to renew our nation." Clinton then reminded listeners of his achievements—how things had changed, even improved, over the past four years. But more work remained to ensure that Americans' "rich texture of racial, religious and political diversity will be a godsend in the twenty-first century." The President intended to use his new lease on political life to toil to that end, presiding over "a government that is smaller, lives within its means, and does more with less."

In the first paragraph alone of his second inaugural address, Bill Clinton mentioned the twenty-first century no fewer than five times. Only two of his predecessors, John Adams and William McKinley, had served at the dawn of new centuries; and neither had witnessed the birth of a new millennium. The President seldom skirted an opportunity to invoke the shape of things to come, detecting in the figure 2000 all the youth and imagination and vitality and optimism he hoped to associate with his administration. "I've tried to reanimate the presidency," he affirmed. "I've tried to redefine it in a way for the new times we are living in and the century we're going into."

Clinton's back-to-back victories over opponents of the World War II generation further reinforced his sense that his Oval Office tenure bestrode a transition in American life and culture. The President looked to the decades between the Civil War and World War I as an analogous period in the country's past. "I still believe the time in history that this most approximates is the shift from the agricultural to the industrial age," he calculated. "We have to define the moment. . . . Primarily it's characterized by enormous globalization of the economy. Number two, it's characterized by a breathtaking revolution in information and telecommunications and the biological sciences. Number three, it's characterized by an increase in the scope and pace of change in the way ordinary people work and live, relate to each other, and relate to the rest of the world. And fourthly, it's characterized by great new challenges to the role of government."

Much like James Monroe, who came to the White House for two terms beginning in 1817 and whose stint was described even by contemporaries as the "Era of Good Feelings," Clinton presided over nearly a decade of relative peace and prosperity. Sectionalism and tariff issues festered enough to make the early-nineteenth-century characterization somewhat misleading, but the title stuck because Monroe's tenure was comparatively more quiescent than the painful embargo of Jefferson's administration or the War of 1812 that marked the Madison years. Similarly, those who saw Bill Clinton's time in office as a "Second Era of Good Feelings" did not necessarily overlook conflict, but rather contrasted the more placid 1990s with the stagflation of the 1970s or the warming-over of the cold war in the 1980s. Monroe straddled two generations. So too Clinton.

For his second term, the President got plenty of free advice. "He changes personae and positions with the skill of a linebacker and the grace of a ballet dancer," charged Charlton Heston. "Now he should try to find himself and be himself." "Stick to your principles," admonished former Reagan press secretary James Brady. From historian Doris Kearns Goodwin: "Use the presidency to empower progressive social movements." And from comic Jay Leno, referring to Clinton's mounting legal woes: "I'd tell him to avoid any sort of prison reform—it could be a potential conflict of interest."

These comments aside, a good scare, it is said, is worth more to a man than good advice. And Clinton the pol had endured two frightening episodes: once in 1980 when he lost his gubernatorial reelection bid; and once in 1994 when Democrats suffered an unexpected drubbing at the polls. The experiences convinced him that the liberal policies on which he had cut his political cyeteeth had become anachronisms. Clinton had also learned that his childhood predisposition to avoid conflict and pursue collaboration was more likely to spell electoral success than being endlessly dogmatic. "I think honorable compromise with people with different views is what makes democracy work," said Bill Clinton at the start of the 1996 campaign season. "I don't think it's a weakness." Eleven months later, on the eve of his reelection triumph, the President reminded listeners, "It is time to put politics aside, join together, and get the job done for America's future. Tonight we proclaim that the vital American center is alive and well. It is the common ground on which we have made our progress."

The let's-play-together-nicely tone of the President's speech rankled some observers, who wondered aloud whether Clinton had drawn the right lessons from his first term and from his scrutiny of past presidential administrations. Worried historian Alan Brinkley, "If President Clinton really expects to govern without conflict by identifying a noncontroversial center, his second term will be even more frustrating than the first. For there is nothing—either in our history or in the present, fractious political moment—to suggest that there is a nonpolitical route to progress." Indeed, that the President would extend the olive branch on even so heady an occasion as election night, when he might be forgiven for some chest-thumping and a rhetorical excess or two, revealed much about Clinton's perception of his Oval Office role.

As he readied for a second term, the President's cabinet appointments also signaled much about that role. Unlike the painfully public missteps of his first term—à la the likes of Lani Guinier and Zoe Baird—Clinton assembled in late 1996 and early 1997 a team that ruffled few feathers. More than policy coherence, the President, by his own admission, sought personalities, teamwork, and chemistry. He wanted as little as possible of the liberal-versus-moderate tension that had peppered his first-term cabinet. Instead, forging "a coalition of the center" predominated his selections. There was Andrew Cuomo at the Department of Housing and Urban Development (HUD) and Dan Glickman at Agriculture. Racial and gender diversity remained important, so Janet Reno stayed on as attorney general; Madeleine Albright earned the nod as secretary of state; Alexis Herman, an African-American, got promoted to secretary of labor; Rodney Slater, another African-American, garnered a position as transportation secretary; and Bill Richardson, a Hispanic, became U.S. ambassador to the United Nations. Clinton even tipped his cap to bipartisanship, appointing former Republican senator William S. Cohen of Maine to the defense secretary post.

As further testimony to his devotion to the political center, the President named as architects of his economic strategy a lineup palatable to Wall Street: Franklin Raines, still another African-American, as Office of Management and Budget director, Robert Rubin as treasury secretary, and William M. Daley as secretary of commerce. In addition, Gene Sperling was installed as head of the National Economic Council, and Erskine Bowles moved in as the new White House chief of staff. Together, these ex–investment bankers and lawyers signaled the President's satisfaction with the stock market and his aversion to rocking the boat. "Bill Clinton," noted one observer, "had become the Mikhail Gorbachev of the Democratic party, issuing calls for renewal and change while appealing for support from those most interested in the preservation of the status quo."

With his administration's most noted liberals—Robert Reich at Labor and Henry Cisneros at HUD—now departed, Clinton had room to signal that he might accept a capital gains tax cut, long derided by liberal Democrats, as part of a balanced budget deal. Was Clinton abandoning his party altogether? "The men who hang on to high office," wrote author Judith Viorst in 1998, "tend to be men who have learned to make peace with a compromised conscience." So too Clinton? The President seemed convinced that moderation had earned him the White House in 1996; with such reinforcement, he saw little reason to wander from the centrist canon.

Less wandering and more wondering—wondering about scholarly assessments of his presidency—set the tone early in Clinton's second term. Five days after his inaugural, at the Alfalfa Club dinner in Washington, Clinton cracked, "We decided we were going to be more proactive about managing our place in history. This week at the White House we operationalized the Posterity War Room. . . . Mike McCurry is going on *A&E Biography*. Erskine Bowles will be on the History Channel. . . . My media team is busy putting together spots that will go negative on James Buchanan and Warren Harding. . . . And James Carville has announced that he is making a full-scale assault on the scholars at the Heritage Foundation." The President was joking, but he was serious too. With a constitutional prohibition on seeking a third term, Clinton realized that the game clock had already begun winding down. Taking rim shots at history now at least partly influenced the strategy Coach Clinton marked out on the chalkboard.

No small factor in Clinton's historical evaluation, he concluded, would be the endurance of his governing principles. Would his ideas be ephemeral, or would they enjoy some shelf life? Might Clintonism become a model of executive leadership for posterity? The President's successor would be instrumental in this regard. Enter Al Gore. The President is "intently committed to having Al Gore elected" president, said the First Lady. Clinton "sees Gore's election as ratification of his own leadership—with Gore as head of the third Clinton administration," affirmed a Clinton friend. The feeling was mutual. "He is very, very, very, very sensitive to his relationship with the President," said Gore friend and former congressman Tom Downey. "He [Gore] doesn't want to hurt it, doesn't want to undermine it, doesn't want to have others undermine it."

Gore, of course, had never been peripheral to the President. Gore directly supervised no less than fourteen major policy areas, including telecommunications, urban policy, the U.S.-Russia relationship, and science and technology; he spoke his mind freely; his staffers occasionally migrated to work for the President; his digs were eighteen strides from the Oval Office; and he and Clinton lunched regularly on Fridays on salad, sandwiches, and peach cobbler to discuss privately a wide range of White House initiatives and strategies. "The American people will never really know, at least until I write my memoirs, all the magnificent things Al Gore has done as Vice President," said Clinton, beaming, at a DNC fund-raiser in May 1996. "But I'm telling you, we should all be grateful to him."

Gore liked to joke that his service to the country included a brief, five-minute stint as president, the consequence of Clinton's late arrival to his January 1997 inaugural. "Now, it was a very special five minutes for me," he intoned. "I am convinced that historians will look back on the Gore administration as a time when America was at peace at home and abroad, our economy was booming with low inflation, and we created 3.1 new jobs, 2.4 of them in urban America. . . . I have selected a presidential library for my papers. It's a shoebox in Nashville."

Long a policy wonk and committed environmentalist, Gore had a sense of humor that was one of the better kept secrets in a city where leaking surpassed politician-gawking and even baseball as the local pastime. Once, while showering, he poked his sudsy head out from the running water, handed his wife, Tipper, a bottle of women's depilatory, and asked whether he had used enough of her shampoo. Tipper screamed, fearful that Gore's hair was going to fall out.

Still, more often than not Gore's image is wooden. The Vice President "is handsome, friendly, and extremely bright, but when you see him standing there in his blue suit and white shirt and solid tie, you don't yet think 'President.' You think 'airline pilot.'" At the bottom of an Oval Office photo in which his former chief of staff Roy Neel is whispering into his ear, the Vice

President scribbled, "To Roy—OK, I've got it: I stand behind him motionless and keep my mouth shut—Al." In contrast to the frenzied free-for-all
image associated with the President's staff, life with Gore seemed a bit more
balanced. He has retained high-powered corporate consultants to help promote teamwork and collegiality. Leadership scholar Warren Bennis's *On
Becoming a Leader* is recommended reading for his advisers, though the
Vice President cautions that it's "not a book that I live my life by."

Perhaps most relevant to Gore—who confessed on the eve of the 1992
New Hampshire primary, "I'd like to be President and I look forward to
the chance to run in the future"—is Bennis's assessment of recent Oval
Office occupants. "Lyndon Johnson, Richard Nixon, and Jimmy Carter
could be described as self-made men, but they failed to win our hearts or
engage our minds, and finally failed as leaders," concluded Bennis. Success
eluded them because "each seemed trapped in his own shadows."

Early into the second administration, Gore himself got trapped in some
shadowy—and shady—allegations of illegal fund-raising during the 1996
presidential race. Barred as an elected official from campaigning on government property such as the White House, the Vice President nonetheless confessed to making "a few" fund-raising phone calls from 1600 Pennsylvania
Avenue. But his carefully parsed mea culpa pleaded that "no controlling legal
authority" prevented him from making the solicitations. Then came news that
scores of calls were made, not just a few. To boot, Gore tap-danced around his
attendance at a Buddhist-temple fund-raiser in Los Angeles in April 1996
that, Republicans charged, laundered illegal foreign funds into several Democratic races. The Vice President variously characterized the occasion as "community outreach," as "finance-related," and finally as "donor maintenance,"
meaning that "no money was offered or collected or raised at the event."

All of this cast Gore in the unlikely role of ethically challenged politician.
Was not Gore the good son, rather than the artful dodger? "He is not about
the art of seduction; he is about the importance of being earnest," quipped a
pundit. The Vice President could only be thankful that the furor was erupt-
ing fully two years before the onset of the 2000 Oval Office campaign.

Bill Clinton also saw to it that Gore continued to earn credit for various
White House initiatives and to take the lead on a number of policy fronts.
The President, from whom Gore had learned to better appreciate "the value
of perseverance," had endured enough questions of ethical behavior to
know that focusing on the proverbial "business of the American people"
eased the sting. In mid-July 1998, Clinton complimented the Vice President
for devising new clean-air regulations; and in budget negotiations the previous summer, Clinton stepped aside to allow Gore to advocate "empowerment zone" tax breaks and other initiatives to clean up inner cities. This sort
of relationship between a president and vice president would have been
largely unimaginable in, say, the Nixon or Reagan White Houses.

Wooing other constituencies also occupied Gore's time. Two days after being sworn in for a second stint as Vice President, he joined Hillary Rodham Clinton at a National Abortion and Reproductive Rights Action League luncheon. And during 1998 he appeared at AFL-CIO rallies, hoping to shore up support from organized labor—and thus carefully avoiding mention of his support of legislation to facilitate the negotiation of free trade pacts. By 1998's end, Gore had appeared at more fat-cat fund-raisers for more candidates and local party chapters in more states than any other presidential aspirant since George Bush in 1986. The 2000 Democratic nomination race seemed his to lose.

A Gore administration would not want for experience. Gore groupies held various posts in the second-term Clinton White House and cabinet, as they had in the first: OMB director Raines, deputy political director Karen Skelton, chief domestic policy adviser Bruce Reed, Environmental Protection Agency administrator Carol Browner, and even 1996 campaign manager Peter Knight. If, as polls showed, Americans admired competence in presidential officeholders, they would have little reason on that score to wrinkle their noses at Gore or his loyalists. Whether Gore *could* exercise leadership that was visionary, collaborative, even energizing, remained tantalizingly speculative. But whether Gore *would* exercise leadership of a different breed from Clinton's centrist stewardship proved the more absorbing riddle.

A Gore administration was appealing to some, revolting to others, and presumptuous to many. The next presidential election was four full years away, and life in the White House—particularly life with Bill Clinton—had already demonstrated that much could happen in those years. Though the 1996 race focused scant attention on them, many important public policy issues longed for attention. Could Clinton and Gore capitalize on their victory and exercise leadership? Or would Clinton's second term be marked by a reluctance to tackle tough problems?

If Harry Truman had been around to witness the labors of the 105th Congress, ushered into office in January 1997, he would likely have treated it to a tongue-lashing of the first order. The President who had derided the 80th Congress during the 1948 elections as the "do-nothing Congress" would have been exasperated at the paltry legislative achievements and ubiquitous partisanship of the 105th. Actually, the "do-nothing Congress" did quite a lot, providing aid to those fighting communism in Greece and Turkey, and passing the Twenty-second Amendment, the Marshall Plan, the Taft-Hartley Act, the National Security Act, and the Water Pollution Act. The 105th Congress of 1997–98 ranked poorly by comparison.

Republicans nestled in for the 105th Congress with their first consecutive majority since the 1928 election. The GOP held 227 seats in the House and 55 in the Senate. Besides seeing the Clinton-Gore ticket returned to the White House, still-in-the-minority Democrats consoled themselves with the realization that their House incumbents surrendered only three seats, while their Republican counterparts suffered seventeen such defeats. And twelve of those seventeen incumbent GOP losers, Democrats noticed, were members of the vaunted 1994 freshman class. So much for the revolution; it appeared to be eating its young.

The leader of the 1994 revolution, Newt Gingrich, presided over a House in 1997 and 1998 that debated and discussed a variety of issues, but got down to enacting noticeably few laws of any real consequence. The '96 presidential election had witnessed two centrists battling for the middle ground, and the ensuing Congress ended up following the Clinton-Dole example, leaving unresolved weighty issues or eschewing them altogether. Efforts to strengthen campaign finance laws, regulate health maintenance organizations, rewrite toxic-waste-cleanup and endangered-species laws, raise the minimum wage, initiate procedures to close obsolete military bases, revamp bankruptcy laws, toughen statutes involving violent juvenile offenders, curb lawsuits over defective products, deregulate electric utilities, overhaul financial-services laws to permit banks and securities firms to compete for each other's business, and grant the president fast-track trade-negotiating authority all failed to pass the House or Senate, or both.

Even more noticeable than these failures was the demise in the Senate of a historic bill, backed by President Clinton and touted in his 1998 State of the Union address, that would have raised cigarette taxes to finance health programs, helped curb teen smoking, and affirmed the government's authority over the tobacco industry. The proposed legislation suffered from contentious provisions and from a $40 million advertising blitz from the tobacco industry. Assessing the by-products of congressional-presidential cooperation, David Gergen teased in July 1998 that "renaming Washington National Airport after Ronald Reagan may be their most memorable achievement." For Speaker Gingrich, the bitterest pill to swallow was the Congress's failure to pass a proposal to cut taxes by $80 billion over five years, a move that would have benefited mostly middle-income families.

Why the missed opportunities? In part, the culprit was divided government: Democrats controlled the White House; Republicans held the reins in Congress. Bickering, finger-pointing, filibustering, speechifying, and gridlock followed. But that explanation weakens upon consideration of the 1948 Marshall Plan, 1970's clean air and water laws, and 1986's tax reform—all of which were enacted during years when the congressional majority was of a different party from the President. Even 1993–94's health care plan was sacked, despite Democratic control of both houses and in the White House.

A second, and somewhat more compelling, explanation for the 105th

Congress's woes was commitment. Unlike the 104th Congress, particularly in the House, Republicans in 1997–98 had not nearly the sort of issue discipline and commitment to voters of two years prior. There was no 1996 version of the Contract with America to which the GOP could be held specifically accountable. Consequently, Republicans were less unified as a group. They were also less certain of their leader, Newt Gingrich, who early in the 105th was reprimanded and fined by the House for rules violations, and who in 1997 suffered the bruises of a failed coup attempt that sought to oust him from his Speaker's perch. Like Robespierre, Gingrich was proving effective as a revolutionary, but poor as a leader. Confidence in him among the Republican House troops was eroding. None of this boded well for substantive legislating.

Allegations surfacing in January 1998 that President Clinton had engaged in an adulterous relationship with White House intern Monica S. Lewinsky—and then lied about it under oath—also contributed to slim pickings among the 105th Congress's achievements. Republicans calculated that voter disenchantment with the President would extend to Democrats nationwide. So rather than act on important but politically risky issues, they reasoned that their prescription for success in the '98 midterm elections was to hunker down and bide their time. Thus Republicans rallied chiefly around noncontroversial issues, such as Internal Revenue Service restructuring, or constituent-support-building issues, such as tax cuts or abortion restrictions, popular with the GOP's social conservative base. On health maintenance organization regulation, tobacco industry regulation, and campaign finance reform, Republicans—majority-wielders in both House and Senate—noticeably declined to take the lead.

"All the major legislative initiatives were doomed to failure," concluded Republican senator Dan Coats of Indiana, "because the atmosphere became so politicized so early and because of this huge dark cloud of the Clinton crisis hanging over the process. Everyone began suspecting everyone else's motives right from the start. Tobacco, managed care, all those issues required a consensus, a strong consensus, that clearly was not going to develop."

All of this is not to suggest that the 105th Congress did nothing of consequence. It passed a $216 billion highway construction bill, approved President Clinton's $1.1 billion proposal to hire more teachers, expanded subsidized housing to include more low- to moderate-income families, and channeled $18 billion to the International Monetary Fund to contend with global financial crises. In a historic move, the Senate also voted to expand the North Atlantic Treaty Organization, admitting three former Soviet bloc countries to a pact originally conceived to thwart communist aggression.

Late in the congressional session, Americans were again treated to a near repeat of the 1995–96 government shutdown showdown, as the President signaled his unwillingness to sign either appropriations bills or continuing resolutions to keep the government running. Clinton wanted Republicans to accommodate his spending priorities and, with the Lewinsky business simmering, was only too ready to shift public attention to budget disputes. The strategy worked, as Democrats salvaged some of their agenda in this final appropriations battle, and the White House could argue with mixed success in the waning weeks before the midterm elections that the President could still command attention. He could still lead.

But these efforts, including the last-minute ones, paled in comparison to the legislative issues left untouched or unresolved. Assessments of the 105th depended very much on party affiliation. "Truly a remarkably successful Congress," said Republican congressman Bill Archer less than one month before the 1998 midterm elections. "The worst Congress that's ever sat in this building," complained House Democratic Minority Leader Richard A. Gephardt.

Even the most heralded of the 105th's achievements, balancing the federal budget and creating a surplus for the first time since 1969, garnered few headlines. When the Senate voted in April 1998 to approve the balanced budget, the next day's issue of the *Washington Post* stuck the story not on its front page, but on its twentieth. Some economists and budget-watchers were hardly any more complimentary, mustering but lukewarm praise. "The surpluses themselves are simply accounting digits," former labor secretary Robert Reich noted, expressing concern over whether the surplus would be directed "toward the bottom half of the American workforce" that really needs the money.

For her part, the First Lady had grown so exasperated at what she perceived as the stubborn refusal of pundits and journalists to give credit where credit was due—and at their tireless scandal-mongering—that she orchestrated a clandestine effort to strike back. In 1996, she ordered White House lawyers to prepare a report critical of the Whitewater reporting of the *Washington Post*'s Susan Schmidt. The idea was to contrast the *Post*'s coverage with that of other papers, insinuating that the *Post*'s reporting was biased.

Rodham Clinton then urged that the report be released as a public document, but she met stiff opposition from the likes of White House press secretary Michael McCurry. "This is the dumbest idea I've ever heard in my life," complained McCurry at a staff meeting. His candor—and ability to squelch the idea—seemed to reveal how much the First Lady's influence had waned in the White House. Who would have dared to make such a comment in, say, 1993? McCurry objected that the report merely analyzed the tone of the coverage and pointed out few if any factual errors. "My general view is that if you've got a problem with a newspaper and a case you can document, you assemble it and take it to the editor," reasoned McCurry. "To declare holy war on someone publicly usually doesn't work very well."

McCurry's admonitions notwithstanding, Rodham Clinton's disquiet over media excesses seemed not entirely unfounded. By 1996, historian Gil Troy noted, 36 books and 1,264 articles had been written about the First Lady, and over 16,000 articles on the President. These numbers are even more striking when contrasted with the comparatively less intense spotlight cast on the Bushes—a paltry 13 books and 149 articles on Barbara Bush, and 8,771 articles written about her husband.

Rodham Clinton found it difficult to hold her tongue. In early 1998, she attributed the Monica S. Lewinsky investigation to a "vast right-wing conspiracy." And she confessed to an Arkansas paper in mid-1998 that much of her husband's difficulties were owing to "prejudice against our state. They wouldn't be doing this if we were from some other state."

All of this stuck in the President's craw too, fueling his aggravation that he was not properly credited with genuine achievements, genuine change. Clinton was leading, he protested, and offered up his first-term deficit-reduction package as a principal ingredient in the robust economy that had marked most of his White House tenure. Republicans in 1993 had donned their soothsayer hats and estimated direly that Clinton's plan would only provoke a recession and actually increase the deficit. Those predictions never materialized, and five years later the President now sought acknowledgment for his steadfastness on the issue. But in fact Clinton had not been as unwavering as he remembered. As late as 1995 he still proposed a budget rife with deficits stretching indefinitely into the future. Now, in 1998, Clinton was counting on "deficit buster" as part of his historical epitaph. "He came in hoping to be Franklin Roosevelt and ended up being Dwight Eisenhower," observed political scientist Steven Schier, referencing FDR's expansion of government spending during the New Deal and Ike's passion for budget cutting during the 1950s.

Did Clinton *really* expect to be remembered for deficit reduction? Other presidents won wars, preserved the union, toppled dictators, forged critical alliances, rolled back communism, negotiated nuclear arms reduction treaties, fought for the civil and constitutional rights of blacks and women, and brokered peace deals between warring nations. Clinton wanted credit because his checkbook balanced.

"In a democracy," wrote former Bush administration official Richard Darman, "the challenge of leadership is not to find the path of least political risk. Society can find that on its own." History rewards the risk-takers. Many Americans complained that the President was taking those risks, but in the wrong arena—the personal instead of the public. The Lewinsky imbroglio made the question most poignant: How would Clinton ever be remembered as "great" if he was struggling with even being regarded as "good"?

The lackluster performance of the 105th Congress, combined with the President's sexual indiscretions, aroused greater interest than usual in the 1998 midterm elections, if only to see which topic would ultimately prove decisive among voters. Frustrated by Republican abdication of leadership on important issues, would voters hand control of Congress over to Democrats? Or would Democrats prove incapable of escaping the stench of scandal emanating from the White House, giving the GOP an even bigger legislative majority? The answers, as it turned out, were no and no. No, Republicans did not lose either chamber. No, Democrats were not noticeably harmed by Bill Clinton's personal improprieties and prevarications.

House and Senate elections largely turned on local, rather than national, issues. And though Republicans retained control of both houses of Congress, the pitch of their celebrations was muffled by the narrowness of their majority. Senate Republicans gained no seats in the 1998 elections, maintaining the same 55–45 margin over Democrats. In the House, Republicans lost five seats, and clung to a paltry six-member majority.

Listening to the comments of prominent GOPers in the election's immediate aftermath made some wonder whether they really did win. From Congressman Steve Largent: "On November third, the Republican Party hit an iceberg." From 1996 vice-presidential candidate Jack Kemp: "Our disappointing performance last week demonstrates that a failure to stand on principle is ultimately a losing strategy. . . . We've had four years in the majority with poor results." The immediacy of these confessions was rivaled only by their candor. A Republican party that had stormed to a fifty-two-seat victory in 1994 now nursed a precariously slim majority. What had happened?

Republicans had expected to gain as many as twenty House seats. "At every level that matters in 1998, we will sweep," roared a confident Newt Gingrich in the weeks preceding the election. Gingrich the historian knew that the opposition-party gains in nonpresidential-year elections since World War II averaged twenty-seven House seats. Not bad. But not in 1998, it turned out. For the first time in decades, the party in the White House did not lose seats in a midterm election.

The First Lady emerged from the November contests, in the words of columnist Mary McGrory, as a "one-woman rescue squad for her party." Hillary Rodham Clinton campaigned openly and aggressively for Democratic candidates, visiting New York eight times to help Representative Charles Schumer in his race against incumbent senator Alfonse D'Amato and appearing six times in California to help Senator Barbara Boxer's cause. "She brought White House glamour to the provinces without any of the President's scandal baggage."

Bill Clinton, it turned out, again snatched victory from the jaws of defeat. Who would have foreseen the November 1998 result earlier in the year when the Lewinsky story first broke? From his public embarrassment, the President endured equally public defections too. Former aide George Stephanopoulos admitted, "It's awkward to advise a man whom you don't fully respect, and it's unnerving to represent a man whom you don't fully trust," and Senator Joseph Lieberman chastised Clinton on the U.S. Senate floor, saying, "I am afraid that the misconduct the President has admitted may be reinforcing one of the worst messages being delivered by our popular culture, which is that values are fungible." A year that Bill Clinton might otherwise have dubbed *"annus horribilis,"* in which he became only the third U.S. president to be the subject of a congressional impeachment hearing, ended with election results that only the most ardent presidential supporters would have predicted.

Clinton unnecessarily risked his historical legacy for a dalliance. The election results were no product of a masterfully orchestrated campaign strategy, no evidence of presidential leadership. This was fumbling through, chance, luck. The President's professed belief in "the God of second chances" again paid dividends. For not the first time in his political career, Clinton was fortunate in his enemies.

Within seventy-two hours of the 1998 election, the other foot dropped for a disconsolate Republican party. Seeing the disaffection with his leadership mounting as the election returns sunk in and hoping to spare his party "divisiveness and factionalism," Gingrich resigned his post as House Speaker. "The ideas are too big, the issues are too important, for one person to put their office above the good of the party and the country," he reasoned. But how would this bode for the Democrats? Gingrich had been their whipping boy through two elections—elections in which they gained seats in the House. Could Democrats as easily caricature the new Speaker as mean and nasty, as they had Gingrich-the-Grinch? If not, what effect would this have on Clinton's leadership ability as he readied for his presidency's swan song? And would Clinton, or his presidential successor in 2000, misinterpret the 1998 election results as an endorsement of centrism?

Gingrich and many Republican strategists had miscalculated the public's continuing ire over the Lewinsky allegations. Earlier in 1998, Gingrich vowed never to give a speech without referencing corruption in the Clinton administration. But by the September 1998 release of Independent Counsel Kenneth Starr's official report outlining possible impeachable offenses against the President, 41 percent of Americans were urging Congress to drop the matter. Voters had apparently had enough and were unwilling to hold Democratic candidates responsible for presidential transgressions.

"A party is perpetually corrupted by personality," noted Ralph Waldo Emerson, and many Republicans became convinced in the wake of the 1998 elections that Newt Gingrich was the personality corrupting the GOP. To some, Gingrich's sudden retirement made clear just how unique Clinton was, exhibiting an extraordinary ability to endure so much stormy political weather and so many legal attacks for so long. To others, the Speaker's retirement and professed willingness to give up his office for the good of the party and of the country only contrasted with Clinton's selfish arrogance in refusing to do the same.

Ideologically speaking, Bill Clinton's second term began not in January 1997, but in November 1994. The center-directed policies initiated in the wake of the Republican Revolution continued unabated from late 1994 through 1998 and into 1999. Clinton's historical blurb was emerging: a rhetorical presidency that tinkered at the margins of policy. His scandal-ridden tenure was unlikely to give him any moral authority to affect grander, more transformational change.

"I would have much preferred being President during World War II," Bill Clinton once confessed. "I'm a person out of my time." Perhaps Clinton envied FDR's crisis because it provided the context for fundamental shifts in the relationship between government and the American citizenry. FDR could create; Clinton had to defend.

The President had on more than one occasion confronted the horse-and-buggy pace at which the Framers intended for change to occur. "I've learned that the system simply won't accommodate big changes, even when in theory you think they're warranted," said Clinton a few weeks prior to his reelection, "but that with a lot of energy and a lot of persistence you can do a very large number of things, which amount to a major shift." That may have been the President's version, no doubt partly inspired by the lofty plat-itudes of the campaign trail. In the governing of 1996 and 1998, though, many voters saw plenty of itty-bitty plans from Clinton, but no "major shift" on the road ahead that necessitated buckling their political seat belts.

After shooting a 79 in a round of golf near San Diego in June 1996, the President boasted, "I was hot. I was smoking 'em. I was having a good time. Even a blind pig finds an acorn sometimes." Now *there* was a complete epi-taph for the Clinton years—optimistic, serendipitous, fortunate, the benefi-ciary of Republican zealotry, and intent on keeping the policy ball in the middle of the fairway, just out of the rough. Yep. Even a blind pig finds an acorn sometimes.

CHAPTER TWELVE

Global Leadership and
Moral Duties

Bill Clinton had not brought to Washington in 1993 a grand strategy for global leadership—indeed, any strategy at all. Immediately upon assuming office, and well into his second term, he found himself competing, at home and abroad, with hosts of other leaders who had their own strategies, well-crafted and long promoted. Clinton entered a complex argument over the American role in world affairs that politicians had been heatedly pursuing for two centuries. Now he would be a pivotal player in—and a key target of—the squabble.

During much of American history the debate had divided into isolationists and interventionists, pitting those who worried over "entangling alliances" with the Old World that George Washington had feared, against those who wished to intervene abroad for a variety of economic, political, and humanitarian reasons. Before the American Civil War, John Quincy Adams captured the isolationist mood this way: America "goes not abroad in search of monsters to destroy. She is the well-wisher to the freedom and independence of all. She is the champion and vindicator only of her own." William Jennings Bryan and, later, Robert A. Taft held similar conceptions of a limited American international role.

Generally strong in the nineteenth century, isolationist sentiment rose and fell in the twentieth as internationally minded presidents such as Theodore Roosevelt and Woodrow Wilson led in projecting the nation into world affairs. Disillusionment in the wake of World War I was strong enough by the 1930s to arouse isolationist feeling that held even FDR at bay. But Pearl Harbor ended all that.

The old debate continued after World War II but on different terms. The issue became not whether to intervene abroad but how. "Hawks" and "doves" fought over ways to contain Soviet power—mainly with arms or mainly with diplomacy. The basic alternatives were toughness and confrontation versus accommodation and conciliation. The quarrel expired with the end of the cold war, each side proclaiming its strategy had worked.

Since the cold war, the great debate over American global strategy has been more subtle and complex but no less contentious and portentous. The struggle now is between—for want of better terms—"pragmatic" and "moral" leadership. The pragmatists, appealing to the teachings of Founders like Washington, want the United States to follow hardheaded, "practical," carefully calculated, closely circumscribed foreign policy tactics as specific threats and crises arise. The moralists, appealing to the preachings of Wilson and FDR, want the nation to intervene abroad against the conditions that in their view breed poverty, insecurity, and violence—conditions that require effective partnerships with other nations, massive economic and social aid, and even institution-building, such as Wilson's League of Nations.

Both sides see security as America's supreme goal and value in global affairs, but they would frame security in different ways. Pragmatists would restrict commitments, conserve resources, rely on predictable and calculable methods of power and leadership. Typically they offer expedient, short-run solutions to festering problems. Moralists see security in much broader terms as depending on a host of moral and psychological as well as economic and technological solutions. While they emphasize the national interest rather than the pragmatists' specific interests and interest groups, moralists do not sharply distinguish between the two, quoting Jefferson's view that "with nations as with individuals our interests soundly calculated will ever be inseparable from our moral duties."

These differing concepts of effective foreign-policy-making call for contrasting strategies of leadership, transactional versus transformational. Transactional leadership calls for skill in quickly sizing up the seriousness of crises, identifying the key players, mobilizing and shifting resources, but above all for on-the-spot and often last-minute mediating among the adversaries. Transformational leadership calls for an analytical and even intellectual capacity to identify deep-seated economic and ideological forces threatening peace and security, and an understanding of the wide range of actions—coalitions with allies or perhaps enemies, long-term mobilization of a variety of social and economic tools, modest or occasionally ambitious institution-building, and even greater patience and persistence than that expected for transactional leaders. Transformational leadership is far more exacting than transactional; the stakes are often higher, and failure more dire, as with the aborted League of Nations.

These leadership strategies have in turn different implications for the process and extent of change. The goal of transactional leadership is often merely to adjust or readjust the status quo and hence limit or even stave off change. Security means stasis. Or change may come incrementally, piecemeal, sporadically. Transformational leadership, on the other hand, usually creates change, often deep and comprehensive change. Transformational leaders define real change as both extensive and intensive, and above all as purposeful and durable.

What kind of change on the world stage would Clinton-the-Second-Termer undertake? Scandals continued to dog him domestically, so he often retreated to foreign affairs. In marked contrast to the imbroglios of his first term—Haiti, Somalia, North Korea—some of the dominant issues of his second—the Middle East, Ireland, even China—were policy areas that the President himself selected, rather than firestorms that erupted unpredictably and demanded his immediate, and frequently divided, attention. But would this change in circumstance make Bill Clinton any more *resolute* in his foreign-policy-making? Would it signal the onset of transformational leadership? Was it an indication that he had, after all, learned some important lessons from the gaffes of his first four years? Would he, only the third Democrat to win a second presidential term this century, be less of a master broker and more of a moral leader in global affairs?

THE PROBLEM FROM HELL

No issue during Bill Clinton's presidency better captured the tension between the pragmatic and the moral precepts of American foreign policy than Bosnia. The end of communism in Yugoslavia in the late 1980s set loose the centrifugal forces of bitter, revanchist nationalism in a nation where ethnic groups had warred and intermingled for centuries. The largest nationality, the Serbs, determined that if Yugoslavia was going to break up, they would not be content with the borders bequeathed to them by the communists. They would not allow their kin to live under the domination of Croats, in Croatia, or Muslims, in Bosnia-Herzegovina.

As Yugoslavia convulsed, the Serbs set about conquering those parts of the country that, while outside the internationally recognized borders of Serbia, they nonetheless considered Serbian. In some cases, the local population was Serbian; in others, it had been Serbian in some past era. Where their troops occupied, the Serbs engaged in "ethnic cleansing," driving out the Croats and the Muslims, raping their women, and imprisoning their men in concentration camps. The Croats, when they were not losing territory to the Serbs, grabbed what they could in the Croatian-populated areas of Bosnia-Herzegovina.

When fighting in Bosnia broke out during George Bush's stint in the White House, he was watchful, but largely inattentive. He pursued economic sanctions against the Serbs, provided the Muslims with humanitarian relief, and imposed an arms embargo on all sides. But little else. European governments—chiefly America's allies in the North Atlantic Treaty Organization—had maintained that the chaos was a European problem. Mired in a who'll-flinch-first contest with Saddam Hussein over Kuwait and oil, and loath to give the impression that Yankee troops would be globe-trotters in the post–cold war world, Bush declined to push the Bosnia matter. Let Europe handle it.

Needing a feather in his foreign policy cap, though, candidate Clinton decided to pluck the Bosnian goose. Clinton spoke boldly of the need for American leadership in central Europe. If he were president, he said, he would stop the slaughter. "We cannot afford to ignore what appears to be a deliberate and systematic extermination of human beings based on their ethnic origin," he protested in August 1992. Clinton specifically mentioned using American airpower to deter Serb aggression, and lifting the arms embargo against the Bosnian Muslims so that they might have a fighting chance.

A novice without any practical experience in conducting foreign affairs as an elected official, candidate Clinton nonetheless challenged President Bush on Bosnia and on a wide range of policy fronts. During the 1992 campaign, "there was scarcely any item on the wish list of contemporary American internationalism—preventing aggression, stopping nuclear proliferation, vigorously promoting human rights and democracy, redressing the humanitarian disasters that normally attend civil wars—where Clinton promised a more modest U.S. role" than Bush. But in pledging so much, Clinton got himself into a fix. Few, if any, presidents could accomplish what he intended to—and certainly no president with such an ambitious domestic agenda. Once in office, many of his promises on Bosnia devolved into hope—to be communicated in powerful sound bites, rather than potent military strikes.

For most of Bill Clinton's lifetime, American foreign policy, whether directed from the White House by a Democrat or a Republican, adhered to a single overriding principle: containment. Contain the Soviet Union's aggression. Contain communism's spread. Contain the disciples of Marx and Lenin to a small and finite area of the globe. The architects of this doctrine, chief among them State Department diplomat George F. Kennan, calculated that though the Soviets were bent on proselytizing in the name of communism, they were not entirely reckless in their pursuit. If they were met with American or American-backed forces wherever they aimed to foment revolution or install communist regimes, their overall expansion could be held in check. Broad consensus that combating communism was a legitimate foreign policy pursuit often assured presidents of congressional and public support when crises arose.

Unlike Korea, Vietnam, and other hot spots of the cold war where the containment refrain could be sung ad infinitum, it was difficult to argue persuasively that the United States had any strategic interest in Bosnia—and certainly none sufficiently compelling to send ground troops there. Yet because of the visibility and scale of the carnage, it was likewise difficult to remain uninvolved. This was a foreign policy conundrum like few before.

The United States in the twentieth century has been unaccustomed to armed action on a wholly humanitarian basis. Presidents have often sent troops to regions under the guise of moral "rightness," but almost without exception an economic or national security imperative accompanied—and was not infrequently the real motivation behind—the intervention. Framing an issue as a struggle for democracy and a struggle against the Soviet Union, pursuant to containment's precepts, kindled popular sentiment.

Not so with Bosnia. The reference points for conducting foreign policy were obscured by the dust from totalitarianism's collapse. "We are living in an era which we don't even have a name for," calculated foreign affairs expert Graham Allison. "We call it for what it [comes] after—[viz., post–cold war]—but we don't know what it [itself] is." The Soviet Union was no longer America's foe; many of its former provinces were now recipients of American economic aid.

What's a lone superpower like the United States to do? History did not really end with communism's fall, as political philosopher Francis Fukuyama maintained; more to the point, it changed directions. Now the enemy for the United States was not as easily discernible. "Without the cold war," implored Rabbit Angstrom, the central character in John Updike's novels, "what's the point of being an American?" That it was a different world was no secret—everyone knew that. The question was how to operate in it, and far fewer policy-makers had an answer to that riddle.

Doves on the Bosnia matter maintained that "in private conduct, altruism is the ideal. For a nation, it can mean ruin." It follows, they reasoned, that "nations are not individuals. Nations live in a state of nature. There is no higher authority to protect them. If they do not protect themselves, they die. Ignoring one's interests, squandering one's resources in fits of altruism, is the fastest road to national disaster."

By contrast, Bosnia hawks demanded action in the Balkans that was forceful and immediate. What good was winning the war against communism—an oppressive system with no tolerance for individuality and under the auspices of which despots executed their rivals—if America now watched idly as similar phenomena came to pass in the former Yugoslavia? America has the military might, they reasoned, and it should act. Unilaterally. Multilaterally. No matter the configuration or the number of allies, if any. America should act.

Bosnia-Herzegovina, where Yugoslavia's Muslims were concentrated, had no history of nationhood and few of the attributes of sovereignty. Much of its territory was occupied by either Serbs or Croats. And the arms embargo disproportionately penalized the Bosnians, since Serbia had inherited much of the former Yugoslavia's defense industry.

So as the Serbs laid siege to the Bosnian capital, Sarajevo, shelling its civilian population mercilessly from the hills around the city, it became Bill Clinton's task to find a way to end the fighting and preserve Bosnian sovereignty. He could not simply ignore the situation, in part because of his glib 1992 campaign pledge that made the Balkans crisis a moral issue.

Yet as Clinton was quickly discovering from his Oval Office perch, Bosnia was a policy enigma of grand proportions, of the damned-if-you-do-and-damned-if-you-don't variety. The centrist course on Bosnia was elusive, if not altogether nonexistent.

The nationalism that had fueled two world wars was one bent on conquering peoples and expanding the nation-state. In contrast, the Balkan crisis of the 1990s evidenced a mutant strand where factions aimed to destroy one another in the name of nationalism and sought to include only the most specific ethnic or religious groups in their state. Nationalism was now as much about breaking up states as conquering them. Nationalism was also significantly more intractable than Clinton or others had estimated.

American policy toward Bosnia during the first two years of the Clinton administration was cruel. "To those suffering appalling hardship in Sarajevo, the Americans were the cavalry who never came charging over the hill," complained journalist Michael Elliott. The White House insisted "that what was happening in Bosnia was unspeakably awful, and of vital interest to the United States. But [it] did precious little about it and on more than one occasion made a bad situation worse."

Bosnia tugged at Clinton's emotions. Many Americans who watched the carnage on television were similarly sickened. That was the problem. It was tempting to react to the crisis on a visceral level, fueled by the media images, rather than on a cerebral plane, motivated mainly by U.S. security interests. It was a dichotomy of the worst sort. Emotionally, there was an impulse to intervene; strategically, that impulse had to be quelled, or at least more carefully considered. It was difficult to keep heart in check. It was dangerous not to.

Rwanda, which was engulfed in the spring of 1994 in mass slaughters that claimed at least one million lives, provoked similarly conflicted reactions. Yet the Clinton administration sat on the sidelines. Genocide on a scale that the world had not seen since World War II—and the American President decided against direct American involvement. Did the Holocaust teach Americans nothing? Clinton's words in Kigali, Rwanda, during his 1998 African tour rang hollow: "The international community, together with nations in Africa, must bear its share of responsibility for this tragedy, as well. We did not act quickly enough after the killing began. We should not have allowed the refugee camps to become safe havens for the killers. We did not immediately call these crimes by their rightful name: genocide. We cannot change the past." Clinton had perfected the art of confession; he was less nimble when it came to bold and decisive, even preventive, action.

Bosnia posed a leadership crisis not merely for Bill Clinton; it posed an equally poignant identity crisis for the whole country. The Balkan quagmire—even more than Somalia and at least as much as Rwanda—forced the United States to confront its democratic core. In part, that was why there was so much tough talk from Clinton, members of Congress, media personalities, erstwhile diplomats, and others. How could the United States, of all countries, witness this brutality and not act? Wasn't the United States the lone remaining superpower? If a "superpower" would not find a way to intervene to halt such bloodletting, then the designation hardly seemed complimentary.

"Bosnia is the greatest collective failure of the West since the 1930s," lamented Assistant Secretary of State for European Affairs Richard Holbrooke. His boss was more direct; Secretary of State Warren Christopher dubbed it "a problem from hell." The military immediately advised the newly sworn-in Clinton in 1993 that there would be no quick and easy combat solution. In contrast to the exposed Iraqi troops that the United States had routed in the Persian Gulf War, the Serbs were hidden away in craggy mountains that would give them shelter from American airpower. If American troops were to enter the Balkan war, they would have to enter en masse, stay for an indefinite time, and expect significant casualties.

The decision-making process was grueling. One official bitterly complained early on that what he saw in the way of White House discussions on Bosnia "wasn't policy-making. It was group therapy—an existential debate over what is the role of America, etc."

Many Bosnia meetings showed Clinton's "ad hocracy" at work. Lower-level officials were given to gabbing as much as—if not more than—senior advisers. Secretary of State Warren Christopher piped up now and again, but was largely silent. Defense Secretary Les Aspin roamed from one topic to the next. Clinton often permitted this to go on. It was positively maddening to Gore, who was hawkish on Bosnia and saw merit in bombing the Serbs.

Gore was generally more decisive than his boss and offered quiet, behind-the-scenes advice to Clinton to act with firmer resolve. Part of this was a luxury afforded him by his vice-presidential status; most of it was simply his personality. An administration official allowed that Gore "is much sharper and firmer" than Clinton in his decision-making—and "more instinctively presidential than Clinton."

This disposition of Gore's appealed to Warren Christopher, who had difficulty scheduling meetings with the President short of a crisis. Christopher knew of the rapport between Clinton and Gore, and he knew too of the Vice President's interest in a reasoned approach to foreign policy. Nor was it lost on Christopher that while serving in the U.S. Senate, Gore had held a seat on the Foreign Relations Committee and earned a reputation for expertise on U.S. nuclear weapons. So in the administration's early going, the two men arranged to meet on Fridays to exchange ideas and discuss policies. Over Bosnia, though, their relationship became strained, as Christopher grew uncomfortable with the Vice President's inclination to use military force in the Balkans.

The differing opinions produced not just stasis, but public disappointment and disaffection. No fewer than five State Department officials resigned because of differences of conscience with the Bush and Clinton policies of inaction in the Balkans. Not since Anthony Lake and two others quit Henry Kissinger's National Security Council staff in 1970 over the U.S. invasion of Cambodia had there been as many resignations on moral grounds. "This is a weak and weakly mandated government," complained one of the officials, Marshall Freeman Harris. "It came into office believing it was elected to deal with a domestic agenda, and it has continued to believe that if it had an activist Bosnian policy, the risks associated with this would jeopardize what the President set out to do domestically."

"The question raised by Clinton's performance [in Bosnia]," said a U.S. diplomat, "is not just his backbone but his basic competence." The unproductiveness of many discussions was apparent less than six months into his presidency when an adviser at a meeting on Bosnia asked aloud, "Isn't there anyone outside the government with some bright ideas? Someone who could help us?"

Such indecision was precisely what concerned Clinton's labor secretary, Robert Reich. In "situations where the public is uncertain about the choices it faces and what's at stake in those choices," lamented Reich, "I worry that his [Clinton's] leadership may fail. He'll become unfocused and too eager to please."

In Bosnia, Clinton eventually came to push for a policy dubbed "lift and strike." It entailed lifting the arms embargo, a step that was thought to be beneficial to the Bosnians, since the Serbs were already well armed. "If there were other countries keeping us from defending ourselves," the President had blurted out, "I'd be pissed as hell or goddamn resentful." The "strike" element of the policy referred to air strikes Clinton wanted the North Atlantic Treaty Organization (NATO) to launch against the Serbs if they continued to shell Bosnian cities. In the spring of 1993, he sent Warren Christopher to Europe to gather support for the idea.

But Clinton and Christopher were not the team to persuade reluctant allies to follow the American lead. France and Britain already had troops on the ground in the Balkans, operating under UN auspices as peacekeepers. They feared that these troops would become Serb targets if NATO struck by air. So they said no. Christopher returned to Washington in defeat. The proposal quietly died.

This was appalling to some former government officials who remembered more vigorous U.S. leadership in NATO. "For an American secretary of state to go and see the allies about a matter on which the President campaigned, and about which the administration was said at the time to have strong feelings, and then to come back and say, 'They won't go along with it, so we're going to change our policy'—well, this was without precedent," said former assistant secretary of defense Richard Perle.

In fact, once Clinton, like Bush, had decided that stopping the war in Bosnia was not worth sacrificing the blood of American ground troops, Christopher's debacle became predictable. Proposing to bomb the Serbs was, in effect, proposing to try to deal with the situation on the cheap, limiting the risk to American pilots and aircraft. The allies, whose troops were on the ground and vulnerable, could readily see that. It was not a game they had any interest in playing.

There was a case, of course, to be made for America's steering clear of the Balkan fire and hoping it would burn itself out. Serbia was not, after all, Nazi Germany. It had no pretensions to a universal ideology, nor any apparent imperial ambitions outside its region. Serbia posed no direct threat to vital American interests. And at a time when voters seemed preoccupied with the size of their own pocketbooks, it was arguable that the wise course was to avoid any expensive and protracted military conflict in an area peripheral to the national interest. This at least was how Clinton rationalized his general inaction.

But America had already puffed on the isolationist pipe in the years leading up to the two world wars—and with dire consequences. Were those lessons already forgotten? What's more, wasn't the task of a leader to educate? Couldn't Clinton embark on a presidential publicity campaign to draw attention to the need and importance of international events? Couldn't he plead his case for American involvement in Bosnia, as he had with Haiti and NAFTA? Yes, of course he could. But this might compromise still further the President's domestic agenda. And Clinton, often risk-averse when it came to policy-making, liked to hedge his bets.

The eighteenth-century French writer Voltaire advised not to judge a man by his answers, but by his questions. And Clinton asked good questions on Bosnia. He pressed advocates of particular policy positions, demanding to know what American objectives would be achieved with a given alternative and inquiring as to how U.S. troops might be extracted if deployed. Such foresight was good, such intricate inquiry even admirable. Psychologists would call Clinton "cerebrally complex," suggesting his capacity to see multiple perspectives and assess policy alternatives from a number of different vantage points. Few would label Clinton tendentious.

Clinton, the first post–cold war president, had a temperament that fit this circumstance well. The old strategy of containment no longer guided American foreign-policy-making. Clinton—the New Democrat, the man who professed disdain for the stridencies of left and right, the man who wanted to locate the vital American center—did not like paradigms, anyway. Politically, Clinton searched for a different way. He was accustomed to blazing a new path, his path.

For Clinton to enter the White House without the cold war guideposts probably mattered less to him than it would have to another Oval Office occupant. For one thing, foreign-policy-making was not high on his priority list. But probably even more important was the President's disposition. Clinton was accustomed to inventing new stratagems, searching for innovative syntheses, creating different approaches. In this narrow sense, Clinton was well suited as the first post–cold war president. He thrived on the chaos and the uncertainty; indeed, as his aides would confess, he himself often created such disorder in policy meetings by soliciting so many opinions and pursuing countless what-if scenarios.

What is not readily appreciated, though, is that just this sort of intellectual wheel-spinning took place in the years before the vaunted containment doctrine came to be so readily agreed upon. The Russian Revolution of 1917 established the Soviet Union. Yet not until 1947 did George F. Kennan publish his seminal article in *Foreign Affairs*, outlining the parameters of containment. And not until 1936 did the United States extend formal diplomatic recognition to the Soviet Union. True, Clinton fumbled for some grand architecture to guide American foreign-policy-making for the post–cold war era. But so has the foreign policy establishment. Scholars and experts in a range of foreign affairs issues have likewise failed to generate an interpretive schema that is as widely accepted as was containment.

Perhaps they won't, either. At least not for some time. Meantime, the world turns. Crises arise. Leaders must lead. They must decide. Clinton may not have "containment," but neither did Wilson or FDR. Yet they still led, making some of the most important foreign affairs decisions in American history.

Particularly on matters of foreign policy, Clinton's first instinct was to debate rather than to act. His penchant for leaving few policy options unexplored, while ensuring many viewpoints an audition, nurtured a dark side: it cultivated an atmosphere of paralysis. The discussions were no substitute for decisions, yet the President occasionally seemed inclined to make them so. "He who wants to defend everything, defends nothing," admonished Frederick the Great, "and he who wants to be everyone's friend has no friends in the end." Clinton's natural indecisiveness exacerbated a situation that was already bound to engender hesitation in nearly anyone. And worse, even when he did decide, he was given to backpedaling on his tough talk when supposed ultimatums went unheeded.

Effective presidential leadership—in international affairs or in any other arena—cannot be conducted "on the fly," as Clinton was given to doing. The President's "ad hocracy" may have encouraged new ideas and given rise to a spirit of equality among some White House staffers, but it also wasted time and unreasonably delayed—or even stymied altogether—decision-making. How did the President expect transformational change—real change—to occur in this way? In many respects, Clinton was not leading. He was managing. More to the point, he was permitting Bosnia to manage him.

BOLDNESS BY DEFAULT

Bosnia perplexed Bill Clinton. For months, even years, he failed to make a consistently strong case, one way or the other, for the official American position in the Balkans. Instead, his rhetoric wobbled between the heroic and the pragmatic, between selfishness and selflessness, between internationalism and isolationism. Bill Clinton really was the first post–cold war president.

"I am appalled by what has happened there," he said. "I am saddened. I am sickened." In February 1993 he revealed, "If the United States doesn't act in situations like this, nothing will happen. A failure to do so would be to give up American leadership."

But a few months later, he would say of the Balkan situation, "I don't want to have to spend any more time on that than is absolutely necessary. Because what I got elected to do was to let America look at our own problems and our own challenges and deal with those things." President-elect Clinton even worried in 1992 that "I might have to spend all my time on foreign policy. And I don't want that to happen."

What a strange—and potentially dangerous—turn it was for a former Georgetown University international relations major and aide to J. William Fulbright, longtime chair of the Senate Foreign Relations Committee, to dispose so casually of items on the international docket. The world on the cusp of the twenty-first century demanded the American President's attention. Clinton's belief that he could relegate it to the backseat of his administration was naive and myopic, even a bit selfish. And it foretold the difficulties he would have conducting foreign policy.

Every cold war president—including those with hefty domestic agendas such as Lyndon Johnson or Jimmy Carter—had assembled his foreign policy team regularly. Not so Clinton. Particularly in his first term, it was not unusual for him to manage problems at the last minute. For domestic issues like NAFTA, this approach occasionally worked. But then NAFTA only risked jobs and reelection prospects. Comparatively speaking, last-minute scrambling on the international front promised to inflict much more harm; it could damage American credibility, compromise American national security, and cost American lives. For a man who so often exercised prudence on policy matters, this frenzied decision-making apparatus was remarkably imprudent.

Foreign affairs frequently garnered less attention than domestic-policy-making in the Clinton White House because the President was, for some time, uncomfortable donning the garb of international spokesman. Too, Clinton genuinely believed he was elected to focus on domestic matters. Some public opinion polls affirmed the priority. An October 1994 survey revealed that most Americans did not consider U.S.-Bosnia relations to be among even the top ten American foreign policy concerns. Nonetheless, when asked to evaluate the administration's performance in Bosnia, Americans had formed a clear opinion: a paltry 24 percent were willing to dub Clinton's efforts "excellent" or "good."

Perhaps Clinton was examining the wrong polls. Why, for instance, did he choose for so long to eyeball polls that confirmed his own predilection to tend to domestic items rather than heed and seek to improve the findings of polls that rated poorly his Bosnia efforts? The President was not challenging himself. He was too long content to rationalize his shilly-shallying in Bosnia on the results of select polls that reported what he wanted to hear—namely, focus on domestic problems and eschew international ones. Turning a blind eye to unwelcome news was hardly leadership.

Polling during Clinton's watch was elevated to an art form—and the President was much maligned for it. It was one thing to occasionally stick a thermometer under the tongue of the body politic on a weighty issue. It was quite another to be led around by the nose on issues large and small by mounds of polling data. Polling wasn't good for leadership. It enervated, even obscured, the role of the leader as educator and opinion-shaper. And it was certainly no prescription for transforming leadership. Clinton was allowing his administration to become "providers" and "servicers" to the whims of public opinion.

As his White House tenure wore on, of course, Clinton came to carve out more and more time for global affairs. In part, this was because the President established genuine friendships with counterparts such as Russia's Boris Yeltsin, Britain's Tony Blair, and Jordan's King Hussein, and because he warmed to his role as proverbial leader of the free world. Too, Clinton calculated that his efforts on the international front permitted him to circumvent the partisan Congress and the scandal-minded media, so as to sketch for himself the contours of his historical portrait. In his second term, matters beyond America's shores occasionally appeared less the intrusion they had been in his first—particularly in Northern Ireland and the Middle East, where periodic successes bumped stories about alleged illegal fundraising or adultery or perjury off the front pages of newspapers.

The amount of time Clinton ultimately ended up devoting to foreign policy issues was as unexpected to him as it had been to Woodrow Wilson eighty years earlier. "It would be an irony of fate," said Wilson shortly before his 1913 inauguration, "if my administration had to deal chiefly with foreign affairs." Within two years, armed conflict broke out in Europe—and in the very same Balkan region that later came to plague Clinton. By the spring of 1917, the United States had officially entered "the Great War." An irony of fate, indeed.

Clinton and Wilson were alike in other ways too. Both had somewhat troubled childhoods—Clinton's pudginess and broken home, and Wilson's dyslexia. Both were born in the South. Both were students of government and held graduate degrees. Both had been teachers. Both were Democrats. Both were among the brightest American presidents. Both served elected terms as governors. Both ran for president on platforms of progressive change. Both broke Republican holds on the presidency (Wilson was the first Democratic president in sixteen years; Clinton the first in twelve). Both were elected to first terms with only a plurality of votes (Wilson with 41 percent; Clinton with 43 percent). And both won their first terms because a third-party candidate siphoned votes from the Republican nominee: Teddy Roosevelt was to William Howard Taft what Ross Perot was to George Bush.

But Clinton was the opposite of Wilson in one significant way. Wilson was principled and uncompromising at times, as in his determined campaign to involve the United States in the League of Nations. Clinton only occasionally—and unpredictably—displayed such devotion to a particular cause. On the international scene, he was often more comfortable speaking of change and hoarding his political capital than he was pushing for genuine change and expending that capital.

Clinton was in any case fast discovering that Bosnia was not an issue to be assessed in terms either of political capital or of the conventional, cold war–vintage, geostrategic guideposts. Decision-making vis-à-vis Bosnia was muddied by the existence of the United Nations—the outgrowth of Wilson's own League of Nations—and the presence of United Nations Protective Forces (UNPROFOR) in the Balkans. Without the UN and UNPROFOR, Clinton and America the Lone Superpower would still have debated the merits of U.S. intervention, but the ensuing arguments would likely have contained fewer twists and turns. Yet as it happened, the looming shadows of the UN and UNPROFOR forced Clinton to wrestle not just with the dicey matter of intervention—but also with the specter of placing American troops under foreign command, with the obligations the United States had made to the international community when it first joined the UN, and with the damage to the UN that might be inflicted if the United States reneged so publicly on those obligations.

There was also the frightening prospect of predicting what might happen if UN troops left at American insistence and then U.S.-dispatched soldiers did no better—or even worse—than the international troops. UNPROFOR, however poorly it performed, still created an evaluatory benchmark that complicated U.S. policy-making. Indirectly, Wilson had made Clinton's work exponentially more difficult. Indirectly, the Wilson precedent of an international peacekeeping body had allowed Clinton to indulge in his innate propensities to work together rather than stand alone, to seek a perfect solution, and to delay important decisions. In this sense, Wilson, the United Nations, and Bosnia brought out some of the worst in Bill Clinton. The President's leadership style was not well suited for the Balkan crisis.

Consequently, Clinton's Balkan policy drifted. Before mid-1995, there were but a sprinkling of air attacks against the Serbs. The downing of a single American pilot, Captain Scott O'Grady in June 1995, was treated by the White House as a matter of intense concern, and his subsequent rescue became a cause for great celebration. It was a rare—and wholly serendipitous—foreign policy "success" in the Balkans, and one that the President and National Security Adviser Anthony Lake enjoyed by puffing cigars on the Truman Balcony.

By summer 1995, Clinton's dillydallying for nearly two years had given rise to the strange spectacle of the U.S. Congress taking the lead in a foreign policy initiative. This was a far cry from the deference to executive leadership in foreign affairs that had prompted the legislative branch in 1964 to grant President Lyndon Johnson considerable latitude in troop deployment in Vietnam via the Gulf of Tonkin Resolution. An American public that had in recent years been treated to Ronald Reagan's invasion of Grenada and bombing of Libya, and George Bush's toppling of Manuel Noriega—none of which was done with congressional assent—now witnessed the Congress exercising leadership in a domain that in recent decades had near exclusively been that of the President.

Clinton risked becoming irrelevant abroad. He appeared to have squandered on Bosnia whatever foreign policy capital he had gained via Haiti or NAFTA. The Congress in August 1995 endorsed a measure to compel him to undertake a plan with many elements of the "lift and strike" option he had earlier advanced and then withdrawn. The President fought back by vetoing the bill, but the Senate threatened to override it.

All of this domestic provocation proved sufficient to push Clinton to action. He ordered U.S. warplanes to participate in a three-day bombing of the Serbs in late August 1995. Instigated by the Serbs' shelling of a Sarajevo marketplace earlier that month, it was the largest NATO combat operation to date. The action brought another halt to the fighting—and engendered another flood of optimism that perhaps this time the carnage would truly end, that perhaps this time was different.

And perhaps it was. Clinton seemed bolder and more determined than ever to keep Bosnia out of the 1996 presidential race. Not long before the bombings, in early August, Tony Lake and Undersecretary of State Peter Tarnoff were dispatched to Europe to brief the allies on a tougher U.S. plan to end the war. In contrast to Warren Christopher's similar trip two years earlier, though, Lake did not solicit opinions. He indicated that the United States was committed to specific actions, whether or not others agreed. Clinton appeared to be learning.

The fruits of this late-summer push were evident by the fall. The presidents of Bosnia, Serbia, and Croatia met with U.S. officials in November 1995 at Dayton's Wright-Patterson Air Force Base and initialed a peace agreement. If it cohered, the plan would be the first time since 1905 that a treaty to end a foreign war was brokered on American soil. Nearly a century ago, Russian and Japanese diplomats had met with President Theodore Roosevelt in Portsmouth, New Hampshire, to settle their feuding over lands in east Asia. For his efforts, TR garnered the Nobel Peace Prize. Would Clinton's efforts pay similar dividends?

The Dayton Accord was the fourth plan since 1992 designed to end the Bosnian conflict. But there was genuine hope surrounding this one. All sides seemed to want the fighting to stop. Moreover, the plan was born of intense and firm efforts—and prior, painfully public failures—by Warren Christopher and his deputy Richard Holbrooke. The two men were dogged in their dealings with the three presidents, even delivering a risky ultimatum when the negotiations seemed hopelessly deadlocked. After days of talks, and in an uncharacteristic moment of raw anger, Christopher seethed to Alija Izetbegovic, Bosnia's founder-president, "Mr. President, I am truly disappointed at the fuzzy, unrealistic, and sloppy manner in which you and your delegation have approached this negotiation. You can have a successful outcome or not, as you wish. But we must have your answer in one hour. If you say no, we will announce in the morning that the Dayton peace talks have been closed down." As Christopher and Holbrooke prepared to leave, Holbrooke added, "Not suspended—closed down. In one hour."

The eventual agreement created a single Bosnian state, divided into a Serb republic and a Muslim-Croat federation. Both the republic and the federation owed at least nominal loyalty to a central government, which was itself presided over by a three-member collective presidency. Too, the Dayton Accords called for the deployment of a "multinational military Implementation Force"—including American soldiers, who were soon on their way.

President Clinton took to the airwaves to rally public support for U.S. involvement. In a late November 1995 nationwide television address he made his case. Only now did his proposed actions seem consistent with his rhetoric. "Nowhere today," said Clinton, "is the need for American leadership more stark or more immediate than in Bosnia." But many Americans remained unconvinced. An early-December *Time*/CNN poll found that 55 percent of voters opposed the decision to send troops to Bosnia.

This time, Clinton stood firm. And he stood firm despite the political cal-culations that advised against American involvement in the region. He knew that neither his positions on Bosnia nor on foreign policy in general explained why he landed in the White House in 1992. Americans had elected him to deal with domestic concerns. Moreover, astute politician that he was, Clinton also understood that complete or even partial success in Bosnia—or North Korea or Haiti, for that matter—would hardly guarantee victory in 1996. LBJ's entanglement in Vietnam overwhelmed and detracted from his Great Society efforts and drove him from the 1968 con-test; Carter's labors at the Camp David Accords brought him no win in 1980; and most recently, Bush's stratospheric popularity following the Per-sian Gulf War failed to keep him from packing for home in '92.

So what propelled Clinton to take such action in the months immediately preceding his reelection bid? There was no significant political benefit, it seemed, even if he accomplished his goal. Americans might think it good that the slaughter in Bosnia had ceased, but would they return Clinton to the White House on this basis alone? Not likely. And what of the criticism Clinton might receive on the campaign trail? Had he stuck with prior policy positions, he might have been chided by Republican opponents for doing nothing in Bosnia, but now he potentially opened himself to the more harm-ful charges of needlessly killing American soldiers. Voters might not reelect Clinton for successful Bosnia efforts, but they would throw him out of office quicker than he could spell H-O-P-E if the Bosnia mission cost too many American lives.

"What gives?" some Americans were asking. Could it be that at last Clin-ton had come unabashedly clean with some firm conviction, regardless of those confounded polls? Had he taken Haiti's lesson to heart—that he could eventually sway opinion in his direction? If so, despite disgruntled Ameri-cans, it was at least refreshing to know where the President stood and to see him make his case.

Alas, the explanation for Clinton's sudden decisiveness was not so san-guine. The single boldest foreign policy move of the Clinton presidency to date—that of deploying American troops to Bosnia—came about not through deliberation, but through default. "The decision was made in so aimless a manner," wrote *Foreign Affairs* associate editor Warren Bass, "that almost all senior officials [including Clinton himself] were caught off guard when the implications of what they had done finally sank in."

The confusion originated in a late-1994 Clinton administration agree-ment that NATO would intervene to help UNPROFOR, the United Nations peacekeeping mission, leave Bosnia *if* the situation became too tense to permit UNPROFOR to function. By consenting to this plan, Clinton also pledged twenty thousand U.S. troops as part of the sixty-thousand-person evacuation team. Less than a year later, the unexpected—and, it seems, the ill-considered—happened: the hypotheticals turned real. In the spring of 1995, with a nod from the American NATO ambassador and U.S. military planners in Brussels, NATO formally approved the rescue mission. American troops were now bound for Bosnia—the consequence of a months-old decision regarding a contingency clause, the profundity of which American policy-makers failed to appreciate adequately.

Clinton had painted himself into a corner. He now faced the prospect of either acknowledging the failure of the UN's Bosnia peacekeeping efforts by sending in U.S. troops to aid in UNPROFOR's withdrawal or angering NATO allies by backing out of the American troop commitment. His options so limited, the President decided to proceed with the deployment of U.S. ground forces. Clinton reasoned that the NATO alliance, sorely in need of a credible mission in the wake of the Soviet Union's demise, would perhaps be enervated irrevocably if America welshed on its promise.

Realizing that American troops were destined for Bosnia anyway, members of Clinton's foreign policy team, notably UN ambassador Madeleine Albright and National Security Adviser Tony Lake, clamored for a Clinton administration initiated peace offensive. This way, the troops might be portrayed as venturing to the Balkans to ratify a success rather than to facilitate the exodus from a failure.

And so began the work of Assistant Secretary of State Richard Holbrooke—work that bore fruit at Dayton.

Dayton proved to be a mixed success. It stopped the fighting. It outlined the creation of a single, multiethnic country with a central government. It provided for the prosecution of war criminals. It called for the return of refugees. And under its auspices, Sarajevo was reunified and partially rebuilt; large quantities of weapons were destroyed; democratic elections were held in September 1998; and no fewer than four airports opened to civilian traffic.

But there was a darker side to each of these points of light. The fighting eventually resumed, notably in Kosovo, in Serbia proper, in 1998 and continued into 1999. Bosnia's division into various ethnic enclaves raised the frightful specter of partition—an outcome that had only led to further violence and mass migration in places where it had been tried, such as Cyprus, India, Palestine, and Ireland. Even the September 1998 elections to select members of the state presidency and of state and regional legislatures, held some three years after Dayton, still evidenced competing visions of Bosnia's future—one of ethnic separatism, the other of ethnic integration.

Moreover, by the fall of 1998, the provisions for war-criminal prosecution and return of the estimated 1.8 million refugees were largely unimplemented. The Muslim-Serbian-Croatian government, based in Sarajevo, convened only after the West protested. The United States still maintained at the end of 1998 some 6,500 troops in Bosnia, part of an overall NATO-led deployment of 34,000. And Dayton necessitated dealing with—and by extension, legitimizing and strengthening—two ethnic nationalists, Serbian president Slobodan Milosevic and Croatian president Franjo Tudjman, who had repeatedly shown disdain for either tolerance or the will of international institutions such as the United Nations. For a man who had wrestled so much with the moral, Wilsonian dimensions of the Bosnian imbroglio, Clinton in the end sanctioned a settlement rife with realpolitik.

The President's solution was inspired not by his own independent resolve, but by a backdoor effort to save face in light of complications arising from a wholly unanticipated American troop commitment. In the end, Clinton was emboldened on Bosnia not out of disgust over what he was witnessing, but out of an eleventh-hour strategy emanating from a largely unforeseen circumstance. "The Clinton administration's decision to reevaluate its Bosnia diplomacy came not from a realization of the failure of its earlier rudderlessness or a renewal of Wilsonian principle," chronicled Warren Bass. "Rather, it came from a decision few could even remember making. . . . The choice to commit U.S. troops to help withdraw UNPROFOR was not the fruit of any formal deliberative process in which the President approved the mission through such standard means as a decision memorandum. Rather, it was made by inertia." What kind of leadership was this?

The President spent more than two years vacillating on Bosnia. Meantime, violence proliferated. Rapes and mass murders continued unabated. Families were torn asunder. All told, the Bosnian war had cost some 150,000 lives by 1998.

Though he did stumble on Bosnia, Clinton did not abdicate leadership on the issue altogether. He could have let the killing continue, as he had for so much of his first term in office, and as so much of the rest of the world had done. But he did not.

Clinton also deftly used Bosnia to finesse the prickly issue of NATO's expansion. Russian leaders protested the alliance's continued existence, pointing to their own dissolution of the pro-communist Warsaw Pact as evidence that the relics of the cold war should be shelved. "Europe, not having yet freed itself from the heritage of the cold war, is in danger of plunging into a cold peace," warned Boris Yeltsin in December 1994. "Why sow the seeds of mistrust? After all, we are no longer enemies. We are all partners."

NATO proponents countered that the pact's perpetuation would continue to fulfill some of the alliance's principal—and, in their minds, still necessary—charter aims, such as security protections and promotion of freedom and democracy. To help make their case that NATO expansion need not necessarily bode ill for Russia, the administration included Russian troops in the Bosnian Implementation Force (IFOR) called for in the Dayton Accords. And not only was the NATO commander an American, but

Russian troops were even placed under direct U.S. command. This was a watershed development, given the prolonged acrimony of the cold war, but one for which Clinton got little immediate credit.

Even the overall decision to expand NATO by admitting Poland, Hungary, and the Czech Republic garnered only fleeting headlines for the President. The Senate endorsed the move in the spring of 1998 with a 80–19 bipartisan vote, giving Clinton one of his biggest foreign policy victories. No doubt learning from its frenzied, last-minute scrambling on earlier issues such as NAFTA, the administration had planned well for the NATO issue, having created more than a year in advance of the vote a State Department office to work with Congress and with outside groups to shore up support. "They were organized for NATO," conceded Republican senator Richard Lugar, "and they should be given credit for that."

But Clinton's success on NATO was also one of the few instances where the post–cold war situation did not demand a wholly new approach or an innovative stitching together of coalitions. NATO had enjoyed bipartisan support since its inception in 1949—part of the unwritten cold war principle that domestic bickering stops at water's edge. Thus, many senators had come to see the merits of NATO's growth, well in advance of Clinton's barrage of pro-expansion arguments.

The beefed-up NATO would not want for items on its to-do list. Demanding much attention by late 1998 was Kosovo, a province of Serbia where the majority ethnic Albanian inhabitants struggled for independence and where Slobodan Milosevic sanctioned ghastly crimes—pitchfork impalements, decapitations, slaughters of pregnant women—all in the name of quelling what he termed an internal rebellion. The American response was firm, at least in word. Secretary of State Madeleine Albright warned in March 1998, "We are not going to stand by and watch the Serbian authorities do in Kosovo what they can no longer get away with doing in Bosnia." But, for months, stand by and watch is precisely what the United States did.

And so was set into motion another refrain to the song that had since 1991 become painfully, even pitifully, familiar in the Balkans: Serbian aggression begat American and world condemnation begat Serbian defiance begat Western military threats begat continued Serbian recalcitrance begat Western ultimatums begat last-minute and ersatz Serbian compliance.

The Kosovo chapter of the Balkan imbroglio continued to show the Clinton administration's ambivalence, backpedaling, and miscalculation in the region. Despite Albright's stern warning in March 1998 on Kosovo—and still sterner American admonitions in late 1998 and early 1999—the United States failed for an entire year to take decisive action to stop Milosevic's ethnic-cleansing campaign. And even this U.S. action, which began in March 1999 under NATO's auspices and consisted of air bombing raids on various military and communication targets in Serbia, was undertaken with scant advance mobilization of American public opinion. That the aerial assault continued for weeks privately worried some administration officials, who had expected Milosevic to fold and call off his Kosovo operation soon after the NATO bombing commenced.

A few bright spots were apparent, though. It was NATO that authorized air strikes against Serbia. It was NATO that coordinated the bombing of a sovereign nation. It was NATO's supreme commander, who, early on, spent time bargaining with Milosevic over conditions necessary to stave off the impending military action. And it was NATO that was charged with coordinating surveillance flights over Kosovo to monitor Serbian troop movements. This did much to demonstrate to naysayers—and to affirm to stalwarts—that NATO could indeed be integral to European peace and security in the postcommunist age. In this respect, because he fought hard for its new lease on life, NATO's achievement was partly Clinton's achievement.

But because the operation was so clearly a NATO undertaking—indeed, the alliance's largest effort ever—the consequences of failure mounted considerably. And some cracks simply could not be painted over. A few weeks into the aerial assault on Serbia, the three newest NATO member countries, bordering or nearly bordering the very region where the strife was occurring, had ponied up little for the cause: "Czech Republic—offered to provide a military hospital, but no soldiers or military equipment. Hungary—ready to contribute medical teams; allowed the use of Hungarian air space and airport facilities. Poland—[nothing]." This led some critics to wonder aloud why these countries had gained admission to the alliance in the first place.

Though the Kosovo intervention was, technically speaking, a NATO operation, American forces remained integral to the campaign's success. NATO's fate in the episode would, to a large degree, be Bill Clinton's fate. In Kosovo, Clinton again discovered how NATO, and the United Nations for that matter, still complicated his leadership efforts in foreign affairs. For one thing, the collective security arrangement of NATO and the international peacekeeping aims of the UN were somewhat at odds—NATO assuming an aggressive posture, regarding an attack on one member nation as an attack on all, the UN painting itself as deliberative, seeking to defuse attacks in the first place. Thus, American participation in both entities was a bit of a balancing act.

For another thing, the team approach inherent in each confederation held out collective, not independent, action as the ideal. For a president like Bill Clinton, predisposed as he was to consensus and centrism, having the group approach so visibly reinforced had the effect of often discrediting autonomous decision-making. The existence of internationally recognized, and historically legitimated, institutions that put a premium on collective thought and action minimized the extent to which anything but a consensus approach was seriously considered among the range of options. Yet at times leaders must go it alone, nations must go it alone. But such was rarely Bill Clinton's way.

When talk among some congresspersons and others in the spring of 1999 turned to the possibility of dispatching NATO (including American) ground troops to Kosovo to repel the Serbs' assault on the independence-minded Kosovo Albanians, President Clinton resisted the notion. Instead, he continued to see in the aerial assault a prudent "middle way" between nonintervention and full-fledged war. The whole Kosovo episode once again illustrated the perils of moderation in foreign affairs, as in domestic.

THE PEACEMAKER

If Bill Clinton's leadership style was ill suited for Bosnia and Kosovo, it was appreciably better suited for the imbroglios in the Middle East and Northern Ireland. In those locales, his indecision morphed into patience, and his genuine distaste for conflict ripened into tenacity.

The hostility in the Middle East and in Northern Ireland, not unlike the antagonism in the Balkans, was deep-seated and historically textured. Generations of Israelis had come of age knowing nothing but hatred for Arabs; thousands of Catholics across Ireland instinctively seethed at Protestants and at the British presence in such places as Belfast.

Bill Clinton's familiarity with the strife in Ireland predated his presidency. His tenure as a Rhodes Scholar at Oxford in the late 1960s coincided with a widespread civil rights campaign by Irish Catholics, protesting British intrusiveness and indeed demanding London's outright withdrawal from Northern Ireland. In the twenty-five years since, Clinton and the world had watched as tensions in the region ebbed and flowed, resulting in the violent deaths of some 3,400 people and showing only intermittent signs of subsiding.

Many Irish had, of course, been objecting to what they regarded as foreign occupation by the British since at least the time of Elizabeth I. Not until 1921 were most of the counties on the island granted independence, eventually forming the Republic of Ireland. For the rest of the twentieth century, the six largely Protestant counties where the British maintained a presence—Northern Ireland—would be for Catholics an ignominy, symbolizing the persistence of London's arrogance and tyranny.

Bill Clinton earned the backing of many Irish Americans in 1992 when he suggested, in the time-honored tradition of presidential candidates suggesting an awful lot of optimistic strategies on the campaign trail, a willingness to dislodge the logjam in Northern Ireland. "I think," mused then-governor Clinton, "sometimes that we are too reluctant to engage ourselves [in Northern Ireland] in a positive way because of our long-standing special relationship with Great Britain and also because it seemed such a thorny problem."

This was the bold Clinton, signaling his willingness to ruffle British feathers over the issue of Ireland. This was the Clinton who inspired hope—the Clinton who many in turn hoped would emerge the victor in his struggle with the indecisive, infidelity-prone Clinton. This was the Clinton prepared to honor sage advice from his campaign manager, James Carville: "If you never want to stumble, stand still." This was the Clinton of change.

President-elect Clinton gave early indication that his comments on the Irish question were not just convenient campaign posturings. He seemed intent on following through. Members of the group Americans for a New Irish Agenda (ANIA) met in Little Rock with Clinton's transition team to discuss concrete steps for bringing the various parties to the bargaining table.

Events moved quickly. In September 1993, the Clinton administration sent a delegation of Irish Americans to Ireland. The Irish Republican Army (IRA), the paramilitary group most identified with anti-British violence, marked the occasion with a cease-fire. Their gesture signified both the group's willingness to consider peace and the importance that it placed on American involvement in any forthcoming negotiations. Clinton gave the Irish nationalists further cause for hope when he sent with his delegation a letter criticizing employment practices in the North that discriminated against Catholics and deploring the "wanton use of lethal force" by pro-British security forces.

Meanwhile, Clinton had decided that the peace process could be advanced by pursuing at least two complementary objectives: naming a peace envoy and granting to the leader of Sinn Fein a visa to enter the United States. The peace envoy notion encountered firm resistance from the British, who resented the possibility of American intrusion into the matter. So incensed was London that Conservatives wasted little time conveying their displeasure; they announced on Clinton's inauguration day in 1993 that they would demand the new President drop the idea.

Was this a case of the it's-the-economy-stupid President shooting from the hip at foreign affairs targets? Would Clinton stick to his guns on the Ireland question? Was the conflict there a threat to American security interests, or more of a moral consideration? In this post–cold war world, where the alliance with England might be as integral as ever to global peace, was Clinton really prepared to bump heads over Ireland?

Apparently, yes, for Clinton continued to push on the visa for Gerry Adams, president of the IRA's political wing, Sinn Fein. With counsel from Senator Edward Kennedy, long a proponent of the peaceful resolution of Irish problems, Clinton came to see that Adams's visit to the United States would help the Catholic leader in his own efforts back home to convince IRA hard-liners of the importance of American involvement in the peace process. As well, in the United States, Adams would witness firsthand considerable sympathy for the pro-Irish, as distinct from the pro-IRA, position.

Adams's visit to the United States in early 1994 brought a firestorm of media attention to him and heaved a barrage of criticism upon the President. In consenting to Adams's visa, the President discounted both the pleas of the British government and the advice of his own State Department. Clinton was lambasted for setting a potentially dangerous precedent—that of not conditioning Adams's entry on his disavowal of violence. The indictment seemed not unwarranted later that spring when the IRA launched dummy rockets at London's Heathrow Airport. Had Clinton miscalculated? Had Gerry Adams duped him? Was the IRA interested in peace? Was Sinn Fein?

The answer came in late August 1994 when the IRA announced for the first time since 1969 "a complete cessation of military operations." Adams had been able, after all, to use his American trip to help advance the cause of peace in Ireland and to convince even the staunchest anti-British elements within the IRA to retreat—at least temporarily—from their martial exploits.

Soon, Adams again visited the United States—first, in the fall of 1994 and then in the spring of 1995, where he was a guest, with Social Democratic and Labour Party (SDLP) leader John Hume, at a St. Patrick's Day dinner at the White House. When Adams and Hume broke into song together, onlookers erupted into a ringing applause.

Clinton deserved his share of the credit for the emotional scene that night. Learning of Adams's White House invitation, British prime minister John Major was so angry at Bill Clinton that he refused for an entire week to accept a phone call from the President.

But Clinton stood tall. He had devoted attention to a question that his predecessors had largely avoided. He had risked injuring, perhaps irreparably, a close alliance with England that had endured for more than a century. He had stood firm in the face of rebukes for giving visibility and legitimacy to Adams, a man whom many considered a disingenuous advocate of peace and complicit in the IRA's bombings. Clinton had articulated to the British, to the Irish, to Irish Americans, and indeed to all Americans the need to heal wounds. He had shown leadership.

Clinton's efforts on the Ireland question were not confined to White House hootenannies and pious platitudes, either. In May 1995, the White House sponsored a three-day Economic Summit on Ireland, representing to the *Irish Times* "the most significant engagement by the United States in the affairs of any European country since President Truman's Marshall Plan after the Second World War." More than fourteen hundred attendees heard from the likes of President Clinton, Vice President Gore, Commerce Secretary Ron Brown, and Secretary of State Warren Christopher about the opportunities for American business investment in Northern Ireland and in the counties of the Republic that border the North. Clinton, the economic president, understood well the importance of economic growth to national strength and to the endurance of Irish peace. At least in Ireland, he was apparently not content with a Band-Aid solution.

Clinton was dogged. Even before the 1995 economic summit, he had tied jobs in Northern Ireland to the peace progress, increasing U.S. aid to the region in 1994 and urging American companies to invest in Belfast. In late 1995, he paid a presidential visit with all the trimmings to Northern Ireland and made heartfelt pleas that helped breathe new life into the peace efforts. That same year he also persuaded the British to accept an American role in the negotiations, materializing in the appointment of former U.S. Senate majority leader George Mitchell as chair of the IRA disarmament talks.

Mitchell performed so well in this role that Britain and Ireland invited him to chair the comprehensive peace negotiations in 1996. Events proved that Clinton, and the British and Irish delegations, had chosen well. By April 1998, after twenty-two months, an agreement had been reached.

The deal, approved by voters in both Northern Ireland and the Republic in May 1998, created a new, popularly elected 108-seat Northern Ireland Assembly to replace the British government as the local governing authority. Still, under the plan Northern Ireland retained its political allegiance to London, though provisions allowed for a majority of voters to decide in the future to break with Britain and unite with the Republic. Other of the agreement's terms arranged for the disarmament of various military groups and the release of prisoners from both sides.

The plan had the solid endorsement of American, Irish, and British leaders. "This is the best chance in a lifetime for peace in Ireland," said British prime minister Tony Blair. Bill Clinton was similarly sanguine, even a bit didactic: "This is the chance of a lifetime for peace in Ireland. You must do it for yourselves and your children. It is too late for those who have already been killed by the sectarian violence of the last three decades, but you can do it and you must—now." Irish prime minister Bertie Ahern joined the chorus of optimists, crediting the United States for its efforts. "The Irish can't do it themselves," he noted. "The pressure and involvement by the United States has been indispensable."

Here was a clear, and rare, foreign policy victory for Bill Clinton. From his days as a student at Oxford, he had witnessed the volatility of the Irish conflict. From his days as a presidential candidate, he had committed to making an effort to promote peace, even if it risked offending England. "The success of the [1998] agreement," wrote journalist John Lloyd, "may lie in its very looseness and ambiguity." The irony abounded, for looseness and ambiguity so often characterized Bill Clinton. And they were frequently arrows flung at him by way of criticism. In Ireland, those same characteristics, combined with patience, were part of the solution, not the problem.

*   *   *

The acrimony in the Middle East appeared no less intractable than it did in Northern Ireland when Bill Clinton assumed office. Presidents for the last half century had contended with ancient hatreds in the region—hatreds inflamed by the creation of the independent Jewish nation-state of Israel and Harry Truman's swift recognition of it in 1948. Since that time, Jews and Arabs in the Middle East had fought not only an incessant war of words, but, intermittently, wars of weapons and of bloodshed. Notable armed conflicts erupted in Egypt in 1956 and 1967, in Israel in 1973, and in Lebanon in 1982.

Even more than in Northern Ireland, the U.S. government kept abreast of the slightest developments in the Middle East. Indeed, the United States sought where possible to play a pivotal role in those developments. The region was strategically valuable: it was a rich source of most of the world's petroleum. The region was also dangerously susceptible to Soviet aggression and influence during the cold war. Few other areas of the globe demanded more of an adherence to containment principles than the Middle East. If communists established a strong foothold there, the American oil supply could be threatened indefinitely. And that was no prescription for waging war against totalitarianism.

And so it was with U.S. strategic interests in mind, as well as his own strong and religiously motivated hankering for peace, that Jimmy Carter set about brokering an end to the Egypt-Israel dispute. The Camp David Accords of 1978 led to the normalization of diplomatic relations between the two countries for the first time since Israel was declared an independent state some thirty years earlier. The agreement was a remarkable turnabout from the climate of the previous decade when Egyptian ruler Gamal Abdel Nasser promised, "We swear to God that we shall not rest until we restore the Arab nation to Palestine and Palestine to the Arab nation. . . . [T]here is no room for Israel within the Arab nation." Less than fifteen years later, Egypt became the first Arab country to formally recognize Israel.

By the time Bill Clinton took office, relations between Egypt and Israel remained agreeable. The same could not be said of the Jewish state's interaction with the neighboring Arabs known as Palestinians, who struggled for the creation of a homeland in the region. Pervasive Israeli-Palestinian wrangling over control of territories within Israel such as the West Bank and the Gaza Strip loomed large and often gave way to terrorist bombings and savagely violent deaths. But since the Soviets no longer threatened the region, many asked what stake did the United States have in fomenting Middle East peace? To paraphrase former Secretary of State James Baker, what dog did America have in the fight? Wouldn't the Middle East be another example of how American foreign policy goals had changed, another casualty of the postcontainment age, another case of America pulling up anchor and setting sail for home? Continued intervention in the region would be motivated by little more than idealism rather than practical, security-oriented reasons, right? And hadn't Bill Clinton's very election in the first place signaled the American public's casual disinterest in foreign affairs?

Yes and no. The Soviet threat had dissipated, but new hazards had surfaced. Rogue leaders such as Libya's Muammar Qaddafi and particularly Iraq's Saddam Hussein still rendered the region unstable. And as the 1991 Persian Gulf War made pointedly clear, the sanctity of America's oil supply was not inviolable. Even if the foreign affairs pragmatists denied the moral imperative to Middle East peace, they could not overlook the strategic merit of continued American engagement in the region.

The engagement took a serendipitous turn in the months leading up to Bill Clinton's first term. Many Israelis had tired of the protracted conflict with Palestinians. The missile attacks on Israeli cities during the Gulf War had sobered even some of the hard-liners. The political beneficiary was the Labour Party, which handed the conservative Likud Party its most decisive defeat in more than a decade in the national elections held in June 1992. Yitzhak Rabin, who had promised to negotiate an agreement with the Palestinians soon after taking office, was elected prime minister. Rabin also signaled his intent to improve relations with the United States, which had soured during Yitzhak Shamir's tenure in office. Perhaps peace was at hand. Perhaps Bill Clinton might play some prominent role and reap the rewards. What a coup this would be for the man who was not expected—indeed, who himself did not expect—to play much of a role on the world stage.

But by the time Rabin met Clinton for the first time in Washington in March 1993, things looked grim. Orchestrated murders and kidnappings in December 1992 had stalled the Israeli-Palestinian peace talks indefinitely. Clinton hinted to Rabin that the paltry progress in the bilateral discussions was making it difficult for the United States to justify setting aside the time and resources to the effort. This jolted Rabin hard, as he had already committed himself to peace and as he saw the Jewish death toll rising and relations with the Arabs ebbing.

For his part, Palestine Liberation Organization (PLO) chairman Yasser Arafat worried over the effect of continuing discord with Israel. Arafat had witnessed in recent months a sizable influx of immigrants to Israel, many from the former Soviet Union, and feared that this might make the Jewish hold on the contested West Bank immutable. Moreover, the PLO's support of Saddam Hussein in the Gulf War had alienated many Arab governments. Arafat could no longer count on the subsidies he had long come to expect. This might weaken his standing among Palestinians and cripple his bargaining position with Israel. When Egyptian president Mubarak dismissed Arafat's diplomatic pleas to intercede at the negotiating table, the chairman sought other venues.

The venue that proved decisive was not the one on which most eyes had been fixed. Official bilateral negotiations between Israel and the PLO had been intermittently a part of the Washington diplomatic scene since late 1991. But in early 1993, backdoor talks opened up in Oslo, Norway. Americans knew of this secret channel and, though not directly involved, strongly endorsed the outcome. The approval was essential because American diplomatic and financial leverage would be key to any enduring peace.

To commemorate the breakthrough at Oslo, the White House hosted a signing ceremony in September 1993 at which Arafat and Rabin essentially agreed to reach an agreement. Just as the John Hume–Gerry Adams duet at the 1995 St. Patrick's Day party presaged a breakthrough on the Northern Ireland issue, when Arafat and Rabin clasped hands, it appeared that a new page in Palestinian-Israeli relations had turned. Rabin acknowledged the PLO's legitimacy as the representative of the Palestinian people; Arafat renounced the PLO's sponsorship of terrorism and affirmed Israel's right to exist. For their efforts, Rabin, Arafat, and Israeli Labour Party leader Shimon Peres were awarded the Nobel Peace Prize in October 1994. Bill Clinton had not specifically brokered the deal, but his commitment to the peace process undeniably played a role in the turn of events.

The White House milked the episode. Presidents Carter and Bush were on hand for the September 1993 ceremony, as were former secretaries of state Henry Kissinger, Cyrus Vance, and James Baker. Less than a year into his presidency, Clinton had scored a foreign policy victory. The presence of dignitaries with solid foreign affairs achievements to their credit accentuated the President's feat. But inasmuch as the Arafat-Rabin deal was long on principles and short on specifics, much work remained. Would Clinton's leadership bring about more successes when Israeli and Palestinian opponents of the deal had aired their dissension and thrown their bombs? Or would Clinton become distracted with domestic affairs and seek cover under the justification he had intimated to Rabin in the spring of 1993, namely that it might not be worth devoting American resources to the peace?

The answer seemed apparent just nine months later when still another Arab state hitched itself to the peace bandwagon. At a White House ceremony in June 1994, Jordan's King Hussein and Israel's Rabin agreed to a "Washington Declaration," ending the "state of belligerency" between their two countries. Later that fall, President Clinton flew to an Israel-Jordan border village for an even more stirring ceremony. Though the Russians were present—as they had been in September 1993 for the Arafat-Rabin deal—few doubted the pivotal American role. Among other things, the peace treaty defined the international boundary between Jordan and Israel and established full and formal diplomatic relations between them.

King Hussein saw in the agreement not just the opportunity to ease tensions with Israel, which he had signaled he was prepared to do once the conservative Likud leadership left power, but also a chance to repair relations with the United States, which had waned when he declined to join the

Allied alliance in the Gulf War. Both Israel and Jordan knew of the important diplomatic leverage and economic benefits that close association with the United States could bring.

Within a year, though, the peace—between Israel and Jordan, between Israel and the PLO—was jeopardized. Yitzhak Rabin was dead, the target of an assassin's bullet in November 1995. The price for peace was high. Having seen the bitter fruit of Rabin's efforts, would his successor, Shimon Peres, stumble? Equally as important, would Clinton continue to push for peace, knowing full well the potentially dire consequences? Could he summon the ability to persuade his counterparts to continue on the road they had staked out? Or would the President's efforts on the peace front be a mere detour in a history of hatred, an ephemeral moment in a story otherwise full of destruction and bloodshed?

When Peres lost his election bid to Likud Party stalwart Benjamin Netanyahu in 1996, prospects looked ominous. Had Israeli voters had their fill of Labour's extension of the olive branch to the Palestinians? Would Rabin's slaying signal the onset of renewed violence and recalcitrance between the two sides? And might the new prime minister, Netanyahu, become the architect of and spokesman for that recalcitrance, much as his Likud predecessor Yitzhak Shamir had done?

Some of the worst fears about Israel's ideological trajectory under Netanyahu's watch were not realized. But the peace process sputtered for nearly two years. Then, in the spring and summer of 1998, there were signals that the train might get back on track. By October 1998, it had built a full head of steam. Over days of negotiations that went on much longer than originally forecast, Bill Clinton invested dozens of hours of his time bargaining with Netanyahu and Arafat in close quarters in a conference center not far from the shores of the Chesapeake Bay in Maryland.

Highlights of the Wye River Pact included the PLO's agreement to eliminate from its charter language calling for Israel's destruction, a Palestinian agreement to exert tighter control over weapons trafficking, an Israeli agreement to surrender 14 percent of West Bank territory to Palestine, and an Israeli agreement to release 750 jailed Palestinians. But the deal had about it a tentative air, with Secretary of State Albright referring to "a way station on the path toward peace" and President Clinton reminding listeners that "the forces of hate will come again." Even the pact's official title—Wye Memorandum, as opposed to Wye Pact or Wye Treaty—struck a cautious chord.

But as with his work in Northern Ireland, Clinton could rightfully claim a foreign policy success with this Middle East deal. The President had not allowed bombings, bickering, or even political assassinations to corrupt his efforts at peace. He was able to cajole Arafat and particularly Netanyahu into making the same calculation.

It was the sort of persuasive argument, moral contention—even browbeating—that could only effectively be delivered from one head of state to another. But it was risky. Clinton's personal presence at Wye River put much on the line, and only days before midterm elections in the United States. Had his negotiators failed, it would have been one thing. But for the President to invest significant amounts of his own time to the enterprise elevated the stakes enormously.

Of course, the political risks were high for others too, notably Netanyahu. The United States threatened to declare an impasse at Wye if he did not agree to certain provisions that could have had dire political consequences for him back home. The prime minister needed to keep the concessions to a minimum to deflect criticism from hard-liners, yet he needed to keep the peace process on track to maintain the swing vote that had put him into power in the first place.

If anyone understood this predicament, it was Clinton, a fellow pol. And Clinton used his ability, so often derided in other contexts, to wheedle the prime minister into making the necessary commitments. Apparently integral to the summit's success was an eleventh-hour pledge by Clinton to consider issuing clemency to a U.S. Navy analyst convicted of spying for Israel. Only accounts differed as to whether Clinton had actually agreed to release the spy or simply to consider the matter seriously. The same rhetorical contortions that incited so much anti-Clinton criticism in the Monica S. Lewinsky matter proved instrumental in brokering the Wye deal.

Clinton's involvement was the first instance in which a President had so busied himself with a Middle East negotiation since Jimmy Carter's Camp David efforts two decades earlier. Clinton's role assumed three distinct forms over the nine days of talks. At times, especially in the early going, Clinton asked many questions and listened. Later, he led the U.S. delegation in trying to isolate the critical issues integral to an agreement. Finally, the President made efforts to keep the talks from collapsing in the face of repeated Israeli threats to leave. At one point, the Israeli delegation even loaded its luggage in vans, theatrically conveying their intent to head home. Clinton was steadfast. He indicated to the Israelis that he had already prepared a speech with poetic lines about missed opportunities. "I'd prefer not to give this speech," he said coyly, "but I'm ready to give it."

The bluff, if it was a bluff, worked. Clinton was a study in diligence, "a warrior for peace," praised Netanyahu. The prime minister continued, "I mean, he doesn't stop. He has this ability to maintain a tireless pace and to nudge and prod and suggest and use a nimble and flexible mind to truly explore the possibilities of both sides, and never just on one side. That is a great gift. I think a precious and unique one, and it served us well." At last, America could see evidence that the President's inchoateness and ambiguity had a functional application.

Jordan's King Hussein, who was battling an ultimately fatal form of non-

Hodgkin's lymphoma and had joined the talks late in the game to lend moral encouragement, was equally unrestrained in his praise. Clinton, said Hussein, exhibited throughout the negotiations qualities of "dedication, clearheadedness, focus, and determination." Clinton had "the tolerance and the patience of Job." Coming from a man who had worked with American presidents since Eisenhower, this was high praise.

Ike's vice president, Richard Nixon, once famously noted that history's most honored title is "peacemaker." The words next to Clinton's name—like those next to Nixon's—in yet-to-be-written textbooks are likely to be checkered. Some of the descriptions are deserved, some are not. Yet for his Middle East efforts, Clinton unquestionably earned "peacemaker."

In the wake of the deal, pundits rightfully pointed out the agreement's flaws and unresolved questions. "Why, Oh Wye," they sarcastically sang, and sought to keep popular attention on the still-brewing intern sex scandal. But voters concluded that, on the Middle East and other issues, Clinton was not performing badly—maybe even demonstrating leadership—and so returned many Democrats to the Congress in the 1998 midterm elections. It was the first time in sixty years that the party in the White House did not lose congressional seats in an off-year election. Bill Clinton really was the man from Hope.

"Anyone dealing with the Middle East," said Jimmy Carter in 1998, "has to be an optimist." Few would begrudge Bill Clinton this title. Perhaps it rivaled even the tag "Slick Willie" for its propriety. How else could the President continue with "the people's business" day after day, amid allegations of sexual shenanigans and ubiquitous calls for impeachment? How else could the President make such strides in locales like Ireland and the Middle East, places of decades-old, even centuries-old, antagonisms? An optimist, indeed.

And then there were the Balkans—a quagmire that would curdle the milk of even the cheeriest romantic. Few admonitions from the international community seemed to stop the bloodletting in the region. Moral pleas went unheard; military threats went unheeded. In Bosnia and Kosovo, Bill Clinton the negotiator, Bill Clinton the leader, fumbled for his sea legs.

Why the difference? Why did attributes—caution, patience, even indecision—that proved so poor in wrestling with a policy dilemma such as Bosnia become so effective in another arena, such as Northern Ireland or the Middle East? Part of the explanation lies in the wear-'em-down approach. Many Americans, powerful and politically connected ones too, of Irish ancestry had worked for decades to stop the fighting in Northern Ireland—and the same with the Middle East. Presidents and policy-makers and private organizations had labored for years to foment peace there. Bill Clinton was not beginning anew in either venue; considerable groundwork had been laid.

Still, even this does not explain Clinton's willingness to antagonize the British, longtime American allies, for the sake of peace in Northern Ireland; this was gutsy. Nor does it explain Clinton's commitment of so much presidential time and presidential capital to the Wye River negotiations; this was risky. Clinton's efforts on both fronts demanded presidential courage. Cold political calculus was not readily evident in either venue; it seemed that Clinton was expending energy for causes he genuinely believed in.

Also noteworthy is that Clinton ascended to the presidency with low expectations in the area of foreign affairs, save where economic considerations came into play as in NAFTA or GATT. The magnitude of Clinton's achievements were thus multiplied several times over because few had expected, or elected, him to perform well in this arena.

Equally instructive is that, in both the Middle East and Northern Ireland—and to some extent in Haiti—America did not set about wooing world opinion. America acted on its own. America's decisions did not hinge solely on the positions of NATO allies or UN Security Council members. America led—Bill Clinton led—instead of seeking permission slips.

None of this, of course, held true in Bosnia. It was a fresh crisis, having only a recent—and perfunctory—history of American involvement. It erupted on the world stage with barbarous force and involved death and destruction on a scale that Europe had not seen in half a century. Unlike the more seasoned stories in the Middle East and Northern Ireland, news organizations were less apt to put reports about Bosnia at the end of the newspaper's A section. And Bosnia—and later Kosovo—precisely because of its scale and proximity to other European and Eurasian nations, set into motion entities such as the UN and NATO. The involvement of these organizations, once consulted, circumscribed the American ability to act independently.

Bill Clinton could, of course, have acted unilaterally in the Balkans if he were so resolved. But given the precedent of consulting the world's deliberative bodies in the first place, breaking free of the UN or NATO and acting independently would have been a difficult move to finesse politically. And Clinton, to boot, had the example of George Bush's coalition building in the Gulf War to reinforce his own predilection to act collaboratively.

In considering the whole of Clinton's leadership in foreign affairs, he was strong—in Northern Ireland, in the Middle East—where the players congregated around a table and reasoned through their differences. This was intellectual argument, creativity, persistence, face-to-face negotiation, at which Clinton had always excelled. The President evidenced weak leadership—in Iraq, in North Korea, in the Balkans—where military action was required or nearly used. This called for decisiveness, bold action, and no backpedaling, at which Clinton often blundered.

Late in his second term, Bill Clinton still had no grand strategy for global leadership. He had dealt with some important crises and made important strides. But his deals were brokered piecemeal, and with no real connective thread to bind them together. His secretary of state surveyed the horizon. "Foreign policy, unlike baseball," noted Madeleine Albright in 1998, "has no world championships; there are no permanent victories and no seventieth home runs. In our era, moreover, neither the adversaries, nor the rules, nor even the location of the playing field, are fully fixed."

Yet "our era" is not unlike others. The American Civil War's climax in 1865, German unification in 1871, and the end of the world wars in 1918 and 1945 marked the genesis of similar periods of confusion and introspection, even discontent. Intellectuals and others fumbled about for meaning in the aftermath of grand events. "We shall not succeed in banishing the curse that besets us, that of being born too late for a great political era," wrote Max Weber in 1895, "unless we understand how to become the forerunners of a greater one."

This was the dilemma that beset Bill Clinton. The world during his presidency was one that called for—but did not demand, as in the days of Wilson and FDR and even Reagan—strong American leadership. Occasionally, the calls were heeded. More often, they were not. A grand design, some interpretive paradigm, still eluded the President and foreign affairs analysts. Meantime, Clinton's conduct on the international scene was often akin to a high-wire act. The scene was inspiring when it was done well. But often even the Comeback Kid, like the Flying Wallendas, fell off.

CHAPTER THIRTEEN

What Kind of Leadership?

At some point a two-term president begins to think more about his place in history and less about his standing in the polls and at the polls. His hope for eternal fame rises most acutely after his reelection, of course, but not only then. Presidents are now held responsible for leading their party to win in congressional elections; thus Clinton, and Hillary Rodham Clinton too, were blamed for the Republican takeover of Congress in 1994, then credited for some Democratic gains in 1998. A president is also expected to help his vice president succeed him, but in 2000 that will be Al Gore's responsibility.

During much of his life—and perhaps as early as seizing JFK's hand—Clinton aspired to be not only president but a "great" president. One of his most crushing reactions to the Monica S. Lewinsky revelations was that his behavior had relegated him to the standing of a run-of-the-mill president. He might even be downgraded to failure—a rating inexplicably accorded Jimmy Carter in one polling of presidential scholars.

What is greatness in the White House? For years scholars have been rating presidents without a clear and agreed-on set of criteria. In our view, the bottom-line answer is conviction and commitment, plus the courage and competence to act on beliefs and promises. The scholarly rating game shows some volatility over the years in the standings of presidents—Harry Truman improved the more we got to know some of his successors—but the continuing "greats" over the years are the committed leaders Washington, Lincoln, and Franklin Roosevelt, with Thomas Jefferson just behind.

Monuments are another form of rating, especially in Washington. There is a pecking order in those memorials. For a century or more Washington and Lincoln have had their monuments, joined by Jefferson a half century ago and by FDR in the past decade. Washington's is the most imposing, Lincoln's the most evocative, Jefferson's the most philosophical, and Roosevelt's the most revealing about himself and his First Lady. Then there is Mount Rushmore, with Washington, Jefferson, and Lincoln carved in mighty stone, along with Theodore Roosevelt. Mean-spirited people complained that TR got there only because he and the sculptor were friends, but admirers of this "near great" are satisfied that he made it on his own.

Could Clinton aspire to a monument in Washington? Of course every president now gets his home library, no matter how great or nongreat. But Clinton might want more. Could he even hope for Mount Rushmore? There appears to be an open spot next to TR. But Franklin Roosevelt idolators see two spots that could be reserved for FDR and—yes—Eleanor. Still, what if someday the South Dakotans might balance the present three easterners and one midwesterner with a famous southerner?

Of course all this is terribly elitist. Dozens of other presidents, along with hundreds of governors, congressmen, local politicos, judges, and even professors are memorialized in thousands of courthouses, libraries, parks, and schools across the country. The warp and woof of American leadership, they are portrayed holding swords, canes, bibles, scrolls, constitutions, the reins of horses. Not one, so far as we know, brandishes a balanced budget law.

THE PRICE OF CENTRISM

A contradiction lay at the heart of Clinton's leadership: if he truly aspired to presidential greatness, the strategy he had chosen ensured that he would never achieve it. Rather, long before his presidency he had resolved on a centrist path that called for the kind of transactional leadership that he would exercise in abundance, especially in foreign policy. As a master broker he raised the art of the deal to world-class levels. But he rejected the kind of transformational leadership that might have placed him among the historic "greats."

What form did their transformational leadership take? Washington consolidated a whole new constitutional system that he had helped create. Jefferson recognized that political parties were necessary to unify and democratize that system, and he, with James Madison, fashioned the first opposition party. Lincoln moved on from demanding union at any price to demanding emancipation at any price and established a moral leadership that would vitalize his country for more than a century. FDR's remarkable foresight in broadening the antigovernment Bill of Rights into an "economic bill of rights" provided a "people's charter" that helped Americans cope with the ravages of the Depression and inequality.

The huge successes of these and other presidents displayed their transformational leadership: creativity in fashioning new policies; the courage to press for reforms and other changes despite popular apathy and opposition; the conviction to stick to grand principles no matter how long their realization might take; the commitment to the people to fight for their welfare at any personal cost. What was required for "greatness," in short, was a lifelong struggle to help achieve real, intended, principled, and lasting change.

Clinton could claim that he was just as committed to centrism as those great leaders had been committed to liberalism or progressivism. But just what was Clinton's centrism? The confusion over the term was vividly dramatized when his and Rodham Clinton's health bill of 1993–94 came to be categorized as a radical departure from his centrism. In fact in most respects the health plan epitomized moderate "mainstream" thinking. Rejecting the Canadian plan, it sought to attain a liberal goal, universal health care, without alienating conservatives, such as highly paid doctors and insurance companies. It had no particular ideology; it was neither socialist nor laissez-faire.

Confusion on this score was understandable because there seemed to be several brands of centrism. To some it was a kind of shopping list including moderate, liberal, and indeed conservative policies, from which the White House could pick items almost at will to meet immediate political and legislative exigencies. For others it was a nice balancing act, choosing conservative stands such as the death penalty and matching it with a liberal position on, say, gun control, without much in the middle.

The White House itself seemed unable to clarify this new form of government, or how it fit into the broader political system. In the summer of 1995, in a speech at Georgetown University, Clinton lamented that politics had become more and more fractured, and "just like the rest of us, pluralized. It's exciting in some ways, but as we divide into more and more and more sharply defined organized groups around more and more and more stratified issues, as we communicate more and more with people in extreme rhetoric through mass mailings or sometimes semihysterical messages right before election on the telephone, or thirty-second ads designed far more to inflame than to inform, as we see politicians actually getting language lessons on how to turn their adversaries into aliens, it is difficult to draw the conclusion that our political system is producing the sort of discussion that will give us the kind of results we need." Clinton seemed less than certain that mere goodwill among elected officials could paint over deep cracks in the polity.

Again and again the President invoked symbols of common ground, national unity, middle-class values, political partnership. Again and again he fell into pieties, such as civility, good citizenship, "strong families and faith," provoking in the minds of some listeners the only response to such shibboleths: "Of course, and who's against them?"

At that point, the President occupied the middle of the middle ground— so tenaciously that the liberal press searched for a Rasputin and found him in Dick Morris, who had come back to advise Clinton in 1995 after having worked for such conservatives as Jesse Helms and Paula Hawkins. But Clinton did not really need an adviser or a speechwriter for the Georgetown address. He was speaking from his heart and mind about his present political lodging place. Still, even this speech, lengthy though it was, omitted vital questions.

What about the Republicans? Were they supposed to suspend their partisanship to join the President on some peaceful ground? Clinton did not seem to recognize that he was confronted by one of the most disciplined and doctrinaire parties in this century, or if he did, he still assumed he could make deals with it. But the Republicans had won in 1994 with a most forthright platform, the Contract with America. Why should they break their promises to the people in order to trade with the President? These Republicans could hardly forget that Clinton had defeated a GOP governor in Arkansas and later driven their own president out of the White House. Who was he to talk conciliation?

And what about the Democrats? The President did not once mention the words *Democrat* or *Democratic party* in his Georgetown speech, though he was still using the old party catchwords—justice, equality, compassion, the Jeffersonian pursuit of happiness. Two hundred years earlier Jefferson and Madison were busy founding the Democratic-Republican party that would pursue the ancient values of liberty, equality, and fraternity. Was the modern Democratic party to stand by impotent while Clinton dickered with Republicans on his newly rediscovered common ground?

"Centrism is fine when it is the result of competing interests," William Safire wrote in late 1997. "Thesis; antithesis; synthesis. But centrism is vapid when it is the suffocator of interests, seeking to please rather than trying to move. Clinton's approach, in most cases, has been to follow the primrose path of polling down the middle: his motto has become a firm 'there must be no compromise without compromise.'"

Clinton's major failure was his inability, during his centrist phases, to frame a coordinated policy program that would make of his centrism not just an electoral strategy but a vital center of change. He was not against a political strategy in principle—he would tell aides that he wanted a "strategy" for some undertaking, as though strategies could be ordered up like tractors from John Deere. He loved strategy so much, someone quipped, that he had several of them, often at the same time. Clinton still clung to his overarching values of fairness and justice, but furthering such values to the degree he wished called for a strategy of change. Would centrist politics produce the kind of transformation that Clinton had so often championed and still seemed to support?

Perhaps it would if Clinton pursued his brokering kind of leadership persistently and skillfully. But in his heart he was not content to be only a dealer—at times his lofty values summoned him to a higher, transforming level of leadership. Such leadership, however, called for steady commitment to values such as equality and justice, priorities among those values, capacity to mobilize support both in his party and in movements that could be linked with the party, tenacity in pursuing his long-run visions and goals. It was not enough to know Niccolò Machiavelli's famous distinction between the courageous lion and the wily fox. He also needed to remember another Machiavelli dictum, which he quoted to a group of *Washington Post* reporters: "It must be considered that there is nothing more difficult to carry out or more doubtful of success, nor dangerous to handle, than to initiate a new order of things." For reformers have enemies, Machiavelli explained, and only "lukewarm defenders."

Clinton had lost many of his liberal defenders within three years of his somewhere-left-of-center 1992 campaign for the presidency. But he had not won over his centrist supporters, who feared another lurch to the left. Close observers had been tracking Clinton's ambivalence. Bob Woodward noted how Clinton sought to placate conservative foes of the energy (BTU) tax, stating, "I've been fighting the wrong folks." Elizabeth Drew reported that the President's ambivalence was raising again the "character issue," which could be overcome only if Clinton could move forcefully ahead on his program. It was not the first time someone pronounced, "Clinton was in a race against himself."

"On the one hand, the President badly wants to look like a problem-solver who will work with anyone to overcome the barriers of party and ideology," E. J. Dionne Jr. wrote in mid-1995. But Clinton also understood that "the Republicans have been dominating the political debate, and to change that, Democrats need to take on the large questions, challenging the Republican view of government fundamentally, and with conviction."

But Clinton could not resort to venomous politics. He could not hate those who hated him—not even the House Republicans who were targeting his favorite programs for extinction. "The Republicans were unanimous in their hatred for me—and I welcome their hatred," Franklin Roosevelt cried out to a roaring Democratic crowd at the height of the 1936 election campaign, as he scorched "economic royalists" who occupied positions similar to those of the Gingrich Republicans sixty years later. Clinton could not speak in such tones. Facing an ideological party, he could not be ideological because he was a transactional broker who was not always persistent and skillful enough to make his dealing stick, and was a would-be transforming leader without the deep conviction necessary to that strategy. No wonder some Americans considered him neither a fox nor a lion, but a chameleon.

The clinching argument for centrism is simple: it works. While the ideologues are out there speechifying and pontificating, New Democrats are out there getting things done—not as fast as the "old" liberals would like, perhaps, but centrists get there step by step.

They have a point. The Clinton-Gore centrists can boast of hundreds of presidential and congressional acts leading to incremental progress. But the problem, as always, is not simply what the centrists have done. It is what they have done in comparison with the enormity of the problem and with the changes, some of them regressive, that others are fashioning. It is not only a battle of leaders but a battle of leaderships, economic and social and ideological as well as political.

"Government bureaucracies built a half or even a quarter century ago," Al From wrote in 1991, "are incapable of coping with the challenges of the 1990s—jobs lost to companies overseas, stagnant family incomes, a burgeoning underclass, homelessness, rampant drug abuse and crime and violence in our cities, crumbling roads and bridges, declining public schools, and a deterioration of moral and cultural values symbolized by the breakdown of the family. We need a new set of political innovations."

Eight years and trillions of dollars later, can we say that any of these fundamental problems have been solved? Some economic improvement, yes, but the problems still stare at us. Take education—a concern of Clinton and Rodham Clinton's from their earliest days in Arkansas and a key test of centrist strategy. "We have to be prepared to reform the systems we have made," Governor Bill Clinton told the Democratic Leadership Council in 1990. "As the governors' statement on national education goals says, we can't get there with the system we've got. That's why restructuring schools nationwide is so important."

Restructuring schools? Restructuring the educational *system*? In eight years we have seen a plethora of proposals and programs for federal loans, grants, testing (for teachers and students), school uniforms, aid to special education, recruiting volunteers to teach fourth-graders to read, the end of "social promotion" in schools, adding one hundred thousand new teachers in the primary grades—most of these worthy and helpful—but nothing that could be described as a transformation of our educational system. Centrism, with its incremental advances, cannot possibly achieve such a huge task. And education continues in crisis in the United States.

The centrists have an excuse—the intractability of the American political system. And one of the key arguments for centrism is that it is flexible enough to allow brokering within the interstices of the constitutional checks and balances. Still, it is the liberals, and the conservatives demanding systemic change, who have the main problem with all the veto traps and institutional blocks in the political system. But transformational leaders have learned that the system will respond if they work at it long enough and hard enough; and if this fails to work, they have ideas about rejuvenating the system. Centrists have hardly been forthcoming with ideas for "reconstruction": centrists don't do that sort of thing.

So, Clinton began his seventh year in office amid a political and institutional shambles. Indeed, as Alison Mitchell observed in the *New York Times*, when the 1997–98 Congress came to an end, "it stood identified less with any signature bill than with the paralysis of American politics near century's end." The lesson seemed clear: centrists can deal and bargain and transact from the center; they can gain incremental changes from the center; they cannot truly lead and transform from the center.

Thus, the cardinal question transcends Bill Clinton's or Al Gore's or Hillary Rodham Clinton's "greatness." It goes to core issues about the dynamics of progress, the role of conflict and consensus in democracy, the capacity of people to bring about far-reaching change, the requirements of leadership. It sharply poses the difference between the truly "vital center" that Arthur Schlesinger Jr. wrote about years ago and the mainstream, bipartisan, flaccid centrism of the 1990s.

THE MYTH OF PRESIDENTIAL VIRTUE

While Clinton had been jibbing and yawing in his search for the political center, right, left, or middle, some close observers had been searching for a center in him, ethical, moral, or virtuous.

No words are more confused or abused than the language of good behavior. Dictionaries don't help; ours defines morality as ethics, ethics as morality, and virtue as both. But the distinctions are crucial. We define *virtue* as approved personal conduct, especially sexual; *ethical* as rectitude or right conduct, especially in nonprivate business or professional behavior; and moral as fidelity to the highest and broadest of national or community values, past and present, especially as proclaimed and continually reiterated in formal pronouncements such as presidential inaugural addresses over a long span of time.

The myth of the virtuous American president began early, with George Washington. The story of the cherry tree, although fabricated, symbolized the honesty and integrity that later ennobled the first president's leadership. Yet, he was succeeded, after the very proper John Adams, by his fellow Virginian Thomas Jefferson, who was shown many years later to have probably slept with his slave Sally Hemmings. This was not only unvirtuous but illegal as miscegenation under the laws of the day. But the myth survived and even flourished during the nineteenth century because the genteel press, though it might criticize a president's policies, would not conceive of investigating and exposing presidential peccadilloes, and even scholarly biographers rarely dug into sexual behavior.

Throughout the twentieth century, rumors drifted around about the extramarital sexual behavior—both before and during their presidencies—on the part of Harding, Franklin Roosevelt, Eisenhower, JFK, LBJ, and perhaps earlier of Woodrow Wilson. But the press was not yet so intrusive, or respectable biographers so bold, as to shatter the benign image of the virtuous president. Only years later did it become known, for example, that Harding had had sex with his young mistress in a White House "closet"; or that FDR had had a romance in his earlier Washington days with his wife's secretary or that the liaison was renewed in the White House during his final years; or that JFK had indulged in numerous trysts in the presidential mansion.

How long could the myth survive? Its destruction would require the combination of a reckless president, some bad luck, and rapacious journalists. This was the unintended feat of Bill Clinton. But when one strips away the exploitation of the "scandal" and considers the titillating specifics of the sexual behavior—the caressing, groping, undressing, and the rest—was there any difference between what literally went on in Harding's closet and in Bill and Monica's lovemaking? Only one difference so far as the myth was concerned—Harding's was never exposed in all its graphic detail by an independent prosecutor and sensationalized in the press.

Clinton was attacked not only for his sexual behavior, of course, but for lying about it. And few Americans would ever forget that indignant finger thrust out from the tube, as the President flatly denied the accusations against him. But the earlier transgressors had lied too—implicitly in the case of Jefferson, or with the covering-up by Harding and Kennedy, with the aid of a complicit press.

At issue is the president's right to privacy, including his right to protect it. Beginning with childhood, we all exercise that right, against intrusive parents, prying friends, interrogating employers. Whatever the law may say about the obstruction of justice, William Buckley Jr. wrote, "it is unrealistic to distinguish sharply between the offense of adultery and the offense of lying about it, inasmuch as the second offense goes hand in hand with the first. Anyone who commits adultery is expected to lie about it."

The right to privacy remains the issue. Perhaps presidents do not need it. Or perhaps they need it most of all.

The tragedy of Monicagate was intensely personal—the horrendous invasions of the privacy of Monica S. Lewinsky herself at the hands of an alleged friend, the privacy of Bill Clinton and countless others at the hands of a rampaging prosecutor, and the intense distress for Hillary Rodham Clinton and daughter Chelsea. Everything revolved around the definition of virtue as sex. The tragedy quickly became political, as a media frenzy turned the ethical lesson of Monicagate upside down, grotesquely overemphasizing sex in the Oval Office and ignoring the nonsexual ethical implications. As a result the whole era rivals the Age of McCarthy in its confused and perverted priorities. It ignored the great lesson of American history that ethical concerns must trump private virtue in the public realms.

To free a president from public accountability for behavior in the private realm does not free him from ethical responsibilities in the public realm. Rather, it is to pinion him all the more tightly to his public obligations. It is to confront him with the ethical standards that Americans learn from their parents, teachers, ministers, scoutmasters, coaches, indeed, from the lofty heritage of Christian and Judaic teachings. The standards are old-fashioned but eternally new—rectitude, integrity, compassion, loyalty, responsibility, trustworthiness, civility, respect for all regardless of status, race, gender, or age.

Both the political and economic demands of transactional leadership require a set of more specific but still significant qualities for brokers and mediators—honesty, accountability, reciprocity, credibility, and prudence. How well would the presidents of this century meet both the broader and narrower tests? The answer is difficult because qualities such as rectitude and credibility are not easily definable and certainly not quantifiable. But we do know that presidents lie, dissemble, cover up, break promises, but that they also show compassion, treat people with respect, work hard for their intended goals. As academics we would grade presidents of this century ethically at around a "gentleman's C," with Richard Nixon lowering the collective grade and Jimmy Carter raising it.

How would Bill Clinton fare in this ethical lineup? Measured by the presidential leadership we have studied, we would place him in the middle of the middle, on the basis of Clinton's promises not met, trust not given him, public integrity questioned, along with his incremental progress and his compassion and respect for Americans not sharing in the promise of America. His standing rises a bit when combined with the "straight arrow" Al Gore, and even more when pooled with the integrity and trustworthiness of Hillary Rodham Clinton. These evaluations, anecdotal and impressionistic, may well be modified when the Clinton-Gore leadership is evaluated in longer perspective, and with more factual information.

A pressing question that allows a more easily measurable answer, based on extensive historical data, is whether presidential ethics have declined over two centuries, and if so, whether the deterioration will continue. From the lofty ethical standards of Washington and most of the other founders, those standards declined during the nineteenth century as our political system became more democratized and more subject to bossism and corruption. This tendency was balanced by relatively strong parties that could enforce a measure of discipline on individual miscreants in order to protect their national image and popular vote appeal. As parties have declined in the twentieth century, this kind of collective control has yielded to highly personalistic politics that encourages candidates and officeholders to set their own ethical standards, if any, free of external influence. Bill Clinton— far more a manipulator of the national Democratic party than a disciplined agent of it—well exemplifies this trend.

Will the apparent overall decline in presidential ethics continue in the twenty-first century? Probably yes, for two reasons, political and intellectual.

Increasingly our political institutions and practices are forcing office seekers and -holders to resort to manipulation and deception. Our constitutional checks and balances have long compelled our political executives and legislators to be extraordinarily skillful in threading their way through the devices that thwart collective action. In the absence of strong parties that can unify and empower the rank and file in Congress and the state legislatures, factional leaders within the parties pursue their narrower ends by mobilizing money, interest groups, and legions of lobbyists. Policy—or the blocking of policy—falls into the hands of "transactional opportunists."

Nothing suggests any improvement in this situation; on the contrary, the problem will only worsen, and with it the tendency of politicians, including presidents, to take ethical shortcuts, fueled by money. The Constitution cannot be reformed to make for more responsible and accountable collective action, and the power of corporate money is bound to increase. The sheer incapacity of Congress to pass any effective control of campaign finance is a symptom of the malaise. Nor can presidents solve this problem; increasingly they are part of it.

Behind these political forces lies a pervasive intellectual doctrine—pragmatism. It is ludicrous how often this pretentious term—which today means only expedient, narrow, and short-run self-interest—is used in the press to defend mediocre political actors. "Don't worry, folks, Senator Smith, who might talk like a visionary, is really down-to-earth, a practical man. He coaches Little League and makes bookcases in his basement. He will not be carried away by his ideals or principles. He's okay—a pragmatist." This kind of pragmatism has come to mean, ethically, "anything goes, if you can get away with it." The test is "what immediately works?"—with no consideration of broader, long-term aspects.

Fashioned by Harvardmen William James and Charles Sanders Peirce and others a century ago, pragmatism was a philosophical theory about truth and a refreshing reaction against the heavy Anglo-Hegelian European dogmas that dominated philosophical teaching in America. Pragmatism called for fresh thinking, intellectual innovation, new truths, practical experience. James described his kind of pragmatist: he "turns away from abstraction and insufficiency, from verbal solutions, from bad *a priori* reasons, from fixed principles, closed systems, and pretended absolutes and origins. He turns toward concreteness and adequacy, toward facts, toward action and toward power." James did not flinch from mentioning pragmatism's "cash-value."

So analytically based was this kind of pragmatism, so clearheaded in clarifying different kinds of thought and action, so relevant to American politics and markets, that the new doctrine established a dominant role in American thought in the twentieth century. But during that century the doctrine has been both trivialized and barbarized. Trivialized in its application to almost any business or political act needing a positive spin. Barbarized in its use as "practicality" to defend ethically dubious persons or acts. Thus the FDR

White House joked about some of the disreputable city bosses who trafficked with it; the Kennedy White House admitted it made use of rascals, but these were "our rascals"; the Bush White House compromised with some of the most egregious Christian-right extremists.

So today's "pragmatism" is not an ethical test of political leadership—it is merely winning votes in the next election. Almost anything legal—and much that borders on the illegal—is justified as the "practical" thing to do. But the pragmatists ignore broader and more long-run aspects of elections. How is the contest being waged? What broader stakes than winning are involved? How will defeat or victory impact the future? Winning elections obviously calls for practicality—but what about the role of vision and idealism?

Above all today's pragmatism is anti-ideology. But the pragmatists have made an ideology of pragmatism.

Pragmatism encourages compartmentalization—the separation of self-serving acts from their ethical implications. Bill Clinton is said to deal with his varied problems by putting them into separate boxes—a personal relations box, a budget box, an election box, a Southern Baptist box, a civil rights box. Perhaps this is understandable since, in a broader sphere, our government itself is compartmentalized, as the constitutional separation of powers distributes authority and accountability among House, Senate, White House, and judiciary, and subdivisions thereof, even apart from the division of powers between the national and state governments.

As the most dynamic and innovative branch, can the presidency regain the moral leadership that certain administrations have displayed in the past?

THE REAL TEST: MORAL LEADERSHIP

"Are you having fun?" *Rolling Stone* reporters asked Bill Clinton. It was around the end of his first year in the White House.

"You bet," he answered. "I like it very much. Not every hour of the day is fun. The country is going through a period of change."

"But are you having fun in this job?"

"I genuinely enjoy it."

Later in the interview one of the reporters told Clinton of a young man who had been disappointed by the President's performance and had asked the reporter to pass on his question: What was Clinton "willing to stand up for and die for"?

The President furiously turned on the reporter, his face reddening as his voice rose.

"But that's the press's fault too, damn it. I have fought more damn battles here for more things than any President in the last twenty years." Clinton raged on: he had not "gotten one damn bit of credit for it from the knee-jerk liberal press, and I am sick and tired of it and you can put that in the damn article." He got up there "every day, and I work till late at night on everything from national service to the budget to the crime bill and all this stuff and you guys take it and you say, 'Fine, go on to something else, what else can I hit him about?' " Clinton ranted on and on. He was amazingly self-revealing, a bit paranoid, and wildly off the mark.

The "knee-jerk liberal press." All Democratic presidents—FDR, JFK, LBJ, Carter—were criticized by liberals farther to the left, sometimes unfairly. It came with the job.

"I have fought and fought and fought and fought." What had he fought about? He had pursued a number of policies tenaciously—as he would in the next five years—but he was hardly the image of the Andy Jackson fighting president.

"I . . ." "I . . ." "I . . ." Clinton was remarkably narcissistic, even for a president. In happier moments Clinton boasted of his "White House team." This was a time when the White House troika of Bill, Al, and Hillary was especially influential.

"So if you convince them I don't have any convictions, that's fine, but it's a damn lie. It's a lie." He pointed to a couple of his policies, such as tax reform. Already the most common criticism of the President was his "lack of principle." And again, this was a standard charge against presidents—it too came with the territory.

"Do I care if I don't get credit? No." Of course Clinton did care immensely—that's what the shouting was about. "And you get no credit around here for fighting and bleeding . . ." But Clinton had not fought and bled—he had brokered and negotiated and compromised on a wide range of policies.

And clearly he was not a happy president, at least at this point. Political psychologist Stanley Renshon noted his "bitter sense of futility," which suggested the active-negative character types. This was a reference to the distinction that presidential scholar James David Barber had drawn between active-positive presidents (FDR, Truman, JFK, Carter), who were the most psychologically healthy, and the active-negatives, who dutifully carried out their presidential chores (Wilson, Hoover, LBJ, Nixon) but gained little happiness on the job. Had the cheery, sunny Bill Clinton who had started office as an active-positive, but then, frustrated by Congress and criticism, turned active-negative?

Perhaps it signified something simpler, and even more significant—Clinton's dissatisfaction with himself. Over and beyond his centrist strategy, his endless brokerage, his incremental steps, perhaps he still visualized himself ideally as a principled and visionary leader. Would he ever be in a position to display that kind of political leadership?

In the next five years he became a more seasoned president, more resilient and self-assured. In part this resulted from the sheer experience of governing, and his winning in 1996 the most glorious prize of American politics, a second presidential term. His job satisfaction also rose, ironically, after the Republican sweep of Congress in 1994, forcing him to define and defend his own policies.

Then Monicagate. Anyone who had seen Clinton reveal his vulnerabilities in the *Rolling Stone* interview, or in other incidents where he had lost his cool, could understand Clinton's excruciating mortification later in the titillating revelations. And now he had no one to blame—no "knee-jerk liberals" or hostile press—for his troubles, only his own reckless behavior.

At the beginning of his presidency Bill Clinton had preached and promised change—big change. His presidential leadership would be measured by the success of his economic and social reform. While he was vague on some details, his and Hillary Rodham Clinton's plans became clearer when they proposed a comprehensive new health program. Facing a Democratic Congress, still in his presidential honeymoon, the President reasonably expected that, like FDR and others, he would be granted support and leeway.

The reaction to the rejection of the health bill still remains a mystery. The rejection itself was understandable—the First Lady's plan, developed with Ira Magaziner, had significant flaws, including overelaborate details that evidently tried to anticipate the flood of executive and administrative orders that usually follow the presidential signing of a major bill. In the long history of reform, first efforts often fail; the measure is revived and the fight goes on. Not so with the health bill. The rejection by a centrist Congress triggered a vituperative reaction against the proposers in the White House, not the destroyers on the Hill. The proposal was not only a failure; it was an outrage.

The most important of the overreactors was the President himself. Of all politicians he should have recognized the enormity of the high-powered and heavily financed attack the pharmaceutical and other lobbies had launched in Congress. But the conservatives won a double victory—the killing of the bill and Clinton's return to the centrist, incremental strategy that he and his Democratic Leadership Council colleagues had embraced in the late 1980s.

So gradualism was back in favor. And over the next few years Clinton offered scores and scores of policy bytes, most of them welcomed by the public as promising to address specific problems and deficiencies. Supported by his Vice President and First Lady, he was imaginative and indefatigable in pressing for these small but benevolent changes. But he was most firm, most willing to spend his political capital, not on controversial liberal policies but on such centrist, DLC-backed programs as NAFTA and budget balancing.

The tragedy of the Clinton administration was its failure to tackle the big changes needed to overcome the most glaring deficiencies and inequalities in American society.

Consider education. Clinton had prided himself on being the Education Governor of Arkansas, but even with the indispensable help of Rodham Clinton and a number of initiatives, Arkansas was still near the bottom of state standings on education when he left Little Rock. Then he would be, above all, the Education President, on the premise that the states could not do the job without ample funding from Washington. Soon he was initiating a host of education policy bytes, most of them worthy. But no teacher or parent could enjoy the illusion in 1999 that public education as a whole had been dramatically improved.

A *New York Times* article reported "leaky school roofs, buckling auditorium floors, antiquated coal furnaces, and dangerously rotted window frames." This was not a depression town in the 1930s but booming New York City in November 1998. Teachers and parents could report thousands and thousands of such situations across the country. Education was still in crisis.

Or remember an even more deep-seated problem—the grotesque income gap between the rich and the poor in America. Here again Clinton offered a host of proposals, some of which alleviated the direct symptoms of poverty. But income data told the real story. "Overall, from the late sixties to the midnineties," according to Douglas A. Hicks of the University of Richmond, "income inequality, measured by the standard indicator called the Gini coefficient, increased by over twenty percent for families, and by almost twenty percent for households." Seen another way—in terms of quintiles of the U.S. population—the top 20 percent of our income distribution now receives almost half of the total national income. This is a greater share than the middle 60 percent earns and thirteen times the share of the poorest 20 percent. Clinton failed to exhibit the moral outrage that could have put inequality at the top of the nation's agenda.

Or take the "environmental challenge," Al Gore's special bailiwick. Early administration initiatives were either junked in Congress, as with the proposed BTU energy tax, or drastically cut, as with the proposed boost of the gasoline tax. After 1994, Clinton's and Gore's main efforts were devoted to thwarting Republican attempts to reverse recent gains in environmental policy. That policy—really a cluster of policies—was so complicated by global, national, regional, and special interest (oil industry) politics as to defy easy generalization, but it can be noted that Clinton and Gore's second term neared its end with their old environmental comrades disenchanted by the administration's centrist and weak leadership in this area.

The great excuse of Clinton and Gore—as of all American leaders trying to fashion major change—was the intractability of a constitutional system that utterly fragmented policy. Yet previous presidents had confronted the two-hundred-year-old Constitution and managed somehow to bring off huge changes—Roosevelt's New Deal programs, JFK's economic policies, LBJ's civil rights achievements. Of course, they enjoyed Democratic Congresses, but consider Ronald Reagan's conservative programs. He faced mainly Democratic Congresses but he put through his right-wing policies. He had two big things going for him: conviction and consistency.

The blockage of Clinton-Gore policies in Congress might have tempted Gore to propose major changes in the constitutional and political system. After all, he was in charge of REGO, the exciting project of Reinventing Government. With his strong philosophical interests, his legal and religious education, and his hands-on experience in politics and journalism, he might have at least proposed some constitutional changes for consideration—most notably the abolition of the midterm congressional elections, which had regularly wreaked havoc on presidents no matter how well or poorly they were leading. But the Vice President limited himself to downsizing the huge federal bureaucracy and experimenting with some managerial improvements. Government was hardly reinvented.

So if it was Government Lite under Clinton and Gore, as critics contended, how could they judge the President's efforts, for all his tenacity and compassion, as anything more than Leadership Lite?

Fall Projection 1999

Barring still another jolting surprise, in hardly more than a year Bill Clinton will conclude one of the most remarkable and problematic presidencies Americans have ever known. He will be one of the youngest ex-presidents ever, along with Franklin Pierce and Teddy Roosevelt. Al Gore may be president or among the youngest of ex–vice presidents, but in either case still pledged to act in the Clinton tradition. Hillary Rodham Clinton will become one of the youngest ex–first ladies.

In the end, perhaps Clinton's finest legacy will be the two persons he chose to be his close and nondisposable comrades. Decades earlier he had spotted a bespectacled, drably dressed woman at Yale—not his usual type— and sensed the brilliance of her mind and the power of her personality; he asked her to marry him. Eight years earlier, from a field of a dozen hopefuls, he had chosen as his running mate virtually a political clone—a young, white southerner—and found a vice president of unconditional loyalty. Together these three, for a brief but exhilarating moment, had created a new institution in American government—a troika testing the leadership qualities of all three.

Seven years ago, when we interviewed Bill Clinton during his first presidential campaign, he had professed a strong hope to be a transformational leader who would shape large and lasting changes in American society. Instead he became the consummate transactional leader in dealing with friend and foe in Washington and in skillful mediation of conflicts abroad. Campaigning month after month and year after year, the troika had become masterful presidential election strategists. But they failed to convert their election victories into transformational governing strategies.

In the early weeks of 1999, as the impeachment proceedings were approaching their climax, Clinton took two steps that would set the stage for legislative action for the rest of the year. His State of the Union message, vigorously applauded by Democratic members and limply by Republican, showcased the President once again as the masterful proposer of a flood of policy ideas. His proposed budget, labeled by the *New York Times* as fiscally conservative, struck us as his latest call for cautious, centrist incrementalism.

Because we have made clear in this volume our reservations about centrism as a governing strategy, in 1998 we had wondered if Hillary Rodham Clinton shared these reservations. Or might she favor a different strategy? So we went to see her.

We met the First Lady in the old Map Room where FDR and Winston Churchill had watched their grand strategy triumphantly unroll during World War II in Europe and the Pacific. Having often visited the quiet and even funereal Clinton West Wing, we were surprised by the liveliness of the East Wing—delegations arriving and departing, a large staff busy with the First Lady's big agenda, the media in full coverage. We had never seen Hillary Rodham Clinton close-up in her working quarters—she seemed fresh, radiant, unmarked by the long-gathering storm over Monicagate.

How did she find a balance between principle and pragmatism? "Well," she told us, "of course I have a very particular perspective and I think that principle has always driven pragmatism. But that we came into an era as a country—whether you determine to call it the post–cold war era or however it is characterized—when there was a real void in political principle and understanding of what politics is about. And I would argue that one of the President's great accomplishments has been to undo to a significant extent the damage that Ronald Reagan and his followers did in undermining the legitimacy of government in our democracy. That is not something I believe, however, that you can go out and preach about or talk about. You have to do it almost incrementally, piece by piece, to kind of reestablish some social contract, if you will.

"And I don't know whether others will see it as I do, but part of what Bill has tried to do is slowly but steadily sort of reverse the undermining of governmental legitimacy and social efficacy as something that can move us toward some concept of common good. And during the first administration certainly there was an enormous amount of attention paid to what would be viewed as steps in policy that average Americans could relate to and see that they affected their lives as a means of implementing the larger principle of re-creating some sense of democratic consent and respect for government.

"So that if you look at a lot of the individual pieces that don't appear to be related in any thematic way, I would argue that they're all part of a larger whole that he and I have talked about—which is giving people some reason once again to feel connected to their government. So whether it's [the] Family and Medical Leave [Act] or the Brady Bill or taking assault weapons off the street or even, as he has done, trumpeting small measures like curfews or school uniforms—that can give people a sense that all is not lost, that they're not living this sort of libertarian wilderness where it's every person for himself.

"So from my vantage point I think one of his great accomplishments has been this slow but steady reknitting of the social fabric. But as I say, I don't think it's something you can actually talk about to any great extent. It has to just be sort of pieced together. . . ."

WE: *Does Clinton fear conflict? We remember FDR proclaiming, "They hate me and I welcome their hatred."*

HRC: I understand, I think, where that perception comes from. I just vehemently disagree with it. I think that part of the reason for that kind of assessment may be due to his temperament, which is different from Roosevelt's perhaps. But I think if you look at, particularly '93 and '94, when much of the base for the administration was laid, it was an extraordinary conflict that he was faced with. I mean, it's rare that you are elected president and, from the very beginning of your administration, it's clear that the other party will not cooperate with you at all. . . .

WE: *Why the overreaction to the health care defeat, why was health care then dropped by the administration?*

HRC: But it wasn't. But what we have done is, rather than going with a comprehensive approach, we have chipped away on key issues. . . . So there are many pieces of the health care legislation which we either have enacted or that we are in the process of trying to enact. But we didn't go back with a comprehensive approach because we knew we'd invite the same opposition. So instead what we have done is to sort of chip away at pieces of it to create some constituency. . . .

WE: *Historians will, we think, view centrism as the President's central strategy. Why—why for example doesn't Clinton take a stronger stand for a more graduated income tax?*

HRC: . . . Because when he was running for office in '92, as you may remember from your interview, he was convinced—both out of his experience in the DLC and his experience in governing a very poor state for a long time—that we were paralyzed politically because of the standoff between the right and the left. . . . And that in any kind of showdown in American political history—except in times of great crisis and emergency—the right would always win. I mean, there's just a kind of ingrained sense of individualism and entitlement to one's own property and to one's own position in our democracy. . . .

WE: *Have you ever been a DLC member or involved in the DLC?*

HRC: No.

WE: *We at the grass roots don't think that the President or any recent Democratic leader has done much to strengthen the party at the local level. Do you feel the President or anyone else has done enough on that score?*

HRC: No, I don't. . . .

On the issue of centrism the First Lady had not given an inch. The President "has tried to take positions that were reasonable and prudent and progressive all at the same time." The "centrist kind of position that he has taken has a lot of substance in it." And she argued her case so cogently, pointedly, forcefully, that even the most rabid anticentrist could not but be impressed—especially considering that our questions had not been cleared with her ahead of time.

But as we analyzed her comments further, we unearthed a different subtext, a different Rodham Clinton. However "reasonable" she felt her husband had been, she took strong positions on almost every policy and political issue mentioned. She targeted the Republican assault on the Brady Bill (the assault weapons ban), the tobacco lobby, the Republican rhetoric, the "Reaganites [who had] deliberately set out to destroy the federal government . . . [and] damn near did it," and above all the lobbyists who had spent hundreds of millions of dollars to destroy her health plan. We believe this to be the real, the liberal Hillary Rodham Clinton, who will strike out on a militantly progressive course once freed of her understandable determination to support her husband, the President.

And we believe this because we see Hillary Rodham Clinton as a potential transforming leader dedicated above all to achieving practical results—real, intended, comprehensive, and durable change. What would transformational leadership mean in the twenty-first century?

It would demand a systemic rather than a fragmented approach to American government. It would focus on fundamental causes of problems rather than surface manifestations, summoning political support behind strong agendas, mobilizing movement and party and left-of-center forces rather than depending on assortments of interest groups alone. It would align politically and intellectually with democracies around the world who are following center-left philosophies and agendas. It would be "pragmatic" to the extent that pragmatism could be made to serve principle, in the spirit of FDR, who talked cunningly about being "a bit left of center" while pursuing a strong progressive course.

Applied to education, a systemic strategy would not advance single-pronged panaceas such as school uniforms, or adding one or two teachers to a school to meet the class-size problem. It would look at public schools in the total context of the economic, social, and cultural forces controlling the lives of schoolchildren and their parents. It would deal with children's environments long before they entered a classroom. It would deal with factors of mental and physical health, psychological sources of self-esteem, language barriers and opportunities, school location and student transportation, school and preschool recreation, improved teacher salaries and conditions and recruitment, school and preschool counseling, crime and drug control, as well as the obvious problems of oversized classes, decrepit school buildings, inadequate facilities and texts, corridor and schoolyard security—but these "obvious" problems cannot be solved unless the fundamentally controlling conditions are dealt with. And above all a systemic approach sees the interaction and mutual reinforcement of all these conditions and their solutions.

Applied to poverty, a systemic strategy would recognize the knotty, interlinked problems of deprivation. It would see poor people as poor not only in money but poor in motivation, nutrition, self-esteem, family support, literacy, schooling, health, housing, job skills. Over sixty years ago FDR saw "one-third of a nation ill-nourished, ill-clad, ill-housed." That one-third numbered about 40 million persons. Today about one-fifth of Americans are defined as poor—about 50 million. Scores of policy tidbits cannot rescue these millions—only a massive, unified effort.

Even more important than coordinated planning would be the values by which transformational leadership would be measured. In the United States these are life, liberty, and the pursuit of happiness. Transformational leaders must set priorities among these supreme values: life as the very preservation of a people and their society, making the other values realizable; individual liberty as the most precious of our possessions; happiness as equality, spreading the material and spiritual riches of our society as broadly as possible.

Democratic ends require democratic means: the essence of democracy is not only the consensus that binds us together but the political conflict over the definition of values that gives voters real choices. Thus we divide over national security as protected mainly by diplomacy or by military power; we clash over liberty as mainly freedom from government or through government; we fight over equality as mainly equality of condition or of opportunity. Transformational leadership has been criticized as tending toward the authoritarian or even dictatorial; on the contrary, as leadership scholar Bernard Bass had long contended, transformational leaders foster in their followers a "higher moral maturity" and authenticity; and as political scientist Ronald Walters insists, under such leadership followers are converted into citizens and then constituents into leaders.

So transformational leadership, with its emphasis on the highest public values, is the most moral form of leadership. It is also the most practical, because at a time when the biggest changes are flowing from private leaders in business and technology, only strong public leadership can hold antidemocratic forces in check. As we recall the exuberant young presidential candidate discussing that form of leadership in the campaign car speeding to Falls Church seven years ago, we cannot project that Clinton, as a double lame-duck President in the second half of his final term, could hope to put a major legislative program through a Republican Congress. But he still has the bully pulpit, however splintered.

*   *   *

Months after his impeachment/acquittal, memories of the severest crisis of Bill Clinton's presidency were still acute among the people. Extreme rightists, "full of passionate intensity," in William Butler Yeats's words, had almost toppled a twice-elected President. On the eve of another millennium, could "rough beasts" of the world threaten American democracy? Could the centrist-left Democrats demonstrate the conviction that Yeats had found so lacking in the "best"—and command the courage so necessary to that conviction?

ACKNOWLEDGMENTS

In writing about an active presidency, aside from research sources and interviews, scholars must depend on the work of journalists, as we have done. We wish to acknowledge our debt to the journalists, many of whom we have cited in our endnotes, who have been covering the Clinton presidency with insight and professionalism.

Though writing this book was the work of several authors, we are indebted to still others whose names do not appear on the title page. For research assistance at various stages, we thank David Alire, David Burns, Deborah Burns, Renee Burstiner, Shari Barsky Dexter, Matt Eisenberg, Brooke Foster, Vinay Gupta, Karen Maley, Monica Negm, Scott Palmer, Beth Rossi, Kara Schmidt, Jon Sims, Keisha Smith, Tina Travisano, Ben Wei, and Hillary Zouck—and particularly Michael Seelman and Peter Shapiro. Duke Ducharme, Molly Granzow, and Vicky Navalancy helped us manage our workload so that this book project remained the top priority. Irv Goldstein and Stew Edelstein were fountains of encouragement, and Nance Lucas too often bore the brunt of additional duties at the Academy of Leadership because of our preoccupation with Bill Clinton; we thank them all. We are also indebted to the Williams College Faculty Secretarial Office—especially to Becky Brassard and Peggy Weyers—for generous work beyond the call of duty.

Judith Bair, Michael Beschloss, Bob Cullen, Susan Dunn, Janice Enright, Pat Greenfield, Harold Ickes Jr., Barbara Kellerman, Jake Klisivitch, Hugh O'Doherty, Arthur Schlesinger Jr., and Ronald Walters weighed in with valuable suggestions. And our many interviewees filled in narrative gaps and offered anecdotal insights that have greatly added to the value of this book.

We are especially indebted to our outstanding editor, Lisa Drew, for her absolute faith, political savvy, and insight, as well as her tireless enthusiasm for a book that would be a serious look at a serious subject. We are also grateful to our agent, Fifi Oscard, an old friend whose steadfast confidence in this project and in us helped get us on the road to publication. Finally, special thanks are owed to our families—Antonia, David, Deborah, Stewart, Suzanna, Ollie, Wyly, Jeff, Gordon, Ariel, Sam, Tony, Holly, J.C., Jim, Millie,

Ruth Ann, Shane, Sherri, Todd, Violet, Wallette, Wayne—for sparring with us on the topic of Clinton.

To all who have asked us over the past several months, "How's the book coming?" and then suffered through our long-winded responses, you can now see just what we've been up to.

LIST OF INTERVIEWS

Interviews were conducted from July 1992 to April 1999.

Acheson, Eleanor
Adams, Ruth
Allison, Graham
Atkinson, Dick
Baggett, Joan
Baker, Jerry
Bassett, Woody
Beschloss, Michael
Blair, Diane
Bradley, Bill
Brantley, Ellen
Brantley, Max
Bratton, Sam
Brummett, John
Campbell, Tom
Carville, James
Clinton, Bill
Clinton, Hillary Rodham
Coleman, William
Crawford, Charles
Cutler, Lloyd
Daughtrey, Larry
Dionne, E. J.
Downey, Tom
Dumas, Ernest
Emanuel, Rahm
From, Al
Galston, William
Gardner, Page
Gauldin, Mike

Gergen, David
Gilliland, Jim
Gingrich, Newt
Gore, Albert, Sr.
Gore, Pauline
Greer, Frank
Griffith, Betsey
Hall, Don
Hayes, Johnny
Henry, Ann
Ickes, Harold, Jr.
Jackson, Cliff
Jones, Don
Jost, Ken
King, Patricia
Kissire, Robert
Lewis, Ann
Lindley, Tom
Magaziner, Ira
Martin, Charles
McGovern, George
Merritt, Gilbert
Moore, Rudy
Moynihan, Daniel Patrick
Neel, Roy
Neustadt, Richard
Osenbaugh, Elizabeth
Pallance, Geri
Panetta, Leon
Penny, Timothy

349

Peretz, Martin
Purvis, Joe
Quinn, Jack
Reed, Roy
Ritter, Frank
Roberts, Bobby
Robinson, Jack, Jr.
Robinson, Tom
Root, Paul
Rule, Herb
Rutherford, Skip
Schechter, Alan
Seigenthaler, John
Shapiro, Howard
Shields, Geoffrey
Shookoff, Andrew
Smith, Steve

Smotherman, Eleanor
Soline, Stephanie
Sperling, Gene
Spragens, Janet
Sprecher, Drexel
Staley, Carolyn Yeldell
Starr, John Robert
Thomases, Susan
Thompson, Jerry
Wallace, Chris
Walters, Ronald
Wexler, Ann
Whillock, Carl
Wilhelm, David
Wofford, Harris
Wright, Betsey
Wright, George

NOTES

Epigraph

11 Permission to reproduce William Butler Yeats's "The Second Coming" was obtained from Yvonne Negron at A. P. Watt Ltd. Literary Agents, London, England.

CHAPTER ONE
Presidential Heroes and Moral Failures

19 Why, we asked Bill Clinton: Authors' interview with Bill Clinton, 9/12/92.

19 Like the party leaders that followed: James W. Davis, *The President as Party Leader* (New York: Praeger, 1992); Roy F. Nichols, *The Invention of the American Political Parties* (New York: Free Press, 1972); Morton Borden, *Parties and Politics in the Early Republic* (New York: Thomas Y. Crowell Publishers, 1967).

20 In choosing George Clinton as his running mate: John P. Kaminski, *George Clinton: Yeoman Politician of the New Republic* (Madison, Wis.: Madison House, 1993); Steven E. Siry, *DeWitt Clinton and the American Political Economy: Sectionalism, Politics, and Republican Ideology, 1787–1828* (New York: Peter Lang, 1989); William M. Goldsmith, *The Growth of Presidential Power—Vol. 1: The Formative Years* (New York: Chelsea House Publishers, 1974).

21 Still, if Roosevelt was the first media: John Milton Cooper, *The Warrior and the Priest: Woodrow Wilson and Theodore Roosevelt* (Cambridge, Mass.: Belknap/Harvard University Press, 1983).

23 Americans had in effect a four-party system: James MacGregor Burns, *The Deadlock of Democracy* (Englewood Cliffs, N.J.: Prentice-Hall,1963).

25 "I'm really humiliated that I'm President": Michael R. Beschloss, ed., *Taking Charge: The Johnson White House Tapes, 1963–1964* (New York: Simon & Schuster, 1997), 114.

26 In effect this intertwining distributes veto power: Richard Neustadt, *Presidential Power and the Modern Presidents* (New York: Free Press, rev. ed., 1991).

26 Eisenhower's support dropped: "Clinton's Big Comeback Shown in Vote Score," *Congressional Quarterly*, 12/21/96, 3455.

26 All the last presidents prior to Clinton: Ibid.

27 Often a limb must be amputated: John G. Nicolay and John Hay, eds., *Complete Works of Abraham Lincoln*, vol. 10 (Lincoln Memorial University, 1894), 66.

27 In 1941, Franklin Roosevelt launched: Arthur M. Schlesinger Jr., *Encyclopedia of the American Presidency*, Leonard W. Levy and Louis Fisher, eds., vol. 2 (New York: Simon & Schuster, 1994), 800.

27 He also sent troops to Iceland: Arthur M. Schlesinger Jr., *The Imperial Presidency* (Boston: Houghton Mifflin, 1973), 112–13.

28 He had good history teachers: Authors' interview with Paul Root, 12/6/94.

351

28 Bill Clinton's assumption of office: For contemporary views of presidential leadership, see Thomas E. Cronin and Michael A. Genovese, *The Paradoxes of the American Presidency* (New York: Oxford University Press, 1998); Robert B. Denton Jr. and Dan F. Hahn, *Presidential Communication: Description and Analysis* (New York: Praeger, 1986); Fred I. Greenstein, ed., *Leadership in the Modern Presidency* (Cambridge, Mass.: Harvard University Press, 1988); Godfrey Hodgson, *All Things to All Men* (New York: Simon and Schuster, 1980); Charles O. Jones, *The Presidency in a Separated System* (Washington, D.C.: Brookings, 1994); Anthony King, ed., *The New American Political System* (Washington, D.C.: American Enterprise Institute Press, 1978); Richard Loss, *The Modern Theory of Presidential Power* (Westport, Conn.: Greenwood Press, 1990); Richard E. Neustadt, *Presidential Power and the Modern Presidents* (New York: The Free Press, 1990); Bert A. Rockman, *The Leadership Question* (New York: Praeger, 1984); Arthur M. Schlesinger Jr., *The Imperial Presidency* (Boston: Houghton Mifflin, 1973); Stephen Skowronek, *The Politics Presidents Make* (Cambridge, Mass.: Belknap/Harvard University Press, 1993); Arthur M. Schlesinger Jr., *A Thousand Days* (Boston: Houghton Mifflin, 1965); Herbert S. Parmet, *JFK: The Presidency of John F. Kennedy* (New York: Dial Press, 1983); Richard Reeves, *President Kennedy: Profile of Power* (New York: Simon & Schuster, 1993); Garry Wills, *The Kennedy Imprisonment* (Boston: Little, Brown, 1981) .

30 The abolitionists made their priorities clear: For more on Abraham Lincoln on preserving the Constitution, see John G. Nicolay and John Hay, eds., *Complete Works of Abraham Lincoln*, vol. 10 (Lincoln Memorial University, 1894), especially 66.

30 Second only to slavery as the supreme: For recent scholarship on women's suffrage, see Christine Stansell, "The Road from Seneca Falls," *The New Republic*, 8/10/98.

34 In 1747, at the age of fifteen: For George Washington's rules of civility, see John Rhodehamel, ed., *George Washington: Writings* (New York: The Library of America, 1997), 3–10; and Charles Moore, ed., *George Washington's Rules of Civility and Decent Behavior in Company and Conversation* (The Riverside Press, 1926).

34 "the proofs you have given of your patriotism": Douglas Southall Freeman, *George Washington*, vol. 6 (New York: Charles Scribner's Sons, 1954), 164.

35 In both character and conviction Washington set a standard: For more on character, see James David Barber, *The Presidential Character* (Englewood Cliffs, N.J.: Prentice-Hall, 1992); Stephen L. Carter, *Integrity* (New York: HarperCollins, 1996); Stephen D. Hudson, *Human Character and Morality* (Routledge and Kegan Paul, 1986); Joel J. Kupperman, *Character* (New York: Oxford University Press, 1991); James Q. Wilson, *On Character* (Washington, D.C.: American Enterprise Institute Press, 1991).

35 "ideas are extremely minute": Alexis de Tocqueville, *Democracy in America*, vol. 2 (New York: Alfred A. Knopf, 1945), 77.

36 "Ha! Undecided voter": Stephen E. Ambrose, *Nixon* (New York: Touchstone, 1988), 557.

36 Still, during his first term Nixon's: For more on the Nixon presidency, see Stephen E. Ambrose, *Nixon*, 3 vols. (New York: Touchstone, 1988); Fawn M. Brodie, *Richard Nixon: The Shaping of His Character* (New York: W. W. Norton, 1981); Joan Hoff, *Nixon Without Watergate: A Presidency Reconsidered* (New York: Basic Books, 1995); Bruce Mazlish, *In Search of Nixon* (New York: Basic Books, 1972); Roger Morris, *Richard Milhous Nixon: The Rise of an American Politician* (New York: Henry Holt, 1991); Herbert S. Parmet, *Richard Nixon and His America* (Boston: Little, Brown, 1990).

37 As governor of California and president: For more on the Reagan presidency, see Martin Anderson, *Revolution: The Reagan Legacy* (Stanford, Calif.: Hoover Institution Press, 1990); James MacGregor Burns, *The Crosswinds of Freedom* (New York: Alfred A. Knopf, 1989), chs. 14–15; Lou Cannon, "Ronald Reagan," *Encyclopedia of the American Presidency*, Leonard W. Levy and Louis Fisher, eds., vol. 3 (New York:

Simon & Schuster, 1994); Dinesh D'Souza, *Ronald Reagan: How an Ordinary Man Became an Extraordinary Leader* (New York: The Free Press, 1997); Robert Dallek, *Ronald Reagan: The Politics of Symbolism* (Cambridge, Mass.: Harvard University Press, 1984); Ronnie Dugger, *On Reagan: The Man and His Presidency* (New York: McGraw-Hill Book, 1983); Jeffrey K. Tulis, *The Rhetorical Presidency* (Princeton, N.J.: Princeton University Press, 1987).

37 *Ideas Are Weapons*: Max Lerner, *Ideas Are Weapons: The History and Uses of Ideas* (New York: Viking Press, 1939).

37 *Ideas Have Consequences*: Richard Weaver, *Ideas Have Consequences* (Chicago: University of Chicago Press, reprint 1984).

CHAPTER TWO
The Education of Three Politicos

41 Bill Clinton told us: Authors' interview with Bill Clinton, 9/12/92.

42 Historians, said Erik Erikson: Erik Erikson, *Identity: Youth and Crisis* (New York: W. W. Norton, 1968), 44.

42 Social historians poke fun: For more on presidential personality, see Alexander L. George and Juliette L. George, *Presidential Personality and Performance* (Boulder, Colo.: Westview Press, 1998); and Stanley A. Renshon, *The Psychological Assessment of Presidential Candidates* (New York: New York University Press, 1996).

42 In the wake of Sigmund Freud: See Erikson, *Identity: Youth and Crisis*; Erikson, *Childhood and Society*, 2nd ed. (New York: W. W. Norton, 1963); and Erikson, *Identity and the Life Cycle* (New York: W. W. Norton, 1959).

42 Because of his abandonments: See, for instance, Stanley A. Renshon, *High Hopes: The Clinton Presidency and the Politics of Ambition* (New York: New York University Press, 1996); Paul H. Elovitz, "Clinton's Childhood, Personality, and the First Year in Office," *Journal of Psychohistory* 21, no. 3 (winter 1994): 264; and Paul M. Fick, *The Dysfunctional President: Inside the Mind of Bill Clinton* (New York: Birch Lane Press, 1995).

42 Hence the key element in Clinton's: For more on Clinton's early years, see David Maraniss, *First in His Class* (New York: Simon & Schuster, 1995); John Brummett, *Highwire: From the Back Roads to the Beltway: The Education of Bill Clinton* (New York: Hyperion, 1994); Virginia Kelley, *Leading with My Heart: My Life* (New York: Simon & Schuster, 1994); and Roger II. Morris, *Partners in Power* (New York: Henry Holt, 1996).

42 The pathbreaking psychologist: Abraham Maslow, *Motivation and Personality* (New York: Harper, 1954), 90; and Maslow, *Toward a Psychology of Being*, 2nd ed. (Princeton, N.J.: Van Nostrand, 1968). For more on leaders' psychological needs, see Harold D. Lasswell, *Psychopathology and Politics* (Chicago: University of Chicago Press, 1930); James C. Davies, *Human Nature in Politics* (New York: Wiley, 1963); and Jeanne N. Knutson, *The Human Basis of the Polity* (Chicago: Aldine-Atherton, 1972).

43 This feeling, like general political awareness: For more on the importance of peer influence on children, see James MacGregor Burns, *Leadership* (New York: Harper and Row, 1978), 89–90; and Judith Rich Harris, *The Nurture Assumption: Why Children Turn Out the Way They Do* (New York: The Free Press, 1998).

43 In Greece, young men: For more on this, see Werner Jaeger, *Paideia: The Ideals of Greek Culture* (New York: Oxford University Press, 1939); Karl Mannheim, *Freedom, Power, and Democratic Planning* (New York: Oxford University Press, 1950); and James MacGregor Burns, *Roosevelt: The Lion and the Fox* (New York: Harcourt Brace Jovanovich, 1956), 15–16.

44 Well tutored by his grandmother: Maraniss, *First in His Class*. More on Clinton's early schooling is noted in Jim Moore with Rick Ihde, *Clinton: Young Man in a Hurry*

(Fort Worth, Tex.: Summit Group, 1992); and Ernest Dumas, ed., *The Clintons of Arkansas* (Fayetteville: University of Arkansas Press, 1993). Also authors' interview with George Wright, 12/13/94.

44 "he was glad to tell you what he knew": Authors' interview with Paul Root, 12/6/94.

45 "It was just kind of fun": Authors' interview with Carolyn Yeldell Staley, 1/4/95. See also Maraniss, *First in His Class.*

46 "Long Island power slate": Authors' interview with Tom Campbell, 12/20/94. See also Tom Campbell, "A Preference for the Future," in Dumas, *Clintons of Arkansas.* Some of the information on Clinton's stint at Georgetown and at Oxford is taken from Maraniss, *First in His Class,* especially chapters 3, 7–8.

47 "catalytic time for the whole nation": Authors' interview with Carolyn Yeldell Staley, 1/4/95.

47 "He wanted to take the torch from Martin": Ibid.

48 "the ubiquitous lists and three-by-five cards": Morris, *Partners in Power.*

48 "was ambitious in the same way": Authors' interview with William T. Coleman III, 12/14/94.

48 The war at home over Vietnam: Specifics on Clinton and Vietnam are taken from Meredith Oakley, *On the Make: The Rise of Bill Clinton* (Washington, D.C.: Regnery Publishing, 1994). See also Renshon, *Psychological Assessment of Presidential Candidates,* especially chapter 10.

49 It was probably the most self-revealing letter: For a different view of Clinton's draft letter, see Scott W. Webster, "Men and Women, Love and War: A Gendered Look at Bill Clinton's Draft Letter," *Journal of Unconventional History* (winter 1994).

50 "I didn't rule it out": Authors' interview with Al Gore Sr., 4/13/95.

50 "I didn't know presidents talked like that": Authors' interview with Al Gore Sr. and Pauline Gore, 4/13/95.

51 "A powerful father and a strong-willed son": Authors' interview with Martin Peretz, 4/12/95.

51 "I think we were both very conscious": Authors' interview with Pauline Gore, 4/13/95.

51 "self-reliant, to teach him to work": Authors' interview with Al Gore Sr., 4/13/95.

51 "He was never unable to make a decision": Authors' interview with Graham Allison, 4/12/95.

51 Gore later wrote a senior thesis: Authors' interview with Richard Neustadt, 3/14/95; and authors' interview with Graham Allison, 2/10/99. Some information here on Gore at Harvard and elsewhere is also taken from Hank Hillin, *Al Gore, Jr.: His Life and Career* (New York: Birch Lane Press, 1988, 1992); and from Thomas Hardy, "The Boy Candidate," *Chicago Tribune,* 7/24/87.

51 "I'll go, obey the law": Authors' interview with Al Gore Sr. and Pauline Gore, 4/13/95.

52 "troublesome questions": Authors' interview with Al Gore Sr. and Pauline Gore, 4/13/95.

52 "He wrote exceptionally well": Authors' interview with John Seigenthaler, 3/15/95 and 3/16/95.

52 "well-prepared, bright" and "would not make a comment": Authors' interview with Don Hall, 2/24/95.

52 A classmate, Andrew Shookhoff, remembered Gore: Authors' interview with Andrew Shookhoff, 3/17/95.

52 Susan Thomases quotes: Authors' interview with Susan Thomases, 1/20/98.

53 It seemed harder than ever: Margaret Talbot, "Wife Story," *The New Republic,* 2/16/98.

53 "tough guy—gruff, big, and overweight": Donnie Radcliffe, *Hillary Rodham Clinton: A First Lady for Our Time* (New York: Warner Books, 1993).

53 On one matter the parents: Material on Hillary Rodham's early years is taken from

Radcliffe, *Hillary Rodham Clinton*; David Brock, *The Seduction of Hillary Rodham* (New York: The Free Press, 1996); Norman King, *The Woman in the White House* (New York: Birch Lane Press, 1996); and Rex Nelson and Philip Martin, *The Hillary Factor* (Gallen Publishing Group, 1993).

54 Rodham was allowed to apply to Radcliffe: Authors' interview with Jerry Baker, 2/17/95.

54 "our prevailing, acquisitive": Rodham, as cited in Maraniss, *First in His Class*, 258.

54 Touting his own self-image: Radcliffe, *Hillary Rodham Clinton*, 44; and authors' interview with Don Jones, 3/1/95.

55 Rather heady stuff for a teenager: Radcliffe, *Hillary Rodham Clinton*, 44–75; and authors' interview with Don Jones, 3/1/95.

55 Jones also introduced her to Saul Alinsky: Radcliffe, *Hillary Rodham Clinton*, 75; authors' interview with Don Jones, 3/1/95; and authors' interview with Alan Schechter, 2/27/95.

55 Events too were turning her left: Rodham's years at Wellesley are informed by authors' interview with Betsey Griffith, 2/23/95; authors' interview with Eleanor Acheson, 3/15/95; authors' interview with Patricia King, 2/13/95; authors' interview with Ruth Adams, 4/14/95; and authors' interview with Geoffrey Shields, 3/11/95.

55 'I can't stand it anymore': Radcliffe, *Hillary Rodham Clinton*, 68.

56 Meantime they had to get their law degrees: Rodham and Clinton years at Yale informed by Morris, *Partners in Power*; and authors' interview with William T. Coleman III, 12/14/94.

56 Quotes from V. O. Key Jr.: V. O. Key Jr, *Southern Politics in State and Nation* (New York: Vintage Books, 1949).

57 With its wide-open Democratic party: For background on Arkansas politics, see Diane D. Blair, *Arkansas Politics and Government: Do the People Rule?* (Lincoln: University of Nebraska Press, 1988); Ernest Dumas, "Introduction," in Dumas, *Clintons of Arkansas*; Fred Williams et al., eds., *A Documentary History of Arkansas* (Fayetteville: University of Arkansas Press, 1984); Diane D. Blair and Robert L. Savage, "The Appearance of Realignment and Dealignment in Arkansas," in Robert H. Swansbrough and David M. Brodsky, eds., *The South's New Politics* (Columbia: University of South Carolina Press, 1988); and Thomas G. Keilhorn, "Party Development and Partisan Change: An Analysis of Changing Patterns of Mass Support for the Parties in Arkansas" (Ph.D. diss., University of Illinois, 1973).

58 "with tears in his eyes": Much of the material on Clinton in Arkansas politics is taken from Maraniss, *First in His Class*; Charles Flynn Allen and Jonathan Portis, *The Comeback Kid* (New York: Birch Lane Press, 1992); Dumas, *Clintons of Arkansas*; and Stephen A. Smith, ed., *Bill Clinton on Stump, State, and Stage: The Rhetorical Road to the White House* (Fayetteville: University of Arkansas Press, 1994). For information on gubernatorial transitions in Arkansas politics, see Thad L. Beyle, ed., *Gubernatorial Transitions: The 1982 Election* (Durham, N.C.: Duke University Press, 1985).

58 "kind of bargain": See Judith Warner, *Hillary Clinton: The Inside Story* (New York: Signet Books, 1993), especially 89. And authors' interview with Ann Henry, 3/6/95.

59 "We talked about it": Authors' interview with John Seigenthaler, 3/15/95 and 3/16/95.

59 "This call came about four in the morning": Authors' interview with Al Gore Sr., 4/13/95.

59 His limited goals as attorney general: Authors' interview with Joe Purvis, 12/14/94; and authors' interview with Woody Bassett, 12/28/94.

59 Clinton's governorship could serve: Authors' interview with Stephen Smith, 12/12/94; and authors' interview with Rudy Moore, 2/9/95.

60 "wunderkind of Razorback politics": Kenneth Bredemeier, "The 1982 Elections: The Arkansas Governor's Race," *Washington Post*, 10/28/82.

61   "irrationality of politics": Rodham, as cited in Maraniss, *First in His Class,* 393. Also authors' interview with Don Jones, 3/1/95.

61   He worked out some political maxims: Oakley, *On the Make*; and authors' interview with Mike Gauldin, 12/14/94.

62   He and Rodham revamped his staff: Authors' interview with Betsey Wright, 10/31/94.

62   It was Clinton's critical victory: Much of this material is informed by authors' interview with George Wright, 12/13/94; authors' interview with Ernest Dumas, 12/8/94; authors' interview with John Brummett, 12/13/94; authors' interview with Skip Rutherford, 12/8/94; authors' interview with Roy Reed, 12/6/94; and authors' interview with John Robert Starr, 1/13/95.

62   "education governor": Authors' interview with Paul Root, 12/6/94; authors' interview with Bobby Roberts, 12/13/94. Material on the Clintons and Arkansas education was taken from Blair, *Arkansas Politics and Government*; Oakley, *On the Make*; and Allen and Portis, *Comeback Kid,* especially 86.

63   "powerful core principles": Authors' interview with Diane Blair, 12/8/94.

63   "Cuomo would have been hell": James Carville and Mary Matalin with Peter Knobler, *All's Fair: Love, War, and Running for President* (New York: Simon & Schuster and Random House, 1994), 96.

64   "I don't think being more specific": *60 Minutes* interview, 1/26/92.

64   "cocandidate": Brock, *Seduction of Hillary Rodham,* 261, 263.

64   Then came Super Tuesday: Information on 1992 presidential campaign taken from Robert D. Loevy, *The Flawed Path to the Presidency, 1992* (Albany: State University of New York Press, 1992); Peter Goldman et al., *Quest for the Presidency* (College Station, Tex.: Texas A&M University Press, 1994); and Gerald M. Pomper, ed., *The Election of 1992: Reports and Interpretations* (Chatham, N.J.: Chatham House Publishers, 1993).

66   He published his views in January 1992: Al Gore, *Earth in the Balance* (New York: Penguin Books, 1992), see especially 3, 14.

67   The brainchild of: Authors' interview with David Wilhelm, 4/19/95.

67   He had elaborately spelled out his policy views: Bill Clinton, *Putting People First* (New York: Times Books, 1992).

68   In 1991, when so many: W. Lance Bennett, "The Clueless Public: Bill Clinton Meets the New American Voter in Campaign '92," in Stanley A. Renshon, ed., *The Clinton Presidency: Campaigning, Governing, and the Psychology of Leadership* (Boulder, Colo.: Westview Press, 1995), 92.

68   Bush assailed his opponent's draft record: For more on Bush's campaign tactics, see Betty Glad, "How George Bush Lost the Presidential Election of 1992," in Renshon, *The Clinton Presidency,* 11–35.

68   For Clinton, Bush was a moving: Bennett, "The Clueless Public," in Renshon, *The Clinton Presidency,* 109.

69   "sense of purpose, direction": Dan Quayle, *Standing Firm: A Vice-Presidential Memoir* (New York: HarperCollins, 1994).

69   Before either Bush or Clinton could even: For more on Perot's 1992 candidacy, see Jerrold M. Post, "The Political Psychology of the Ross Perot Phenomenon," in Renshon, *The Clinton Presidency,* 37–56.

69   When the returns came in on election night: Goldman et al., *Quest for the Presidency 1992.*

69   "a lifetime of service": Bill Clinton, as cited in Loevy, *Flawed Path to the Presidency,* 243.

70   No one could gainsay the sweep: For general information on the southern trend to Republicanism, see Jerome M. Mileur, chapter 6, in James MacGregor Burns et al., eds., *The Democrats Must Lead* (Boulder, Colo.: Westview Press, 1992).

70 By the end of the campaign: Robert E. Denton Jr., *The 1992 Presidential Campaign* (Westport, Conn.: Praeger Publishers, 1994), 230.

70 While 77 percent of a national sample: Kathleen A. Frankovic, "Public Opinion in the 1992 Campaign," in Pomper, *The Election of 1992*, 126.

70 "In the microcosm of Bill Clinton's election": Bennett, "The Clueless Public," in Renshon, *The Clinton Presidency*, 93.

71 "The result": Ibid.

CHAPTER THREE
Leadership—for a Change?

75 Change vs. more of the same: James Carville and Mary Matalin with Peter Knobler, *All's Fair: Love, War, and Running for President* (New York: Simon & Schuster and Random House, 1994), 244.

76 The national debt had quadrupled: Shirley Anne Warshaw, *Powersharing: White House Cabinet Relations in the Modern Presidency* (Albany: State University of New York Press, 1996), 3.

76 Americans' faith in government: Burns Roper, "Democracy in America: How Are We Doing?" *The Public Perspective*, The Roper Center for Public Opinion Research, April/May 1994, 3.

76 In Roosevelt's time, the vast majority: "Devolutionary Thinking Is Now Part of a Larger Critique of Modern Government Experience," *The Public Perspective*, The Roper Center for Public Opinion Research, April/May 1995, 28.

76 Historical cross-cultural comparisons: John Gastil, "A Definition and Illustration of Democratic Leadership," *Human Relations*, vol. 47, no. 8 (1994): 955.

76 He knew that "virtually all major": Bert Rockman, "The American President, Integrator or Divider?" (paper prepared for the 1997 annual meeting of the American Political Science Association, Washington, D.C., 8/28–8/31/97), 1.

77 The strategy in essence was sincere: Warshaw, *Powersharing*, 4.

77 he had decided against establishing a preelection transition office: James Rigglesperger and James King, "Getting Started: Transitions in the Modern Presidency," (paper prepared for delivery at the 1998 annual meeting of the American Political Science Association, Boston, Mass., 9/3–9/6/98).

78 "She wanted mostly to listen": Bob Woodward, *The Agenda* (New York: Simon & Schuster, 1994), 87.

78 "It's a real problem": Authors' interview with James Carville, 5/15/95.

79 John Kennedy had asked Clark Clifford and Richard Neustadt to prepare separate memorandums: Rigglesperger and King, "Getting Started."

79 He knew historically that cabinets were: Thomas Cronin and Michael Genovese, *The Paradoxes of the American Presidency* (New York: Oxford University Press, 1998).

79 Bush's Vice President: Ibid., 273.

79 As presidential scholar Harold Laski suggested: Harold Laski, *The American Presidency: An Interpretation* (New York: Harper & Brothers, 1940), 257–58.

79 "Each session began with a kind of high-minded": Authors' interview with Roy Neel, 3/30/95 and 4/26/95.

80 They would not have the "Cabinet Government": Warshaw, *Powersharing*, 12.

80 Thus collegiality among the cabinet: Ibid., 13.

80 They chose three women: Center for the American Woman and Politics, "Women Appointed to Presidential Cabinets Fact Sheet," 1998.

80 The paucity of senior black campaign staffers: Warshaw, *Powersharing*, 14.

80 Eight of the fourteen members had received: Thomas Dye, "The Friends of Bill and Hillary," *PS: Political Science and Politics*, vol. 26, no. 4 (December 1993): 693.

81 Still, her vetting required more than two hundred phone calls: G. Calvin Mackenzie,

ed., *Obstacle Course: The Report of the Twentieth Century Fund Task Force on Presidential Appointment Process* (Twentieth Century Fund Press, 1997), 69.

81 "the mix of new and old hands": Authors' interview with Bill Clinton, 9/12/92.

81 Agriculture was wide-open when: Dan Balz, "Picking the Clinton Cabinet: The Winners, the Losers and Those Who Got Lost in the Shuffle," *Washington Post Magazine*, 5/9/93.

81 And too, searches for women and minorities: Mackenzie, *Obstacle Course*, 68.

81 U.S. senator Harris Wofford: Authors' interview with Harris Wofford, 1/19/95.

82 When the Tennessee senator entered: Authors' interview with Albert Gore Sr., 4/13/95.

83 "needed to coordinate several intersecting power centers": Mackenzie, *Obstacle Course*, 69.

83 They were filled: Richard Neustadt, as quoted in Martha Joynt Kumar, "Preparing the White House Staff to Govern," Academy of Leadership internal document, 1998, 7.

83 "Not only had the process": Warshaw, *Powersharing*, 6.

84 Although DLCers were notably absent: Donald Lambro, "President-Elect Names 48 to Transition Team," *Washington Times*, 11/13/92.

84 One Democratic insider: Warshaw, *Powersharing*, 19.

84 "All of these things conspired to slow down": Authors' interview with Roy Neel, 3/30/95 and 4/26/95.

85 "The White House is not simply": Harrison Wellford, as quoted in Kumar, "Preparing the White House Staff," 1. Authors' possession.

85 fifteen thousand a week: Mackenzie, *Obstacle Course*, 51.

85 Some had the endorsement: Ibid., 52.

85 "In political times, windows of": Ibid., 5, 52, 72.

86 The great prestige and independence of the Senate: V. O. Key Jr., *Southern Politics in State and Nation* (New York: Vintage Books, 1949).

86 "Newness, haste, hubris, and": Anthony J. Eksterowicz and Glenn Halstedt, "Modern Presidential Transitions: Problems, Pitfalls, and Lessons for Success," *Presidential Studies Quarterly* (spring 1998): 299–319. See also Carl Brauer, *Presidential Transitions: Eisenhower Through Reagan* (New York: Oxford University Press, 1986); James Pfiffner, *The Strategic Presidency: Hitting the Ground Running* (Lawrence: University Press of Kansas, 2nd ed., 1996).

87 Vernon Jordan's ten agency-cluster: Warshaw, *Powersharing*, 10, 11.

87 The tall, loosely framed Virginian: James MacGregor Burns, *Vineyard of Liberty* (New York: Alfred A. Knopf, 1982), 159.

88 The address itself, written by a squad: Bill Clinton, "Second Inaugural Address," *Presidential Studies Quarterly* (winter 1997).

89 Though his inaugural address: This line is similar to Mario Cuomo's famous quip to a Yale University audience in 1985, "We campaign in poetry, but when we're elected, we're forced to govern in prose," as cited in Margaret Miner and Hugh Rawson, eds., *American Heritage Dictionary of American Quotations* (New York: Penguin, 1997), 394.

CHAPTER FOUR
The Gauntlet of Leadership

91 "a place for what Franklin Roosevelt called": Bill Clinton, "Inaugural Address," 1/20/93, in *Weekly Compilation of Presidential Documents*, 1/25/93, vol. 29, 75–77.

91 "I am convinced that what this nation": Bill Clinton, "Remarks to the National Governors' Association in Tulsa, Oklahoma," 8/16/93, in *Weekly Compilation of Presidential Documents*, 8/23/93, vol. 33, 1629–38.

91 "I don't know any president": Authors' interview with Harris Wofford, 1/19/95.

91 Fifty-one percent of Americans: *Washington Post*-ABC News poll, as cited in "Public Holds Great Expectations for New President, Survey Shows," *Washington Post*, 1/19/93.

92 "Nobody could have filled": Authors' interview with Joan Baggett, 1/95.

92 No other Democratic president this century: David S. Broder, "Between Gridlock and Lock Step: An Opening for Clinton," *Washington Post*, 1/20/93.

93 "when I think somehow": Bill Clinton, as quoted in *Newsweek*, 12/13/93.

94 "One of the best preparations": Authors' interview with William Galston, 4/9/97.

94 If not chaotic: Ibid.

94 "Clinton has a preference for people": Robert Reich, as quoted in Elizabeth Drew, *On the Edge: The Clinton Presidency* (New York: Simon & Schuster, 1994), 105.

95 "I love the power and the order": Bill Clinton, as quoted in David Mixner, *Stranger Among Friends* (New York: Bantam, 1996), 301.

95 "meetingest fellow": Lloyd Bentsen, as quoted in Bob Woodward, *The Agenda: Inside the Clinton White House* (New York: Simon & Schuster, 1994), 328.

95 "There was nobody there": Robert Reich, as told to American Political Science Association annual meeting, Boston, Mass., 9/3/98.

95 "He was good at playing": Lani Guinier, *Lift Every Voice: Turning a Civil Rights Setback into a New Vision of Social Justice* (New York: Simon & Schuster, 1998), 113.

96 Most damaging of all: David Brock, *The Seduction of Hillary Rodham* (New York: The Free Press, 1996), 378, 381.

97 "They really weren't ready": Authors' interview with Daniel Patrick Moynihan, 4/18/96.

97 Previous presidents had understood: Grace Tully, *FDR, My Boss* (New York: Charles Scribner's Sons, 1949), 78.

97 "He knows that one way": Unnamed aide, as quoted in Drew, *On the Edge*, 95.

97 "I have been living with": Clinton in *Boston Globe* interview, 1991, as cited in Drew, *On the Edge*, 95.

97 Even on his honeymoon: Gil Troy, *Affairs of State: The Rise and Rejection of the Presidential Couple Since World War II* (New York: The Free Press, 1997), 345.

98 And it was a bill that: Authors' interview with Hillary Rodham Clinton, 6/15/98.

98 "Where would we be today": Mixner, *Stranger Among Friends*, 313.

98 In a telephone call: Ibid., 305.

99 "My disappointment is at": Drew, *On the Edge*, 250.

100 Clinton had entered office: For more on this point, see Doris Kearns Goodwin, "Lessons of Presidential Leadership," *Leader to Leader* (summer 1998).

101 Into this unstable equilibrium: Woodward, *Agenda*, 68–71, 106–7.

101 "The dynamic is inside himself": Drew, *On the Edge*, 64.

102 "Why," implored Paul Begala: Woodward, *Agenda*, 126.

102 Clinton's hour-long address: For text of speech, see *Reuters Limited: The Reuter European Business Report*, 2/18/93.

102 Some aides even pointed to: Authors' interview with David Gergen, 2/28/97.

102 "It really doesn't make sense": Authors' interview with Pauline Gore, 4/13/95.

102 The Clinton-Gore intimacy: Authors' interview with Lloyd Cutler, 9/21/95.

103 Clinton's concession of power: Authors' interview with Diane Blair, 12/8/94.

103 "She is a litigator": Authors' interview with Harold Ickes Jr., 7/25/97.

103 When it came to interacting: Authors' interview with Hillary Rodham Clinton, 6/15/98.

103 "It was hard for her to know": Authors' interview with David Gergen, 2/28/97.

104 She would mention: Woodward, *Agenda*, 110.

104 In May 1993: *People*, 5/10/93, 86, as cited in Troy, *Affairs of State*, 359.

104 One journalist even proclaimed: Ann Devroy, as cited in *Washington Post*, 10/24/97.

104 At a late-January 1993: Woodward, *Agenda,* 111.
104 Reflecting on his years: Lyndon Johnson to Richard Nixon, quoted in Bobby Baker with Larry Nixon, *Wheeling and Dealing* (New York: W. W. Norton, 1978), 265, as cited in Thomas E. Cronin and Michael Genovese, *The Paradoxes of the American Presidency* (New York: Oxford University Press, 1998), 110.
104 Clinton had swallowed: Clinton, as cited in Carl M. Cannon, "To Lead Is to Learn, Clinton Finds," *Baltimore Sun,* 4/25/93.
107 Ross Perot, who had made: Dan Balz, "Perot Slams the President," *Washington Post,* 5/27/93.
109 "For a very long time": Drew, *On the Edge,* 262.
110 When the President telephoned Kerrey: Woodward, *Agenda,* 287.
111 Kerrey voted aye: Ibid., 272; and *Congressional Record,* 8/6/93.
111 "What we heard tonight": Drew, *On the Edge,* 272.
111 "In the thirty years": Authors' interview with Leon Panetta, 4/9/97.
111 Clinton informed his cabinet: Drew, *On the Edge,* 227.
111 Recalled economic adviser Gene Sperling: Authors' interview with Gene Sperling, 11/15/96.
112 As well, members of the: Authors' interview with Jack Quinn, 6/20/97.
112 "The Vice President rarely": Authors' interview with Roy Neel, 2/3/99.
112 On this score: Authors' interview with William Galston, 4/9/97.
113 To Lani Guinier: Guinier, *Lift Every Voice,* 36.
113 Ann Lewis, eventual: Authors' interview with Ann Lewis, 2/19/97.
113 "When the phone rings at midnight": Authors' interview with Skip Rutherford, 12/8/94.
113 "I think he is one of the most intellectual": Authors' interview with Stephen Smith, 12/12/94.
113 "It just blows me away": Authors' interview with Timothy Penny, 12/20/94.
113 "President Clinton uses": Robert Reich, address to American Political Science Association annual meeting, Boston, Mass., 9/3/98.
113 They needed his enthusiasm: Authors' interview with Hillary Rodham Clinton, 6/15/98.
113 Although the economy was: Drew, *On the Edge,* 62.
114 She also harbored: Troy, *Affairs of State,* 363.
114 "Heck," he noted, "half the time": Mary McGrory, "Timid Democrats Should Embrace Clinton," Universal Press Syndicate, in *The Berkshire Eagle,* 9/27/93.
114 Journalists and historians questioned: Michael Beschloss, "Seven Ways to Win Friends," *The New Yorker,* 1/30/95, 43–44.
114 Persistent president-bashing: Burns Roper, "Democracy in America: How Are We Doing?" *The Public Perspective,* March/April 1994, 3–4.
114 Favorable White House stories: Michael Grossman and Martha Joynt Kumar, *Portraying the President: The White House and the News Media* (Baltimore: Johns Hopkins University Press, 1981). See especially chapters 10 and 11.
114 Clinton made lots of news: Study by the Center for Media and Public Affairs, cited in Howard Kurtz, "The Bad News About Clinton," *Washington Post,* 9/1/94.
115 During that time: Ibid.
115 Many reporters had turned into: Erika King, "From Slick Willie to Homer Simpson: *The New York Times'* Assessment of Clinton's Character During the First One Hundred Days" (paper presented at the eighteenth meeting of the International Society of Political Psychologists, Washington, D.C., 7/5/95–7/6/95), table 1. See also Thomas E. Patterson, "Trust Politicians, Not the Press," *New York Times,* 12/15/93.
115 "Reporters have to have": Tom Rosenstiel, *The Beat Goes On* (New York: Twentieth Century Fund Press, 1994), 32.
115 In a downward cycle: Kurtz, "The Bad News About Clinton." See also Howard

Kurtz, *Spin Cycle: Inside the Clinton Propaganda Machine* (New York: The Free Press, 1998).

115 "He has always been an enigma": Authors' interview with Mike Gauldin, 12/14/94.

115 "Voters mistrust Clinton in part": Kurtz, "The Bad News About Clinton."

116 Early in the Clinton presidency: Woodward, *Agenda,* 110.

116 In his time, he grumbled: Bruce Miroff, *Icons of Democracy* (New York: Basic Books, 1993), 66–67.

116 But his son later denied: Ibid., 83–124.

116 "The climactic spectacle": Ibid., 169–70, 173.

117 Wirthlin's efforts in creating: W. Lance Bennett, "The Clueless Public: Bill Clinton Meets the New American Voter in Campaign '92," in Stanley A. Renshon, ed., *The Clinton Presidency: Campaigning, Governing, and the Psychology of Leadership* (Boulder, Colo.: Westview Press, 1995), 98.

117 "Anyone who glances at the headlines": Howard Kurtz, "The Press in Campaign Land," *Washington Post Magazine,* 7/16/95, 10.

117 "It's possible for a candidate": Ibid.

117 "yet to establish in the minds": William Raspberry, "The Clinton Thing," *Washington Post,* 11/29/94.

117 "no fixed views": David Brock, "The Agenda," *American Spectator,* August 1994.

117 "near terminal ambivalence": Ibid.

117 "indecisive, emotionally needy": Michiko Kakutani, "Two Views of Clinton, Both Unflattering," *New York Times,* 11/4/94.

117 "indiscipline and incoherence": Paul Fick, *The Dysfunctional President* (New York: Birch Lane Press, 1995), 26.

117 "His thriving on chaos": Margaret G. Hermann, "Advice and Advisers in the Clinton Presidency: The Impact of Leadership Style," in Renshon, *Clinton Presidency,* 158.

117 "He was energized by self-created": Fick, *Dysfunctional President,* 7.

118 "difficulty making decisions": Kakutani, "Two Views of Clinton."

118 "caves in to pressure": Mickey Kaus, "The Cure," *The New Republic,* 9/12/94, 6.

118 "vacillating, passive,": Molly Ivins, "Cut Clinton Some Slack," *St. Augustine Record,* 6/11/95.

118 "undisciplined, indecisive, emotional": Brock, "The Agenda."

118 "We've hit a point where": Robert Lichter, "Regard for Government Officials: Comparison to Other Fields," The Roper Organization, October 1992.

118 We asked Clinton shortly before: Authors' interview with Bill Clinton, 9/12/92.

120 An October 1997 report: Vice President Al Gore, *Businesslike Government: Lessons Learned from America's Best Companies* (Washington, D.C.: National Performance Review, October 1997).

121 Government shrank by: Stephen Barr, "Marking a Milestone with Testimonials," *Washington Post,* 3/4/98. See also E. J. Dionne, "Reinventing Reinventing," *Washington Post,* 4/28/98.

121 "Sure as hell did": Authors' interview with Roy Neel, 4/7/95 and 4/26/95.

121 A 1998 Pew Research Center: Al Kamen, "In the Loop," *Washington Post,* 3/10/98.

121 Well into Clinton's second term: David S. Broder, "Trust in Government Edges Up," *Washington Post,* 3/10/98.

122 His position prevailed: *Congressional Quarterly Reports,* 12/19/92, 3896, as cited in Cronin and Genovese, *Paradoxes of the American Presidency,* 180.

122 Some of the President's: Charles O. Jones, "Campaigning to Govern: The Clinton Style," in Colin Campbell and Bert A. Rockman, eds., *The Clinton Presidency: First Appraisals* (Chatham, N.J.: Chatham House Publishers, 1996), 41.

122 In a sense, Clinton's: Authors' interview with Timothy Penny, 12/20/94.

122 Said Robert Reich: Robert Reich, address to American Political Science Association annual meeting, Boston, Mass., 9/3/98.

122 "He's not trying to overpower": Authors' interview with Stephen Smith, 12/12/94.
122 Betsey Wright, another former aide: Authors' interview with Betsey Wright, 10/31/94.

CHAPTER FIVE
The Tragedy of Health

123 "Jobs, education, health care": Haynes Johnson and David S. Broder, *The System: The American Way of Politics at the Breaking Point* (Boston: Little, Brown, 1996), 81–82.
123 "If criminals have a right": Theda Skocpol, *Boomerang: Clinton's Health Security Effort and the Turn Against Government in U.S. Politics* (New York: W. W. Norton, 1996), 27.
124 up to 2 million more: Ibid., 20–25.
124 The nation's health care system: For more on the health care industry and the need for reform, see Max Heirich, *Rethinking Health Care: Innovation and Change in America* (Boulder, Colo.: Westview Press, 1998); Henry J. Aaron, *The Problem That Won't Go Away: Reforming U.S. Health Care Financing* (Washington, D.C.: Brookings Institution, 1996); Ronald M. Anderson and Gerald F. Kominski, *Changing the U.S. Health Care System: Key Issues in Health Services, Policy and Management* (San Francisco: Jossey-Bass, 1996); Tim Porter-O'Grady and Cathleen Krueger Wilson, *The Leadership Revolution in Health Care: Altering Systems, Changing Behaviors* (Aspen Publishers, 1995); David F. Drake, *Reforming the Health Care Market: An Interpretive Economic History* (Washington, D.C.: Georgetown University Press, 1994); Harry A. Sultz and Kristina M. Young, *Health Care USA: Understanding Its Organization and Delivery* (Aspen Publishers, 1997); James A. Morone and Gary S. Belkin, *The Politics of Health Care Reform: Lessons from the Past, Prospects for the Future* (Durham, N.C.: Duke University Press, 1994).
124 He put Clinton: Authors' interview with E. J. Dionne, 1995.
124 "full-scale effort at responsive leadership": Stanley Renshon, ed., *The Clinton Presidency: Campaigning, Governing, and the Psychology of Leadership* (Boulder, Colo.: Westview, 1995), 208.
124 Ambitious and confident: Stanley Renshon, "A Preliminary Assessment of the Clinton Presidency: Character, Leadership and Performance," *Political Psychology*, June 1994, 376.
124 "vast social good": James L. Sundquist, ed., *Beyond Gridlock?: Prospects for Governance in the Clinton Years and After* (Washington, D.C.: Brookings Institution, Committee on the Future of the Presidency, 1993), 23.
125 "middle way between market tendencies and government involvement": Skocpol, *Boomerang*, xii.
125 "liberal to liberals and centrist to centrists": David Greenbert, "It Wasn't Harry and Louise," *New York Times Book Review*, 3/23/97, 15.
125 "leadership committed to change": "Announcement Speech" by Bill Clinton, Old State House, Little Rock, Ark., 10/3/91.
126 "a social planner": Morton Kondrake, "Apprentices' Sorcerer: Clinton's Best New Idea," *The New Republic*, July 1992, 14–16.
126 He saw her as a clearheaded: Authors' interview with Ira Magaziner, 1/29/97.
126 agreed to the closed process: Johnson and Broder, *System*, 140.
127 In an era when ideological politics: William Schneider, "The New Populism," *Political Psychology*, December 1994, 779.
127 Choosing the form the plan: For more on the reform plan generally, see Paul Starr, *The Logic of Health Care Reform: Why and How the President's Plan Will Work* (New York: Viking Penguin, 1994); Theodore R. Marmor, *Understanding Health Care*

Reform (New Haven, Conn.: Yale University Press, 1994); Howard M. Leichter, *Health Policy Reform in America: Innovations from the States* (New York: M. E. Sharpe, 1997).

127 Their hope was to move the bill quickly: Authors' interview with Ira Magaziner, 1/29/97.

128 "Not only would they oppose the health care": Ibid.

128 "both health reform and the President": Skocpol, *Boomerang*, 81.

128 Public opinion–poll support: Ibid., 75.

128 "If there was any doubt about whether": Dana Priest, "Health Care Testimony from the Top," *Washington Post*, 9/29/93, A1.

129 "Hillary," said former senator: Authors' interview with Harris Wofford, 1/19/95.

129 Magaziner remembered promises: Authors' interview with Ira Magaziner, 3/5/97.

129 "remembered as putting the last piece": Peter Baker, "Mt. Rushmore or Bust: Clinton's Quest for a Legacy," *Washington Post*, 8/3/97.

129 "this kind of sweeping reform": Johnson and Broder, *System*, 639.

129 "liberal or conservative": "Announcement Speech" by Bill Clinton.

130 "base of political leadership": Schneider, "New Populism," 783.

130 "conflict and dissent rather than clarification": Johnson and Broder, *System*, 634.

131 "in the classic sense": Skocpol, *Boomerang*, 118.

131 "We just got outspent and outsmarted": Authors' interview with Hillary Rodham Clinton, 6/15/98.

131 "Whatever you do, don't get caught up": Skocpol, *Boomerang*, 118.

131 "people to the merits and limitations": Renshon, "Preliminary Assessment," 392.

131 "mastery and belief in his political and policy understandings": Ibid., 387.

131 "politically tone deaf": Sundquist, *Beyond Gridlock?*, 23.

132 "bureaucratic takeover by welfare state liberals": Skocpol, *Boomerang*, 146.

132 "public trust in public policy": Renshon, "Preliminary Assessment," 334.

132 "either indifferent or incompetent": Johnson and Broder, *System*, 607.

132 "I get listened to on the Hill": Michael Weisskopf, "Lining Up Allies in the Health Care Debate," *Washington Post*, 10/3/93.

133 "tools, techniques, and philosophy": Sundquist, *Beyond Gridlock?*, 23.

133 "communications and the political war": Bob Woodward, *The Choice* (New York: Simon & Schuster, 1996), 126.

134 "need a party or an ideology": William Schneider, "The New Populism," *Political Psychology*, December 1994, 779.

134 "Why," asked Dick Armey: Armey and Kristol, as quoted in Alissa J. Rubin, "Health Leaders Using Fervent Approach to Convert Wavering Members," *Congressional Quarterly*, July 1994, 1866–72.

135 But Johnson, Nixon before his resignation: Ronald Elving, "GOP's Field of Dreams Sows Nightmare for Democrats," *Congressional Quarterly*, 10/22/94, 2992.

136 Democrats desperately tried to keep their races local: Juan Williams, "Will Clinton Fail His Midterms?" *Washington Post*, 3/20/94.

136 "The whole Republican campaign is based": Fred Barnes, "White House Watch: Back Again," *The New Republic*, 11/21/94, 10.

137 Voters viewed the President as a failure: Harold W. Stanley, "The Parties, the President, and the 1994 Midterm Elections," in Colin Campbell and Bert A. Rockman, eds., *The Clinton Presidency: First Appraisals* (Chatham, N.J.: Chatham House 1996), 189.

137 "abiding image of the 103rd Congress": Elving, "GOP's Field of Dreams," 2992.

137 In October the President's: Paul Richter, "President Going on Campaign Trail—for Bill Clinton," *Los Angeles Times*, 10/31/94.

138 The House of Representatives would be led: William Greider, "Electoral Post-Mortem," *Rolling Stone*, December 1994.

138 During presidential election years: Michael Lind, "What Bill Wrought," *The New Republic*, 12/5/94, 19.

138 They left the Republicans to exploit: Ibid.

139 The President's focus on the deficit: Greider, "Electoral Post-Mortem," 153.

139 Vice President Gore had: Stephen Barr, Ann Devroy, "Clinton Vows Commitment to Centrism," *Washington Post*, 12/7/94, A1.

139 "when you're messing up": Ibid.

139 "trying to lead a cynical": Robert Wright, "TRB: The Inner Circle," *The New Republic*, 11/21/94, 6.

139 "join me in the center of the debate": Text of news conference, "Clinton Reaches Out to GOP," *Congressional Quarterly*, 11/12/94, 3293.

139 "We're dragging the Clinton administration": Ann Devroy, "Clinton Revs Up, Steers to the Center," *Washington Post*, 12/8/94, A1.

139 Many white males with high school degrees: Paul Taylor, "Behind the Broom of '94: Wealthier, Educated Voters," *Washington Post*, 6/8/95, A12.

139 The Democratic party: Thomas B. Edsall, "The Implosion of the Democrats," *Washington Post*, 11/20/94, C3.

139 "We are not seeing the pauperization": Joel Klein, "The Contemplative Bomb-Thrower," *Newsweek*, 1/30/95, 37.

140 "They looked at us": Text of news conference, "Clinton Reaches Out to GOP," 3294.

140 Gephardt did not mince words: Jessica Lee, "Distance Grows Between Clinton, Democrats," *USA Today*, 2/14/95.

140 By January, as the President's: Fred Barnes, "Zero Hour," *The New Republic*, 1/23/95, 18.

140 He implored Americans in a July 1995 speech: Paul Richter, "Clinton Hints of Veto, 'Train Wreck' on Spending Bill," *Los Angeles Times*, 7/25/95.

140 "What we are seeing is dealignment": Thomas B. Edsall, "Huge Gains in South Fueled GOP Vote in '94," *Washington Post*, 6/27/95.

141 "Clinton's 1994 plan was an effort": Jonathan Chait, "Reform Placebo," *The New Republic*, 1/19/98, 15.

141 A popular movie of 1997: James L. Brooks and Mark L. Andrus, *As Good As It Gets* (1997).

CHAPTER SIX
Squarely in the Center

146 "How do you stump a liberal?": Richard L. Berke, "Who's a Liberal! Is Clinton One? Was Nixon?" *New York Times*, 9/29/96.

146 "protean president": Thomas Byrne Edsall, "The Protean President," *The Atlantic Monthly*, May 1996, 42–47.

146 never was chummy with organized labor: Berke, "Who's a Liberal!"

146 On the eve of the 1996 election: *New York Times*/CBS News polls, as cited in Berke, "Who's a Liberal!"

147 "a liberal, responsible Democratic party": Tom Hamburger and Eric Black, "How Did Liberal Get to Be Such a Dirty Word?" *Minneapolis Star Tribune*, 9/30/96.

147 "New Choice": Robin Toner, "Democrat Session Previews '92 Race," *New York Times*, 5/8/91.

147 The English word: Hamburger and Black, "How Did Liberal Get to Be Such a Dirty Word?"

147 "The natural liberty of man": John Locke, *Second Treatise of Government* (1690), as cited in Mitchell Cohen and Nicole Fermon, eds., *Princeton Readings in Political Thought: Essential Texts Since Plato* (Princeton, N.J.: Princeton University Press, 1996), 249–50.

147 "most cogent reason": John Stuart Mill, *On Liberty*, ed. Currin V. Shields (1859; reprint, New York: Macmillan Publishing, 1956), 134.

147 "both the cheapness": Ibid., 115.

148 "the mischief": Ibid., 140.

148 Only in the twentieth-century: Hamburger and Black, "How Did Liberal Get to Be Such a Dirty Word?"

148 In the 1980 elections: Ronald Radosh, *Divided They Fell: The Demise of the Democratic Party, 1964–1996* (New York: The Free Press, 1996), 191.

148 "He literally felt his life was over": Authors' interview with Harold Ickes Jr., 7/25/97.

149 "We were brought up to believe": Bill Clinton, address to Democratic National Convention, 1980, as cited in David Maraniss, *First in His Class: The Biography of Bill Clinton* (New York: Simon & Schuster, 1995), 382–83.

149 "more creative and realistic": Ibid., 382.

149 detractors of Warren Harding: James MacGregor Burns, *The Workshop of Democracy* (New York: Alfred A. Knopf, 1985), 471.

149 or cartoonist Gary Trudeau's: James MacGregor Burns, *The Crosswinds of Freedom* (New York: Alfred A. Knopf, 1989), 636.

150 "A president's words": Bill Clinton, transcript of address to City Club of Cleveland, Ohio, 5/21/92.

150 "Government cannot solve our problems": Jimmy Carter, 1978 State of the Union speech, as cited in Robert Dallek, *Hail to the Chief: The Making and Unmaking of American Presidents* (New York: Hyperion, 1996), 35.

151 "present liberalism of the Democratic party": Herbert S. Parmet, *The Democrats: The Years After FDR* (New York: Macmillan Publishing, 1976), 289–91.

151 "emerging Republican majority": Kevin P. Phillips, *The Emerging Republican Majority* (New Rochelle, N.Y.: Arlington House, 1969).

151 "I am a centrist": Parmet, *Democrats*, 305.

151 CDM attracted many erstwhile: David Shribman, "Group Goes from Exile to Influence," *New York Times*, 11/23/81. See also David Shribman, "Democrats of 'Mainstream' Regroup to Try Again," *New York Times*, 5/23/83.

151 CDM adherents urged Democrats: Howard Kurtz, "A Pundit Puts It All on the Line," *Washington Post*, 11/8/95.

151 "We're a funny organization": Shribman, "Democrats of 'Mainstream' Regroup."

151 He had toiled since the late 1960s: Ben J. Wattenberg and Richard M. Scammon, *The Real Majority* (New York: Coward-McCann, 1970).

151 Yet to win the White House: John Dillin, "Democratic Hopefuls Face 'Vicious Circle,'" *Christian Science Monitor*, 9/2/87. See also Walter Goodman, "Why Things Are Looking Up for the Democrats," *New York Times*, 10/16/92.

152 Michael Harrington: Michael Harrington, *The Other America: Poverty in the United States* (New York: Macmillan, 1962).

152 New York congressman: Parmet, *Democrats*, 306.

153 "Your leaders are out of touch": William E. Farrell, "Democrats Pore Over the Results and Discuss Some New Formulas," *New York Times*, 11/29/84.

153 This bit of election ingenuity: Radosh, *Divided They Fell*, 209.

154 "The Democrats' 1988 defeat": Jon F. Hale, "The Making of the New Democrats," *Political Science Quarterly*, summer 1995.

154 "First, that growth, not redistribution": Al From, "Democrats in the Center," *Louisville Courier-Journal*, 11/3/96.

154 "Just as the New Deal": Al From, "The New Politics," *The Mainstream Democrat*, March 1991, 4.

155 "Extending property to the propertyless": Joel Kotkin, "Forget Moderation," *The New Democrat*, December 1993, 25.

155 The New Democrats' critique: Ibid., 26.

155 Democrats also come under fire: Ibid.

155 "operates better in a bipartisan": Authors' interview with Al From, 4/18/95.

156 Instructively, Clinton's active involvement: Much of the DLC information is taken from Hale, "The Making of the New Democrats."

156 "We're obsessed with our process": James R. Dickenson, "Democrats Seek Identity After Loss," *Washington Post,* 12/17/84.

156 "We're about at the level of bereft": CNN's *Evans & Novak,* 5/11/91, transcript #60.

156 Clinton and the DLCers disagreed: Jack Quinn maintained in his 6/20/97 interview with the authors that Gary Hart was the first modern Democratic candidate to have much success in offering a third way in Democratic politics.

156 Since the mid-1970s: For more on think tanks and Republicans, see Donald E. Abelson and Christine M. Carberry, "Policy Experts in Presidential Campaigns: A Model of Think Tank Recruitment," *Presidential Studies Quarterly,* fall 1997, 679–97.

156 "We are more akin": Lloyd Grove, "Al From, the Life of the Party," *Washington Post,* 7/24/92.

157 "not been 100 percent faithful": *New York Times,* 12/7/94, B10.

157 "The change I seek": Hale, "The Making of the New Democrats."

157 "don't work anymore and they do not": Authors' interview with Betsey Wright, 10/31/94.

157 "I think that the President": Authors' interview with Jack Quinn, 6/20/97.

157 "I think Hillary": Authors' interview with Ann Wexler, 4/21/95.

157 "[W]e feel that for too long": Maraniss, *First in His Class,* 258.

157 Indeed, she talked at times like a centrist: Elizabeth Drew, *On the Edge: The Clinton Presidency* (New York: Simon & Schuster, 1994), 187. Also, authors' interview with Hillary Rodham Clinton, 6/15/98.

158 "To boil it down to a slogan": David Osborne, *Laboratories of Democracy* (Boston: Harvard Business School Press, 1988), 327, 330–31.

158 "Leaders of the 'third way'": Stephen Skowronek, "President Clinton and the Risks of 'Third Way' Politics," *Extensions: A Journal of the Carl Albert Congressional Research and Studies Center,* spring 1996, 10–15. See also Skowronek, *The Politics Presidents Make: Leadership from John Adams to Bill Clinton* (Cambridge, Mass.: Belknap/Harvard University Press, 1997), especially 447–64.

158 "Our approaches to issues": Memo to Bill Clinton from Drexel Sprecher, dated 3/92. Authors' possession.

158 Significantly, with its May 1991 issue: "Introducing the New Democrat," *The New Democrat,* May 1991, inside front cover.

159 "The left has been the conscience": Peter Grier, "Democrats' Values Moving to Suburbs," *Christian Science Monitor,* 8/27/97.

159 In the South: Richard K. Scher, *Politics in the New South: Republicanism, Race and Leadership in the Twentieth Century* (Armonk, N.Y.: M. E. Sharpe, 1997), 303.

159 "I was a peacemaker": Linda Diebel, "Admirers Say He's 'Very Bright,' the Right Man for the Times," *Toronto Star,* 10/25/92.

159 The New Democrat Coalition, for instance: Michael Doyle, "32 Democrats Join Forces for Clout," *Sacramento Bee,* 3/7/97; and Michael Doyle, "Role of 2 Valley Democrats Could Be Crucial on Budget," *Sacramento Bee,* 3/2/97.

159 Slightly older were the so-called: Guy Gugliotta, " 'Blue Dog' Democrats May Have Their Day in a Kinder, Gentler Congress," *Washington Post,* 11/24/96; and David Goldstein, " 'Blue Dogs' Get Attention on Capitol Hill," *Kansas City Star,* 6/19/95.

160 In early 1997, Indiana senator Dan Coats: David Goldstein, "They've Set the GOP on Social Issues," *Kansas City Star,* 3/18/97.

160 endorsing ideas like a charitable tax credit: David Brooks, "The New Bleeding Hearts," *Washington Post,* 2/16/97.

160 Calling itself the Main Street Coalition: "Pushing Both Parties to the Center," *Chris-*

tian Science Monitor, 3/6/97; and David S. Broder, "Endangered Species of Republican," *Washington Post,* 10/29/97.

160 "At some point": Suzanne Fields, "Politics and Statesmanship," *Atlanta Constitution,* 1/18/96.

160 Democrats for the Leisure Class: Thomas W. Still, "DLC Pulls Democrats to Center," *Wisconsin State Journal,* 7/15/92.

160 In 1986, Michael Harrington: John Dillin, "Democrats, Left and Right, Searching for a Comeback Formula," *Christian Science Monitor,* 5/2/86.

160 "He doesn't know shit from Shinola": Grove, "Al From, the Life of the Party."

160 "the future of the Democratic party": David S. Broder, "Hill Liberals Launch Democratic Coalition," *Washington Post,* 5/14/90.

160 "My conviction": George McGovern, "A Word from the Original McGovernik," *Washington Post,* 12/25/94.

161 "some who now label themselves": John E. Yang, "Looking Back to Theodore Roosevelt, Gephardt Calls for 'New Progressivism,'" *Washington Post,* 12/3/97.

161 Beyond the Washington Beltway: Jim Hightower, *There's Nothing in the Middle of the Road but Yellow Stripes and Dead Armadillos* (New York: HarperCollins, 1997).

161 "If fainthearted Democrats": Arthur M. Schlesinger Jr., "For Democrats, Me-Too Reaganism Will Spell Disaster," *New York Times,* 7/6/86.

161 An August 1997 poll: Al From, as cited in Paul Leavitt et al., "Poll: Americans Getting to Like Bipartisanship," *USA Today,* 8/7/97.

161 Tracked in the polls throughout: Roper Center for Public Opinion Research, *The Public Perspective,* March/April 1994, 77. Also, Roper Center for Public Opinion Research, "Public Opinion and Demographic Report," November/December 1994, 105, 109.

163 These could have been chapter headings: Fred Barnes, "Tactics, Tactics," *The New Republic,* 5/15/95, 12.

163 "I was not then elected president": *Berkshire Eagle,* 4/8/95.

165 Why not then imitate: For more on the Harry Truman precedent, see David McCullough, *Truman* (New York: Simon & Schuster, 1992); Alonzo L. Hamby, *Beyond the New Deal: Harry S Truman and American Liberalism* (New York: Columbia University Press, 1973); and Robert J. Donovan, *Conflict and Crisis* (New York: W. W. Norton, 1977).

165 More than two centuries ago: Gary Hart, *The Good Fight: The Education of an American Reformer* (New York: Random House, 1993), 238.

166 "Since we are being followed": Russell Baker, "Don't Look Back," *New York Times,* 8/3/95.

166 "presidents who carry the latest polls": Herbert B. Asher, "Polls and Popularity," *Encyclopedia of the American Presidency,* vol. 3 (New York: Simon & Schuster, 1994), 1187.

166 "If you think about our most": Barnes, "Tactics, Tactics."

166 He would also speak out politically: *Berkshire Eagle,* 8/29/95.

166 "troubling and dangerous": *New York Times,* 7/13/95.

168 "have not been much interested in the": Daniel J. Boorstin, *The Genius of American Politics* (Chicago: University of Chicago Press, 1953), 2.

CHAPTER SEVEN

The Intrusion of Foreign Affairs

169 "literally blows you away": Authors' interview with Joe Purvis, 12/14/94.

169 "quagmire": E. J. Dionne, "Clinton's Problems with Promises," *Arizona Republic,* 5/8/94.

169 Indeed, Lake and Christopher well understood: Elizabeth Drew, *On the Edge: The Clinton Presidency* (New York: Simon & Schuster, 1994), 28.

170 Less than one month before: John E. Reilly, ed., *American Public Opinion and U.S. Foreign Policy, 1995* (Chicago Council on Foreign Relations, 1995), 10.

170 "A great president": Henry Kissinger, *Diplomacy* (New York: Simon & Schuster, 1994), 39.

170 Around the end of 1918: William Butler Yeats, "The Second Coming"; Richard Ellmann, *The Identity of Yeats* (New York: Oxford University Press, 1964); B. L. Reid, *William Butler Yeats: The Lyric of Tragedy* (Norman: University of Oklahoma Press, 1961); A. Norman Jeffares, *A Commentary on the Collected Poems of W. B. Yeats* (Stanford, Calif.: Stanford University Press, 1968).

171 The United States has always sought: For more on American efforts at economic hegemony, see Thomas J. McCormick, *America's Half-Century: United States Foreign Policy in the Cold War* (Baltimore: Johns Hopkins University Press, 1989).

171 "Today is not a time": Eric Alterman, "When Democracy and Liberty Collide," *New York Times,* 10/3/98.

172 Secretary of State Warren Christopher: Karen Breslau and Bob Cohn, "Al Gore: Talk a Lot, and Carry a Big Stick," *Newsweek,* 10/31/94, 30.

172 "The first is to grasp": *New York Times,* 8/14/92.

173 The end of the cold war: For more on presidents, leadership, and foreign-policy-making, see Barbara Kellerman and Ryan J. Barilleaux, *The President as World Leader* (New York: St. Martin's Press, 1991); Thomas F. Eagleton, *War and Presidential Power: A Chronicle of Congressional Surrender* (New York: Liveright, 1974); Edward R. Drachman et al., *Presidents and Foreign Policy: Countdown to Ten Controversial Decisions* (Albany: State University of New York Press, 1997); James E. Winkates et al., eds., *U.S. Foreign Policy in Transition* (Chicago: Nelson Hall Publishers, 1994); Joshua Muravchik, *The Imperative of American Leadership: A Challenge to Neo-Isolationism* (Washington, D.C.: American Enterprise Institute, 1996); Steven Schlosstein, *The End of the American Century* (New York: Congdon & Weed, 1989); and Joseph S. Nye Jr., *Bound to Lead: The Changing Nature of American Power* (New York: Basic Books, 1990).

174 "What is very difficult and very dangerous": Les Aspin, "Challenges to Values-Based Military Intervention," 11/30/94. This was a luncheon keynote address delivered at the U.S. Institute of Peace's conference "Managing Chaos: Coping with International Conflict into the 21st Century."

175 By the spring of 1994: David E. Sanger, "North Korea Foils Efforts to Halt Its Nuclear Plans," *New York Times,* 5/29/94.

175 "We had hoped": Drew, *On the Edge,* 138.

175 The new Korean crisis: Elaine Sciolino, "For Carter, a Thrust onto the Front Pages Again," *New York Times,* 6/3/94.

176 In 1991, for instance: Michael Kelly, "It All Codepends," *The New Yorker,* 10/3/94, 82.

176 Carter flew to Pyongyang: David E. Sanger, "Two Koreas Agree to Summit Meeting on Nuclear Issue," *New York Times,* 6/19/94.

176 But, Carter said, he was in: Kelly, "It All Codepends."

176 "very firm": Bill Clinton, on NBC's *Meet the Pess,* 11/7/93, as cited in Michael Wines, "Present Arms," *New York Times,* 9/18/94.

176 At a news conference: Sciolino, "For Carter, a Thrust."

177 When formal talks between: Barton Gellman, "U.S., Allies Struggling to Fulfill N. Korea Pact," *Washington Post,* 5/2/98. See also Dana Priest and Sandra Sugawara, "North Korea Missile Test Threatens Nuclear Pact," *Washington Post,* 9/1/98.

177 "While it was not unconditional": This quote and N. Korean episode taken from accounts in R. Jeffrey Smith, "U.S. Tickets Funds for N. Korea Nuclear Pact," *Washington Post,* 12/1/94; William Safire, "Clinton's Concessions," *New York Times,* 10/24/94; and Lally Weymouth, "Questioning the Korea Deal," *Washington Post,* 1/25/95.

178 Clinton was also facing: For more on Clinton and Haiti and North Korea, see Thomas H. Henriksen, *Clinton's Foreign Policy in Somalia, Bosnia, Haiti, and North Korea* (Stanford, Calif.: Hoover Institution Press, 1996).

178 Some leading members of Congress: See, for instance, Senator Richard Lugar's comments in Thomas W. Lippman, "U.S. Considered Attacks on N. Korea, Perry Tells Panel," *Washington Post*, 1/25/95.

178 First, it did not guarantee: Priest and Sugawara, "North Korea Missile Test Threatens Nuclear Pact."

178 "The failure to deal with": Jeane Kirkpatrick, statement made at U.S. Institute of Peace conference on "Managing Chaos," 11/30/94.

178 U.S. intelligence analysts discovered: Priest and Sugawara, "North Korea Missile Test Threatens Nuclear Pact."

178 "In a crisis": Monica Crowley, *Nixon in Winter* (New York: Random House, 1998), 219.

179 Shortly after the battle of Antietam: For quotes, see Stephen B. Oates, *With Malice Toward None: The Life of Abraham Lincoln* (1977; reprint, New York: Mentor Books, 1978), 352.

180 Combining his own political: Drew, *On the Edge*, 332.

180 "I don't suppose". Ibid., 139.

180 He openly endorsed: Wines, "Present Arms."

181 At the rate things were going: Lawrence A. Pezzullo, "Clinton's Errors. Where Policies Went Awry," *The Sun*, 9/25/94.

181 Approaching that international body: For criticism of American overindulgence in United Nations approval, see Thomas L. Friedman, "Forgive and Forget," *New York Times*, 8/11/98.

181 He and some of the uniformed: Drew, *On the Edge*, 428.

182 "In meetings, when a lot": Paul Kengor, "The Foreign Policy Role of Vice President Al Gore," *Presidential Studies Quarterly*, winter 1997, 20.

182 Both Clinton and Gore telephoned: Ibid., 30.

182 With nearly twenty U.S.: Wines, "Present Arms."

182 The final decision to send: For more on Gore's foreign-policy role, see Kengor, "The Foreign Policy Role."

182 General Powell seemed to impress: Elaine Sciolino, "On the Brink of War, a Tense Battle of Wills," *New York Times*, 9/20/94.

183 "deserves credit for seeking a diplomatic": David E. Rosenbaum, "On Both Sides of the Aisle, the Resolutions on Haiti Abruptly Turn from Opposition to Praise," *New York Times*, 9/20/94.

183 "Let it be noted": Kevin Fedarko, "Deliverance," *Time*, 10/24/94, 30–31.

183 Illinois congressman Henry J. Hyde: Rosenbaum, "On Both Sides of the Aisle."

183 He spent most of the first two years: For more on Clinton and his early foreign policy, see Larry Berman and Emily O. Goldman, "Clinton's Foreign Policy at Midterm," in Colin Campbell and Bert A. Rockman, eds., *The Clinton Presidency: First Appraisals* (Chatham, N.J.: Chatham House Publishers, 1996).

184 Michel railed against: "House Backs Pact in Big Clinton Victory," *New York Times*, 11/18/93.

184 It comported with a host: For instance, see Winston S. Churchill, *The Age of Revolution* (New York: Dodd, Mead, 1957); Eric Hobsbawm, *The Age of Empire, 1875–1914* (New York: Vintage Books, 1987); Richard Hofstadter, *The Age of Reform* (New York: Vintage Books, 1955); Nicolaus Mills, ed., *Culture in an Age of Money: The Legacy of the 1980s in America* (Chicago: Ivan R. Dee Publishers, 1990); and Eric Hobsbawm, *The Age of Extremes* (New York: Random House, 1994).

185 Complimenting Franklin Roosevelt: "Excerpts from Remarks at Global Lenders' Talks," *New York Times*, 10/7/98.

185 At least as much as Republicans: For a discussion of the primacy of economic issues

in Clinton's worldview and of the frequency with which Clinton references economic issues in his foreign policy addresses, see Aubrey W. Jewett and Marc D. Turetzky, "President Clinton's Foreign Policy Beliefs: A First Term Appraisal" (paper presented at the annual meeting of the American Political Science Association, Boston, Mass., September 1998).

186 Much was riding on NAFTA: Kenneth J. Cooper, "NAFTA Split Parties, Shuffled Politics as Administration Overtook Opponents," *Washington Post*, 11/18/93.

186 By itself, the agreement: See USA*NAFTA's brochure entitled "NAFTA: Our Economy, Our Future" (1993), 4.

187 Opponents charged that anywhere: The AFL-CIO's Task Force on Trade cited statistics in a press release titled "The Jobs Debate" (#7, 1993). The Economic Policy Institute projected 550,000 jobs lost; Koechlin and Larudee estimated 490,000 jobs lost; the Economic Strategy Institute estimated 220,000 jobs lost; and the Institute for International Economics projected 5,400 jobs lost.

187 Statistically, these figures meant little: "House Backs Pact in Big Clinton Victory," *New York Times*, 11/18/93.

187 Opinion polls even demonstrated: Douglas Jehl, "Scramble in the Capital for Today's Trade Pact Vote," *New York Times*, 11/17/93.

187 Clinton knew in NAFTA: Foley and White House aide, as quoted in R. W. Apple, Jr., "A High-Stakes Gamble That Paid Off," *New York Times*, 11/18/93.

187 Nine months into his tenure: Drew, *On the Edge*, 298.

188 "Clinton," he said afterward: Ibid., 299.

188 The day after the President's: Gwen Ifill, "56 Long Days of Coordinated Persuasion," *New York Times*, 11/19/93.

188 While he met with fence-sitting: Michael Duffy, "Attention NAFTA Shoppers," *Time*, October 1993.

188 Bentsen might personally: Ifill, "56 Long Days."

188 Transportation Secretary Federico Peña: Duffy, "Attention NAFTA Shoppers."

188 From mid-September through: Ifill, "56 Long Days."

188 In all, since his East Room kickoff: Ibid.

189 The day before the House vote: Jehl, "Scramble in the Capital."

189 Central to the highlight reel: John Brummett, *Highwire: From the Back Roads to the Beltway: The Education of Bill Clinton* (New York: Hyperion, 1994), 225.

189 Broadcast on *Larry King Live*: Drew, *On the Edge*, 344.

189 "I cannot imagine" Elaine Sciolino and Todd S. Purdum, "Gore, a Vice President Who Eludes the Shadows," *New York Times*, 2/19/95.

189 Gore's former chief of staff: Authors' interview with Roy Neel, 3/30/95 and 4/26/95.

190 Clinton was known: Margaret Carlson, "Where's Al?" *Time*, 9/13/93.

190 Gore was so connected: Sciolino and Purdum, "Gore, a Vice President."

190 The Vice President confessed: Ibid.

190 Gore had jumped: Drew, *On the Edge*, 344.

190 During the 1992 campaign: Brummett, *Highwire*, 218.

190 In a news conference: "Unions Vow to Punish Pact's Backers," *New York Times*, 11/19/93.

191 In an early November 1993: Drew, *On the Edge*, 343.

191 The final tally sheet: Cooper, "NAFTA Split Parties."

191 "Great Showdown": Kevin Merida and Tom Kenworthy, "For Some, a Bitter NAFTA Taste," *Washington Post*, 11/18/93.

191 Commented one administration official: Duffy, "Attention NAFTA Shoppers."

191 Among the White House deals: Keith Bradsher, "Clinton's Shopping List for Votes Has Ring of Grocery Buyer's List," *New York Times*, 11/17/93.

192 Nearly $33 million: The Clinton quote and all figures are in Charles Lewis, "The NAFTA-Math," *Washington Post*, 12/26/93.

193 A former gubernatorial aide: Authors' interview with Bobby Roberts, 12/13/94.

193 An itinerant White House: Ann Devroy and Dan Balz, "For President, Coalitions Are in Constant Flux," *Washington Post,* 11/18/93.

193 Representative Louise Slaughter of New York: Merida and Kenworthy, "For Some, a Bitter NAFTA Taste."

193 Clinton's pragmatism: Authors' interview with Bobby Roberts, 12/13/94.

193 Aides agreed that Hillary: Ibid.

194 Consistent with the attention: Drew, *On the Edge,* 341.

194 A staged interruption: Cooper, "NAFTA Split Parties."

194 Lawmakers who had spent weeks: Merida and Kenworthy, "For Some, a Bitter NAFTA Taste."

194 Majority Leader Gephardt: "House Backs Pact in Big Clinton Victory."

194 Before the year's end: For more on Clinton's NAFTA fight, see C. Don Livingston and Kenneth A. Wink, "The Passage of the North American Free Trade Agreement in the U.S. House of Representatives: Presidential Leadership or Presidential Luck?" *Presidential Studies Quarterly,* winter 1997.

195 Near the end of 1994: U.S. Department of Commerce, "NAFTA: The First Nine Months," NAFTA Facts Document No. 4006. As of 11/14/94, the document read, "Approximately 12,122 employees are being provided with assistance . . . "

195 Despite those 12,000 lost jobs: Ibid.

195 By early 1995, the Department: U.S. Department of Commerce, "NAFTA: First Year Snapshot," NAFTA Facts Document No. 4003, 2/17/95.

195 "The intensity came": Ifill, "56 Long Days."

196 On NAFTA: For more on the positive impact of these economic pacts, see John Spanier and Steven W. Hook, *American Foreign Policy Since World War II* (Washington, D.C.: Congressional Quarterly Press, 1998), 336–39.

196 "Until NAFTA": Brummett, *Highwire,* 225.

196 Les Aspin did not make: Drew, *On the Edge,* 366.

197 "What is astonishing": Authors' interview with Newt Gingrich, 4/12/99.

CHAPTER EIGHT

Forward, About-Face, March

201 From statehouses and legislatures: For more on midterm election results, see Harold W. Stanley, "The Parties, the President, and the 1994 Midterm Elections," in Colin Campbell and Bert A. Rockman, eds., *The Clinton Presidency: First Appraisals* (Chatham, N.J.: Chatham House 1996), 192.

202 "Not since 1867": Walter Dean Burnham, "Realignment Lives," Ibid., 367.

202 Not a single aide predicted: Elizabeth Drew, *Showdown: The Struggle Between the Gingrich Congress and the Clinton White House* (New York: Simon & Schuster, 1996), 34.

203 "an age-old way to conduct midterm elections:": David R. Mayhew, "Innovative Midterm Elections," in Philip A. Klinker, ed., *Midterm: The Elections of 1994 in Context* (Boulder, Colo.: Westview Press, 1996), 157.

203 "party and a movement that is based on ideas": Newt Gingrich, acceptance speech to the House Republican Conference, http://dolphin.gulf.net/Gingrich, 12/3/94, 5.

203 "a brain-dead Congress is a bad Congress": Ibid.

204 "was a political mirror image": E. J. Dionne, *They Only Look Dead* (New York: Simon & Schuster, 1996), 77.

204 Aimed at voters: Ibid., 78.

204 "subordination of social to fiscal issues": Russell L. Riley, "Party Government and the Contract with America," *Political Science & Politics,* December 1995, 706.

204 "running solely against an unpopular president": John J. Pitney Jr. and William F.

Connelly Jr., "Permanent Minority No More: House Republicans in 1994," *Political Science & Politics*, December 1995, 50.

204 "the intellectual energy had again shifted back to the right": Dionne, *They Only Look Dead*, 76.

205 "preeminent political leader in America": Karen Tumulty, "Man With a Vision," *Time*, 1/9/95, 22.

205 Perceived as dogmatic and arrogant: Ibid.

205 Just days after the election: Newt Gingrich, speech to Washington Research Group, http://dolphin.gulf.net/Gingrich, 11/11/94, 3.

205 "What has gone wrong is a welfare system": Newt Gingrich speech to Republican governors in New Hampshire, http://dolphin.gulf.net/Gingrich, 2/21/95.

205 By April 7, 1995, a NBC News/*Wall Street Journal* poll: Drew, *Showdown*, 184.

205 "nationalism, aggressive expansionism": David R. Mayhew, "Innovative Midterm Elections," in Klinker, *Midterm*, 159.

206 The result revealed a party: Walter Dean Burnham, "Realignment Lives," in Campbell and Rockman, *The Clinton Presidency*, 382.

206 "leading by including": Drew, *Showdown*, 74.

207 Leadership will bring change: Ibid., 8.

207 "We should not be happy just": Newt Gingrich, Inauguration Speech, Part II http://dolphin.gulf.net/Gingrich, 1/4/95, 4.

207 "set and create a focus": Drew, *Showdown*, 15.

207 "he's the greatest leader we ever had": Ibid.

207 "be another Ronald Reagan": Ibid., 278.

208 "were intended to strengthen the role": James G. Gimpel, *Legislating the Revolution, the Contract with America in Its First 100 Days* (Needham, Mass.: Allyn & Bacon, 1996), 125.

208 "heavily sedated and deep in therapy": Ibid., 122.

208 "discovered his center of gravity": Authors' interview with William Galston, 4/9/97.

208 Comparing the aftermath of the 1994 elections: Ibid.

209 His campaigning partisans: David McCullough, *Truman* (New York: Touchstone, 1992), 522.

209 "would run forty-five minutes at a minimum": Authors' interview with Harold Ickes Jr., 7/25/97.

209 "we'd beat their ass": Ibid.

209 Asked to agree or disagree: John F. Bibby, *Return of Divided Party Government* (Washington, D.C.: Congressional Quarterly Press, 1995), 5–6.

210 Notably, turnout among African-Americans: Alfred J. Tuchfarber, Stephen E. Bennett, Andrew E. Smith, Eric W. Rademacher, "The Republican Tidal Wave of 1994: Testing Hypotheses About Realignment, Restructuring, and Rebellion," *Political Science & Politics*, December 1995, 690.

210 "mostly younger, non-college-educated voters": Dionne, *They Only Look Dead*, 85.

210 "Great Protestant White Middle.": Burnham, "Realignment Lives," 380.

210 the "southernization of the GOP": Michael Lind, "The Southern Coup," *The New Republic*, 6/19/95, 20.

210 "rather than urge massive new forms": Dionne, *They Only Look Dead*, 156.

210 For Democrats to retain their majority: See generally ibid., 84–85.

210 "they weren't even getting into the car": Tuchfarber et al., "The Republican Tidal Wave," 689.

210 "major political or social disruptions ": Ibid., fn 6.

210 "midst of a historic period of party realignment": Ibid., 694.

211 "Probably no President since Andrew Johnson": McCullough, *Truman*, 524.

211 "about the importance of a number of pieces of legislation": Burt Solomon, "At Both Ends of the Avenue," *National Journal*, 1/7/95, 38.

211 The day after the election: For text of Clinton's address, see http://library.white-house.gov., 10/9/94.

212 "drawing the line on Congress would give us momentum": Drew, *Showdown,* 60.

212 "They don't want a legislator in chief": Authors' interview with Frank Greer, 4/26/95.

213 "every bit as much on the line as Clinton's": Drew, *Showdown,* 61.

213 Another wondered simply why the President: Ibid., 109–10.

213 Two years before the results: Dave Kaplan, "Texas Map Allowed for '94 Election," *Congressional Quarterly,* 9/10/94, 2540.

213 Voters thought he lacked common sense: Ibid.

214 "just over half the number the President's party": Rhodes Cook, "An Outspoken Clinton Might Rally the Party" *Congressional Quarterly,* 10/8/94, 2934.

216 "as a party . . . we have some conflicting interests": Drew, *Showdown,* 101–2.

216 "prepared to stake everything to get to a balanced budget": Ibid., 35.

217 Hatfield would retire from the upper chamber: Timothy Egan, "Oregon's Senator Hatfield Confirms He Will Retire," *New York Times,* 12/2/95.

218 "We were doing fine until Newt stumbled": Suneel Ratan, "The Most Unkindest Cut," *Time,* 5/15/95, 38.

218 "This man needs to have spontaneity": Authors' interview with Betsey Wright, 10/31/94.

219 "Was he the fiscally restrained free trade centrist?": Authors' interview with William Galston, 4/9/97.

219 "that he was never going to get caught": Authors' interview with Harold Ickes Jr., 7/25/97.

219 Clinton claimed to have had: Remarks by the President to American Society of Newspaper Editors, White House Press Releases Database, http://library.whitehouse.gov/cgi, 4/7/95.

220 was "only occasionally willing to include": Blanche Wiesen Cook, *Eleanor Roosevelt,* vol. 1 (New York: Penguin Books, 1992), 424.

220 "impossible for husband and wife": Ibid., 425.

220 "play a leadership role . . . [for] women": Barbara Crossette, "Hillary Clinton Asks U.N. to Do More for Women," *New York Times,* 3/15/95.

220 "I was not involved in most of the work ": Todd S. Purdum, "First Lady Holds Forth, Long Distance," *New York Times,* 3/20/95.

220 "If we can send missiles down chimneys": Roxanne Roberts, "The First Lady's Women's Crusade," *Washington Post,* 5/6/95, D1.

221 "transform whole communities": Hillary Rodham Clinton, "Arts for Our Sake," *New York Times,* 6/21/95, A19.

221 "But we must," she said: Authors' notes, Service Employees International Union conference, 5/95.

221 "I can't be worried ": Roberts, "The First Lady's Women's Crusade," D1.

221 "a bit weary, if resigned": Ibid., D1.

221 "the orthodox views of the two parties": Dick Morris, *Behind the Oval Office* (New York: Random House, 1997), 80.

221 "a way to change, not abandon": Ibid.

221 "them to constitute a third force": Ibid.

221 "triangulated third way": Ibid., 118.

222 "an alarming tendency to abandon": Lloyd Grove, "How to Triangulate an Oval Office," *Washington Post,* 11/28/95, C1.

223 "a great public relations opportunity": Newt Gingrich, *Lessons Learned the Hard Way* (New York: HarperCollins, 1998), 55.

223 "Hear this, before or after a veto": *The National Journal,* 12/2/95.

223 But Clinton had his foil: Authors' interview will Bill Bradley, 7/10/96.

223 "weak President who would ultimately feel required": Gingrich, *Lessons Learned,* 59.

223   In early October 1995: Katharine Q. Seelye, "Democrats Fleeing to GOP," *New York Times,* 10/7/95, A1.
224   "probably the greatest one-way exodus": Ibid.
224   "a party under siege": Ibid.

CHAPTER NINE
Welfare and Illfare

225   "exhilarating to have the opportunity": William Greider and Jan S. Wenner, "President Clinton," *Rolling Stone,* 12/9/93, 41.
225   Deputy Chief of Staff Harold Ickes Jr. said: Authors' interview with Harold Ickes Jr., 11/6/97.
225   Now, after eighteen months of congressional squabbling: Jeffrey L. Katz, "After 60 Years, Most Control Is Passing to States," *Congressional Quarterly,* 8/3/96, 2190.
225   The change was undeniable: For more on welfare reform generally, see: Klaus Funken and Penny Cooper, *Old and New Poverty: The Challenge for Reform* (Paul & Co., 1996); Charles P. Cozic, Bruno Leone, and Scott Barbour, *Welfare Reform* (San Diego, Calif.: Greenhaven Press, 1997); James S. Denton and Daniel Moynihan, *Welfare Reform: Consensus or Conflict?* (Lanham, Md.: University Press of America, 1988); Joel F. Handler, *The Poverty of Welfare Reform* (New Haven: Yale University Press, 1995); Edward D. Berkowitz and Kim McQuaid, *Creating the Welfare State: The Political Economy of the Twentieth Century Reform* (Westport, Conn.: Greenwood Publishing, 1988); James L. Payne, *Overcoming Welfare: Expecting More from the Poor—and from Ourselves* (New York: Basic Books, 1998); Gary C. Bryner, *Politics and Public Morality: The Great American Welfare Reform Debate* (New York: W. W. Norton, 1998); Anne Marie Commisa, *From Rhetoric to Reform?: Welfare Policy in American Politics* (Boulder, Colo.: Westview Press, 1998); Richard L. Koon, *Welfare Reform: Helping the Least Fortunate Become Less Dependent* (New York: Garland Publishers, 1997); Michael L. Murray, *And Economic Justice for All: Welfare Reform for the 21st Century* (New York: M. E. Sharpe, 1997); Lawrence M. Mead, ed., *The New Paternalism* (Washington, D.C.: The Brookings Institution Press, 1997); Alfred DeGrazia, *American Welfare* (New York: New York University Press, 1961); Ralph Segalman, *Poverty in America: The Welfare Dilemma* (Westport, Conn.: Greenwood Press, 1981); Robert Bremner, *The Discovery of Poverty in the United States* (New Brunswick, Conn.: Transaction Publishers, 1992); William M. Epstein, *Welfare in America: How Social Science Fails the Poor* (Madison: University of Wisconsin Press, 1997); Walter L. Trattner, *From Poor Law to Welfare State: A History of Social Welfare in America* (New York: Simon & Schuster, 1999).
226   "a bill that America wants and America needs": Richard Berke, "Fulfilling '92's Promise, Capturing a '96 Issue," *New York Times,* 8/1/96, A25.
226   "leave a moral blot on his presidency and on our nation": Katz, "After 60 Years," 2195.
227   "Today, we have a historic opportunity": Ibid., 2190.
227   The First Lady had published: Hillary Rodham Clinton, *It Takes a Village, and Other Lessons Children Teach Us* (New York: Touchstone, 1996).
227   "Washington has decided to end the War on Poverty": Jeff Jacoby, "One Small Step Towards the Reformation of Welfare," *Times-Picayune,* 8/8/96, B7.
227   "deficiencies cloud the . . . forecast for welfare reform": Katherine Boo, "Most DC Daycare Centers Have Expired Licenses," *Washington Post,* 10/6/97.
227   "legislative child abuse": Peter Edelman, "The Worst Thing Bill Clinton Has Done," *The Atlantic Monthly,* March 1997, 45.
227   "My President will boldly throw one million into poverty.": Katz, "After 60 Years," 2195.

227 "the behavior of certain adults can be changed": Ibid., 2190.
228 "and benefit reductions unrelated to welfare": Edelman, "The Worst Thing," 43.
228 many of them affecting working families: Ibid.
228 People like Vanessa Cooke: Barbara Vobejda and Jon Jeter, "Though Welfare Rolls Are Down, True Test of Reform Is Just Starting," *Washington Post*, 8/22/97, A13.
229 "the [welfare] debate is over": Ibid.
229 In addition, child-nutrition programs: Edelman, "The Worst Thing," 49.
229 "We now know that": John F. Harris and Judith Havemann, "Welfare Rolls Continue Sharp Decline," *Washington Post*, 8/13/97, A1.
229 At no time in the country's history: For more on this point, see generally: Felice D. Perlmutter, *From Welfare to Work: Corporate Initiatives and Welfare Reform* (New York: Oxford University Press,1997); Robert M. Solow, *Work and Welfare* (Princeton, N.J.: Princeton University Press, 1998); Gwendolyn Mink, *Welfare's End* (Ithaca, N.Y.: Cornell University Press, 1998).
229 "The people with skills found jobs": Simon Lee, *Arkansas Business*, 9/8/97, 1.
230 In Eldridge Cassidy's grocery store: David Maraniss, *First in His Class: A Biography of Bill Clinton* (New York: Simon & Schuster, 1995), 31.
231 "In the aftermath of Mondale's defeat": Ibid., 417.
231 "comprehensive bipartisan welfare reform policy": Carol Matlack, "Clinton Backs Overhaul of Welfare System," *Arkansas Democrat-Gazette*, 2/18/87.
231 "I come from a state": Ibid.
232 as "moral enforcers" of the system: Barbara Vobejda, "After Sixty Years, a Basic Shift in Philosophy," *Washington Post*, 8/1/96, A7.
232 Clinton reflected the shift: For more on this point, see generally Vaughn Davis Bornet, *Welfare in America* (Norman: University of Oklahoma Press, 1960); David A. Rochefort, *American Social Welfare Policy: Dynamics of Formulation and Change* (Boulder, Colo.: Westview Press, 1986).
232 The law was a compromise for Democrats: Edelman, "The Worst Thing," 44.
232 According to a local citizen activist: George Church, "How Clinton Ran Arkansas," *Time*, 4/13/92, 24.
233 "as an opportunity to gain support": Frances Fox Piven and David Ellwood, "Controversy," *The American Prospect*, July-August 1996, 14–15.
233 "Joe Duffey, who knew Clinton": E. J. Dionne, *Why Americans Hate Politics* (New York: Touchstone, 1992), 80.
234 "People are not really often reacting to me": Hilary Stout, "Hillary Clinton Looks at Her Strange Role," *Wall Street Journal*, 9/30/94.
234 A real estate agent in Florida: *Fort Lauderdale Sun Sentinel*, 10/20/96.
234 Aides referred to the "end welfare as we know it": David Elwood, *The American Prospect*, May-June 1996, 26.
234 By the 1950s, antipathy to handouts: Robert Samuelson, *The Good Life and Its Discontents* (New York: Times Books, 1996), 12.
234 Clinton's promise was propelled: Jared Bernstein and Irwin Garfinkel, "Welfare Reform: Fixing the System Inside and Out," in John Hansen and Robert Morris, eds., *The National Government and Social Welfare*, (Westport, Conn.: Auburn House, 1997), 147.
234 "nothing to brag of": Michael Parenti, *Democracy for the Few* (New York: St. Martin's Press, 1995), 50.
234 In the early nineteenth century: Ibid., 64.
234 "the same government that had": Ibid., 65.
234 By the late 1920s a study showed: Richard Boyer and Herbert Morais, *Labor's Untold Story* (New York: Cameron Assoc., 1955), 237.
234 "Continued dependence upon relief induces": Samuelson, *The Good Life and Its Discontents*, 181.

235 "War is going on in the White House": Robert Pear, *New York Times*, 7/31/96, A11.

236 "I doubt most Americans are even aware": Elwood, *The American Prospect*, 26.

237 "stars don't align that often": Todd Purdum, "The Welfare Bill," *New York Times*, 8/1/96, A22.

237 "I think everybody was leavened": Ibid., Al.

237 Al From, from his perch at the DLC: Ibid., A23.

238 "a second chance, not a way of life": State of the Union speech, 1/25/94.

238 The decrease accelerated each year: GAO report to the chairmen, Committee on Finance, U.S. Senate, and Subcommittee on Human Resources, Committee on Ways and Means, House of Representatives, June 1998, 7.

238 Some officials in the states: Spencer S. Hsu, "Faring So-So After Leaving Welfare," *Washington Post*, 10/11/98, B1.

239 States were spending more for welfare-to-work: President Bill Clinton, Remarks on Welfare Reform, Office of the Press Secretary, White House, 8/4/98, http://www.pub.whitehouse.gov.

239 In early 1999: "Survey of Those Leaving AFDC or W-2," January to March 1998, Preliminary Report, State of Wisconsin, Department of Workforce Development, 1/13/99.

239 "Changing values and expectations": Bill Archer, "Welfare Reform's Unprecedented Success," *Washington Post*, 8/10/98, A17.

CHAPTER TEN
True North

241 Often in the life: For more on this, see Georgia J. Sorenson, "Emergent Leadership: A Phenomenological Study of Ten Political Transforming Leaders" (Ph.D. diss., University of Maryland, 1992).

241 For Bill Clinton: Kerry White, "Little Rock Mobilizes to Preserve a Landmark," *Education Week*, 8/7/98, http://www.edweek.org/ew/vol-15/41rock.h15.

241 The televised event mesmerized: Associated Press, "Clinton Offers Hand in Healing," *Daily Kent Stater* (Kent State University, Ohio), 9/26/97, 8.

241 He watched as President Eisenhower: Ibid.

241 "It was Little Rock that made": Remarks by the President in Ceremony Commemorating the 40th Anniversary of the Desegregation of Central High School, Little Rock, Arkansas, 9/25/97, Office of the Press Secretary, White House.

241 A decade later, in July 1969: Kenneth Walsh and Julian Barnes, "Handholding as Policy," *U.S. News & World Report*, 6/23/97, 20.

241 "There was a lot of racial": Ibid.

242 Robert Kissire remembered: Authors' interview with Robert Kissire, 7/20/98.

242 "We're here to swim": Walsh and Barnes, "Handholding as Policy," 20.

242 But over the next few weeks: Ibid.

242 "My entire public life": Remarks by the President in meeting with the Advisory Board of the President on Race, 6/13/97, http://www.whitehouse.gov/Initiatives/1997061614199.html.

242 Hillary Rodham Clinton too would note: Authors' interview with Hillary Rodham Clinton, 6/15/98.

242 Harold Ickes, a veteran of the civil: Authors' interview with Harold Ickes, 7/25/97. And authors' interview with Rahm Emanuel, 1/29/97.

242 Cassidy had only a sixth-grade: Remarks by the President in Ceremony Commemorating the 40th Anniversary of the Desegregation of Central High School.

243 Young Clinton's friends remember him: Randall Mikkelsen, "Clinton to Attend Desegregation Commemoration," *Reuters News Service*, 9/25/97.

243 As a young delegate from Arkansas: President Clinton's Remarks on Affirmative

Action (National Archives, Washington, D.C., 1995), http://www.rain.org/-open-mind/affirm1.htm.

243 President Kennedy cited their courage: David Maraniss, *First in His Class: The Biography of Bill Clinton* (New York: Simon & Schuster, 1995), 19.

243 "I was in my living room in Hot Springs": "Civil Rights Activists Support Clinton," World African Network, 8/31/98, http://www.wanonline.com.

243 Later the following year: David Kusnet "Can Clinton Back Up His Rhetoric on the Race Issue?" *Houston Chronicle*, 6/13/97.

243 with Bill Coleman, Lani Guinier, and others: Maraniss, *First in His Class*, 238.

243 He identified with the black students: Authors' interview with William T. Coleman III, 12/14/94.

243 As governor, he appointed more blacks: President Clinton's Remarks on Affirmative Action. See also Maraniss, *First in His Class*, 453.

243 and he appointed the first black: Maraniss, *First in His Class*, 453.

243 His commitment was not token: John Brummett, *Highwire: From the Back Roads to the Beltway: The Education of Bill Clinton* (New York: Hyperion, 1994), 115.

243 Longtime Clinton observer: Ibid., 267.

243 "divided by race too long": Maraniss, *First in His Class*, 462.

243 On the corner outside the statehouse: Ibid.

244 First identified by Stan Greenberg: Stanley Greenberg, *Report on Democratic Defection, Report Prepared for the Michigan House Democratic Campaign Committee* (Washington, D.C.: The Analysis Group, 1985).

244 so-called wedge issues: Howard Winant, "Behind Blue Eyes: Whiteness and Contemporary U.S. Racial Politics," in Michelle Fine, Lois Weis, Linda Powell, L. Mun Wong, eds., *Off White: Readings on Race, Power and Society* (New York: Routledge, 1997), 42.

244 But the "racism wedge": Ibid.

244 Thurmond's "Dixiecrats": Monroe Billington, *Southern Politics Since the Civil War* (Malabar, Fla.: R. E. Krieger, 1984). We are indebted to Peter Shapiro for his excellent review of the Southern Strategy, "Retrenchment: Clinton, New Democrats, and the Politics of Race" (University of Maryland, 1994).

244 but perpetuation of racial segregation: Background drawn from, V. O. Key, *Southern Politics in State and Nation* (New York: Vintage, 1949).

245 He cleverly aligned himself: Kenneth O'Reilly, *Nixon's Piano* (New York: The Free Press, 1995), 284.

245 "Here was the birth of the Southern strategy": Ibid., 283.

245 Wallace's campaign also brought: Winant, "Behind Blue Eyes," 44.

245 Even *color-blind*: O'Reilly, *Nixon's Piano*, 361.

245 Justice Department nominee: Lani Guinier, "Clinton Spoke the Truth on Race," *New York Times*, 10/19/93.

245 In an age of political correctness: Ibid.

245 Nobel Prize–winning author: Stephan and Abigail Thernstrom, "We Have Overcome," *The New Republic*, 10/13/97, 24.

245 He rounded up southern black leaders: O'Reilly, *Nixon's Piano*, 336.

245 But Carter did not commit: Robert C. Smith, "Black Appointed Officials: A Neglected Area of Research in Black Political Participation," *Journal of Black Studies* 14 (1984): 376.

245 Despite his unfortunate use of the term: O'Reilly, *Nixon's Piano*, 339, 340, 335, 336.

245 Reagan in 1980 extended the: David Oshinsky, "What Became of the Democrats," *Washington Post Book Section*, 10/20/91, 26.

246 For campaign purposes: Ibid.

246 Atwater later claimed: Michael Duffy and Dan Goodgame, *Marching in Place: The Status Quo Presidency of George Bush* (New York: Simon & Schuster, 1992).

246 virtually all progressive symbols and themes: Jerry Watts, "Clinton and Blacks: Evading Race," *New Politics*, 4, no. 2 (winter 1993).

246 In 1992, Clinton deliberately sidestepped: Betty Glad, "How George Bush Lost the Election," in Stanley A. Renshon, ed., *The Clinton Presidency: Campaigning, Governing and the Psychology of Leadership* (Boulder, Colo.: Westview Press, 1995), 18.

246 They knew that in states with: Jack Germond and Jules Witcover, *Mad as Hell: Revolt at the Ballot Box, 1992* (New York: Warner Books, 1993), 291.

246 Blacks were consistently more liberal: Ronald Walters and Robert C. Smith, *Black Leadership: Theory, Research, and Praxis* (Albany: State University of New York Press, 1999), 85.

247 Like Carter, Clinton rounded up: Brummett, *Highwire*, 183.

247 What united Macomb's residents: O'Reilly, *Nixon's Piano*, 366.

247 Dick Morris, also examining: Bob Woodward, *The Choice* (New York: Simon & Schuster, 1996), 143.

247 Judged from the primaries onward: O'Reilly, *Nixon's Piano*, 143.

247 "Race" failed to make the list: C. Vann Woodward, "The Bubbas," *The Atlantic Monthly*, July 1992.

247 The "Civil Rights" section: Bill Clinton and Al Gore, *Putting People First* (New York: Times Books, 1992), 33–36, 63–66.

248 "He was a genius at counterscheduling": Brummett, *Highwire*, 28.

248 More notable was his attack: Ibid.

248 While not acknowledging that the Souljah: O'Reilly, *Nixon's Piano*, 409–10, 414.

249 At the end of the election season: Authors' interview with Bill Clinton, 9/12/92.

249 In it, she forgave the sins of the Southern: Guinier, "Clinton Spoke the Truth on Race."

249 He spoke of the "physical differences": See O'Reilly, *Nixon's Piano*, 43, 46; and James MacGregor Burns, *Vineyard of Liberty* (New York: Alfred A. Knopf, 1981), 584.

249 "God's will . . . every drop": Kusnet, "Can Clinton Back Up His Rhetoric?"

250 "If my name ever goes into history," Burns, *Vineyard of Liberty*, 627.

250 Lincoln was later to say that: Kusnet, "Can Clinton Back Up His Rhetoric?"

250 In his 1881 inaugural address: Kusnet, Ibid.

250 He used his inaugural address: O'Reilly, *Nixon's Piano*, 55.

250 Though black Americans had turned: James MacGregor Burns and Stewart Burns, *The People's Charter* (New York: Alfred A. Knopf, 1991), 275.

250 During the 1944 campaign: William Leuchtenburg, *In the Shadow of FDR* (Ithaca, N.Y.: Cornell University Press, 1983), 25.

250 Speaking in 1947 at the Lincoln: Kusnet, "Can Clinton Back Up His Rhetoric?"

251 The task force findings so enraged: Leuchtenburg, *In the Shadow of FDR*, 26.

251 Hardly supporting this carryover: O'Reilly, *Nixon's Piano*, 169, 171–72.

251 John F. Kennedy, vowing a fresh: Kusnet, "Can Clinton Back Up His Rhetoric?"

251 Calling upon the moral authority: O'Reilly, *Nixon's Piano*, 189.

251 In her book: Lani Guinier, *Tyranny of the Majority: Fundamental Fairness and Representative Democracy* (New York: The Free Press, 1994).

251 Seizing the moral capital: Authors' interview with Ronald Walters, 11/22/98.

252 Not long after JFK's death: O'Reilly, *Nixon's Piano*, 241.

252 This edition of the report: Glenn Loury, "Unequalized," *The New Republic*, 4/6/98, 10.

252 The Thernstroms had insisted in a recent: Stephan and Abigail M. Thernstrom, *America in Black and White: One Nation Indivisible* (New York: Simon & Schuster, 1997).

252 But in the years since 1975: Loury, "Unequalized," 10.

252 In 1998, almost one-third: Alan Wolfe, "The Facts and the Feelings," *The New Republic*, 9/29/97, 32.

253 And the racial disparity was evident: Radio address by the President to the nation, 2/21/98, http://www.whitehouse.gov/WH/html/1198-02-21.html.

253 Clinton insisted that the directors: Shirley Anne Warshaw, *Powersharing: White House Cabinet Relations in the Modern Presidency* (Albany: State University of New York Press, 1996), 9.

253 The cabinet selection process: Ibid., 14, 25.

253 A solid 13 percent: Speech by President Clinton at 86th Annual Holy Convocation, 11/13/93, Memphis, Tenn., http://www.whitehouse.gov/Initiatives/OneAmerica/19970610-1134.html.

253 Eleven of the sixteen top positions: Warshaw, *Powersharing*, 19.

253 Christopher Edley Jr. noted: Christopher Edley Jr., *Not All Black and White* (New York: Farrar Straus Books, 1996).

253 He appointed more African-Americans: "30 Years After Memphis: What If King Were Alive Today, What Would He Say?" *Ebony*, April 1998, 134.

254 A protracted effort on the part: Terry Neal, "A Turnout You Shouldn't Stereotype," *Washington Post*, 11/8/98.

254 The welfare reform bill of Clinton's first term: http://www.whitehouse.gov/Initiatives/19970616-14199.html.

254 But he took the criticism in stride, commenting: Remarks by the President in meeting with the Advisory Board to the President on Race, 6/13/97, http://www.whitehouse.gov/Initiatives/19970616-14199.html.

255 Nathan Glazer reflected: Nathan Glazer, "In Defense of Preference," *The New Republic*, 4/6/98, 18.

255 At the time of his assassination: "30 Years After Memphis," 134.

255 Clinton's approach to race as President: Winant, "Behind Blue Eyes," 46.

255 The answer appeared to be no: James Q. Wilson, *The New Republic*, 5/11/98, 37.

256 Clinton and his team: David Sears, Carol Van Laar, Mary Carrillo, and Rick Kosterman, "Is It Really Racism? The Origins of White Americans' Opposition to Race-Targeted Policies," *Public Opinion Quarterly* 61, no. 1 (1997): 16–53.

256 Some twenty-seven other items: "Accomplishment Document," President's Initiative on Race, 11/5/98.

256 A group of prominent conservative: "A New Race Relations Panel," *Washington Post*, 4/30/98.

256 Still others predicted that the work itself: Robert Blendon, John Benson, Mollyann Brodie, Drew Altman, Mario Brossard, "The Public and the President's Commission on Race," *The Public Perspective*, February/March 1998, 66.

257 "I think we ought to be thinking": Remarks by the President to students and others from the Akron community, University of Akron, 12/3/97, Office of the White House Press Secretary.

257 More than four in ten white Americans: Blendon et al., "The Public and the President's Commission on Race," 66.

257 Rodham Clinton was the first to speak: Confidential source.

257 According to Clinton: Paul Ritcher, "Clinton Urges Dialogue Between Races," *Atlanta Constitution*, 10/17/95.

258 Racial problems, he asserted: Clinton comments at the University of Texas at Austin, 10/16/95.

258 In a major speech on affirmative action: "President Clinton's Remarks on Affirmative Action" (National Archives, Washington, D.C., 1995), http://www.rain.org/-openmind/affirm1.htm.

258 Before Johnson's time: Thernstrom and Thernstrom, *America in Black and White*, 24.

258 The president, Roosevelt said: Thomas Cronin and Michael Genovese, *The Paradoxes of the American Presidency* (New York: Oxford University Press, 1998), 137.

259 "I expect this to be": Michael Fletcher, "Race Board Comes to Familiar Conclusions,

Washington Post, 9/17/98. This chapter has also benefited from several books, including: Andrew Hacker, *Two Nations: Black and White, Separate, Hostile, Unequal* (New York: Ballantine Books, 1995); Gunnar Myrdal, *An American Dilemma: The Negro Problem and Modern Democracy* (New York: Harper and Brothers, 1944); Cornell West, *Race Matters* (New York: Vintage Books, 1994); William Julius Wilson, *The Declining Significance of Race: Blacks and Changing American Institutions* (Chicago: University of Chicago Press, 1978).

259 "Black Americans know that Clinton": Authors' interview with Ronald Walters, 11/22/98.

CHAPTER ELEVEN

God and Second Chances

263 Upon winning an unprecedented: Thomas Bailey and David Kennedy, *The American Pageant* (Lexington, Mass.: D. C. Heath and Co., 1991), 858.

263 Newt Gingrich noted soberly: William C. Berman, *America's Right Turn: From Nixon to Clinton* (Baltimore: Johns Hopkins University Press, 1998), 177.

264 The Whitewater scandal: William Safire, *New York Times,* 1/8/96.

264 Rodham Clinton's own: *Los Angeles Times,* 1/25/96.

264 "If you'll give me": "The Choice '96," Frontline Productions, Helen Whitney (producer), air date 11/4/96.

264 "The God I believe in": Ibid.

264 Surveying the Republican primary: Bob Woodward, *The Choice* (New York: Simon & Schuster, 1996), 366–67.

265 "adult leadership": Steven V. Roberts et al., "Looking for Mr. Un-Dole," *U.S. News & World Report,* 1/15/96, 30.

265 Said a Republican congressman: Ibid.

266 Before the results were known: Woodward, *Choice,* 386.

266 "Nothing as significant as this": John Hohenberg, *Re-electing Bill Clinton: Why America Chose a "New" Democrat* (Syracuse, N.Y.: Syracuse University Press, 1997), 51.

266 "All of the forces of the old order": Woodward, *Choice,* 387.

266 Two days after Delaware: Ibid., 395.

267 "In 1984, they had us": "Out Loud," *Time,* 2/26/96, 25.

267 As the race evolved: Nancy Gibbs and Michael Duffy, "Battling the Party Crashers," *Time,* 2/19/96, 28.

267 Keeping these disparate elements: Steven V. Roberts et al., "Crashing the Party," *U.S. News & World Report,* 2/26/96, 26.

268 Dole's denunciation: Gibbs and Duffy, "Battling the Party Crashers," 28.

268 "In the great tradition": Ibid.

268 "I'm not in this for politics": Woodward, *Choice,* 409.

268 Forbes too surrendered: Hohenberg, *Re-electing Bill Clinton,* 59.

268 " a great leader, a great friend": Ibid., 58.

269 "Let's you and I fly off": Kenneth T. Walsh and Bruce B. Auster, "Taking the Offensive," *U.S. News & World Report,* 1/29/96, 28.

269 When Steve Forbes, for instance: Nancy Gibbs, "Is Forbes for Real?" *Time,* 2/12/96, 30.

269 That's why pollster: Stanley Greenberg's July 1995 memo, "Here Come the Dole Democrats: Excerpt from a Memo to President Bill Clinton," *Harper's,* October 1995.

270 "There is no one": Authors' interview with Betsey Wright, 10/31/94.

270 To boot, inconsistencies: Judy Keen, "Dole's Record: Action Over Ideology," *USA Today,* 5/17/96.

270   To the extent that Dole: Woodward, *Choice*, 418.

271   Dole concluded that he needed: Richard Nixon, Pat Buchanan, and Bob Dole quotes as cited in Michael Kramer, "The Danger of Dullness," *Time*, 3/11/96, 30.

271   Someone once jokingly asked: Gotti-Bush joke told by Warren Bennis to National League of Cities National Conference, Philadelphia, Pa., 12/4/97. C-SPAN aired the event on 12/27/97.

271   An April conference call: Michael Duffy and Nancy Gibbs, "The Soul of Dole," *Time*, 8/19/96, 36–37.

271   "every country needs a president": William Safire, "The Job Is Open," *Berkshire Eagle*, 2/9/98.

271   "It was horrible": Duffy and Gibbs, "The Soul of Dole," 37.

271   "I will seek the presidency": Hohenberg, *Re-electing Bill Clinton*, 71.

272   In the speech's immediate aftermath: Richard Stengel, "The Hard Way," *Time*, 5/27/96, 25.

272   "If a month from now": Jerelyn Eddings et al., "Reinventing Bob Dole," *U.S. News & World Report*, 5/27/96, 28–29.

272   Two decades earlier: Duffy and Gibbs, "The Soul of Dole," 32.

272   "His convictions are for very prudent". Rudman quote and ACU statistics from Keen, "Dole's Record."

272   In 1995, Dole supported: Ibid.

273   "I don't have any risky ideas": Dole quote and Burke quote from Duffy and Gibbs, "The Soul of Dole," 37.

273   "It's a southern, anti-union": "Viewpoint," *U.S. News & World Report*, 5/20/96, 22.

273   "His obsession is to stop": Keen, "Dole's Record."

273   "Psychologically": Stengel, "The Hard Way," 25.

273   "It ain't the New Deal": George J. Church, "The Learning Curve," *Time*, 9/2/96, 32.

274   Noted historian Michael Beschloss: Eric Pooley, "The Last Action Hero," *Time*, 7/22/96, 32.

274   First, two Clinton partners: Brian Duffy and Edward T. Pound, "Summer on the Grill," *U.S. News & World Report*, 7/1/96, 24.

275   Clinton apologized and saw to the: Hohenberg, *Re-electing Bill Clinton*, 90–91.

275   "smells to high heaven": Ibid., 90.

275   Frustrated by the: Nancy Gibbs, "The Rough Politics of Virtue," *Time*, 6/3/96, 22.

275   In accepting the Green: "Viewpoint," *Time*, 9/2/96, 20.

275   In 1993, fresh out of the: Church, "The Learning Curve," Ibid., 32.

275   "The good news is that we": E. J. Dionne Jr., "Clinton Swipes the GOP's Lyrics," *Washington Post*, 7/21/96.

275   When asked at that time what would make: Nelson Polsby, as quoted in A. L. May, "A Hopeless Mismatch?" *Atlanta Constitution*, 9/1/91.

275   Recounting a Dole anecdote": "Stump Wit," *Time*, 10/28/96, 26.

276   Wryly predicting a Dole upswing: John Buckley, as quoted in "Verbatim," *Time*, 8/12/96, 9.

276   Though General Colin Powell: Jeffrey H. Birnbaum, "Powell: No. 1 for No. 2," *Time*, 8/18/96, 42.

276   Dole-Kemp was an uneasy: Richard Lacayo and Michael Duffy, "Punching Up the Ticket," *Time*, 8/18/96, 21–22.

276   The President's move to the center: "Viewpoint," *U.S. News & World Report*, 12/23/96, 24.

276   Now, on the very morning: Morris scandal and Bob Dole quote, see Richard Lacayo, "Skunk at the Family Picnic," *Time*, 9/9/96.

277   Clinton, he determined: Richard Stengel, "When Foxes Pose as Hedgehogs," *Time*, 10/7/96, 63.

277   Neither man was without: Lacayo and Duffy, "Punching Up the Ticket," 22.

277 "The fox": Stengel, "When Foxes Pose as Hedgehogs," 63.

277 A summer 1996 poll: Gloria Borger and Linda Kulman, "Does Character Count?" *U.S. News & World Report*, 6/24/96, 35–36. For more on character and presidents, see Robert Wilson, ed., *Character Above All: Ten Presidents from FDR to George Bush* (New York: Simon & Schuster, 1995).

278 Among five factors: Borger and Kulman, "Does Character Count?" 36.

278 Clinton may have mastered American politics: David M. Shribman, "Era of Pretty Good Feelings: The Middle Way of Bill Clinton and America's Voters," in L. Sandy Maisel, ed., *The Parties Respond: Changes in American Parties and Campaigns* (Boulder, Colo.: Westview Press, 1998), 354.

278 Actor Mel Gibson complained: "Verbatim," *Time*, 11/18/96, 23.

278 Former Democratic presidential candidate: Authors' interview with George McGovern, 4/19/95.

278 And Newt Gingrich offered this assessment: Authors' interview with Newt Gingrich, 4/12/99.

278 Taking a cue: Nancy Gibbs, "The New Age of Anxiety," *Time*, 4/1/96, 34.

278 "preferred the middle way of Bill": Shribman, "Era of Pretty Good Feelings," 354.

278 Though he garnered: Hohenberg, *Re-electing Bill Clinton*, 268.

279 In the 1996 bout: Shribman, "Era of Pretty Good Feelings," 353.

279 Though, as one scholar noted: Ibid., 342.

279 "When we last gathered": Bill Clinton, "Second Inaugural Address," *Presidential Studies Quarterly*, winter 1997, 107–8.

280 "I've tried to reanimate": Kenneth T. Walsh, "The Second Start," *U.S. News & World Report*, 1/27/97, 34.

280 "I still believe the time": Kenneth T. Walsh, "Learning from Big Jumbo," *U.S. News & World Report*, 1/26/98, 33, 37.

281 For his second term, the President: "A Little Advice," *Time*, 11/18/96, 43.

281 "I think honorable compromise": Kenneth T. Walsh and Bruce B. Auster, "Taking the Offensive," *U.S. News & World Report*, 1/29/96, 29.

281 "It is time to put politics aside": Michael Duffy and Nancy Gibbs, "Our Journey Is Not Done," *Time*, 11/18/96, 34.

281 Worried historian Alan Brinkley: Alan Brinkley, *New York Times Magazine*, 1/19/97, 32.

281 More than policy coherence: Johanna McGeary, "Mix and Match," *Time*, 12/16/96, 29, 31.

281 "a coalition of the center": Kenneth T. Walsh, "Stop Me Before I Wobble Again," *Time*, 12/23/96, 36.

282 Racial and gender diversity remained important: For more on Albright, see Ann Blackman, *Seasons of Her Life: A Biography of Madeleine Korbel Albright* (New York: Scribner, 1998).

282 "Bill Clinton," noted one observer: Morley Winograd and Dudley Buffa, *Taking Control: Politics in the Information Age* (New York: Henry Holt, 1996), 23.

282 Together, these ex–investment bankers and lawyers: George J. Church, "Meet the Firm of . . . Raines, Rubin, Daley, & Bowles," *Time*, 12/23/96, 30.

282 "The men who hang on to high office": Judith Viorst, "How Power Begets Weakness," *Washington Post*, 3/19/98.

282 Five days after his inaugural: "Historical Wit," *Time*, 2/10/97, 21.

283 The President is: Authors' interview with Hillary Rodham Clinton, 6/15/98.

283 Clinton "sees Gore's": Kenneth T. Walsh, "Is He Clinton's Real Legacy?" *U.S. News & World Report*, 9/8/97, 22.

283 "He is very, very, very": Authors' interview with Tom Downey, 4/21/95.

283 Gore directly supervised: Walsh, "Is He Clinton's Real Legacy?" 24, 26.

283 and he and Clinton lunched regularly: Ibid., 24.

283 "The American people will never": Washington Convention Center, 5/8/96. Authors' notes.

283 "Now, it was a very special": Roger Simon, "With Strings Attached," *Capital Style,* November 1997, 51–52.

283 Once, while showering: Ibid., 51.

283 The Vice President "is handsome": Ibid.

283 At the bottom of an Oval Office: Richard L. Berke, "The Good Son," *New York Times Magazine,* 2/20/94.

284 He has retained high-powered: Gore on Bennis and quotes from Bennis book, Ibid.

284 Early into the second administration: Ruth Marcus, "GOP Hits Gore on Temple Fund-Raiser," *Washington Post,* 2/10/98.

284 "He is not about the art of seduction": Michael Kelly, "The Artful Dodger and the Good Son," *Washington Post,* 12/17/97.

284 The Vice President could only: Attorney General Janet Reno decided in late 1998 not to appoint an independent counsel to further investigate the allegations against Gore. See Roberto Suro, "Reno Rejects Probe of Gore on Lying," *Washington Post,* 11/25/98.

284 "the value of perseverance": Kenneth T. Walsh, "Learning 'to Recognize the Feelings in Myself,' " *U.S. News & World Report,* 9/8/97, 24.

284 In mid-July 1998: Walsh, "Is He Clinton's Real Legacy?" 24.

285 Two days after being sworn in: John Nichols, "How Al Gore Has It Wired," *The Nation,* 7/20/98, 14, 12.

285 Republicans nestled in: Richard E. Cohen, "Campaining for Congress: The Echo of '94," in Larry J. Sabato, ed., *Toward the Millennium: The Elections of 1996* (Boston: Allyn and Bacon, 1997), 186–88.

286 Efforts to strengthen: Helen Dewar, "Capitol Tally: One Big Win Followed by Many Losses," *Washington Post,* 10/23/98. See also Sarah A. Binder and Thomas E. Mann, "The 105th: It Could've Been a Contender," *Washington Post,* 10/18/98.

286 Even more noticeable: Saundra Torry, "After a Year of Legal Setbacks, Tobacco Looks Bigger Than Ever," *Washington Post,* 8/15/98.

286 Assessing the by-products: David Gergen, "Headline Happy in D.C.," *U.S. News & World Report,* 7/20/98, 64.

287 Republicans calculated that: Binder and Mann, "The 105th."

287 "All the major legislative initiatives": Dewar, "Capitol Tally."

287 It passed a $216 billion: Ibid.

288 "Truly a remarkably": Archer and Gephardt quotes, Ibid.

288 When the Senate voted: Eric Planin, "Senate Passes Balanced Budget, First in 30 Years, by a 57–41 Vote," *Washington Post,* 4/3/98.

288 "The surpluses themselves": John F. Harris, "It's a Brave New World Where Politicians Will Bicker Over Surpluses," *Washington Post,* 10/1/98.

288 In 1996, she ordered White House lawyers: Howard Kurtz, "First Lady Ordered 1996 Critique of Coverage," *Washington Post,* 2/14/98.

289 By 1996, historian Gil Troy noted: Gil Troy, *Affairs of State: The Rise and Rejection of the Presidential Couple Since World War II* (New York: The Free Press, 1997), 362.

289 In early 1998, she attributed: Ruth Marcus, "First Lady Sees Anti-Arkansas Bias," *Washington Post,* 8/12/98. Comments originally appeared in *Arkansas Democrat-Gazette,* 8/11/98.

289 Republicans in 1993: Ibid.

289 "In a democracy": Richard Darman, "Zero-Risk Leadership," *New York Times,* 2/9/97.

289 The Lewinsky imbroglio: This question is poignantly posed in Michael J. Gerson, "Words He Dare Not Speak," *U.S. News & World Report,* 9/21/98, 33.

290 Senate Republicans gained no seats: Helen Dewar, "Senate GOP Mulls Chance of Shake-Up," *Washington Post,* 11/8/98.

290 From Congressman Steve Largent: Ceci Connolly, "Three Years of Missteps, One Sudden Fall," *Washington Post*, 11/8/98.

290 From 1996 vice-presidential: Jack Kemp, "With No Agenda, What Can You Expect?" *Washington Post*, 11/8/98.

290 Republicans had expected to gain: Connolly, "Three Years of Missteps."

290 "At every level that matters": Dan Balz, "Ready, or Not?" *Washington Post Magazine*, 10/25/98, 9.

290 Gingrich the historian: Connolly, "Three Years of Missteps."

290 The First Lady emerged: Mary McGrory, "Mr. and Mrs. Comeback Kid," *Washington Post*, 11/8/98. See also Debra Rosenberg, "Hillary's Splendid Season," *Newsweek*, 11/16/98. For more on the contours of the Clintons' marriage, especially in the wake of the Lewinsky scandal, see Gail Sheehy, "Hillary's Choice," *Vanity Fair*, February 1999.

290 Former aide George Stephanopoulos: George Stephanopoulos, "The Betrayal," *Newsweek*, 8/31/98, 45.

291 "I'm afraid that the misconduct": Joseph Lieberman, " 'It Is Wrong and Unacceptable,' " *U.S. News & World Report*, 9/14/98, 16.

291 "The ideas are too big": Dan Balz, "Gingrich Says He's Leaving to Spare Turmoil in Party," *Washington Post*, 11/10/98.

291 But by the September 1998 release: Mark Shields, "Unfair to Newt," *Washington Post*, 11/8/98.

291 "A party is perpetually": Margaret Miner and Hugh Rawson, eds., *American Heritage Dictionary of American Quotations* (New York: Penguin, 1997), 390.

292 Clinton's historical blurb: Walter Shapiro, "Tale of the Textbook in 2048: Six Versions of the Clinton Years," *USA Today*, 7/8/98.

292 "I would have much preferred": Andrew Ferguson, "Poor, Poor, Pitiful Me," *Time*, 2/17/97, 42.

292 "I've learned that the system": "If You Try It All at Once . . . ," *Time*, 9/2/96, 22.

292 "I was hot": "Viewpoint," *U.S. News & World Report*, 6/24/96, 28.

CHAPTER TWELVE

Global Leadership and Moral Duties

293 Before the American Civil War: Ernest R. May, " 'Who Are We?': Two Centuries of American Foreign Relations," *Foreign Affairs*, March/April 1994, 136.

294 The struggle now is between: For more on the late-twentieth-century foreign policy paradigm—or rather, the multiplicity of competing paradigms—see Richard N. Haass, "Paradigm Lost," *Foreign Affairs*, January/February 1995, 45. Also see Henry Kissinger, "Photo-Op Foreign Policy," *New Perspectives Quarterly*, summer 1994, 43; and William G. Hyland, *Clinton's World: Remaking American Foreign Policy* (Westport, Conn.: Praeger, 1999).

294 While they emphasize: Thomas Jefferson, "Second Inaugural Address," March 4, 1805.

295 He pursued economic sanctions: Michael Kelly, "Surrender and Blame," *The New Yorker*, 12/19/94, 46.

296 "We cannot afford to ignore": Ibid., 47.

296 During the 1992 campaign: David C. Hendrickson, "The Recovery of Internationalism," *Foreign Affairs*, September/October 1994, 27.

297 The reference points for conducting: Authors' interview with Graham Allison, 2/10/99.

297 "We are living in an era": Ibid.

297 History did not really end: Francis Fukuyama, *The End of History and the Last Man* (New York: The Free Press, 1992).

297 "Without the cold war": Samuel P. Huntington, "The Erosion of American National Interests," *Foreign Affairs*, September/October 1997, 29.

297 Doves on the Bosnia matter: Charles Krauthammer, "How the Doves Became Hawks," *Time*, 5/17/93, 74.

298 "To those suffering appalling": Michael Elliott, "The Lessons of Bosnia's War," *Newsweek*, 4/20/98, 35.

298 Clinton's words in Kigali: "Clinton's Painful Words of Sorrow and Chagrin," *New York Times*, 3/26/98.

299 Bosnia posed a leadership crisis: For more on presidential leadership, see Richard Nixon, *Leaders* (New York: Simon & Schuster, 1982); Lance Blakesley, *Presidential Leadership: From Eisenhower to Clinton* (Chicago: Nelson-Hall Publishers, 1995); and Erwin C. Hargrove, *The President as Leader: Appealing to the Better Angels of Our Nature* (Lawrence: University Press of Kansas, 1998). For some recent scholarship on leadership more generally, see Harvard Business Review, *On Leadership* (Cambridge, Mass.: Harvard Business School Press, 1998), and Barbara Kellerman, *Reinventing Leadership: Making the Connection Between Politics and Business* (Albany: State University of New York Press, 1999).

299 "Bosnia is the greatest collective": ABC News *Nightline*, 7/12/95.

299 His boss was more direct: Elizabeth Drew, *On the Edge: The Clinton Presidency* (New York: Simon & Schuster, 1994), 162.

299 One official bitterly complained: Ibid., 150.

299 Lower-level officials were given: Bruce W. Nelan, "Reluctant Warrior," *Time*, 5/17/93, 29.

299 An administration official: Drew, *On the Edge*, 228.

299 So in the administration's early going: Karen Breslau and Bob Cohn, "Al Gore: Talk a Lot, and Carry a Big Stick," *Newsweek*, 10/31/94, 30.

300 Over Bosnia, though: Drew, *On the Edge*, 160, 411. Still, Christopher was given to pushing for a more firm U.S. stand in Bosnia. After a mortar shell hit a Sarajevo marketplace killing many people, Christopher wrote a memo to the President and confided, "I am acutely uncomfortable with the passive position we are now in."

300 "The question raised by": Nelan, "Reluctant Warrior," 28.

300 The unproductiveness of many: Ibid., 29.

300 Such indecision was precisely: Robert Reich, *Locked in the Cabinet* (New York: Alfred A. Knopf, 1997), 7.

301 What's more, wasn't the task: Authors' interview with Michael Beschloss, 4/17/95.

301 He pressed advocates: Drew, *On the Edge*, 150.

302 Scholars and experts in a range: For some efforts at a post–cold war paradigm, see Samuel P. Huntington, *The Clash of Civilizations and the Remaking of World Order* (New York: Simon & Schuster, 1996); and Zbigniew Brzezinski, *The Grand Chessboard: American Primacy and Its Geostrategic Imperatives* (New York: Basic Books, 1997). For a broader perspective on U.S. interaction with the world, see also Walter A. McDougall, *Promised Land, Crusader State: The American Encounter with the World Since 1776* (New York: Houghton Mifflin, 1997).

302 "He who wants to defend": Zbigniew Brzezinski, "A Plan for Europe," *Foreign Affairs*, January/February 1995, 28.

302 The President's "ad hocracy": For more on the ad hocracy, see Richard N. Haass, "Bill Clinton's Adhocracy," *New York Times Magazine*, 5/29/94.

303 "I am appalled": Kelly, "Surrender and Blame," 48.

303 In February 1993: Drew, *On the Edge*, 146.

303 But a few months later: Nelan, "Reluctant Warrior," 28.

303 President-elect Clinton even: Lance Morrow, "William J. Clinton: The Torch Is Passed," *Time*, 1/4/94.

303 Every cold war president: Drew, *On the Edge*, 144.

304   An October 1994 survey: Chicago Council on Foreign Relations, "American Public Opinion and U.S. Foreign Policy, 1995" (Chicago: Chicago Council on Foreign Relations, 1995), figure II-2, 14.

304   Nonetheless, when asked to evaluate: Ibid., figure II-5, 17.

305   "It would be an irony of fate": Morrow, "William J. Clinton."

307   The two men were dogged in their: Richard Holbrooke, *To End a War* (New York: Random House, 1998), 305.

308   "The decision was made in so aimless": Warren Bass, "The Triage of Dayton," *Foreign Affairs*, September/October 1998, 99.

309   Dayton proved to be a mixed success: Richard Holbrooke, "Why Are We in Bosnia?" *The New Yorker*, 5/18/98, 45.

309   Bosnia's division into various: For more on partition, see Radha Kumar, "The Troubled History of Partition," *Foreign Affairs*, January/February 1997, 22–34. See also Richard L. Holbrooke's response in letter to the editor, *Foreign Affairs*, March/April 1997, 170–72.

309   Even the September 1998 elections to select: R. Jeffrey Smith, "Bosnians to Decide on Path Toward Future," *Washington Post*, 9/12/98.

309   Moreover, by the fall of 1998: Bass, "The Triage of Dayton," 96. Information also taken from Aleksa Djilas, "Imagining Kosovo," *Foreign Affairs*, September/October 1998, 126.

310   "The Clinton administration's decision": Bass, "The Triage of Dayton," 100–101.

310   All told, the Bosnian war: Smith, "Bosnians to Decide."

310   "Europe, not having yet freed": Daniel Williams, "Yeltsin, Clinton Clash Over NATO's Role," *Washington Post*, 12/6/94.

310   To help make their case: Bass, "The Triage of Dayton," 104.

311   "They were organized for NATO": Helen Dewar, "Victories as Convincing as NATO Unlikely in Other Foreign Issues," *Washington Post*, 5/2/98.

311   Demanding much attention by late 1998: George Will, "Ersatz Seriousness About Serbia," *Washington Post*, 10/8/98.

311   The American response was firm: Mary McGrory, "Balkan Roulette," *Washington Post*, 10/15/98.

312   It was NATO that authorized: William Drozdiak, "NATO Faces Deadline on Attacks," *Washington Post*, 10/27/98.

312   And it was NATO: R. Jeffrey Smith, "Dramatic Kosovo Negotiations Had a Predetermined Last Act," *Washington Post*, 10/15/98.

312   A few weeks into the aerial assault: David S. Broder, "Words vs. Deeds," *Washington Post*, 4/14/99. For more on events leading to Kosovo intervention, see Elaine Sciolino and Ethan Bronner, "How a President, Distracted by Scandal, Entered Balkan War," *New York Times*, 4/18/99.

313   "I think": Tim Pat Coogan, *The Troubles: Ireland's Ordeal 1966–1996 and the Search for Peace* (Boulder, Colo.: Roberts Rinehart Publishers, 1996), 351.

314   This was the Clinton prepared: Margaret Carlson, "Remaking of the President," *Time*, 5/17/93, 41.

314   In September 1993: Coogan, *The Troubles*, 352.

315   The answer came in late August 1994: Ibid., 378.

315   Soon, Adams again visited: Ibid., 392.

315   But Clinton stood tall: Much of the preceding is taken from Coogan, *The Troubles*, 351–92.

316   "This is the best chance": T. R. Reid and Dan Balz, "Ireland's Twin Referendums," *Washington Post*, 5/22/98.

316   Bill Clinton was similarly sanguine: Thomas W. Lippman, "Clinton Makes Case for Peace in N. Ireland," *Washington Post*, 3/18/98.

316   Irish prime minister: Ibid.

316 "The success of the": John Lloyd, "Ireland's Uncertain Peace," *Foreign Affairs*, September/October 1998, 122.

317 "We swear to God": Howard M. Sachar, *A History of Israel from the Rise of Zionism to Our Time* (New York: Alfred A. Knopf, 1996), 615.

319 The White House milked the episode: Much of the preceding discussion is taken from Ibid., 988–1001. See also, Noam Chomsky, *The Fateful Triangle: The United States, Israel, and the Palestinians* (Boston: South End Press, 1983).

319 King Hussein saw in the agreement: Sachar, *A History of Israel*, 1000.

320 Highlights of the Wye River Pact: Serge Schmemann, "After All the Talk, a Hesitant Peace," *New York Times*, 10/24/98.

321 The United States threatened to declare: Barton Gellman, "Ultimatums Were a U.S. Tool in Middle East Talks," *Washington Post*, 11/4/98.

321 "I'd prefer not to give": John F. Harris, "Clinton Ambiguity Proves a Strength in Summit Role," *Washington Post*, 10/25/98. Much of this paragraph is taken from the Harris article.

321 Clinton was a study in diligence: Anthony Lewis, "The Three Clintons," *New York Times*, 10/27/98.

322 "Anyone dealing with the Middle East": Jimmy Carter, Anwar Sadat Lecture for Peace, University of Maryland, College Park, 10/25/98.

324 "Foreign policy, unlike baseball": Madeleine K. Albright, "The Testing of American Foreign Policy," *Foreign Affairs*, November/December 1998, 51.

324 "We shall not succeed": Charles S. Maier, "Democracy and Its Discontents," *Foreign Affairs*, July/August 1994, 54.

CHAPTER THIRTEEN

What Kind of Leadership?

325 What is greatness in the White: Richard J. Ellis and Aaron Wildavsky, "Presidential Greatness and Cultural Dilemmas," *Encyclopedia of the American Presidency*, vol. 3 (New York: Simon & Schuster, 1994), 209–13.

325 Monuments are another form of rating: Stephen W. Stathis, "Monuments, Presidential," ibid., 1043–44; Peter Baker, "Mount Rushmore or Bust: Clinton's Quest for a Legacy," *Washington Post*, 8/3/97.

325 In the summer of 1995: Bill Clinton, "Remarks by the President on Responsible Citizenship and the American Community," Georgetown University, White House Office of the Press Secretary, 7/6/95. See also, *New York Times*, 7/7/95, A14.

328 "Centrism is fine": William Safire, "The Demo-Labor Party," *New York Times*, 11/12/97.

328 It was not enough to know Niccolò Machiavelli's: Haynes Johnson, *Divided We Fall: Gambling with History in the Nineties* (New York: W. W. Norton, 1995), 61, 365, 367. See also Susan Dunn and James MacGregor Burns, "The Lion, the Fox, and the President," *Harvard Magazine*, February 1995, 40–44.

329 "I've been fighting the wrong folks": Bob Woodward, *The Agenda: Inside the Clinton White House* (New York: Simon & Schuster, 1994), 205.

329 Elizabeth Drew reported that: Elizabeth Drew, *On the Edge: The Clinton Presidency* (New York: Simon & Schuster, 1994), 395.

329 "On the one hand": E. J. Dionne Jr., "The Unspoken Conspiracy," *Berkshire Eagle*, 6/15/95.

329 "The Republicans were unanimous in their hatred": Franklin Delano Roosevelt, *The Public Papers and Addresses of Franklin D. Roosevelt*, vol. 5 (New York: Random House, 1938), 568.

330 "Government bureaucracies built a half": Al From, "The New Politics," *The Mainstream Democrat*, March 1991.

330 "We have to be prepared": Bill Clinton, "The Road Ahead," *The Mainstream Democrat*, May 1990.

330 Indeed, as Alison Mitchell observed: Alison Mitchell, "Outlook for Political Dynamics: More of the Same," *New York Times*, 10/22/98.

331 It sharply poses the difference: Arthur M. Schlesinger Jr., *The Vital Center: The Politics of Freedom* (Boston: Houghton Mifflin, 1949).

331 But the distinctions are crucial: For more on ethics and leadership, see Joanne B. Ciulla, ed., *Ethics, the Heart of Leadership* (Westport, Conn.: Quorum Books, 1998); Stanley A. Renshon, ed., *The Clinton Presidency: Campaigning, Governing, and the Psychology of Leadership* (Boulder, Colo.: Westview Press, 1995); Bernard M. Bass, *Leadership and Performance Beyond Expectations* (New York: The Free Press, 1985); Robert K. Greenleaf, *Servant Leadership* (New York: Paulist Press, 1977); Ronald A. Heifetz, *A Leadership Without Easy Answers* (Cambridge, Mass.: Belknap/Harvard University Press, 1994); Joseph Rost, *Leadership for the Twenty-First Century* (New York: Praeger, 1991); James MacGregor Burns, *Leadership* (New York: Harper, 1978); William J. Byron, "Ten Building Blocks of Catholic Social Teaching," *America*, 10/31/98; Bernard M. Bass and Paul Steidlmeier, "Ethics, Character, and Authentic Transformational Leadership," Center for Leadership Studies, Binghamton University, 1998.

332 Whatever the law may say about: William F. Buckley Jr., "U.S. v. Clinton," *National Review*, 9/28/98, 43.

332 Everything revolved around the definition: For more on virtues, see William J. Bennett, *The Book of Virtues: A Treasury of Great Moral Stories* (New York: Simon & Schuster, 1993).

332 The tragedy quickly became political: For more on the Lewinsky outrage, see William J. Bennett, *The Death of Outrage: Bill Clinton and the Assault on American Ideals* (New York: The Free Press, 1998).

334 "transactional opportunists": Ciulla, *Ethics*, 170.

334 Fashioned by Harvardmen: For more on pragmatism see William James, *Pragmatism, and Four Essays from the Meaning of Truth* (Meridian Books, 1950); Charles Morris, *The Pragmatic Movement in American Philosophy* (George Braziller, 1970); Morton White, *Pragmatism and the American Mind* (New York: Oxford University Press, 1973); James Bissett Pratt, *What Is Pragmatism?* (New York: Macmillan, 1909), a critique; Morris Dickstein, ed. *The Revival of Pragmatism* (Durham, N.C.: Duke University Press, 1999).

335 "Are you having fun?": Jann S. Wenner and William Greider, *Rolling Stone*, 12/9/93, 40–45; Stanley A. Renshon, *The Psychological Assessment of Presidential Candidates* (New York: Routledge, 1998).

336 This was a reference to the distinction: For more on James David Barber's theory, see Michael Nelson, "Presidential Character," *Encyclopedia of the American Presidency*, vol. 3, 1200–1202; James David Barber, *The Presidential Character: Predicting Performance in the White House* (Englewood Cliffs, N.J.: Prentice-Hall, 1972).

338 A *New York Times* article: *New York Times*, 11/18/98, A26.

338 But income data told the real: Daniel H. Weinberg, "A Brief Look at Postwar U.S. Income Inequality," *Current Population Reports—Household Economic Studies*, 60–191, U.S. Census Bureau, 1, based on Census Bureau data, as cited in Douglas A. Hicks, "Inequalities, Needs, and Leadership," Jepson School of Leadership Studies (1998) (presented at Leaders/Scholars Association Conference, 11/13/98–11/15/98, Los Angeles, Calif.), 2.

339 The blockage of Clinton-Gore policies: For more on the Constitution and governmental deadlock, see David W. Brady and Craig Volden, *Revolving Gridlock* (Boulder, Colo.: Westview Press, 1998); James L. Sundquist, *Back to Gridlock?* (Washington, D.C.: Brookings Institution, 1995); David R. Mayhew, *Divided We*

Govern (New Haven, Conn.: Yale University Press, 1991); Lloyd Cutler, "Some Reflections About Divided Government," *Presidential Studies Quarterly* 17, 490ff; James MacGregor Burns, *The Deadlock of Democracy* (Englewood Cliffs, N.J.: Prentice-Hall, 1963).

EPILOGUE
Fall Projection 1999

341 His proposed budget: *New York Times*, 2/1/99, 1, 19.

343 Have you ever been a DLC member: Authors' interview with Hillary Rodham Clinton, 6/15/98. This particular question was posed earlier in the interview than is suggested by its appearance at this point in the text. In integrating the raw interview transcript with the book text, the order of some questions has been changed for clarity's sake. In quoting from the interview, we have summarized our own questions, but quoted exactly the First Lady's responses.

345 Over sixty years ago: *The Public Papers and Addresses of Franklin D. Roosevelt*, 1937 volume (New York: The Macmillan Co., 1941), 121.

345 Transformational leadership has been criticized: For more on transformational leadership as fostering "higher moral authority," see Bernard M. Bass and Paul Steidlmeier, "Ethics, Character, and Authentic Transformational Leadership," Center for Leadership Studies, Binghamton University, 1998. On converting followers into citizens, see Ronald Walters, "The Legitimacy to Lead" (keynote address at Leaders/Scholars Association Conference, 11/13/98–11/15/98, Los Angeles, Calif.).

345 It is also the most practical: For more on accelerating change, see Warren Bennis and Philip Slater, *The Temporary Society* (San Francisco: Jossey-Bass Publishers, rev. ed., 1998).

INDEX

401